Stress and adversity over the life course

Although stress occurs at every stage of life, much research studies its effects over short-term periods, typically within circumscribed life stages. Little attention has been given to the possibilities that the impact and consequences of stress depend critically on the life stage in which the stress occurs, or that a sequence of prior stressors acts as a context for such effects.

This book attempts to map the influence of early stressful experiences on later life outcomes, studying the trajectories of stressors over the life course. It examines the ramifications of stressful events at key life-course transition points and explores the diversity of outcomes for individuals who have suffered through trauma. Finally, the book suggests new methods for study of stress and adversity through the life course, where issues of timing and sequence of stressors are crucial.

Stress and adversity over the life course

Trajectories and turning points

Edited by

IAN H. GOTLIB
Stanford University

BLAIR WHEATON
University of Toronto

CAMBRIDGE UNIVERSITY PRESS
Cambridge, New York, Melbourne, Madrid, Cape Town, Singapore, São Paulo

Cambridge University Press
The Edinburgh Building, Cambridge CB2 2RU, UK

Published in the United States of America by Cambridge University Press, New York

www.cambridge.org
Information on this title: www.cambridge.org/9780521550758

First published 1997
This digitally printed first paperback version 2006

A catalogue record for this publication is available from the British Library

Library of Congress Cataloguing in Publication data
Stress and adversity over the life course : trajectories and turning
points / edited by Ian H. Gotlib, Blair Wheaton.
p.   cm.
Includes bibliographical references.
ISBN 0-521-55075-0
1. Stress (Psychology)   2. Life cycle, Human – Effect of stress on.
I. Gotlib, Ian H.   II. Wheaton, Blair.
BF575.S75S754   1997
155.9′042 – dc21   96-45176
                                                              CIP

ISBN-13 978-0-521-55075-8 hardback
ISBN-10 0-521-55075-0 hardback

ISBN-13 978-0-521-02971-1 paperback
ISBN-10 0-521-02971-6 paperback

Contents

Contributors

Robert Aseltine, Jr. *Center for Survey Research, University of Massachusetts - Boston*
Deborah Belle *Department of Psychology, Boston University*
Mary Ellen Colten *Center for Survey Research, University of Massachusetts - Boston*
Hope Cooper *Human Development and Family Studies, Cornell University*
David Dooley *School of Social Ecology, University of California - Irvine*
Lindon J. Eaves *Department of Human Genetics, Virginia Commonwealth University*
Walter M. Ensel *Department of Sociology, State University of New York - Albany*
Jacquelyn Gillis-Light *Department of Psychology, Kalamazoo College*
Susan Gore *Department of Sociology, University of Massachusetts - Boston*
Ian H. Gotlib *Department of Psychology, Stanford University*
John Hagan *Department of Sociology, University of Toronto*
Kimberlee Hall *Department of Sociology, University of Toronto*
Carolyn S. Holmes *Department of Sociology, University of Michigan*
Kenneth S. Kendler *Department of Psychiatry, Virginia Commonwealth University*
Ronald C. Kessler *Department of Health Care Policy, Harvard Medical School*
Wan-foon Gina Lai *Department of Sociology, National Singapore University*
Anthony Lewis *Arizona Boys Ranch*
Bin Lin *Center for Survey Reserch, University of Massachusetts - Boston*
Nan Lin *Department of Sociology, Duke University*
William J. Magee *Department of Sociology, University of Toronto*
Bill McCarthy *Department of Sociology, University of Victoria*
Elizabeth G. Menaghan *Department of Sociology, Ohio State University*
Phyllis Moen *Human Development and Family Studies, Cornell University*
Sara Norell *Department of Psychology, Boston University*
JoAnn Prause *School of Social Ecology, University of California - Irvine*
Patricia Roszell *Department of Sociology, University of Toronto*
Judith D. Singer *Graduate School of Education, Harvard University*
Robert S. Weiss *Gerontology Institute, University of Massachusetts*
Donald Wertlieb *Eliot-Pearson Department of Child Study, Tufts University*
Elaine Wethington *Human Development and Family Studies, Cornell University*
Blair Wheaton *Department of Sociology, University of Toronto*
John B. Willett *Graduate School of Education, Harvard University*

1 Trajectories and turning points over the life course: concepts and themes

Blair Wheaton & Ian H. Gotlib

The life course is a path. For most people, this path is far from straight. We use the ideas of trajectories and turning points to divide the life course into complementary parts. A trajectory is the continuation of a direction. It is the inertia in our lives that results from the sum of the forces that propel us toward a destination. A turning point is a disruption in a trajectory, a deflection in the path. Indeed, the essential characteristic of a turning point is that it changes the direction of a trajectory.

The concepts of trajectories and turning points require each other in order to be understood. If we concentrate on trajectories, it leads naturally to the question: What intervenes and disturbs these trajectories? What pushes people away from the path they were on? What puts people back on their former path? Similarly, we cannot conceive of turning points without defining the trajectory as the "norm." To see an event or a transition as a turning point requires time, stability, and an established baseline.

We think most clearly of turning points as "events," as crucially important moments in a life history. But turning points need not be dramatic events, or unusual events, or even a single discrete event. Turning points may be difficult to see as they are occurring, because they are only recognized to be turning points as time passes and as it becomes clear that there has been a change in direction. This fact points to two essential features of turning points: they are more than temporary detours in the current trajectory, and they are knowable only after the fact.

It is possible to represent the life course as a road on which we are traveling, the trajectory component in our lives. Forks in the road represent potential turning points, but they are not necessarily so. Sometimes, two alternative paths will actually lead down parallel routes to the same life destination. Thus, every fork, every choice point, or every alternative presented is not by necessity a potential turning point. Only when an event or circumstance truly takes us in a new direction, with an altered destination, have we experienced a turning point.

Time is a consideration in defining both trajectories and turning points. Every perturbation in the life course cannot be considered a new trajectory, or

1

taken as evidence that a turning point has occurred. Apparent new directions can sometimes be no more than the equivalent of random error in a time series. Indeed, there are reasons for small and/or temporary changes in direction that should not (yet) be seen as evidence of an altered probability of life changes. Although there can be no definitive guidelines concerning how much time must pass for a new direction to become a new trajectory, there are clues that the change in direction is more than temporary. These clues could involve any of the following possibilities: (1) stability of a new direction across life transitions; (2) resistance to efforts to re-establish a former trajectory; (3) transformation of identity to accommodate a new trajectory; and (4) evidence of a role commitment implied by a new direction.

Defining concepts

Life-course trajectories

We begin by providing an initial definition of the twin concepts of trajectories and turning points; this will help to locate these concepts both in existing work on the life course and in the chapters in this book. *A trajectory is the stable component of a direction toward a life destination and is characterized by a given probability of occurrence.* A trajectory refers to the tendency to persistence in life-course patterns, but not necessarily as defined by an unchanging probability of a life outcome. Rather, a trajectory can be defined by a linearly increasing probability over time, by a nonlinearly decreasing probability, or by other combinations of these possibilities.

Figure 1 presents a trajectory reflecting a nonlinear increase in the chances of a life outcome occurring (e.g., marriage, having children, getting a good job) over time. The figure depicts the nature of the trajectory as a "built-in" process. For example, the longer the individual stays in school, the more likely it is that beneficial life outcomes will occur. The trajectory in Figure 1 implies that early experiences in the life course make a greater difference with respect to this outcome than will later experiences. This conclusion is reflected by a faster rise in the curve over childhood and adolescence than at later adult stages, where the net change is much smaller. This pattern would be typical of a trajectory defined by early educational performance.

Figure 1 raises a question about life trajectories: Can trajectories be defined without reference to an endpoint or a destination? We think not. To define or think of a trajectory in the life course, we must have in mind some endpoint to which it is leading – in essence, a criterion that reflects a long-term impact of something that occurred earlier in life. Thus, in this book we consider long-term impacts on mental health as evidence of the trajectories set in motion by earlier stressors or, alternatively, by available resources.

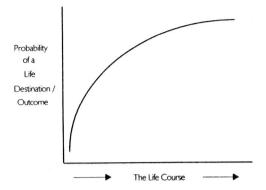

Figure 1. An example of a nonlinear life-course trajectory.

Life trajectories may be defined by stressful experiences in childhood. The experience of chronic sexual abuse, for example, may decrease the chances of attaining a college-level education, a stable marriage or relationship, emotional well-being, or even a successful career. This abuse changes the person's trajectory by virtue of a number of possible mechanisms, such as altering one's identity at crucial developmental junctures, or leading to leaving home at a younger age, or lowering self-esteem or through poorer performance in school. These mechanisms, in turn, underscore the *chain reaction* notion of a trajectory: once a trajectory is defined, events tend to have accumulating consequences.

Turning points and reference points

In contrast to trajectories, turning points are more difficult to define and are open to alternative formulations. Although turning points have an intuitive meaning, there is a definite lack of precision in their identification and definition. Yet turning points represent an essential life-course concept.

It is clear that the notion of a turning point in life has retrospective explanatory value as individuals review their lives (Clausen 1990). The idea that a given decision was crucial in setting the stage for a different life course is attractive, but sometimes problematic. Turning points are often the embodiment of wisdom in hindsight, and there is a convenience to such an explanation that begs the question: Why is that decision, or that transition, or that event, a turning point? It is likely that outcomes in life are formed by many such decisions and events that alter probabilities of life outcomes. What is it that makes some experience attain the status of a "turning point?"

Obviously, a turning point must have lasting effects, producing change in one or more life trajectories. Further, a turning point implies alternative pathways that have real and important differences in life changes attached to them – whether or not the alternative pathways seemed to differ only slightly from each other at the time of the choice point. It is often the case that small decisions, decisions based on little information, and naive decisions are unable to anticipate the divergence in future outcomes. Thus, for example, although the mainstreaming of children in schools can appear as though all children are being exposed to essentially the same curriculum, subtle differences in expectations or enrichment of a program can lead to widely divergent probabilities of school success in the future. This concept is not unlike the realities associated with small differences in starting job income for a woman versus an equally qualified man. After ten years of proportionally equal raises, the man will have a significantly higher income than will the woman; the apparently trivial difference at the beginning of their jobs is now substantial.

Examples of turning points will help to define the concept. Many academics or professionals were at some point forced to decide which graduate school they would attend. The important aspect of this example is that, to an undergraduate facing a far-away reality, this decision is often based either on the wrong indicators or on extremely limited indicators of differences among schools. But differences in the content, goals, philosophy, and expectations of various postgraduate and professional environments can often affect one's entire future work identity, if not one's identity as a whole. Values acquired at a formative period are values that stick; as such, the nature of one's work, the goals of one's work, and the amount of work one does are all informed by these differences in training philosophy. The turning point in this example is the decision to choose school A over school B; the effects are both lasting and significant.

Another example: An individual whose closest friend dies unexpectedly from a drug overdose goes through an "epiphany" (in his words) about the dangers in his own drug addiction. He is fundamentally frightened by the experience and decides, because of his friend's death, to end his own use of drugs. The death of his friend is a *stressor* that has the effect of an intervention, a turning point that either sets him back on a previous life course or leads him on a different course.

These examples suggest a number of different perspectives to the concept of a turning point. In these examples, a turning point is a change in direction in the life course that is nonnormative given an established baseline. This baseline is the stable trajectory in the life course that existed prior to the turning point. The nature of the trajectory is rendered normative, in this use of the term, by virtue of the person's own life history, and not necessarily (or only) by social norms about appropriate roles or stages of achievement. This is necessary because we can define changes in direction only with respect to the individual's own prior trajectory. In this approach, we define the person as his or her own "control group" in specifying what a turning point can be.

It is also possible to define turning points with reference to social norms, or even to historical norms. This view treats common or normative life transitions as turning points by definition, such as in the cases of graduation from high school, becoming a parent, or retiring from a job or career. In these cases, the transition automatically precipitates changes in life trajectories, necessitating acquisition of and adjustment to new roles, and often the re-arrangement of values, time, priorities, and responsibilities.

A turning point can also have the connotation of an intervention, an *attempt* to change direction in the life course. Such interventions can be natural events, or they can be programs designed specifically to change life trajectories (such as Alcoholics Anonymous). Thus, a turning point can also be a compensation for a loss in trajectory, something that in fact sets a person back on an original course. This usage of the term, however, still requires that the prior trajectory be well-established (alcoholism) and heading toward a clear decrement in future outcomes. The mirror possibility also applies: a special intervention that gives a child a head start in school can be counteracted by a poor school environment, thus putting the child back on a "normative" (for him or her) trajectory.

We define a *turning point,* most generally, as *a change in direction in the life course, with respect to a previously established trajectory, that has the long-term impact of altering the probability of life destinations.* All of our prior examples are captured by this general definition. Note that short-term changes in trajectory are not included as turning points. Note also that multiple turning points are possible and even likely – some resulting in lives going "off track" and some resulting in lives getting back "on track."

Figure 2 presents a life trajectory elaborated by the impact of turning points. The dotted line shows the trajectory from Figure 1. The solid line is the actual life trajectory affected by multiple turning points. Somewhere in adolescence, let us say, the individual in this plot experiences a clear turning point (A), perhaps a parental divorce followed by a sustained period of withdrawal from social activities and deteriorating school performance. After a few years, he falls in love (B), and his new partner encourages him to return to former interests and to apply himself; his path changes again. He gets married (which is not a turning point in this example) and continues to do well until into adulthood, when he is transferred to a different city by his company (C). He has never left the town in which he grew up and has trouble adjusting to the realities of a new environment. He withdraws again, as before, isolating himself from his family, and his path again shows a changed trajectory. Thus, there are three turning points in this example: the parental divorce, falling in love with his future wife, and a geographic move in adulthood.

Figure 2 presents multiple turning points, some of which function specifically to cancel the effects of previous turning points. There is no easy distinction

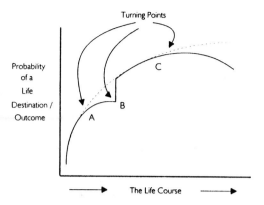

Figure 2. A life-course trajectory with multiple turning points.

between temporary detours in the life course and the occurrence of two coun-
teracting turning points. To distinguish between these situations, one must ask
two questions: (1) Would the trajectory return to its former course on its own?
That is, is the change in direction self-limiting or does it require some further
change event or intervention? (2) Is the individual's identity consistent with the
demands of the changed trajectory, or with the original trajectory? As long as
the individual is holding on to a former identity despite circumstantial changes
in life-course direction, and as long as there is still a chance that the new trajectory is temporary and self-limiting, we cannot count this situation as evidence
of a turning point.

The forms that turning points take

Even with general guidelines about the nature of turning points, it is difficult
to specify their operational meaning (i.e., how they are manifested in empirical data). As we shall see, events, transitions, crises, or changes in role requirements can all be the basis of turning points that have major life-course consequences. A basic question is how these factors can be specified in empirical
models representing long-term trajectories in the life course. Given that trajectories are represented simply by the net long-term impacts of earlier events – in
our case, usually stressors or adverse circumstances – how do we specify the
effects of turning points?

There are at least two ways in which turning points can exert changes in life
trajectories. Turning points can be either *universal* (i.e., they apply to virtually
everyone that experiences them) or *conditional* (i.e., they exert different effects

on different people). Because of the importance of social, historical, and biographical contexts in the meaning and consequences of life transitions and events (Elder 1985, 1991), it is likely that many, if not most, turning points are conditional. Nevertheless, some events may be so serious and so clearly defined in their implications that their effect is universal. Moreover, variables that reflect a social or psychological context can have general effects as turning points. The latter is clear in the case of "school effects" in the life course. Attendance at different schools that vary widely and reliably in quality may have a net effect on the life-course destinations of large groups of people; these, too, are turning points.

Conditional turning points can be specified as interactions, for example, between a prior trajectory (e.g., marital conflict) and an event that changes the direction of this trajectory (e.g., divorce). Any event, transition, or change in social or role responsibilities that shifts the net probability of the life-course destination permanently, without further intervention, is a turning point. Often such interventions in the life course will be manifest as the conditional effect of a *trajectory predictor* on some outcome that depends on the occurrence of a turning point. In contrast, unconditional turning points occur as main effects that do *not* depend on the state of contextual or prior factors. At first blush, it seems unlikely that such turning points can occur. However, if an intervention program for street children reveals a net impact on returning home relative to street children not in a program, it is legitimate to think of the program as a turning point, and it is clearly a main effect that has a generalized impact.

Main-effect turning points will usually play one of a number of roles. Taking the occurrence of an earlier traumatic experience as setting in motion a new life trajectory, turning points that can counteract this change will tend to be one of two types: either they will be relatively independent of the earlier trauma (in effect, uncorrelated and randomly occurring for people who experience this trauma), or they will be events or situations that tend to be activated by the stressor and that eventually counteract the stressor (Wheaton 1985). This effect of "canceling" the earlier stressor occurs because the event or situation activated by the stressor tends to have the opposite effect on the life-course outcome, compared to the stressor, thus reducing or nullifying its impact. There are a number of examples of this kind of turning point. For instance, if the death of a loved one first leads to increased distress but also tends to activate and increase the support of an old friend, then the new support may become a turning point that counteracts the effect of the death. Of course, this is only the case if the distress is prolonged in the first place and if the effect of the support accumulates with time. Similarly, if marital problems tend to increase or exacerbate depression but also increase the chances of seeking and receiving effective marital therapy, then therapy can act to counteract the course of the marital problems.

Life transitions and life-course concepts

Elder (1991) points out the complementarity of the concepts of life trajectories and turning points by noting that "the life course is defined by trajectories that extend across much of the life course, and by short-term changes or transitions" (p. 2). In our approach, some of these transitions and changes may also be turning points. Importantly, however, the trajectories give meaning to the transitions and thus help to determine whether they will be turning points (Elder 1991; Wheaton 1990).

Life transitions define points in the life course when roles are transformed, redefined, or left behind for new roles. Life is full of such transitions: starting school, entering puberty, graduating from high school, ending school, getting a first job, leaving home, getting married, having a first child, buying a house, menopause, retirement, the loss of parents, and so forth. Life is also full of decisions and opportunities that create the possibility of turning points, such as a move, a change of school, a new partner in business, a change in occupation or work, or leaving a long-term relationship.

In all of these cases, the decision concerning whether a transition should be considered to be a turning point essentially involves a consideration of other fundamental concepts in the study of the life course. As Elder (1991) pointed out, "the life course represents a concept and a theoretical perspective." Of the defining concepts in this tradition, we wish to emphasize the central role of three: sequence, timing, and context. Each of these concepts affects whether a transition will be more or less important as a possible change in life direction.

The importance of *sequence* involves the normative order or disorder of events or transitions (Elder 1985; Hogan 1981). An event such as getting a first job will have different meanings and different consequences if it occurs before, rather than after, getting married, or before, rather than after, completion of school. The effect of years of education will most certainly depend on whether education occurs as a continuous role during childhood and adolescence, or rather is a role re-entered in mid-adulthood. In these cases, the likelihood that completion of school will be a turning point is affected by whether it occurs as part of a normative sequence of life tasks. Such normative orderings have an impact, not only because of their social meaning, but also because they are related to the age at which transitions occur. If one completes an MBA at 38 instead of at 25 years of age, there are likely to be ongoing and inertial commitments and prior decisions – children, prior occupations – that will affect how the MBA affects future life directions. In contrast, at age 25, the accumulated realities of prior decisions are less likely to influence the options available.

The sequence of events is thus closely related to the *timing* of events. As noted by Elder (1991), the concept of a "normative timetable" for events governs their implications for the life course:

> Age expectations specify appropriate times for major transitions. There is an appropriate time for entering school, leaving home, getting married, having children, and retiring.... Departures from the usual timetable entail social and psychological consequences, from informal sanctions to lost opportunities and life-course disorder. (p. 10)

When events occur "off time" (i.e., at an age or stage of life that deviates from these normative expectations), the consequences of these events can also be markedly different than expected. However, historical societal changes mean that many timing norms have evolved and are continuing to evolve. Twenty-five to fifty years ago, the transition to parenthood was expected to occur in one's early to mid-twenties. Entering parenthood during mid-adolescence, whether alone or partnered, portended a difficult future. On the other side of the norm, late parenthood (e.g., during one's thirties) had fewer implications than early parenthood, but there was clear pressure not to become an "older" parent. The norm has drifted over time, as has the variability around the mean. Thus, the norm about an *expected* age for parenthood may itself be weaker and so produce fewer adverse consequences for childless people in their thirties and greater support for nonparenthood in general (owing to the increasing societal value and acceptance of a career path for women). Thus, the "necessity" of getting married and having children early may have declined with time. Nonetheless, the implications of teenage parenthood have probably changed much less. Thus, historical context can bend and shape the region of appropriate timing, while leaving some parts of the distribution intact. Clearly, it is not simply the mean age of important life events that is at issue.

We note that the timing of life transitions will surely affect the chances that they will become major life turning points. It continues to be the case that off-time parenthood will have profound implications for the choices one faces concerning jobs, marriage, or school. Even with changes in norms, the social change attending the meaning of later parenthood is far from complete. Thus, job trajectories may still be affected for women who have children after 35, in part because family support institutions are not as generally available as they could be, and in part because job interruptions still have a significant impact on income, promotions, and job training.

Context may be the essential element in specifying whether a transition becomes a turning point. There are many contextual factors that could be considered in understanding the meaning of a given life transition. These include the role context (Moen 1994; Wheaton 1990); the biographical or life history context – the story leading to the transition; the social context – social circumstances that apply at the moment the event or transition occurs; and the historical context – how macro historical events that are themselves causally related affect the manner in which life transitions or difficulties play out over the life course (Elder 1991; Elder & Clipp 1989; Elder & Liker 1982). Elder credits Ryder (1965) with the important concept of an interaction between social and personal life history. Thus, when one enters the labor force (e.g., during the Great Depression or during the 1950s), and at what historical point in time one comes of age to attend university, will significantly affect the life course.

Role context is specified by referring to the "role history" that precedes and informs the meaning of role-exit or role-redefinition events. When retirement occurs, whether it will be a positive or negative life change may depend on such factors as the kind of job left behind, whether the job was chronically physically tiring, whether the environment was cold or dirty, whether there was security or constant uncertainty about job status, whether co-workers were close friends, whether there was substantial commitment to the work role, and so on. In contrast, biographical context goes beyond role specifics to include the history of situations and interdependencies across a number of roles in the life course. Thus, retirement will also be affected by such factors as whether one has a spouse, whether one has grandchildren, whether physical health is intact, whether there are children available to offer support in the event of illness, whether alcohol abuse has been a problem earlier in the life course, whether one has surviving parents or siblings, and the relationship with family members in later life. Each of these may alter the meaning of the retirement experience, directing it toward or away from the notion of a turning point.

A general truism in the life-course literature is that the specification of context is essential in distinguishing events and transitions that mark significant turning points. Some characteristics of a transition event that are informed by context may help to predict which events will also be turning points. One of these is the *contrast* between new situations or roles and former situations or roles. The greater the contrast, the more likely it is that the change will be a turning point. Another aspect of transitions that may be important is whether they have unpredictable or uncertain features, or whether their initial occurrence was unexpected. A final important factor is the ability of the transition event to change or alter identity, to resolve conflict, or to provide escape from prior stress. The greater the extent to which the transition has some instrumental function, the more likely it is that it will be experienced as a turning point.

The role of psychosocial resources

While it may seem obvious, we should add at this point that the concepts typically studied under the rubric of psychosocial resources (e.g. social support, mastery, etc.) may function as protective resources that prevent potentially upsetting transitions from becoming turning points; that is, they may buffer transitions and lead to a lack of change in trajectory. Alternatively, these resources may enhance the consequences of potentially positive transitions and so *allow* them to become turning points. Thus, under conditions of challenge, mastery may potentiate the positive effects of the challenging situation and lead to a change in life trajectory by producing a promotion or changing one's aspirations. The resetting of aspiration or expectation levels with successfully met challenges is a common example of positive turning points.

Psychosocial resources, therefore, typically play an ameliorative or clearly positive role in deflecting life trajectories. In a sense, the states of social support and other social environmental conditions, as well as the given states of personal resources, act as contextual factors that modify the consequences of transitions and events that may qualify as major turning points.

Examples of trajectories and turning points in the literature

The fundamental interplay of life trajectories (continuity) and turning points (change) is a recurring focus of the life-course literature. Before we turn to the examples provided by the chapters ahead, we will review several of the examples provided in discussions by Rutter (1989), Caspi and Elder (1988), Elder and Liker (1982), and Clausen (1990) that illustrate these, or closely related, concepts.

Rutter's pathways from childhood to adult life

Rutter's (1989) concept of pathways through the life course takes as its focus the constant interplay between trajectories and turning points. His examples of the continuities and contingencies that arise in the life course demonstrate both additive and interactive versions of the concept of turning points, as well as the importance of sequence and context in understanding turning-point experiences.

Rutter uses tree diagrams to illustrate the branches in the life course and the role of important contingencies. Some of these tree diagrams represent fully specified arguments for continuity in trajectories, as presented in Figure 3. The process involved here is essentially a chain argument – in this case, a chain of adversity. The argument is that early poor schooling in inner London increases the chances of poor school attendance and that poor attenders had twice the probability of leaving school early (without national examinations), which implied a relative absence of scholastic qualifications in the job market, which led to unskilled work and/or a poor employment record.

Having mapped this trajectory, Rutter (1989) points out that a number of influences managed to break the links in the chain. He notes, for example, that compared with Caucasian girls, girls of color were less likely to have a good attendance record and to stay in school longer, given the same poor schooling background. This is an argument for a contextual interactive effect specifying a turning-point experience for some individuals relative to others in the same situation. In this case, being a girl of color prevented the poor schooling from being a turning point, given an already relatively poor trajectory.

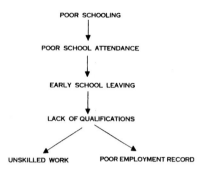

Figure 3. The pathway from poor schooling to lack of job success.

An example of an independent but main-effect type of turning point – much like a natural intervention – is also provided in discussing the cross-generational consequences of parenting breakdown. Parenting breakdown refers to the disruption of parental presence during childhood, for a variety of reasons, leading to institutional rearing. The usual outcome in this group revealed an increased probability of marital breakdown in the next generation and an increased risk of poor parenting. However, a policy of the Children's Homes at the time provided a random intervention that became a turning point for some. This policy was to distribute children across a number of schools, some of which were much better than others. Those with good school experiences were three times more likely than were those with poor school experiences to show planning in choice of career and marriage partner. This led to greater and more continuous marital support from a partner, and increased chances of successful parenting. Here, the turning point is the school placement, which for some meant the continuation of a trajectory, yet for others afforded the opportunity of a change in trajectory.

Caspi and the trajectories resulting from childhood explosiveness

Caspi and Elder (1988) have studied the life-course consequences of childhood explosiveness – in effect, numerous temper tantrums – in girls. Their data provide a useful example of a conditional turning point. Regardless of whether they marry an assertive man, girls who had little difficulty controlling their anger as children have about the same level of control problems in adulthood. In contrast, girls who had clear problems with anger control in childhood have very different trajectories depending on whether they married an assertive man. When they married a nonassertive man, their control problem worsened, but when they married an assertive man, their control problem scores were actually lower than women who had exhibited few control problems in childhood. Thus, it appears that the "fit" between each woman and her chosen marital partner created a clear deflection in the trajectory of anger control over the life course, resulting in more divergent levels than was the case among those women who did not have anger control problems in childhood.

Elder and the women of the Great Depression

Elder's now-classic study of women in Berkeley circa 1930, followed up 40 years later in 1969, reflects his focus on the interaction between biographical and social context and the conditional effects of life transitions and difficulties on long-term life destinations. Elder and Liker (1982) focus on the interaction between social class in the 1930s, as the Depression started, and the long-term impact on later health of the individual variability in economic loss resulting from the Depression. Their work emphasizes the variability in lives resulting from the interaction of personal history (viz., initial social class) and social history (viz., the effects of a systemwide economic trauma that had variable consequences at the individual level). As Elder and Liker point out, although middle-class women may have had relatively more to lose than did working-class women, they also had more resources for dealing with loss. Consequently, the Depression may have had the ironic impact of precipitating greater independence in middle-class women and enhanced feelings of personal competence as they entered economic spheres independent of their husbands. Indeed, for middle-class women, economic hardship in the 1930s predicted *better* emotional health 40 years later; for working-class women, economic deprivation led to worse emotional health 40 years later. Thus, the Depression indirectly functioned as a turning point in a trajectory of emotional well-being for middle-class women relative to working-class women early in their childbearing years in the 1930s.

Clausen's survey of turning points

Clausen's (1990) work has explicitly addressed the types and prevalence of turning points that define new trajectories in the life course. His discussion is unique in its consideration of turning points. Clausen allowed subjects to review and define various events or experiences as turning points in their life course, thus gleaning a sense of how people construct their own life histories. Interestingly, more than 85% of his subjects felt there had been turning points in their lives. Thus, while turning points are ubiquitous, it is nevertheless the case that some individuals experience their lives as "determined," whether due to the unfolding of the disadvantages of poverty or to a middle-class *Ozzie and Harriet* life-course scenario. The point here is that at least some lives do not reveal obvious turning points.

Clausen (1990) expresses surprise at some of the cited turning points, noting that they were sometimes not dramatic or major events but instead subtly evolving changes in the roles or in the organization of life that had greater effects with time. Seemingly innocuous or ill-considered choices, such as the choice of a major in college or a move to a new city, took on added significance with time. This fact underscores our contention that time is important in identifying turning points. Clausen also found that many events that were perceived negatively at the time took on a more positive meaning in retrospect, perhaps with the ability to understand or rationalize their impact with time. For example, a person who was on the edge of suicide and six months pregnant at age 23 noted that the subsequent birth of her child changed her perspective dramatically. She remembered the inability to follow through and commit suicide as her turning point, leading to the ability to know and love her child. She eventually married happily.

Trajectories and turning points in this book: an overview

In preparing this book, we had the unusual opportunity of meeting with the contributors at a small conference and discussing the core concepts of trajectories and turning points. This meeting proved to be both enlightening and sobering. Three essential conclusions emerged from our discussions. First, despite attempts to delineate these concepts as specifically and completely as possible, it was difficult to capture the full range of connotations that the concepts of trajectories and turning points have for the life-course approach. Second, it was clear that the various chapters in this book would produce a number of somewhat different perspectives on these concepts. (In the end, we concluded that this was a good outcome.) Finally, although this book is divided into two main substantive sections – one on trajectories and one on turning points – most of the authors found it difficult to discuss one concept without reference to the other. This follows from the preceding remarks: turning points can be defined only with respect to defined trajectories, and a sole focus on trajectories seems to beg the question of *changes* in trajectories. The chapters in this volume reflect this interdependence, although each chapter emphasizes one of the two concepts in terms of the life course.

The setting of trajectories

The book begins in Part I with a series of chapters on factors that affect life trajectories. Whereas some chapters focus on the trajectories – the life changes set in motion by crucial stressful experiences in childhood, adolescence, or in adulthood – others focus on the salutary trajectories following from protective resources across the lifespan. The first two chapters share an interest in the adverse effects of early childhood stressors and an emphasis on the mapping of trajectories set in motion by these stressors.

Whereas Kessler and his collaborators use the term "childhood adversity," Wheaton and his colleagues discuss "childhood traumas." Although "adversity" is a broader term that captures both the discrete and dramatic nature of traumas as well as the more chronic ongoing social conditions of early life that can so profoundly affect life changes, both groups of authors include discussions of an array of early life stressors that vary in discreteness and chronicity.

These two chapters also share a common perspective concerning the issue of studying multiple traumas (or adversities) simultaneously. Both Kessler and Wheaton point to a number of problems that can accompany the "one-at-a-time" approach to studying childhood stressors. Of course, there are separate literatures for parental divorce, parental death, sexual abuse, school failures, parental substance abuse, and for the other adversities discussed in these chapters. Kessler and associates rightly point out that this approach can miss essential interactions among stressful experiences. Both chapters underscore the need to study particular stressors in the context of accumulating prior stress exposure. Thus, parental divorces often occur against a background of substance abuse, violence, or parental mental health problems. Unless these prior issues are taken into account, the estimation of the risk effects of divorce on adult psychopathology will be biased.

Both chapters also share an interest in using retrospective data to examine the long-term effects of earlier stress on psychiatric disorder. At various points in this book, authors note that retrospective data will continue to be used, and must be used, in the study of lives. Moreover, they point out that we must understand the characteristics of retrospective reporting of stress and onsets of psychiatric episodes, rather than assuming such approaches to be uniformly flawed. In fact, Lin and associates focus on this issue in their chapter discussing the use of the life history calendar to report past stressors.

Kessler and colleagues are interested not only in the long-term effects of early life stressors, but also in the mechanisms by which early adversity affects later mental health; they make clear that the early onset of disorders must be taken into account in explaining the process by which early stress is linked to later (recurrent) mental health problems. If most later problems are recurrent, then two issues must be addressed: the processes that account for early life shifts in mental health that persist across the life course, and whether the relevance of later stressors or resources is lessened by the impact of early-onset disorder (i.e., beginning in early adulthood) on the risk of later stressors and/or the depletion of later resources.

Given the common focus on the trajectories set off by early stressors, a basic question addressed in both of the first two chapters is whether the effects of adversities vary with age. Using survival model approaches, these chapters – together with the concluding chapter by Willett and Singer – point to the importance of the timing of experiences and the essential fit between certain approaches to analyzing data and core life-course concepts. For example, if we believe that sexual abuse will have particularly deleterious effects at younger ages, then the methods we use to assess this hypothesis should be maximally sensitive to this interaction.

The chapter by Kessler and his colleagues is unique in addressing the issue of genetic confounding of early stressors. In designs developed to address and capture genetic variability, an important finding is that early adversity has a relatively independent influence on later psychopathology. This finding supports the importance of understanding the role of environmental stressors and the context and accumulation of stressors across the entire life course.

Wheaton and collaborators utilize data concerning the occurrence of 20 childhood and adult traumatic experiences to estimate overall effects separately for the odds of both psychological disorders (depression, dysthymia, generalized anxiety, and panic) and substance abuse. By studying a wide range of traumatic stressors, it is possible to gauge their ultimate relative importance to psychiatric risk. This chapter, like Kessler's before it, attempts to compare the trajectory-setting implications of early stressful experiences. Wheaton and associates also consider traumatic experiences that can occur in adulthood, although prior to the first onset of a major disorder. Two types of contingencies are considered in these trajectories: the effects of the age at occurrence of the stressor, and the effects of the total accumulated burden due to prior stressors on the impact of newly appearing stressors. The findings of Wheaton and collaborators generally suggest that prior stress, forming a cluster of stress experience, substantially reduces the effects of each new stressor as it occurs. Thus, whether a personal divorce has a major or minor impact will depend to a great degree on whether it is preceded by other stressors or occurs rather in a relative "stress vacuum."

Wheaton and colleagues also present new evidence concerning the extent of the impacts of earlier life traumas. This evidence suggests that the sensitivity of survival-model approaches to estimating risk may produce higher, and more accurate, estimates of risk than do methods that cannot as effectively take into account timing or sequencing of traumas. For example, the impact of parental death is considerably higher in this study than is often reported in the literature. If these estimates are a function of the increased sensitivity to timing inherent in these approaches, then we must conclude that the long-term effects of early stressors are often underestimated, and that at least some stressors have much higher impacts than is currently believed to be the case.

The next two chapters dramatically change the time frame in studying trajectories, focusing on more delimited time periods (early adolescence to early adulthood) that set in motion long-term trajectories. A common approach in studying the life course is to identify such crucial junctures in setting future trajectories. Early to mid-adolescence is believed to be a particularly sensitive period for changes in the future life course, in large part because of the increased influence of peers and increasing personal independence. Hagan and McCarthy focus on early to mid-adolescence, whereas Dooley and Prause focus on late adolescence to early adulthood. This period of life is also considered further in subsequent chapters, but with a primary focus on turning points rather than on trajectories.

Hagan and McCarthy focus on a unique type of future trajectory: although the time focus is short-term (studying a sample of street kids over the course of a summer), the perspective of the chapter is long-term, considering intergenerational transmission of trajectories into criminal involvement. In effect, a parental background of trouble with the law only lays the groundwork for the criminal involvement of the offspring; the actual mechanism of transmission appears to involve labeling (i.e., official sanctioning) of delinquent acts of the young person. The charged offense has a net impact on future tendencies to commit offenses. In demonstrating this kind of effect in the short run, we are witnessing the beginnings of divergent trajectories. We are also witnessing a demonstration of a turning point, where some kids on the street are formally charged, some are not, and the difference is significant in defining future life directions.

The effect of labeling in Hagan and McCarthy's chapter is substantial. But even if it were not, their chapter is consistent with the important point (made previously by Elder, Rutter, and other life-course analysts) that seemingly small or unique events that have no immediate visible or major impact can, in fact, amplify in effect over time, in part because the change in direction becomes self-reinforcing and self-maintaining. Identities become reconciled and consolidated under new labels, and this consolidation can increase the divergence in future life courses.

Dooley and Prause are interested in the transition from high school to early adulthood, specifically, the postschool employment experiences of those who choose not to go on to university or other forms of schooling. The time frame here extends to seven years, using data from the National Longitudinal Survey of Youth. Like Hagan and McCarthy, Dooley and Prause's concern is with crucial junctures in the determination of long-term trajectories. Dooley and Prause are interested in early work experience and its effects on occupational careers as well as on the development of personal resources such as self-esteem – a factor that has been repeatedly demonstrated to be important as a protective resource in dealing with life stressors and difficulties (Pearlin et al. 1981; Pearlin & Schooler 1978).

Dooley and Prause increase our understanding by linking the concepts of social selection and trajectories, and the concepts of social causation and turning points. This distinction highlights differences among the typical ways that social selection and social causation are interpreted: whereas social selection emphasizes the effects of particular personal characteristics (such as self-esteem) on social destinations, social causation has the imagery of an intervention by the social environment, of changing the direction of a prior trajectory. Dooley and Prause provide important evidence that both social selection ("drift") and social causation can coexist and operate dynamically. The operation of social selection is evident in Dooley and Prause's finding that self-esteem in high school predicts the category and chances of employment seven years later. Similarly, the operation of social causation is reflected in the finding that satisfactory early employment leads to important relative gains in self-esteem. Again, the imagery of divergence in the future life course is essential to the notion of turning points.

Dooley and Prause further specify important differences in the various forms that turning points can take, remarking that early employment may operate in different ways on self-esteem. The *developmental* model specifies the difference in self-esteem as a greater gain in esteem for the employed than for the unemployed, whose developmental trajectory for self-esteem is either delayed or permanently set to a lower growth trajectory. The *stress* model would predict greater losses in self-esteem for the unemployed than for the employed, who either have stable self-esteem or gain in self-esteem. By specifying the shape and content of the turning point, Dooley and Prause introduce important distinctions concerning how future life trajectories are determined.

The next two chapters, by Menaghan and Moen, return to a longer-term focus on the concept of trajectories. In Menaghan's chapter, we see the explicit concern with trajectories that extend not only across life spans, but across generations. This, of course, has been a central concern in sociology for some time, typically manifested as an interest in the transmission of poverty or in social inequality in general. Menaghan's own words in outlining her conceptualization of trajectories are worth including here, and reflect a view of the content of trajectories that raises possibilities not emphasized in other chapters. Menaghan is interested in the ongoing, less dramatic social conditions of life that keep trajectories in place, rather than in the transitions in life that set new trajectories. She likens the effects of these conditions on life trajectories to "the cumulative effects of a steady, day-after-day drip of water on a rock." In this emphasis we see the power of the ordinary, the cumulating advantage or disadvantage of the structural givens in daily life.

Menaghan's focus is on occupational conditions for parents that either promote or detract from the quality of home environments for children. Menaghan argues that intergenerational transmission occurs through a number of indirect effects of these conditions – for example, from parents under stress at work to distraction and preoccupation at home and to lower support and supervision of children. These conditions may, in turn, affect the child's educational performance and emotional well-being. At the same time, Menaghan's chapter also emphasizes the importance of combinations of circumstances that together lead to problems in the home environment, implying that these problems can be avoided in a number of ways. For example, good occupational conditions can offset home difficulties; personal resources can help offset the effects of difficult working conditions; and one parent's difficulties can be offset by the other's efforts.

We also see that self-esteem again is a key element in ensuring positive trajectories, even for one's children. Echoing Dooley and Prause's findings, Menaghan demonstrates that early maternal self-esteem puts women on a trajectory for better working conditions and higher spousal earnings. Thus, both Dooley and Prause's chapter and Menaghan's chapter highlight the importance of personal resources in setting and maintaining trajectories, as well as the additional "social causation" effects of the social environments through which we pass.

Moen elaborates this notion of continuity in trajectories from early to later adulthood. Her discussion emphasizes that both social and personal resources (jointly conceived of as "resilience") earlier in life result in pathways that maintain relative advantages in resilience into later adulthood. A continuing theme in the treatment of trajectories is the finding that small differences in advantage early in life may accumulate into greater relative advantages later on. There can be both "maintenance" and "development" trajectories, depending on whether the effects of earlier advantageous circumstances are primarily to avoid negative outcomes or to enhance the probability of positive outcomes.

Moen identifies certain "markers" early in adulthood that predict greater resilience in adulthood in a sample of women studied for over 30 years. Self-esteem is again implicated in resilience. In addition, however, Moen identifies multiple role involvements as a resource that has lasting benefits into later life. Like Menaghan, Moen emphasizes the importance of stable features of life in determining trajectories.

The specification of turning points

Part II of the book considers turning-point experiences or transitions and the issues involved in detecting and defining important turning points. In the previous section, Menaghan eloquently described the pervasive interest in turning points: "It is precisely because continuing in the same direction in which one is already headed is so much expected . . . that we find the exceptions interesting." Indeed, given the discussions in the first section of this volume concerning the stability of trajectories in lives and the power of stress and adversity in defining these trajectories, it is apparent that turning points hold out both the promise of recovering a positive trajectory and the fear of the negative changes endemic in trajectories that attend some social roles or situations.

In the first chapter in this section, Belle and her colleagues explore the issues involved in defining as a turning-point experience the transition to self-care among children. A fundamental issue is whether the onset of self-care represents a turning point to the extent that is often expected. Concerns are frequently expressed about children at home alone after school with undue responsibilities and too much time alone. The image of the "latchkey" child is questioned in a straightforward manner by Belle and associates in their review of existing studies (which more often than not show no differences between children in self-care and children of the same age in other forms of care) and in their own study of care situations for children.

This chapter is persuasive in underscoring the importance of contextual factors, and in specifying the meaning of situations with the potential to become a turning point. This is not a discussion simply of broad conditions, but of the myriad issues that contribute to the form and substance of children's self-care experience. There are many important factors here: the neighborhood, whether the time that the child is unsupervised is spent inside or outside the home, whether the mother is working, the number of unsupervised hours, and the presence of siblings, to name but a few. A crucial issue that arises through the qualitative data presented in this chapter involves the difference in interpretation of the care situation by parents and their children. When a parent reports that she is at home nearly every day when her child comes home, and the child reports independently that he doesn't know the whereabouts of his mother when he comes home, one can begin to appreciate the complexity of attempting to conduct empirical investigations in this area. It appears that interpretation of the circumstances surrounding the care situation may be more important than the fact of self-care itself. As Belle and collaborators succinctly state: "Absent parents are sometimes experienced as psychologically present, and those who are present can be experienced as psychologically absent." It is obvious that turning points cannot be defined broadly but rather by careful specification of a number of features of the turning point – to the extent that contextual factors predominate in the definition.

In the next chapter, Wertlieb addresses a widely studied and deliberated turning-point experience: parental divorce. The number of modifying and exacerbating factors involved in the sequelae of divorce, thereby determining whether or not the divorce *is* a turning point (at least for the child), is itself an issue. As Wertlieb notes, the multiplicity of consequences of divorce for a child, and the pervasiveness of the changes in the structure and opportunities of life, likely affect whether the divorce becomes a turning point. If only one or two areas of life are affected, it is less likely that the experience of parental divorce will function as a turning point. If, however, the entire fabric of life is changed by the divorce – including changes in educational, occupational, and relationship trajectories, income level, subsequent risk of divorce, time of childbearing, and so forth – then it is likely that divorce, by virtue of the *array* of effects, will be a major turning point in life. Thus, delimitation of the consequences is as important as the magnitude of any one consequence.

Wertlieb draws on the Hetherington metaphor of winners, losers, and survivors after divorce to argue that a range of outcomes follows from this event. This viewpoint represents a continuing theme in this section of the book: an array of outcomes, from positive to negative, suggests the overwhelming conditionality built into turning points. Losers turn out to be persistently aggressive and insecure; the survivors cope more successfully but remain unhappy over time despite higher self-esteem and better success in social roles; and the winners combine optimal levels of caring and competence in social roles and are particularly skillful at sharing and helping.

Like Dooley and Prause, Gore and her colleagues focus on transitions from late adolescence to early adulthood. The issues here are broader, in that a variety of roles following from high school are compared for their potential in setting future trajectories. If the life-course literature is accurate, the sequencing and timing of events at crucial developmental junctures should be critical in understanding long-term trajectories. Gore and associates study four groups of young adults after high school: those living in a residential college situation, those in a commuting-to-college role, those working full-time, and those with employment difficulties and not in school. This chapter makes the important point that this period of life is characterized by a number of simultaneous changes, including greater economic independence for some, career decisions, marital possibilities, parenting decisions, new relationships, changing networks, moving, and living on one's own for the first time. Periods of life with this degree of structural change are likely to contain higher rates of turning-point experiences, in part because the divergence in futures is determined by the variability in decisions, roles, and goals.

Gore's chapter reminds us, importantly, that studying multiple outcomes of transition points is essential in understanding the complexity of life transitions, which are seldom exclusively positive or negative in their connotations. For example, whereas full-time workers demonstrate the greatest improvement in reducing levels of depression following high school, it is residential college students who report the greatest gains in the quality of their lives. Thus, whether one or the other experience would constitute a turning point varies, depending on the outcome chosen. In fact, the lesson is that we must examine a range of outcomes to decide whether a particular "track" (the term used by Gore et al.) operates as a turning point. When more outcomes are affected, and all in a similar fashion, it is more likely that a turning point has occurred.

In the next chapter, Wethington describes a unique opportunity to study turning points as they are retrospectively constructed and reported in people's lives. By utilizing data from a survey designed to gather information on turning points, Wethington allows us to see how individuals, by their own accounts, view and conceptualize the major turning points in their lives. From this, and the reasons these turning points are chosen, we learn what issues and common threads seem to be definitive in designating a past experience as a turning point in life. Although the most prevalent turning points reported range widely in content, several consistent themes emerge. It is true that major normative or commonly experienced transitions are viewed as turning points. Events such as becoming a parent or moving are often seen in retrospect as a major change in direction in life. But unscheduled and unanticipated events are also mentioned. Interestingly, it is the *responses* to past stressors, as much as the stressors themselves, that are seen as turning points. Thus, a major depression or an emotional breakdown are seen as irrevocable changes, affecting future life changes. But stressors themselves are less often seen as immutable; in fact, how they turn out seems to be more important than their occurrence per se. Wethington's discussion and data, across a wide age range, are critical in helping to identify and elucidate some of the primary features of turning points from both a conceptual and an empirical perspective.

The final chapter by Weiss shifts attention to later life stages – specifically, the retirement transition. As with earlier turning points discussed in this section, it is the range and variability in the experience of retirement that is most obvious. In contrasting the satisfactions and dissatisfactions of retirement, we see the ambivalence and complexity of the retirement role. As Weiss notes, the distress of retirement involves "the emptiness of what is, not the loss of what was." Thus, the focus in this transition is the role that one adopts on retirement, rather than the role that is left. Respondents in Weiss's interviews have much to say about the former work role, but they do not so much long to return to work as to find constructive ways of staying in touch with their former co-workers. Again, retirement constitutes a turning point in part because of the number of changes that are faced simultaneously. Identities are altered and reorganized, and by definition the structure of life changes. In fact, the destructuring of life becomes an essential descriptor of retirement as a turning point.

Part III of this volume contains two chapters concerning methodological issues and techniques that should be considered in life-course stress research. Both chapters discuss new approaches to the structuring and analysis of data in order to better represent and understand the consequences of stress across life stages. Both chapters also focus on methods that are appropriate for retrospective studies, although the survival-model methods discussed by Willett and Singer could also be based on data collected prospectively.

Lin and his colleagues discuss their application of the life history–calendar method to the measurement of past stressors. As discussed in earlier chapters by Kessler and Wheaton, Lin also emphasizes the need to study multiple stressors simultaneously. The life history–calendar method allows the reporting and specific dating of targeted events of interest that have already occurred. This chapter reports important results on the plausibility and validity of this method for studying stressors. Indeed, Lin and associates have a unique opportunity to examine the validity of this method, using data from a multiwave panel study that began in 1979. In the most recent waves of data collection, the life history calendar was used to gather information about past stressors in the 1979 and 1980 waves. This allows comparison of retrospective reporting of stress with the stress reported at the time. Results are encouraging along a number of fronts. For example, error rates are acceptably low, and most errors are due to under- rather than to overreporting. Investigations of sources of bias in reporting past stressors reveals some patterns, but the size of the bias is usually small and not consequential to the results. The important message of Lin's chapter is that such retrospective methods may be not only useful but actually central to the agenda of studying stress over the life course.

The same can also be said about the final chapter by Willett and Singer, who present a didactic discussion of the basics of survival-model techniques for studying the occurrence of events in the life course. Their discussion emphasizes the fit of these methods to the questions and requirements of life-course research. A number of features of survival modeling are particularly important: the sensitivity of the method to the timing and spacing of events, the flexibility in studying the effects of transitions and other time-varying states across life stages, and the ability to investigate the importance of changes in impact of predictors by age or (more broadly) by period of the life course. Survival models, known in some disciplines as "event history" models, make time an explicit component of both the model and the explanation. Willett and Singer build the basics of the survival-modeling approach piece by piece using a running example based on the data described earlier by Wheaton and his colleagues. Thus, the applicability of this method to the study of the effects of stressors on the risk of psychiatric disorder is not merely hypothetical. Typical of their work in this area, Willett and Singer offer a clear, concise, and compelling overview of an exciting technique for analyzing life-course data.

What lies ahead

The specifics of these chapters aside, we must remember that our common concern is the mapping of life trajectories set in motion by stress and adversity, together with the concomitant circumstances that define these experiences as important and the identification of turning points that either produce decrements in trajectories or "correct" for these decrements.

Although stress occurs at every stage of life, we should also remember that most studies of stress tend to examine its effects primarily over relatively short periods of time, typically within life stages. Theories about the varied unfolding life consequences of early childhood stress speculate about long-term consequences; nevertheless, it is clear that we are only beginning to acquire evidence that allows us actually to assess the continuing and pervasive effects of these stressors over the life course.

We should remember that questions concerning the long-term effects of childhood stressors on life-course destinations have been posed more often in terms of the effects of childhood behavior or affective problems (the typical outcomes in stress research) than in terms of the stress itself. Thus, for example, we often ask whether children with conduct disorder or depression grow into adults with the same or related problems, with impaired coping repertoires or impaired social achievements; we do not typically integrate such issues into one model and ask whether the observed effects of continuity of problems are indirectly reflecting the long reach of stress, maintained by its consequential impairments.

In this volume, we begin from the premise that we have yet to understand the full impact of the stress experience as it unfolds over the life course. In addition to an interest in the long-term consequences of stress experience, however, we are equally interested in factors and conditions that modify or reverse the trajectory of consequences – the turning points that support recovery or precipitate deterioration in functioning in later life. We emphasize that stress sometimes occurs at major transition points in development, and sometimes it does not; the temporal occurrence of stress has implications for both the meaning of the stressor and its consequences. We argue that under some conditions transitional processes across life stages may act to maintain and exacerbate the damage of earlier stress, but under other conditions these same processes may serve to counteract the effects of prior stress.

In addressing such issues, we believe that this volume makes contributions to both the stress and the life-course literatures. First, we present new data, using new methods, that address the importance of childhood experiences in understanding lifetime mental health and well-being. Second, we emphasize the complexity and contingencies of circumstances surrounding possibly stressful situations, as well as the need to understand the circumstances that make it more or less likely that important transitions in life will also be turning points. Third, this volume emphasizes the diversity of outcomes for individuals who have experienced stressful backgrounds, rather than the overall average differences in outcomes between this group and others. Fourth, we draw on the core ideas of the life-course perspective to underscore the necessity of attending to the timing, spacing, and sequencing of stressors. And fundamentally we believe in the importance of studying the cumulative effects of stress over time, throughout lives. Thus, we take seriously the notion of a life history of stress that includes a perspective from the earliest experiences of childhood to the circumstances that life presents across the life course.

References

Caspi, A., & Elder, G. H., Jr. (1988). Emergent family patterns: the intergenerational construction of problem behaviors and relationships. In R. A. Hinde & J. Stevenson-Hinde (eds.), *Relationships within Families: Mutual Influences*. Oxford: Clarendon.

Clausen, J. A. (1990). Turning point as a life course concept. Paper presented at the American Sociological Association meetings (Washington, DC).

Elder, G. H., Jr. (1985). Perspectives on the life course. In Glen H. Elder, Jr. (ed.), *Life Course Dynamics: Trajectories and Transitions 1968-1980.* Ithaca, NY: Cornell University Press.

Elder, G. H., Jr. (1991). The life course. In Edgar F. Borgatta & Marie L. Borgatta (eds.), *The Encyclopedia of Sociology.* New York: Macmillan.

Elder, G. H., & Clipp, E. C. (1989). Combat experience and emotional health: impairment and resilience in later life. *Journal of Personality* 57: 311-41.

Elder, G. H., Jr., & Liker, J. K. (1982). Hard times in women's lives: historical influences across forty years. *American Journal of Sociology* 88: 241-69.

Hogan, D. P. (1981). *Transitions and Social Change: The Early Lives of American Men.* New York: Academic Press.

Moen, P. (1994). Women's roles and resilience: trajectories of advantage or turning points? [Chapter 7 in this volume]

Pearlin, L. I., Lieberman, M. A., Menaghan, E. G., & Mullan, J. T. (1981). The stress process. *Journal of Health and Social Behavior* 22: 337-56.

Pearlin, L. I., & Schooler, C. (1978). The structure of coping. *Journal of Health and Social Behavior* 19: 2-21.

Rutter, M. (1989). Pathways from childhood to adult life. *Journal of Child Psychology and Psychiatry* 30: 23-51.

Ryder, N. B. (1965). The cohort as a concept in the study of social change. *American Sociological Review* 30: 843-61.

Wheaton, B. (1985). Models for the stress-buffering functions of coping resources. *Journal of Health and Social Behavior* 26: 352-65.

Wheaton, B. (1990). Life transitions, role histories, and mental health. *American Sociological Review* 55: 209-24.

I Trajectories: long-term effects of adverse experience

2   Childhood adversity and adult psychopathology

Ronald C. Kessler, Jacquelyn Gillis-Light,
William J. Magee, Kenneth S. Kendler, & Lindon J. Eaves

This chapter presents an overview of research that we have been pursuing for the past several years to study the long-term effects of childhood adversity on adult psychopathology. This work involves secondary analysis of three large-scale population surveys of adults wherein retrospective reports about childhood adversities are related to reports about adult psychiatric disorders. Although this work is still in progress, preliminary results are sufficiently compelling to warrant presentation. We begin with a brief review of previous research in this area and then turn to a discussion of our main findings to date.

Introduction

Previous research

Much evidence from a wide variety of studies in both psychiatric patient samples and general population samples confirms that adults who were exposed to adversity during their childhood years are more likely than the unexposed to have adult psychopathology (e.g., Birtchnell, Evans, & Kennard 1988; Brown

From the Department of Health Care Policy, Harvard Medical School, Boston, MA (Kessler); the Department of Psychology, Kalamazoo College, Kalamazoo, MI (Gillis-Light); the Department of Sociology, the University of Toronto, Toronto, Ontario (Magee); the Department of Human Genetics (Eaves, Kendler); and the Department of Psychiatry, Medical College of Virginia/Virginia Commonwealth University, Richmond, VA (Kendler). Kessler's work on this paper was supported by MERIT Award R37-MH42714, Research Scientist Award K05-MH00507, Research Grants R01-MH46376 and R01-MH52861, all from the National Institute of Mental Health (NIMH), and by The John D. and Catherine T. MacArthur Foundation Research Network on Successful Midlife Development. The work of Light and Magee was supported by Training Grant T32 MH16806 from NIMH. The work of Kendler was supported by Research Scientist Award K05-MH01277 from NIMH. The work of Eaves was supported by Research Grant R01-MH-45268 from NIMH. The data reported here come from the Americans' Changing Lives (ACL) Survey, the National Comorbidity Survey (NCS), and the Virginia Twins Project (VTP). The ACL data collection was supported by Grant P01 AG05561 from the National Institute of Aging. The NCS data collection was supported by Grant R01-MH46376 from the NIMH. The VTP data collection was supported by Grant R01-MH40828 from the NIMH and Grant R01-AA09095 from the National Institute of

& Anderson 1991; Bryer et al. 1987; Earls et al. 1988; Faravelli et al. 1986; Fendrich, Warner, & Weissman 1990; Holmes & Robins 1988; McLeod 1991; Rutter 1989; Tennant 1988; West & Prinz 1987). However, these studies suffer from several limitations. First, the vast majority focus on only a single aspect of adversity at a time. For example, there have been separate studies of the effects of poor maternal care (e.g., Parker 1984; Plantes et al. 1988), death of or separation from a parent (e.g., Faravelli et al. 1986; Tennant 1988), family violence (e.g., Fergusson, Dimond, & Horwood 1986; Hess & Camara 1979), and parental substance abuse (e.g., Weissman et al. 1987; West & Prinz 1987). We know very little, though, about how these different adversities cluster in the lives of particular children, or about how the effects of these adversities interact to cause adult psychopathology, or whether some aspects of adversity explain others in multivariate analyses.

A second limitation is that most previous studies of the long-term effects of childhood adversities have focused only on a single adult psychiatric disorder, usually depression, and have made no attempt to determine whether particular forms of childhood adversity predispose individuals to different adult disorders. What little work has been done on this issue suggests that there may, in fact, be specificity in the effects of some childhood adversities (Kolvin et al. 1988; Rutter 1989), but a clear assessment of this possibility requires a large-scale analysis of the effects of a number of different adversities on a range of adult disorders. Such an analysis has not yet been carried out.

A third limitation of the existing literature is that the causal pathways involved in the long-term effects of childhood adversities have not been extensively examined. Those studies that have attempted to carry out such an analysis have documented a number of presumably significant mediating effects (e.g., Harris, Brown, & Bifulco 1990; Rutter 1989; Sroufe & Rutter 1984). For example, some forms of childhood adversity have been shown to be associated with difficulties in forming a successful marriage and in making a successful role transition into early adulthood (e.g., Brown et al. 1986; Lauer & Lauer 1991; Quinton, Rutter, & Liddle 1984). Other childhood adversities have been shown to be related to intrapsychic vulnerabilities such as helplessness, low self-esteem, and interpersonal dependency (e.g., Harris et al. 1990; Testa et al. 1990). These mediators, in turn, are widely thought to increase risk of adult mental disorder (e.g., Barnett & Gotlib 1988; Lewinsohn, Hoberman, & Rosenbaum 1988; O'Connell & Mayo 1988). However, for reasons discussed in what follows, serious questions can be raised about the validity of the results of these investigations in light of limitations in their methods of analysis.

Alcohol Abuse and Alcoholism; the Virginia Twin Registry is supported by Grant HD-26746 from the National Institute of Child Health and Human Development and Grant NS-25630 from the National Institute of Neurological and Communicative Disorders and Stroke.

Current research

By simultaneously examining the effects of a number of important childhood adversities on multiple measures of adult psychopathology in several different large community epidemiologic surveys of adults, our work is designed to take a first step toward resolving the limitations just described. This is important both for the advancement of theory and as a way of providing the basic empirical data required to target future in-depth investigations of particular constellations of childhood adversities.

An especially important aspect of our work concerns the strategy we have used to address the third listed limitation: the problem of misspecification of causal pathways. In virtually all previous research in adult samples, the causal pathways involved in the long-term effects of childhood adversity have been misspecified, perhaps seriously so, because earlier history of disorder has not been controlled. Our work corrects this problem by using a more elaborate disaggregrated specification of the causal pathways linking childhood adversities with adult disorders than has been used in previous research.

The misspecification, in short, involves the fact that virtually all previous work in this area has focused on current disorder as the outcome while ignoring lifetime disorder. Research on children shows that several different childhood adversities are associated with child and adolescent psychopathology (e.g., Fleming & Offord 1990; Goodyear 1990). It is also known that childhood disorders are often chronic (Harrington et al. 1990; Kovacs & Paulaukas 1984). These results imply that the relationships between childhood adversities and adult disorders could be due to the mediating effects of early-onset lifetime disorders. Yet studies of causal pathways between childhood adversities and adult psychopathology have consistently failed to include history as a mediating or modifying variable. This is true even though theoretical discussions point to the possibility that early-onset disorders can shape the subsequent environment in ways that might incorrectly be interpreted as evidence for mediating effects of environmental variables (Rutter 1989).

This misspecification has the potential to bias interpretations of the effects of mediators other than lifetime history. A good illustration of this potential problem is a study by Parker and Hadzi-Pavlovic (1984) of women whose mothers died during the subjects' childhoods. Lack of care from fathers and stepmothers following the death of the mother, retrospectively assessed by the Parental Bonding Instrument (Parker, Tupling, & Brown 1979), was significantly associated with high adult levels of depression. These associations were, however, attenuated among respondents with supportive spouses, leading the authors to conclude that success in forming intimate relationships "largely corrected any diathesis to greater depression created by uncaring parenting." Yet this conclusion ignores an alternative hypothesis – that lack of success in form-ing a supportive marriage and current depression might both be due to a history of depression prior to marriage.

This alternative hypothesis could have been evaluated by obtaining informa-tion about age of onset of depression and distinguishing between respondents with onsets prior to marriage and those with subsequent onsets. Analyses of this sort, which are being carried out in our work, have the potential to enrich greatly our understanding of developmental psychopathology. The significance of these analyses is enhanced, furthermore, by elaborating the basic model to study the possibility that some childhood adversities are associated with risk of recurrence in adulthood and (when this is shown to be the case) by exploring whether environmental and/or intrapsychic mediators account for the effects of these childhood adversities on adult chronicity and recurrence.

The Americans' Changing Lives survey

The effects of adversity on first onset and recurrence of depression

Our first attempt to investigate these ideas empirically was based on data col-lected in a large two-wave household survey that included retrospective reports concerning eight childhood adversities obtained in the first interview and a brief screening measure of major depression in both the first and second interviews. The two interviews were separated by a period of 30 months. The survey, en-titled Americans' Changing Lives (ACL), was carried out by the Survey Re-search Center at the University of Michigan in a nationally representative sam-ple of noninstitutionalized persons aged 25 and over living in the coterminous United States that was based on a multistage, stratified, area probability sam-pling design. The purpose of the survey was to study productivity and success-ful aging in the midlife period and the later years of life. The sample size was 3,617; the response rate was 70%. The time-2 survey reinterviewed 2,867 of the time-1 respondents, representing 83% of those who were surviving at the time of recontact. More details on the ACL design are presented elsewhere (House et al. 1990).

Neither childhood adversity nor adult psychopathology were areas of central importance to the ACL investigators. Therefore, the measures of these con-structs were quite brief. Childhood adversity was assessed in a series of eight questions, each dealing with an experience that occurred before the respondent was 16 years of age: death of mother, death of father, serious parental marital problems, parental divorce, family violence, serious family drinking problems, family mental illness, and absence of a close and confiding relationship with any adult. For purposes of our initial analyses, each of the eight adversities was treated as a dichotomous yes–no measure.

Psychopathology was assessed with a reworded version of the stem question from the depression section of the Diagnostic Interview Schedule (DIS) version III-A (Robins et al. 1981). A positive response to this single question was used to define lifetime history of depression. Questions were also included to date the age of onset, to record lifetime number of episodes, to date the most recent episode, and to record the length of the most recent episode. Among respondents who reported that their most recent episode occurred in the twelve months prior to the interview, additional questions were asked about symptoms of depression during that episode using the wording developed by Endicott and her associates to assess Family History Research Diagnostic Criteria (FHRDC) symptoms of major depression (Endicott, Andreason, & Spitzer 1978). Responses to the FHRDC questions were used to make best-estimate diagnoses of recent major depressive episodes based on the A criteria of the DSM-III-R diagnostic system (APA 1987).

Our initial analyses of these data used time-1 information on age of onset of depression and time-2 information on episode prevalence during the twelve months prior to the second interview. These data were used to study the separate effects of the childhood adversities on first onset across the lifespan and on recurrence during the past twelve months. The analysis began by replicating previous research in documenting associations between the eight childhood adversities and recent (twelve-month) episodes of major depression (MD). Five of the eight adversities were found to be significantly associated with MD in the past twelve months (family drinking problems, family mental illness, family violence, parental marital problems, and parental divorce) with odds ratios (ORs) ranging from 1.4 to 2.6.

Our investigation of the possibility that these associations were due to indirect influences through history began with an analysis of first onset based on discrete-time survival analysis (Kessler & Magee 1993). An important part of this analysis was the evaluation of interactions between age and the childhood adversities. We hypothesized that these interactions would be negative, which means that the influences of childhood adversities on first onset of depression would decline with age. The only previous data we are aware of on this possibility come from research showing that family histories of depression are greater among early-onset cases than later-onset cases (Mendlewicz & Baron 1981; Weissman et al. 1987), a result which has been interpreted as evidence for a strong genetic influence on early-onset depression. Another plausible interpretation, though, is that the adversities associated with having a mentally ill parent have their most powerful effects early in life. If this latter interpretation is the case, we would expect to find a general pattern of childhood adversities more strongly affecting early onset of depression than later onset.

The analysis yielded results generally consistent with this prediction. Seven of the eight childhood adversities were found to have significant effects on life history of depression (the exception being parental divorce), based on analyses using discrete-time survival analysis methods like those described by Willett and Singer (1995). Five of these seven were found to have effects that decreased significantly with age. All five of the latter (family violence and mental illness, early death of either mother or father, and lack of a close relationship with an adult) significantly predicted early onset, which (following earlier research) was defined as first onset prior to age 20 (Giles et al. 1989; Turnbull et al. 1990; Weissman et al. 1987). The ORs for onsets after age 20, in comparison, were all quite weak, with only one of the five adversities (family violence) continuing to be associated with a significant risk of first onset. It is noteworthy that the two adversities with effects that were found to persist throughout the life course had lower ORs than the other measures in predicting early onset of MD, suggesting that the persistence of these two particular effects beyond age 20 cannot be attributed to a greater initial emotional impact than other childhood adversities.

The next part of the analysis examined whether various forms of childhood adversity influence recurrence of MD. This was done by estimating a series of logistic regression models – in the subsample of respondents with a history of depression prior to the year before the time-2 interview – to predict the recurrence of an episode of MD at any time during that twelve-month period. The results showed that only three of the eight adversities (family history of mental illness, family history of violence, and parental divorce) significantly predicted recurrence of MD. Consistent with previous research (Coryell, Endicott, & Keller 1991; Sorenson, Rutter, & Aneshensel 1991), no significant main effect on risk of recurrence was found for age at onset. Nor did the effects of any of the childhood adversities on recurrence vary as a function of either current age or age at onset.

Investigating mediators of the effects of adversity on recurrence

These initial results suggest that some childhood adversities are more important than others because they affect adult recurrence of depression. Recurrence is an important outcome because the vast majority of episodes of depression in adulthood are recurrences (Burke et al. 1991). Previous research on the causal pathways linking childhood adversity to recurrence have suggested that some childhood adversities interact with early-onset mental disorders to create subsequent environmental experiences that exacerbate initial symptoms and reduce resources for long-term resolution and recovery (Turnbull et al. 1990). However, most of this evidence comes from research on the long-term effects of adolescent conduct disorder and substance abuse (Maughan, Gray, & Rutter 1985). We know very little about such interactions and their effects on the continuity of depression into adulthood.

An initial attempt to provide information of this sort in the ACL data considered the effect of twelve potential mediators, all of them measured in the time-1 ACL interview and used to study recurrence of depression between time 1 and time 2 among respondents who had a lifetime history of MD as of time 1 but who were not depressed at the time-1 interview. These mediators included three measures of sociodemographic characteristics that might be influenced by childhood family violence and might be consequential for adult MD (educational attainment, income, and marital status); three measures of social networks and social support; three measures of personality (extroversion, neuroticism, and personal efficacy); and three measures of chronic stress (financial stress, chronic interpersonal stress, and chronic health problems). Most of these potential mediators had previously been shown to be affected by childhood adversities (Amato & Keith 1991; Brown & Harris 1978; Browne & Finkelhor 1986; Hojat, Borenstien, & Shapurian 1990; McLeod 1991; Rodgers 1990). There is also evidence from the broader epidemiologic literature that all of these variables are significantly associated with prevalence of depression in adulthood (Brown & Harris 1978; McGonagle & Kessler 1990; Weissman et al. 1991).

The analysis began by examining the joint effects of parental mental illness and childhood family violence, the two measures of adversity found in the earlier ACL analyses to predict recurrent depression. Results showed that childhood family violence explained the effect of parental mental illness (Kessler & Magee 1994). More detailed analysis showed also that violence from siblings or multiple adults was a more important predictor of adult recurrent depression than other types of childhood family violence. We also found that these effects were stronger among respondents from lower than middle SES (socioeconomic status) backgrounds and that such status was best operationalized by dividing the sample by father's education.

The examination of mediator effects began by estimating a pair of regression equations for each of the twelve potential mediators in each of the two subsamples defined by SES origins to investigate whether there was a significant effect of childhood family violence (FV) on the mediator and whether there was a significant effect of the mediator on recurrent MD net of FV. Only one of the twelve potential mediators – chronic interpersonal stress – passed this pair of tests. This variable was significant in both the lower and higher father education subsamples, a consistency that argues against the otherwise plausible interpretation that one significant association out of twelve could occur by chance.

But what causal processes explain the occurrence of this mediating effect? One plausible possibility is that childhood FV increased emotional vulnerability to some more proximate risk factor of recurrent MD, a possibility consistent with the notion that childhood adversity can promote adult depression by increasing emotional vulnerability to adult stressful experiences (Rutter 1989).

The vulnerability factors that have most frequently been hypothesized to explain this stress-exacerbating effect are enduring features of the self, such as self-efficacy and conceptions of others in relation to oneself that can influence maintenance of support networks (Harris et al. 1990; Masten, Best, & Garmezy 1990; Metalsky & Joiner 1992). This possibility was investigated by estimating a series of models in which we determined whether any of the time-1 potential mediators interacted with FV to predict recurrent MD. The only significant interaction to emerge from this exploratory analysis was for chronic interpersonal stress on MD. As the interaction was significant in both the lower and higher father education subsamples, we interpreted it as genuine rather than due to a single chance occurrence in a set of twelve separate tests.

Respondents who experienced childhood family violence were found to be much more likely than others to have high levels of chronic adult interpersonal stress. However, FV was associated with increased risk of recurrent MD only in the presence of high chronic adult interpersonal stress. Respondents with a history of FV who did not subsequently have adult interpersonal stress had no higher rates of adult MD than respondents with neither FV nor adult interpersonal stress. There are at least two plausible interpretations of this finding.

One is that the interaction was due to selection rather than to causation. This could occur if the vulnerability to recurrent depression associated with FV also causes chronic interpersonal stress, in which case the existence of these stressors would be more a marker of vulnerability than an exacerbating factor. An indirect test of this interpretation was carried out by estimating interactions of FV with age of onset of depression, number of lifetime episodes of depression, and "density" of depression (defined in terms of average number of episodes per year since first onset). If selection was at work, we would have expected that these measures of the severity and course of depression would have had powerful explanatory effects on the interaction between FV and interpersonal stress. However, the interaction between FV and interpersonal stress remained statistically significant and unchanged in magnitude when these additional interactions were used as controls, arguing against the selection interpretation.

The second plausible interpretation is that the interaction between FV and interpersonal stress comes about because FV is associated with vulnerability factors that increase emotional reactivity to adult stress. If this is true, though, then these vulnerability factors must be quite specific to interpersonal stress, because FV was not found to interact with other measures of chronic stress in the ACL. If true, this specificity would be in some ways heartening, because it would imply that interventions that focused on the interpersonal relationships of those at risk due to early exposure to violence might be more effective than interventions that attempted to change the more global conditions of their lives.

Some small amount of previous research has been done on specific vulnerabilities of this sort (see Metalsky & Joiner 1992), and there are several ways they could come into play in the interaction between FV and interpersonal stress. One is that FV might create disturbed attachment styles (Alexander 1992), which in turn increase emotional reactivity to interpersonal stress (Barnett & Gotlib 1988). Family violence might also increase the tendency to make more extreme appraisals or to use relatively maladaptive coping strategies to manage interpersonal stress. Consistent with this possibility, previous research has shown that denial, repression, regression, and dissociation are frequently adopted by those exposed to extreme childhood adversity (Coons & Milstein 1984). These coping strategies may have survival value during childhood in the context of insecure and disorganized family relationships, but are maladaptive in adult interpersonal contexts (Sroufe & Rutter 1984). Another possibility is that adult interpersonal stress may reactivate depressogenic memories of childhood violence (Millon 1990). Depending on the mechanisms involved, it is conceivable that the link between FV and recurrence of depression could be broken by interventions aimed at modifying attachment styles, or at providing social-skills training that would either reduce exposure to interpersonal stress or change coping and appraisal processes in order to enhance the efficacy of conflict resolution or reduce emotional reactivity to interpersonal stress.

The National Comorbidity Survey

Replicating and expanding the ACL results

The ACL results were useful in suggesting that we were correct in our original concern about the importance of history of depression as a mediator and modifier of the relationship between childhood adversity and adult depression. However, the analysis raised at least as many questions as it answered, owing to limitations in the measures. For example, the coarse assessment of predictor variables increased chances of biased recall (Gotlib et al. 1988; Lewinsohn & Rosenbaum 1987). Moreover, even though past-year depression was defined by the co-occurrence of multiple symptoms, the single-item measure of lifetime depression was overinclusive (McLeod et al. 1990). It was all the more striking, in light of these limitations, that although we documented fairly substantial gross associations between most of the childhood adversities and recent episodes of depression, these associations were consistently attenuated when the analysis was confined to respondents with a history of depression. This led us to believe that specification in terms of history was truly important. However, we realized that this pattern of results needed to be replicated in data sets with more adequate measures before we could conclude that these childhood adversities have much stronger effects on first onset of depression than on recurrence, or that history of depression mediates the effects of some important childhood adversities on recent depression.

Soon after completing the ACL analyses, we had an opportunity to lay the groundwork for replication as part of the design of the National Comorbidity Survey (NCS), which was designed to obtain nationally representative data on the prevalence, risk factors, and consequences of psychiatric morbidity and comorbidity. The NCS was carried out by the Survey Research Center at the University of Michigan in a nationally representative sample of noninstitutionalized persons living in the coterminous United States based on a multistage, stratified, area probability sampling design. The sample size was 8,098; the response rate was 82%. More details on the NCS design are presented elsewhere (Kessler et al. 1994).

Based on the results of the ACL analysis, we included a long series of questions about childhood adversity in the NCS. One group of these questions used the FHRDC method to generate diagnoses of maternal and paternal psychopathology (depression, generalized anxiety disorder, alcoholism, drug dependence, and antisocial personality disorder) during the respondents' childhood years. Another group assessed the parenting styles of the respondents' mother and father in terms of warmth and overprotectiveness with scales developed by Parker and Parker (1991). A third group assessed verbal and physical violence of the respondents' parents toward each other and toward the respondents, using scales developed by Straus (1990). A final group of questions asked about a wide range of potentially traumatic childhood events such as separation from a parent, death of a loved one, and sexual abuse.

Measures of adult psychiatric disorders were based on a modified version of the CIDI (Composite International Diagnostic Interview; WHO 1990), a fully structured diagnostic interview developed in a collaborative WHO/ADAMHA project (Robins et al. 1988) to foster epidemiologic and cross-cultural comparative research by producing diagnoses according to the definitions and criteria of both DSM-III-R (APA 1987) and the Diagnostic Criteria for Research of the ICD-10 (WHO 1991). The version of the CIDI used in the NCS required an average of more than one hour to administer and was used to generate diagnoses of DSM-III-R mood disorders (major depression, dysthymia, mania), anxiety disorders (generalized anxiety disorder, panic disorder, phobia, post-traumatic stress disorder), substance use disorders (alcohol abuse, alcohol dependence, drug abuse, drug dependence), and other disorders (conduct disorder, adult antisocial behavior, schizophrenia, and other nonaffective psychoses). Good reliability and validity of these assessments were documented in a series of international studies carried out as part of the WHO field trials of the CIDI (Wittchen et al. 1990) as well as in an NCS clinical re-appraisal study (Wittchen et al. 1995; Wittchen et al., submitted).

Our initial analyses of these data used information on age of onset of the separate NCS/DSM-III-R disorders and episode prevalence during the twelve months prior to the interview to replicate and extend the ACL analyses. We began by examining bivariate associations of over 30 different measures of childhood adversity in predicting twelve-month prevalences of the separate NCS disorders. Two important results emerged. First, the vast majority of dichotomously measured childhood adversities were found to be significantly and positively associated with recent prevalences of not only depression but also almost all other adult disorders assessed in the NCS, with ORs ranging between 1.3 and 4.6. Second, the adversities differed in the adult disorders that they affected most powerfully. For example, whereas the experience of being in a life-threatening accident as a child had its strongest effect on adult agoraphobia (OR = 3.9), exposure to childhood family violence had its strongest effect on adult depression (OR = 4.2).

We next investigated the effects of childhood adversities on first onset of the NCS disorders. As in the more limited investigation of the ACL data, results showed that the vast majority of the adversities were significantly associated with each of the lifetime disorders, and that the majority of these effects decreased significantly with age. Further, although most adversities were significant predictors of early-onset disorders (defined as disorders that began earlier than age 20), only a minority of the adversities predicted later-onset disorders, and with effects that were generally weaker than in predicting early-onset disorders.

We then examined whether various forms of childhood adversity influence twelve-month persistence of the NCS disorders among respondents with a lifetime history of psychiatric disorders. Results showed that for the most part they do not. Nor could we document that the effects of the adversities on recurrence varied as a function of either current age or age at onset.

The joint effects of multiple adversities

The NCS data were also used to study the joint effects of various adversities on adult psychiatric disorders. This was done by estimating multivariate models of the joint effects of all the adversities considered in the bivariate models described previously. The effects of most childhood adversities on adult disorder became statistically insignificant in these multivariate models. More detailed analyses were then carried out to determine whether it is possible to create composite risk scores of the significant childhood adversities in a fashion similar to the way risk factors for heart disease have been combined to create the Framingham Index for coronary heart disease (Truett, Cornfield, & Kannel 1967). We found that this was not possible owing to the powerful and complex interactions among the adversities in predicting most adult disorders.

These interactions were examined using an empirical search strategy that created optimally predictive interactive risk profiles among multiple predictor variables (Kraemer et al., submitted). Preliminary results suggested that a number of these profiles exist and that most of them involve some combination of disturbed attachment relationships and traumatic experiences of either interpersonal loss or interpersonal violence. We are still in the process of investigating these profiles.

One of the most intriguing parts of this ongoing analysis concerns the long-term effects of parental divorce, which has increased so dramatically since the end of World War II (Bumpass & Castro 1987; Cherlin 1981) that today nearly 50% of all children in this country have experienced it (Bumpass 1984). A review of the considerable body of research that has emerged to examine the impact of parental divorce on children suggests that it has a variety of adverse effects on mental health that persist into adulthood (Chase-Lansdale 1990; Wertlieb 1995). However, almost all of this research has been based on simple comparisons between children in maritally intact homes and those in disrupted homes, without adjusting for the fact that children of divorce are much more likely than others to have been exposed, prior to the breakup, to such other adversities as family violence and parental psychopathology.

We are currently evaluating whether the long-term mental health of children is affected by parental divorce if the divorce brings with it the resolution of the adversities that led to the marital breakup. This is being done by comparing – within subsamples that are otherwise alike in exposure to childhood adversities – the mental health outcomes of adult respondents whose parents divorced with those of respondents whose parents did not. The analyses are sensitive to whether or not the custodial parents in divorced homes were the ones who were violent and/or psychiatrically impaired, as well as to the effects of custodial parent remarriage and changes in family socioeconomic resources after the marital breakup.

Although still incomplete, two consistent patterns are already clear in the preliminary results of these analyses. First, the long-term adverse effects of exposure to childhood family violence and parental psychopathology on adult psychiatric disorder are considerably greater than the adverse effects of coming from a broken home. For example, the OR associated with a dichotomously coded measure of parental marital distress is 1.5 in predicting adult depression, whereas the OR associated with parental divorce among respondents who did not report prior parental marital distress is only 1.2.

Second, there are pervasive negative interactions between divorce and other childhood family adversities; that is, the adverse effect of parental divorce is significantly less powerful in the subsample of respondents who were exposed to other childhood adversities. For example, while parental divorce is associated with an OR of 1.7 in predicting adult alcoholism among respondents whose fathers were reported not to suffer from a psychiatric disorder, there is a significant negative interaction between these two adversities (OR = 0.6) which can be interpreted as showing that there is no meaningful impact of parental divorce on adult alcoholism (i.e., 60% of 1.7 = 1.0, an equal relative OR) among respondents whose fathers had a psychiatric disorder. In subsamples characterized by multiple adversities that were in some sense resolved by the divorce – for example, in cases where the father was not only mentally ill but also violent and unable to hold a job – preliminary analyses suggest that parental divorce is associated with a significantly reduced risk of adult psychopathology.

The Virginia Twins Project

The possibility of confounding due to genetic effects

An important possibility that should be considered when evaluating effects of the sort described here is that unmeasured common causes might explain the relationships between childhood adversities and adult psychopathology. Perhaps the most plausible possibility of this sort is that genetic factors induce both family adversities and psychiatric disorders, creating the false impression that adversities cause adult disorders. Consistent with this possibility, twin research shows that there is a significant genetic component in most common psychiatric disorders (Kendler et al. 1995b), which means that genetic liability to these disorders is transmitted by inheritance from parent to child. We also know that parental psychiatric disorder can take a variety of behavioral forms that create adversities for children, including family violence, financial problems, and marital disruption (Kendler et al. 1993). Together, these effects could induce an association between adversity and disorder even if childhood adversity has no causal impact on adult disorder.

We are currently in the process of evaluating this possibility by working with survey data collected in a longitudinal general population survey of same-sex white female twin pairs selected from the population-based Virginia Twin Registry (VTR; Kendler et al. 1995b). This survey was carried out by a team of interviewers who possessed master's degrees in social work or psychology or bachelor's degrees and two or more years' clinical experience, and who were trained to administer psychiatric research diagnostic interviews. The purpose of the survey was to provide information on genetic and environmental risk factors for common psychiatric disorders. The sample was made up of 1,033 twin pairs, consisting of 590 monozygotic pairs, 440 dizygotic pairs, and three pairs of unknown zygosity. The cooperation rate during the personal interview phase was 92%. More details on the twin survey design are presented elsewhere (Kendler et al. 1995b).

The interview included a subset of the questions about childhood adversity used in the NCS. One group of questions used the FHRDC method to generate diagnoses of maternal and paternal psychopathology (depression, generalized anxiety disorder, alcoholism, drug dependence, and antisocial personality disorder) during the respondents' childhood years, based on respondent reports and supplemented by in-person diagnostic interviews with the parents themselves (if they were still alive and could be contacted). Another group of questions assessed the parenting styles of the respondents' mothers and fathers in terms of warmth and overprotectiveness with scales developed by Parker and Parker (1991). A final group of questions asked about a number of potentially traumatic childhood events such as separation from a parent and death of a loved one.

Measures of adult psychiatric disorders were based on a modified version of the Structured Clinical Interview for DSM-III-R (SCID; Spitzer et al. 1990), a semistructured research diagnostic interview designed to be administered by experienced clinicians. The version of the SCID used in the survey required an average of more than one hour to administer and was used to generate diagnoses of DSM-III-R major depression, generalized anxiety disorder, panic disorder, phobia, alcohol dependence, and bulimia nervosa.

Phenotypic associations

Our work with the twin data has pursued two lines of investigation. The first is studying the effects of childhood parental loss due to death or separation on a number of different adult disorders, including depression, anxiety disorders, and eating disorders. Results so far have shown that these effects vary as a function of the kind of loss, the parent involved, and the form of adult psychopathology (Kendler et al. 1992). For example, adult generalized anxiety and depression are associated with separation from either parent but not with parental death, while adult panic disorder is associated with parental death and maternal separation, but not paternal separation.

The second line of analysis is studying the effects of eleven childhood adversities on adult disorders, with a focus on depression. The adversities include four measures of parental psychopathology (maternal and paternal depression and alcoholism), five measures of relationship loss (death of mother, death of father, death of another close loved one, parental divorce, other long separation from one or both parents), and two other measures (parents cold and overprotective, any other major childhood adversity). Eight of these (the exceptions being death of mother or father and maternal alcoholism) have been found in bivariate survival analysis to be significantly and positively related to lifetime MD, with ORs ranging between 1.3 and 1.9. Consistent with the results of the ACL and NCS analyses, there is a general trend for the ORs to be larger in predicting early-onset than later-onset MD. However, none of these differences is statistically significant in the twin data.

Multivariate analysis has been used to study the joint effects of the five significant adversities. Three of these five remained significant in an initial multivariate survival model (mother depression, parental divorce, and cold/overprotective parenting). Interaction terms to assess the nonadditive joint effects of multiple adversities were found to be consistently insignificant but always less than 1.0. It was found that a composite risk score could be created based on the number (from 0 to 3) of significant adversities experienced, with ORs of 1.5 for exactly one, 2.3 for exactly two, and 2.9 for all three. Comparisons of overall model fit showed that this composite risk score model fits the data better than more complex models that include adversity-specific slopes or interactions.

Genetic associations

Ongoing analyses are evaluating the possibility that the significant associations between childhood adversities and adult disorders are due to unmeasured genetic influences. Although a number of analytic approaches are being explored to carry out this work, the approach that has been most illuminating up to now is one in which genetic liability to a particular disorder has been assessed in a regression framework by using a dummy variable representing genetic risk. Specifically, twins were assigned to one of four categories of increasing "genetic risk" on the basis of their co-twins' lifetime history of major depression: (1) monozygotic twin and co-twin unaffected, (2) dizygotic twin and co-twin unaffected, (3) dizygotic twin and co-twin affected, and (4) monozygotic twin and co-twin affected. The genetic effects in these four groups are assumed to be proportional to -1.0, -0.5, 0.5, and 1.0, respectively (see Kendler et al. 1995a). We would expect to find a significant two-way interaction between these variables in predicting a particular disorder if this disorder is under genetic control. In fact, this is what has been consistently found in these models. Furthermore, we would expect to find significant three-way interactions involving measures of childhood adversity if the effects of these adversities are due to genetic influences. This type of model has been used to specify the results concerning the significant effects of mother depression, cold/overprotective parenting style, and parental divorce on lifetime depression. Models that treated the three adversities separately yielded consistent evidence for positive interactions between genetic liability and childhood adversity in predicting lifetime risk of depression. However, none of these interactions was larger than OR = 1.2 and none was statistically significant, suggesting that the effects of individual adversities are only weakly affected by genetic liability.

A different result emerged, however, in a multivariate model that combined the three adversities into a composite risk score. It was found here that although there are no meaningful interactions between genetic liability and the impact of being exposed to either one (OR = 1.1) or two (OR = 1.0) of the three adversities, there is a powerful interaction between this liability and exposure to all three adversities (OR = 2.1). This result argues that while the effects of exposure to individual adversities on depression are largely due to environmental effects, the stronger relationship that exists between exposure to a large number of adversities and depression is due, at least in part, to the fact that people who are exposed to many childhood adversities may have a strong genetic liability to depression.

Overview and implications

Although still in progress, the results reported here make it clear that there are consistent significant relationships between many different retrospectively reported measures of childhood adversity and several dimensions of adult psychopathology. We have also found that the effects of individual adversities often disappear in multivariate analyses, and that there are a number of interactions among adversities in predicting adult disorders. These interactions are sometimes negative. Indeed, in the extreme, events normally considered adversities (such as parental divorce) were found to be associated with mental health benefits if they led to the resolution of other more powerful adversities.

The documentation of these complex associations between childhood adversities and adult psychopathology shows that caution is needed in research that focuses on a single adversity and a single form of psychopathology, in order not to overinterpret specific associations. For example, even though it may be true that the well-documented relationship between parental loss and adult depression is due, at least in part, to the mediating effect of early loss on depressogenic intrapsychic vulnerability (Harris et al. 1990), it would be a mistake to think that this is the dominant pathway in light of the following facts: the effects of early loss have been shown to be confounded with the effects of other childhood adversities; early loss has been found to predict not only adult depression but also adult anxiety disorder and substance use disorder; depression has often been found to occur secondary to these other disorders (Kessler et al. 1996).

Our research has also produced clear evidence that the effects of childhood adversities on adult psychopathology are largely due to effects on first onset rather than persistence of disorder. Our results suggest that childhood adversities have their most consistent and powerful effects on early-onset disorders, weaker effects on later-onset disorders, and generally insignificant effects on persistence of disorders. These are important distinctions to make for purposes of advancing our understanding of the causal pathways involved in the development of psychopathology, and for purposes of informing preventive intervention efforts.

If these preliminary results are true, it means that many of the factors that mediate the effects of childhood adversities on adult psychopathology are either in place prior to the first onset of disorder or are mediated by the effect of early onset on persistence. One important implication of this for risk-factor research is that lifetime history should routinely be included as a modifier variable in analyses of the relationships between childhood adversities and adult disorders, as failure to do so could lead to incorrect inferences about the importance of variables that are related to early onset but have no active impact on adult onset or persistence. An important implication for intervention research is that ideas about the timing of interventions and intervention targets need to be rethought in order to recognize that children exposed to many forms of adversity have a window of vulnerability to psychopathology that seems to end with the transition into adulthood. The determinants of the decreased vulnerability during the adult years is currently unclear, but could be due to decreasing exposure to the adversities over time, increasing resilience, the increasing importance of adult risk factors that dilute the effects of early adversities, selection of vulnerable children into early-onset disorders, or some combination of these different processes. Genetic influences could be involved as well, to the extent that they control exposure to some types of childhood adversities and also increase risk of early-onset disorder.

The weak link in this approach is that the data on childhood adversities are based on retrospective reports from adult respondents. Systematic recall bias could lead to incorrect inferences about causal pathways, although recent research suggests that this problem may not be as severe for some dimensions as previously supposed (Brewin, Andrews, & Gotlib 1993). The obvious way to resolve this problem is to carry out prospective studies from childhood into adulthood using large samples with oversamples of high-risk children. In order to design and execute such a massively expensive study, however, prior work based on retrospective data is needed. We know that results based on retrospective studies of adults cannot be definitive, but such results can be useful in advancing our knowledge of developmental psychopathology in a number of ways. First, such results can help build an argument for the importance of childhood experiences on adult disorders, a requirement for justifying future prospective studies. Second, they can be used to isolate the particular types of childhood adversities likely to be most important to assess in prospective studies and to take as a focus of intervention in prevention trials. Third, they can be used to pinpoint particular periods of the lifespan when effects are likely to occur. Fourth, they can help identify the environmental and intrapsychic mediators and modifiers that are likely to be involved in these effects. Our hope is that our ongoing work in this area, by focusing on the limitations of previous research that can be addressed with retrospective adult data and by recognizing the limits inherent in this type of study, will help us provide as firm a foundation as possible for future prospective research and intervention efforts.

References

Alexander, P. C. (1992). Application of attachment theory to the study of sexual abuse. *Journal of Consulting and Clinical Psychology* 60: 185-95.

Amato, P. R., & Keith, B. (1991). Separation from a parent during childhood and adult socioeconomic attainment. *Social Forces* 70: 187-206.

American Psychiatric Association [APA] (1987). *Diagnostic and Statistical Manual of Mental Disorders*, rev. 3rd ed. (DSM-III-R). Washington, DC: American Psychiatric Association.

Barnett, P. A., & Gotlib, I. H. (1988). Psychosocial functioning and depression: distinguishing among antecedents, concomitants, and consequences. *Psychological Bulletin* 104: 97-126.

Birtchnell, J., Evans, C., & Kennard, J. (1988). Life history factors associated with neurotic symptomatology in a rural community sample of 40-49 year old women. *Journal of Affective Disorders* 3: 271-85.

Brewin, C. R., Andrews, B., & Gotlib, I. H. (1993). Psychopathology and early experience: a reappraisal of retrospective reports. *Psychological Bulletin* 113: 82-98.

Brown, G. R., & Anderson, B. (1991). Psychiatric morbidity in adult inpatients with childhood histories of sexual and physical abuse. *American Journal of Psychiatry* 148: 55-61.

Brown, G. W., Andrews, B., Harris, T., Adler, Z., & Bridges, L. (1986). Social support, self-esteem, and depression. *Psychological Medicine* 16: 813-31.

Brown, G. W., & Harris, T. O. (1978). *Social Origins of Depression: A Study of Psychiatric Disorder in Women*. New York: Free Press.

Browne, A., & Finkelhor, D. (1986). Initial and long-term effects: a review of the research. In D. Finkelhor (ed.), *Sourcebook on Childhood Sexual Abuse*. Beverly Hills, CA: Sage, pp. 143-79.

Bryer, J. B., Nelson, B. A., Miller, J. B., & Krol, P. A. (1987). Childhood sexual and physical abuse as factors in adult psychiatric illness. *American Journal of Psychiatry* 144: 1426-30.

Bumpass, L. L. (1984). Children and marital disruption: a replication and update. *Demography* 21: 71-82.

Bumpass, L. L., & Castro, T. (1987). Recent trends and differentials in marital disruption. Working paper no. 87-20, Center for Demography and Ecology, University of Wisconsin, Madison.

Burke, K. C., Burke, J. D., Rae, D. S., & Regier, D. A. (1991). Comparing age at onset of major depression and other psychiatric disorders by birth cohorts in five U.S. community populations. *Archives of General Psychiatry* 48: 789-95.

Chase-Lansdale, P. L. (1990). The impact of divorce on life-span development: short and long term effects. In P. B. Baltes, D. L. Featherman, & R. M. Lerner (eds.), *Life-Span Development and Behavior*. Hillsdale, NJ: Erlbaum, pp. 105-50.

Cherlin, A. (1981). *Marriage, Divorce, Remarriage: Changing Patterns in the Postwar United States*. Cambridge, MA: Harvard University Press.

Coons, P. M., & Milstein, V. (1984). Rape and posttraumatic stress in multiple personality. *Psychological Reports* 55: 839-45.

Coryell, W., Endicott, J., & Keller, M. B. (1991). Predictors of relapse into major depressive disorder in a nonclinical population. *American Journal of Psychiatry* 148: 1353-8.

Earls, F., Reich, W., Jung, K. G., & Cloninger, C. R. (1988). Psychopathology in children of alcoholic and antisocial parents. *Alcoholism: Clinical and Experimental Research* 12: 481-7.

Endicott, J., Andreason, N., & Spitzer, R. L. (1978). *Family History Research Diagnostic Criteria*. New York: Biometrics Research, New York State Psychiatric Institute.

Faravelli, C., Sacchetti, E., Ambonetti, A., Conte, G., Pallanti, S., & Vita, A. (1986). Early life events and affective disorder revisited. *British Journal of Psychiatry* 148: 288-95.

Fendrich, M., Warner, V., & Weissman, M. M. (1990). Family risk factors, parental depression, and psychopathology in offspring. *Developmental Psychology* 26: 40-50.

Fergusson, D. M., Dimond, M. E., & Horwood, L. J. (1986). Childhood family placement history and behavior problems in 6-year-old children. *Journal of Child Psychiatry* 27: 213-26.

Fleming, J. E., & Offord, D. R. (1990). Epidemiology of childhood depressive disorders: a critical review. *Journal of American Academy of Child and Adolescent Psychiatry* 29: 571-80.

Giles, D. E., Jarrett, R. B., Biggs, M. M., Guzick, D. S., & Rush, A. J. (1989). Clinical predictors of recurrence in depression. *American Journal of Psychiatry* 146: 764-7.

Goodyear, I. M. (1990). Family relationships, life events and childhood psychopathology. *Journal of Child Psychology and Psychiatry* 31: 161-92.

Gotlib, I., Mount, J. H., Cordy, N. I., & Whiffen, V. E. (1988). Depression and perceptions of early parenting: a longitudinal investigation. *British Journal of Psychiatry* 152: 24-7.

Harrington, R., Fudge, H., Rutter, M., Pickles, A., & Hill, J. P. (1990). Adult outcomes of childhood and adolescent depression. *Archives of General Psychiatry* 47: 465-73.

Harris, T., Brown, G. W., & Bifulco, A. (1990). Loss of parent in childhood and adult psychiatric disorder: a tentative overall model. *Development and Psychopathology* 2: 311-28.

Hess, R. D., & Camara, K. A. (1979). Post-divorce family relationships as mediating factors in the consequences of divorce for children. *Journal of Social Issues* 35: 79-96.

Hojat, M., Borenstien, B. D., & Shapurian, R. (1990). Perceptions of childhood dissatisfaction with parents and selected personality traits in adulthood. *Journal of General Psychology* 117: 241-53.

Holmes, S. J., & Robins, L. N. (1988). The role of parental disciplinary practices in the development of depression and alcoholism. *Psychiatry* 51: 24-36.

House, J. S., Kessler, R. C., Herzog, R., Mero, R. P., Kinney, A. M., & Breslow, M. J. (1990). Age, socioeconomic status, and health. *The Milbank Quarterly* 68: 383-411.

Kendler, K. S., Neale, M. C., Kessler, R. C., Heath, A. C., & Eaves, L. J. (1992). Childhood parental loss and adult psychopathology in women: a twin study perspective. *Archives of General Psychiatry* 49: 109-16.

Kendler, K. S., Neale, M. C., Kessler, R. C., Heath, A. C., & Eaves, L. J. (1993). A twin study of recent life events and difficulties. *Archives of General Psychiatry* 50: 789-96.

Kendler, K. S., Kessler, R. C., Walters, E. E., MacLean, C., Neale, M. C., Heath, A. C., & Eaves, L. J. (1995a). Stressful life events, genetic liability, and onset of an episode of major depression in women. *American Journal of Psychiatry* 152: 833-42.

Kendler, K. S., Walters, E. E., Neale, M. C., Kessler, R. C., Heath, A. C., & Eaves, L. J. (1995b). The structure of the genetic and environmental risk factors for six major psychiatric disorders in women. *Archives of General Psychiatry* 52: 374-83.

Kessler, R. C., & Magee, W. J. (1993). Childhood adversities and adult depression: basic patterns of association in a U.S. national survey. *Psychological Medicine* 23: 679-90.

Kessler, R. C., & Magee, W. J. (1994). Childhood family violence and adult recurrent depression. *Journal of Health and Social Behavior* 35: 13-27.

Kessler, R. C., McGonagle, K. A., Zhao, S., Nelson, C. B., Hughes, M., Eshleman, S., Wittchen, H.-U., & Kendler, K. S. (1994). Lifetime and 12-month prevalence of DSM-III-R psychiatric disorders in the United States: results from the National Comorbidity Survey. *Archives of General Psychiatry* 51: 8-19.

Kessler, R. C., Nelson, C. B., McGonagle, K. A., Liu, J., Swartz, M., & Blazer, D. G. (1996). Comorbidity of DSM-III-R major depressive disorder in the general population: results from the U.S. National Comorbidity Survey. *British Journal of Psychiatry* 168: 17-30.

Kolvin, I., Miller, F. J., Fleeting, M., & Kolvin, P. A. (1988). Social and parenting factors affecting criminal-offence rates: findings from the Newcastle Thousand Family Study (1947-1980). *British Journal of Psychiatry* 152: 80-90.

Kovacs, M., & Paulaukas, S. L. (1984). Developmental stage and the expression of depressive disorders in children: an empirical analysis. *New Directions for Child Development* 26: 59-80.

Kraemer, H. C., Kazdin, A., Offord, D., Kessler, R. C., Jensen, P., & Kupfer, D. J. (submitted). Coming to terms with the terms of risk.

Lauer, R. H., & Lauer, J. C. (1991). The long-term relational consequences of problematic family backgrounds. *Family Relations* 40: 286-90.

Lewinsohn, P. M., Hoberman, H. M., & Rosenbaum, M. (1988). A prospective study of risk factors for unipolar depression. *Journal of Abnormal Psychology* 97: 251-64.

Lewinsohn, P. M., & Rosenbaum, M. (1987). Recall of parental behavior by acute depressives, remitted depressives, and nondepressives. *Journal of Personality and Social Psychology* 52: 611-19.

Masten, A. S., Best, K. M., & Garmezy, N. (1990). Resilience and development: contributions from the study of children who overcome adversity. *Development and Psychopathology* 2: 425–44.

Maughan, B., Gray, G., & Rutter, M. (1985). Reading retardation and antisocial behavior: a follow-up into employment. *Journal of Child Psychology and Psychiatry* 26: 741–58.

McGonagle, K. M., & Kessler, R. C. (1990). Chronic stress, acute stress, and depressive symptoms. *American Journal of Community Psychology* 18: 681–705.

McLeod, Jane D. (1991). Childhood parental loss and adult depression. *Journal of Health and Social Behavior* 35: 205–20.

McLeod, J. D., Turnbull, J. E., Kessler, R. C., & Abelson, J. M. (1990). Sources of discrepancy in the comparison of a lay-administered diagnostic instrument with clinical diagnosis. *Psychiatry Research* 31: 145–59.

Mendlewicz, J., & Baron, M. (1981). Morbidity risks in subtypes of unipolar depressive illness: differences between early and late onset forms. *British Journal of Psychiatry* 139: 463–6.

Metalsky, G. I., & Joiner, T. E., Jr. (1992). Vulnerability to depressive symptomatology: a prospective test of the diathesis-stress and causal mediation components of the hopelessness theory of depression. *Journal of Personality and Social Psychology* 63: 667–75.

Millon, T. (1990). The disorders of personality. In L. A. Pervin (ed.), *Handbook of Personality*. New York: Guilford, pp. 339–70.

O'Connell, R. A., & Mayo, J. A. (1988). The role of social factors in affective disorders: a review. *Hospital and Community Psychiatry* 39: 842–51.

Parker, G. (1984). The measurement of pathogenic parental style and its relevance to psychiatric disorder. *Social Psychiatry* 19: 75–85.

Parker, G., & Hadzi-Pavlovic, D. (1984). Modification of levels of depression in mother-bereaved women by parental and marital relationships. *Psychological Medicine* 14: 125–35.

Parker, G., & Parker, H. (1991). Female victims of child sexual abuse: adult adjustment. *Journal of Family Violence* 6: 183–97.

Parker, G., Tupling, H., & Brown, L. B. (1979). A parental bonding instrument. *British Journal of Medical Psychology* 52: 1–10.

Plantes, M. M., Prusoff, B. A., Brennan, J., & Parker, G. (1988). Parental representations of depressed outpatients from a U.S.A. sample. *Journal of Affective Disorders* 15: 149–55.

Quinton, D., Rutter, M., & Liddle, C. (1984). Institutional rearing, parenting, difficulties and marital support. *Psychological Medicine* 14: 107–24.

Robins, L. N., Helzer, J. E., Croughhan, J., & Ratcliff, K. L. (1981). National Institute of Mental Health Diagnostic Interview Schedule: its history, characteristics and validity. *Archives of General Psychiatry* 38: 381–9.

Robins, L. N., Wing, J., Wittchen, H., Helzer, J. E., Babor, T. F., Burke, J. D., Farmer, A., Jablenski, A., Pickens, R., Regier, D. A., Sartorius, N., & Towle, L. H. (1988). The Composite International Diagnostic Interview: an epidemiologic instrument suitable for use in conjunction with different diagnostic systems and in different cultures. *Archives of General Psychiatry* 45: 1069–77.

Rodgers, B. (1990). Behavior and personality in childhood as predictors of adult psychiatric disorder. *Journal of Child Psychology and Psychiatry* 31: 509–18.

Rutter, M. (1989). Pathways from childhood to adult life. *Journal of Child Psychology and Psychiatry* 30: 23–51.

Sorenson, S. B., Rutter, C. M., & Aneshensel, C. S. (1991). Depression in the community: an investigation into age of onset. *Journal of Consulting and Clinical Psychology* 59: 541–6.

Spitzer, R. L., Williams, J. B. W., Gibbon, M., & First, M. B. (1990). *Structured Clinical Interview for DSM-III-R, Patient Edition* (SCID-P, version 1.0). Washington, DC: American Psychiatric Press.

Sroufe, L. A., & Rutter, M. (1984). The domain of developmental psychopathology. *Child Development* 55: 17–29.

Straus, M. A. (ed.) (1990). *Physical Violence in American Families: Risk Factors and Adaptations to Violence in 8,145 Families*. New Brunswick, NJ: Transaction.

Tennant, C. (1988). Parental loss in childhood: its effect in adult life. *Archives of General Psychiatry* 45: 1045–50.

Testa, M., Miller, B. A., Downs, W. R., & Panek, D. (1990). Long-term effects of childhood victimization: the moderating impact of social support. Paper presented at the annual meeting of the American Society of Criminology (7–10 November, Baltimore).

Truett, J., Cornfield, J., & Kannel, W. (1967). A multivariate analysis of the risk of coronary heart disease in Framingham. *Journal of Chronic Diseases* 20: 511–24.

Turnbull, J. E., George, L. K., Landerman, R., Swartz, M. S., & Blazer, D. G. (1990). Social outcomes related to age of onset among psychiatric disorders. *Journal of Consulting and Clinical Psychology* 58: 832–9.

Weissman, M. M., Bruce, M. L., Leaf, P. J., Florio, L. P., & Holzer, C. III. (1991). Affective disorders. In L. N. Robins & D. A. Regier (eds.), *Psychiatric Disorders in America*. New York: Free Press, pp. 53–80.

Weissman, M. M., Gammon, G. D., John, K., Merikangas, K. R., Warner, V., Prusoff, B. A., & Sholomskas, D. (1987). Children of depressed parents: increased psychopathology and early onset of major depression. *Archives of General Psychiatry* 44: 847–53.

Wertlieb, D. (1995). Children whose parents divorce: life trajectories and turning points. [Chapter 9 in this volume]

West, M. O., & Prinz, R. J. (1987). Parental alcoholism and childhood psychopathology. *Psychological Bulletin* 102: 204–18.

Willett, J. B., & Singer, J. D. (1995). Using discrete-time survival analysis to study event occurrence across the life course. [Chapter 14 in this volume]

Wittchen, H.-U., Kessler, R. C., Zhao, S., & Abelson, J. (1995). Reliability and clinical validity of UM-CIDI generalized anxiety disorder. *Journal of Psychiatric Research* 29: 95–110.

Wittchen, H.-U., Kessler, R. C., Zhao, S., & Abelson, J. (submitted). Reliability and procedural validity of UM-CIDI DSM-III-R phobic disorders. *Psychological Medicine*.

Wittchen, H.-U., Robins, L. N., Cottler, L. B., & Participants in the Multicentre WHO/ADAMHA Field Trials Interrater Reliability of the Composite International Diagnostic Interview (CIDI). (1990). Results from the Multicenter WHO/ADAMHA Field Trials (Wave I). In C. N. Stefanis, A. D. Rabavilas, & C. R. Soldatos (eds.), *Psychiatry: A World Perspective*, vol. 1 (International Congress Series, vol. 900). Amsterdam: Elsevier, pp. 125–32.

World Health Organization [WHO] (1990). *Composite International Diagnostic Interview* (CIDI, version 1.0). Geneva, Switzerland: World Health Organization.

World Health Organization [WHO] (1991). *International Classification of Diseases* (ICD-10). Geneva, Switzerland: World Health Organization.

3 The impact of twenty childhood and adult traumatic stressors on the risk of psychiatric disorder

Blair Wheaton, Patricia Roszell, & Kimberlee Hall

Introduction

The word "stress" has come to have many connotations. Whereas research on life stress focused almost exclusively on life change events through the 1970s, research and theory since then have resulted in a differentiated stress universe, with multiple stress concepts (Wheaton 1994) . Beyond life events, one can identify at least five other types of stressors, including chronic stressors (Pearlin 1989; Wheaton 1983), daily hassles (Kanner et al. 1981), macrosystem stressors such as economic downturns (Dooley & Catalano 1984); "nonevents," that is, the non-occurrence of expected events (Gersten et al. 1974); as well as various forms of childhood and adult traumas, considered individually or collectively (Cadoret et al. 1990; Garmezy 1983; Kessler et al. 1995; Rutter & Quinton 1977; Terr 1991).

In Chapter 2 of this volume, Kessler and his colleagues explored their ongoing research program on childhood adversities. These childhood adversities overlap considerably with the traumatic stressors studied in this chapter. Both refer to serious, often overwhelming, stressful experiences. The term "adversity" clearly allows for both discrete traumatizing experiences and more chronically difficult life conditions. In this chapter, we consider both types of stressors.

The potential importance of traumatic events and situations for long-term mental health is hardly in doubt. Research attention to such traumas has been intense in recent years, especially for certain "core" traumas thought to be crucial in setting long-term trajectories of mental health problems. These include issues such as sexual abuse in childhood (Browne & Finkelhor 1986; Burnam et al. 1988; Green 1993; Kendall-Tackett, Williams, & Finkelhor 1993), physical violence and abuse (Bryer et al. 1987; Gelles & Conte 1990; Holmes & Robins 1988; Kessler & Magee 1994), parental death (Brown, Harris, & Bifulco 1986; McLeod 1991; Saler 1992; Tennant 1988), and parental divorce (Amato & Booth 1991; Amato & Keith 1991; Aro & Palosaari 1992; Glenn & Kramer 1985). Sample findings are as follows: sexual abuse has a substantial association with psychiatric disorders, for some disorders resulting in relative risks in the range of 2 to 3 (Burnam et al. 1988); parental divorce is more moderately but still consistently related to psychiatric outcome (Amato & Keith 1991); the evidence that parental death causes any long-term impact is, despite widespread expectations, at least in doubt (Tennant 1988). However, even in cases where little net impact is demonstrated, there is no doubt that such events are *conditionally* important for some segment of the population, depending on the context of the occurrence of the trauma – for example, a close versus distant relationship with the parent who died (Umberson & Chen 1994).

Despite the clear interest in traumas, this interest tends to coexist in a number of parallel literatures, each one focusing on a particular trauma. As a consequence, these literatures are more successful in focusing on the distinctive features and course of each trauma than on commonalities or interdependence across traumas. As noted by Kessler in the previous chapter, a number of problems in our understanding of traumatic stressors flow from the study of individual, rather than sets of, traumas. We offer three points in this regard. First, the lack of comparative research across traumas means that we really do not know which traumas are more or less important as risk factors in psychiatric disorder. Rather, we often have estimates of risk that do not take into account, for example, the attendant risk due to other stressors that would be estimated in the same data. Second, a related point is that we must control for prior stress, as well as for prior social background, if we are to understand the actual risk consequences of particular stressors. For example, we may find that the effect of parental divorce in part disappears when we control for pre-existing mental health problems in the parents. The more general problem here is that particular stressors may occur as part of a "matrix of disadvantage" (Mullen et al. 1993), suggesting that there are clusters of stressors that tend to co-occur and are in part dependent on each other. Thus, studying a stressor on its own could be essentially misleading.

Finally, the very *level* of impact of a trauma may conditionally depend on the cumulative burden resulting from prior stress, or the presence of specific prior stressors. For example, the actual effect of a divorce may vary considerably, depending on the level of prior stress in the marriage (Wheaton 1990). This point is echoed by Kessler and associates in Chapter 2; as their discussion shows, the implications could take many forms. One is that interactions among stressors occurring over time cannot be discovered unless multiple stressors are measured, and these interactions may be crucial to understanding both the scope and actual size of risk effects for specific stressors. Another implication is that the effect of a traumatic experience may depend on the ordering and content of stressors experienced (Roszell 1996).

These points suggest that studying sets of traumatic stressors across the life course, accompanied by information on age and the ordering and spacing of occurrence of these stressors, may be crucial in properly understanding their long-term role in psychiatric disorders.

Defining traumatic stress

We should clarify our use of the term "traumatic stress" relative to, for example, the usual stressful life-change event. The DSM-III-R manual defines a traumatic event as one "that is outside the range of usual human experience and . . . would be markedly distressing to almost anyone" (APA 1987, p. 250). This definition emphasizes one of the essential characteristics distinguishing traumas from the kinds of life events commonly seen in life event inventories: the magnitude of the stressor. Norris (1992, p. 409) defines traumas in terms of a population of events marked by a sudden or extreme force and denoting "violent encounters with nature, technology, or humankind." Both this and the APA definition point to important classes of traumas, but they are incomplete along two dimensions. First, not all traumas occur only as events. For example, a single rape would be considered a traumatic event, but repeated, regular, and therefore *expected* sexual abuse is best thought of as a chronic traumatic *situation*. Including chronic situations allows us to broaden the definition to include Terr's (1991) consideration both of events and of situations marked by "prolonged and sickening anticipation" (p. 11). Although we ordinarily think of traumas as "shocks," conforming to the notion of an event, we also can think of traumas as involving a long-term repeated pattern of stressful encounters and anticipation of such encounters, leading to increasing numbness, withdrawal, or dissociation (Terr 1991). Second, it should also be clear that not all traumas need be violent.

Spelling out the implications of these definitions, we can see a number of elements of traumas that are important: (1) they must be more severe in level of threat than the usual life-change event; (2) they may occur either as isolated events or as long-term chronic problems; and (3) because of their severity, they are thought to have greater potential for long-term impacts than most other types of stressors.

Designs and methods for studying traumas

The large and varied literature on the psychiatric risk of childhood and adult traumas can be characterized as having a number of methodological tendencies, three of which we address in this chapter.

First, many literatures on specific traumas (e.g., parental death) have relied heavily on retrospective designs using clinical samples, with a case-control logic (Crook & Eliot 1980). Usually, the approach in these studies is to utilize "known cases" of subjects in treatment for a psychiatric disorder and compare their trauma history to a group of either medical patients or some other in-treatment control group. The complexities, and possible methods biases, due to using patients in treatment have been well documented in various critical commentaries (e.g., for parental death), but more important for our purposes is the nonrepresentativeness of the populations used in these studies.

The true risk consequences of traumatic stressors may not be estimated properly in selected or specialized samples. The problem is that any observed risk in such samples may be suspect due to the possibility that the risk effect is activated by a specific but unmeasured characteristic of the sample. For example, people in treatment share *some* experience of poor health or health problems. If there is an interaction between prior psychosocial trauma and recent health troubles of any kind, such that the effect of the trauma is reduced in the presence of attendant health problems, then the lack of a difference across case-control groups where both are drawn from different types of clinical samples is suspect. In this case, there may be a risk effect of the trauma, but it is masked by the relatively constant level of one variable in the samples that are compared.

Whether or not matching helps does depend to some degree on how many essential confounding variables can be matched across groups, but the fundamental problem remains. What matching achieves, at best, is holding constant the potentially confounding factors in comparisons; however, if the samples involved are selected for a characteristic that is related to the outcome at issue (e.g., patients in treatment), then it is also likely to show restricted variability on some important characteristics. The result of this will be that control by matching will only match on certain values of control variables, and this cannot take into account the possibility of interactions between a risk factor and a second factor when it is measured across its full range.

The implication is that risk estimation may benefit as a result of sampling from some sufficiently general or heterogeneous population. This allows estimation of effects under conditions which, at least, average out differences in effects of risk factors across other variables, so that we are observing an average impact rather than an impact in a specific group.

Second, some approaches to detecting the effect of traumatic stress cannot fully take into account the timing of events in a way that allows a sensitive or unbiased estimate of risk. To take a standard example, we could use the prior occurrence of a trauma to predict the later occurrence of psychiatric disorder, which may have considerable variability in onset across the adult life course, using a technique such as logistic regression to estimate the increased risk of disorder due to the trauma experience. However, the actual amount of time between the traumas and the onset of disorder will vary across cases, and the model does not include information about this timing. Nothing in this example is specific to this technique; it applies to any attempt to estimate risk that cannot take timing into account.

In this chapter, we use an event history approach – also more generally known as survival modeling – to estimate risk due to the occurrence of 20 childhood and adult traumatic stressors, estimated in a sample of 1,393 randomly selected respondents of the Toronto metropolitan area. (The event history model is discussed in detail by Willett and Singer in Chapter 14 of this volume.) An essential feature of this approach for our purposes is that it considers each time period in a person's life – each year – as a separate observation. Thus, the exact timing of stressors and the onset of disorder are captured by the data. Because it now appears that the average age of first onset is around 19 to 21 years old (Kessler et al. 1994), an age we replicate in our data, it is essential that we have and use timing information to separate traumas that precede first onsets from traumas that occur after, such as those that predominantly occur during the adult life course. Thus, following the recent work of Kessler and his colleagues, and as reiterated in Chapter 2, we must separate the prediction and understanding of *first onset* from the issue of *recurrence*.

There is still considerable uncertainty about how best to represent the effect of traumas in these models. For example, we could represent the trauma as a binary variable occurring only in the year it occurred. We could also consider the trauma as a "toggle" stressor that is turned on by the event, but exists as a continuing presence throughout life once it occurs. These are the two extremes discussed by Willett and Singer. Here we take a middle-ground approach between these two extremes by specifying each trauma as a *bounded process.* This means, specifically, that we test for the possibility that each trauma may have a lagged effect on the onset of psychiatric disorders. For example, in the case of parental divorce, we can imagine that the year the divorce actually occurred is just the fruition of a process that began one to two years earlier, and in fact will continue for a few years more. To evaluate this possibility, we can specify the effect of divorce as occurring over a set of years before and after the actual year, and test for the continuing impact over a range of years.

A final point about our approach should be noted. Because we are assessing the impacts of a range of traumatic stressors in one sample, this means we can raise the same analytical issues with respect to the impact of these traumas. That is, we can control for the same confounding background factors, we can estimate the relevance of age for each trauma studied, and we can estimate the importance of prior stressors as contextual modifiers of the risk consequences of each trauma.

Analytical objectives

This chapter considers the impact of 20 commonly measured childhood and adult traumatic stressors (see Table 1) on the risk of first-onset psychiatric disorder as measured by the UM-CIDI (Kessler et al. 1994). The focus of our analysis is the overall impacts of these traumas, but we also address four essential issues about these impacts: (1) whether part of the estimated risk at the bivariate level is due to the effect of controls for prior psychosocial and sociodemo-graphic risk factors; (2) whether part of the estimated risk is due to the indirect influence of family psychiatric history simultaneously on the risk of disorder for the respondent as well as the risk of exposure to traumas; (3) whether the effects of traumas vary with age or stage of life; and (4) whether the effects of traumas vary with the level of prior accumulated trauma exposure existing at the time the trauma occurs.

Data and measures

The data we use in this chapter are from a recent longitudinal study of the Toronto area undertaken to assess the risk effects of a range of sources of stress on mental health (Turner & Wheaton 1991). The sampling frame in this study included all person aged 18–55 years in the metropolitan Toronto area. A multi-stage sampling procedure was used, starting with census enumeration areas, then household units within areas, and finally randomly selected household re-spondents within households.

Two waves of interviews were conducted over 1990–92; for each respondent, the two interviews were approximately one year apart. The final N at the first wave was 1,393; this represents over a 75% response rate. The follow-up in-cluded 1,206 of these respondents, representing over 86% of the original re-spondents. Although sample weights have been developed for these data, they cannot be applied to the event history data here because we analyze a "person-period" data set in which each person in the data set contributes as many ob-servations (years) to the final data set as there are years before and up to the onset of a disorder (or their current age, if no disorder has occurred).

Our primary measure of psychiatric disorder is the UM-CIDI, the version of the original CIDI (Wittchen et al. 1991) that was developed at the University of Michigan by Kessler for the National Comorbidity Survey in the United States (Kessler et al. 1994). This is a highly structured interview, in the tradition of the DIS, that allows for assessment of lifetime and current prevalence of a range of DSM-III-R disorders. Age of onset was gathered for each disorder considered here. We note that our prevalence rates for these disorders in Toronto are quite close to those reported by Kessler et al. (1994).

In assessing the effects of the trauma measures, we considered a number of possible controls. We were specifically concerned with background factors that could simultaneously increase the risk of trauma exposure and the disorders we were studying. A number of socioeconomic and demographic differences were considered. In the end, two had consistently important effects in our models: gender, and the average of parental education (measured in years). We also in-corporate a measure of family psychiatric history that is based on a series of questions in the interview about the actual treatment for, or life difficulties due to, problems with "depression or nerves" or with substance abuse for the respondent's biological mother, father, children, siblings, aunts and uncles, and grandparents. This measure could simply stand for the environmental impact of growing up in such a family. On the other hand, although we cannot determine what the family history really stands for in this kind of design, it is important to mention that it may be correlated with genetic influences as well.

The actual stressors we include are shown in Table 1. When a respondent reported any of these situations or events, follow-up questioning was used to determine age of occurrence. For any stressor under study, we constructed a count of prior exposure to all other stressors that had occurred before the time of occurrence of the stressor in question. This allowed us to assess the contextual effect of prior accumulated exposure on the impacts of each stressor in turn.

These stressors are reported retrospectively, sometimes over many years and stages of the life course. Chapter 13 in this volume reports some encouraging and important results about the types of errors that tend to occur in reporting past stressors: specifically, underreporting is much more common, and biases do not change estimated impacts greatly (other than underestimating these impacts). We are working on assessments of the validity of reporting of the items in Table 1 as well, taking advantage of the fact that the same past stressors are reported twice, one year apart. Our results on this issue suggest that most items are reported with acceptable to very good levels of reliability, and that "state-dependent" biases, reflecting changes in reporting the occurrence of a past stressor concurrent with changes in diagnostic status between waves I and II, occur for only a minority of items.

Results

The low prevalence rates observed for individual DSM-III-R psychiatric disorders necessitated collapsing them into more general categories. In the results, we consider two aggregate measures: "psychological" disorders, including the diagnoses of depression, dysthymia, generalized anxiety, and panic disorder; and "substance" disorder, including alcohol or drug abuse or dependence. Just under 35% ($n = 482$) of the sample experienced one or more psychological disorders in their lifetime, and 27% ($n = 375$) of the sample experienced a substance disorder.

The underlying hazard profiles for onset of any psychological disorder and any substance disorder are illustrated in Figures 1 and 2, respectively. The likelihood of onset of psychological disorder gradually increases over childhood, peaking at about 18 to 20 years of age, and slightly decreases thereafter with additional high-risk periods at approximately 25, 30, and 40 years of age. The likelihood of onset of a substance disorder dramatically increases over

Table 1. *Measurement and prevalence of childhood and adulthood trauma exposure, Toronto metropolitan area, 1990–92*

| | Prevalence | | Main-effect measurement | |
Trauma	*n*	Percent	Psychological disorder[a]	Substance disorder[b]
1. Did you ever have a major illness or accident that required you to spend a week or more in the hospital?	389	28.0	discrete	discrete
2. Did you have to do a year of school over again?	344	24.7	discrete	discrete
3. Did your father or mother not have a job for a long time when they wanted to be working?	202	14.5	4 back to 1 forward	1 back
4. Were you ever sent away from home because you did something wrong?	49	3.5	1 back to 1 forward	3 forward
5. Did either of your parents drink or use drugs so often or so regularly that it caused problems for the family?	247	17.8	discrete	discrete
6. Were you regularly physically abused by one of your parents?	83	6.0	1 back	discrete
7. Are you currently separated or divorced? Have you ever been divorced?	228	16.5	1 back to 2 forward	discrete
8. Have you ever ended a relationship with someone you were still in love with?	524	37.9	2 back	discrete
9. Has one of your parents died?	552	39.7	discrete	discrete
10. Did your parents ever get divorced?	190	13.7	discrete	2 back to 2 forward
11. Has a spouse or other loved one, including other children, died? Have you ever had a child who died at or near birth or had to be given up shortly after birth?	685	49.4	1 back to 2 forward	discrete

Table 1 *(cont.)*

| | Prevalence | | Main-effect measurement | |
Trauma	*n*	Percent	Psychological disorder[a]	Substance disorder[b]
12. Have you ever seen something violent happen to someone or seen someone killed?	538	38.7	3 back to 1 forward	3 back to 2 forward
13. Have you ever been in a major fire, flood, earthquake, or other natural disaster?	238	17.1	discrete	discrete
14. Have you ever had a serious accident, injury, or illness that was life-threatening or caused long-term disability?	310	22.3	2 back to 1 forward	discrete
15. Has one of your children ever had a near-fatal accident or life-threatening illness?	117	8.4	discrete	discrete
16. Have you ever been in combat in a war, lived near a war zone, or been present during a political uprising?	238	17.1	discrete	discrete
17. Have you ever discovered your spouse or partner in a close relationship was unfaithful?	354	25.5	3 back to 2 forward	4 back to 2 forward
18. Have you ever been either sexually abused or sexually assaulted?	127	9.1	5 forward	1 forward
19. Have you ever been physically abused by your current or a previous spouse or partner?	137	9.8	2 back	1 back
20. Has your spouse, partner, or child been addicted to alcohol or drugs?	172	12.4	5 back to 2 forward	3 back

[a] Psychological disorder includes diagnosis of depression, dysthymia, generalized anxiety, or panic disorder.
[b] Substance disorder includes diagnosis of alcohol abuse or dependence or drug abuse or dependence.

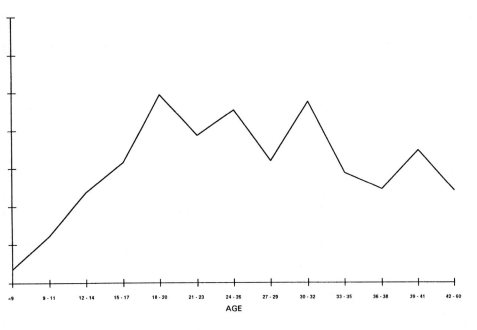

Figure 1. Probability of onset of any psychological disorder by age group.

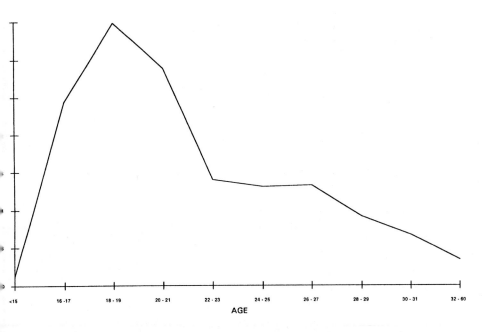

Figure 2. Probability of onset of any substance disorder by age group.

adolescence, reaching peak levels at 18 to 19 years of age, and declines to a relatively low likelihood subsequent to 23 years of age.

Prevalence rates for each traumatic stressor under investigation are reported in Table 1. The rates range from a low of 3.5% for the experience of being sent away from home during childhood to almost 50% for experiencing the death of a spouse, child, or other loved one. In general, these stressors are not that rare: the average prevalence is over 20%. Approximately 40% report the death of a parent, ending a nonmarital relationship, or witnessing violence. Approximately 20–25% report hospitalization requiring a week or more stay; a personal accident, injury, or illness; spousal or partner infidelity; or repeating a year of school. Between 10% and 20% have experienced parental alcohol or drug use; chronic parental unemployment; parental divorce; a personal marital separation or divorce; spouse, partner, or child substance addiction; or living through a war, political uprising, or natural disaster. Fewer than 10% have been exposed to parental physical abuse, spouse or partner physical abuse, sexual abuse or assault, or a child's near-fatal accident or illness.

As mentioned earlier, for each psychiatric outcome under consideration, we incrementally tested for the presence of lagged trauma effects for each year prior and subsequent to event occurrence. In Table 1, a "discrete" specification of the stressor at issue indicates the absence of statistically significant lagged effects, either leading to or after the year of occurrence of the stressor. Otherwise, the reported range of lagged effects indicates the number of years for which statistically significant lags are observed. For example, whereas parental divorce (item 10) has an effect on psychological disorder only in the year of stress occurrence (a discrete effect), its effect on substance disorder extends to include two years prior and two years subsequent to divorce occurrence (2 back to 2 forward). For each stressor, the measurement of stress exposure is similarly operationalized as either a discrete or lagged effect for both psychological and substance disorder.

Analyses of the risk of first onset of any psychological disorder are presented separately for stressors having main effects only (Table 2), stressors that interact with age at time of occurrence (Table 3), and stressors that interact with prior cumulative stress (Table 4). To facilitate interpretation, we interpret risk effects in the hazard models in terms of odds. Stressors are, by necessity, considered one at a time; however, we do control for the sum of prior reported stressors in each case.

In Table 2, estimates are presented in the absence of control measures ("bivariate effect"), controlling for family psychiatric history, gender, and parental education ("partial controls"), and additionally controlling for prior cumulative stress experience ("full controls"). In the absence of controls, all but two of the stress experiences have statistically significant risk effects. In fact, a number of strong risk estimates are observed in this first column. The odds of psycho-

Table 2. *Odds for onset of any psychological disorder[a] by trauma exposure, Toronto metropolitan area, 1990–92*

Trauma	Bivariate effect	Partial controls[b]	Full controls[c]
2. Repeat a year of school	2.03[†]	2.17*	2.03[†]
4. Sent away from home	3.80**	2.89*	2.46*
5. Parental alcohol or drug use	2.14[†]	1.51	1.44
6. Physically abused by parent	3.93***	2.93**	2.52*
8. Ended a nonmarital relationship	2.93***	2.83***	2.73***
9. Parental death	4.11***	4.35***	4.37***
10. Parental divorce	3.88**	2.93*	2.71*
13. Natural disaster	1.12	1.15	1.05
14. Personal accident, injury, or illness	2.50***	2.34***	2.02***
15. Child near-fatal accident or illness	2.55	2.51	2.22
17. Spouse or partner infidelity	3.92***	3.62***	3.22***
19. Spouse or partner physical abuse	4.62***	3.42***	2.85***

[a] Psychological disorder includes diagnosis of depression, dysthymia, generalized anxiety, or panic disorder.
[b] Partial controls include gender, parental education, and family psychiatric history.
[c] Full controls include partial controls and prior cumulative trauma exposure.
[†] $p \leq .10$. *$p \leq .05$. **$p \leq .01$. ***$p \leq .001$.

logical disorder are increased by a factor of about 4 for items such as being sent away from home for doing something wrong (reported for childhood only), experiencing physical abuse by a parent, parental death, parental divorce, spouse or partner infidelity, and spouse or partner physical abuse. Many of the stressors showing the largest effects fall into two categories: losses of important relationships and victimization experiences. We believe these two categories capture a majority of the important deleterious effects of traumatic stress in general.

This set of items also includes a number of stressors drawing the widest attention and most concern in the literature. Further, we note that many of these risk estimates are higher than is often reported in the respective literatures for these stressors. This could be due to the sensitivity of our method to the timing of occurrence of both stressors and disorder. In addition, because event history estimates vary depending on the categorization of time intervals, our employment of finely defined intervals may be more sensitive than aggregate intervals broadly defined according to stages of the life cycle.

The effects of parental death and parental divorce are particularly worthy of note. Here parental deaths increase the odds of some psychological disorder by over 4, whereas there are serious questions in the literature about whether there is an overall effect at all. Parental divorce multiplies the odds of psychological disorders by just under 4, whereas the literature often implies that the effects are modest, or at most, moderate (Amato & Keith 1991). Of course, these estimates measure only short-term risk, but we should remember the results reported by Kessler and his colleagues that earlier onsets of disorder set in motion a pattern of recurrence over time. Thus, long-term mental health *is* at issue here.

A number of other stressors show substantial increases in odds ratios (ORs), including ending a nonmarital relationship (OR = 2.93), repeating a year of school (OR = 2.03), parental alcohol or drug use (OR = 2.14), and experiencing an accident, injury, or illness (OR = 2.50).

In general, the statistical significance and magnitude of the estimates are retained with the introduction of control measures. However, in some notable cases, estimates are reduced in the presence of controls. These include being sent away from home in childhood, parental physical abuse, parental divorce, and spouse or partner physical abuse. It is difficult to attribute these reductions to a particular factor, but we speculate that gender and/or family history of psychiatric problems are involved. In most of these cases, the major reduction occurs in comparing the bivariate effect to the effect under partial controls. Where abuse is at issue, it is likely that part of the reason for the reduction in effect is the joint effects of gender on the risk of being victimized by abuse and the risk of psychological disorders in particular. In the case of parental divorce, or being sent away from home, it is more likely that a family history of psychiatric problems plays a major role. In most cases, further controls for prior stressors do not reduce effects as much, although there is a notable drop for some. In the end, the final estimates, which represent a better assessment of the true risk effect due to each stressor, range more typically from 2 to 3 – except for the persistent and surprisingly strong effect of parental death, which is unaffected by controls.

A predominant hypothesis in the literature on traumatic stress is that the effects of these stressors are sensitive to the age at which the stressor occurs. For these disorders at least, we did not find interactions with age involving the stressors in Table 2. This is surprising in a few cases, such as parental divorce and parental death (for reviews see Maccoby 1983; Rutter 1983; Wallerstein 1983). This may be due to low power to detect age variations in effects in these data, or it may be due to an overestimation of the relevance of age using other methods.

In testing for interactions with age, and to take into account the possibility that changes in the effects of traumas over time may not be constant (i.e., there can be changes in the rate of change), we tested for both linear and nonlinear interactions by allowing for either accelerating or decelerating rates of change in impacts over the life course. Results for stressors demonstrating either linear or nonlinear age-varying effects are reported in Table 3. Age-specific odds are presented at the average age of stress exposure, at one standard deviation above

Table 3. *Age-varying odds[a] for onset of any psychological disorder[b] by trauma exposure, Toronto metropolitan area, 1990–92*

Trauma	Age-specific effect	Partial controls[c]	Full controls[d]
11. Death of a spouse, child, or loved one			
−1 SD (15 years)	2.97	2.72	2.55
Mean (25 years)	2.27	2.20	2.09
+1 SD (35 years)	1.73	1.78	1.71
20. Spouse, partner, or child addiction			
−1 SD (19 years)	4.77	3.45	2.94
Mean (28 years)	2.90	2.23	1.94
+1 SD (38 years)	1.67	1.37	1.23
12. Witness violence or murder			
−1 SD (11 years)	4.37	3.69	3.40
Mean (21 years)	1.93	1.88	1.72
Minimum (28 years)	1.62	1.66	1.52
+1 SD (31 years)	1.67	1.72	1.58
18. Sexual abuse/assault			
−1 SD (6 years)	15.34	8.87	7.66
Mean (14 years)	3.63	2.37	2.06
Minimum (20 years)	2.51	1.81	1.56
+1 SD (23 years)	2.62	1.99	1.71

[a] Odds estimated at the mean age of trauma exposure, one standard deviation below, and one standard deviation above mean age.
[b] Psychological disorder includes diagnosis of depression, dysthymia, generalized anxiety, or panic disorder.
[c] Partial controls include gender, parental education, and family psychiatric history.
[d] Full controls include partial controls and prior cumulative trauma exposure.

and below this mean age, and – in the case of nonlinear interactions – at the age of the minimum effect of the stressor. Although death (of a spouse, child, or other loved one) and addiction (of a spouse, partner, or child) generally increase the odds for onset of any psychological disorder, the increased risk effect linearly attenuates with age. Because multiple relationships qualify in these items, we believe that the difference in effects may reflect differences in the role relationship to the person involved in the death or addiction. Largest risks are not likely to be due to a child (a rare event), since the largest effects are at younger ages. Also, parental deaths are covered by a separate item. For these reasons, it is plausible that these effects are largest when involving a partner or friend at young ages.

The nonlinear age-varying effects observed for witnessing violence or murder, and for sexual abuse/assault, indicate significant odds of psychological disorder across the life cycle and particularly when experienced during childhood and later adulthood. Minimal risk estimates are observed for witnessing violence at age 28 and for sexual abuse or assault at age 20. It is also clear that the nonlinear effect here is not symmetrical. In fact, sexual abuse at ages prior to puberty are clearly very damaging, relative to later ages; in somewhat more muted form, so is the witnessing of violence. The pattern of differential sensitivity across the life cycle could be contingent on the relatively lower prevalence of the experience of the particular stressor during the specific stage in the life cycle.

Although the introduction of background controls (family psychiatric history, gender, and parental education) differentially reduces the age-specific risk effects, additionally controlling for prior cumulative stress experience has minimal explanatory relevance. Death of a spouse, child, or loved one is relatively unaffected by the introduction of controls. Spouse, partner, or child addiction and witnessing violence or murder demonstrate modest reductions in effect when controlling for background characteristics, most notably at ages below the average age of stress exposure. The greatest reduced effect is observed for sexual abuse or assault. Again, the reduction is particularly evident at younger ages, with the risk estimate at age 6 declining from 15.34 to 8.87 with the introduction of background controls. In fact, more than half of the original risk estimate for sexual abuse disappears in the full-controls model. This could be due primarily to gender, since women are at a higher risk for sexual abuse and are also at greater risk for these disorders. At the same time, the remaining impact of sexual abuse at younger ages is still substantial. The greater effect of background controls at younger ages is intuitively logical, since factors such as family psychiatric history are likely to decline in importance with increasing age.

The mental health implications of traumatic stressors may also be conditional on prior stress experience. We hypothesize that prior stress will generally reduce the impact of further stressors as they occur. This is consistent with the notion of a "ceiling effect" with regard to stressors: as the level of burden accumulates, the threat posed by each new stressor is progressively smaller. In addition, the effects of stressors will be attenuated if experience with prior traumas provides the opportunity for development of coping skills that render later stress exposure less problematic. It is also possible, and in contrast to these attenuating effects, that the effects of some stressors may be magnified by prior stress exposure if personal and social coping resources are severely depleted by the prior experience.

The results presented in Table 4 indicate that the effects of some of our stressors are contingent on prior cumulative traumatic exposure. Odds specific to four levels of prior stress exposure are shown: at the average number of prior stressors reported, at levels one standard deviation above and below this mean, and when no prior stressors are reported. This last condition is important because it is relatively common and is often the condition of maximum vulnerability to traumatic stress. This is plausible in view of the fact that a condition

Table 4. *Prior stress-varying odds[a] for onset of any psychological disorder[b] by trauma exposure, Toronto metropolitan area, 1990–92*

Trauma	Trauma-specific effect	Full controls[c]
1. Hospitalization		
0	5.86	6.07
−1 SD	2.52	2.53
Mean	0.71	0.68
+1 SD	0.31	0.28
3. Parental unemployment		
0	5.47	4.75
−1 SD	3.57	3.04
Mean	1.88	1.55
+1 SD	1.23	0.99
7. Personal marital separation/divorce		
0	10.09	9.31
−1 SD	6.66	6.29
Mean	3.57	3.50
+1 SD	2.36	2.36
16. War or political uprising		
0	0.01	0.01
−1 SD	0.07	0.05
Mean	0.96	1.07
+1 SD	5.25	7.80

[a] Odds estimated at the mean of cumulative trauma exposure ($n = 5$) and one standard deviation below ($n = 2$) and one standard deviation above ($n = 7$).
[b] Psychological disorder includes diagnosis of depression, dysthymia, generalized anxiety, or panic disorder.
[c] Full controls include partial controls and prior cumulative trauma exposure.

of "zero stress" implies the absence of practice in coping with challenging difficulties.

In the absence of prior stress exposure, the odds of psychological disorder are increased by 5.86 for hospitalization, by 5.47 for parental unemployment, and by 10.09 for personal marital separation or divorce. As the quantity of prior stress exposure increases, these odds are dramatically attenuated. For individuals who have extensive prior stress repertoires, such experiences must be perceived as relatively less problematic or threatening. In contrast to these attenuating effects, each additional prior traumatic experience significantly *increases* the impact of living through a war or political uprising. This may be due in part

Table 5. *Odds for onset of any substance disorder[a] by trauma exposure, Toronto metropolitan area, 1990–92*

Trauma	Bivariate effect	Partial controls[b]	Full controls[c]
1. Hospitalization	0.58	0.62	0.55
2. Repeat a year of school	3.61***	3.33***	3.06***
5. Parental alcohol or drug use	2.84**	3.04**	2.75**
6. Physically abused by parent	5.16***	4.36**	3.31*
7. Personal marital separation/divorce	3.91**	4.23**	3.74*
9. Parental death	0.77	0.73	0.70
10. Parental divorce	3.50***	2.88***	2.58***
11. Death of spouse, child, or other loved one	1.73†	1.76†	1.62
12. Witness violence or murder	2.50***	2.15***	1.83**
14. Personal accident, injury, or illness	3.12**	2.84**	2.06*
15. Child near-fatal accident or illness	1.60	1.76	1.46
16. War or political uprising	1.83	1.68	1.50
19. Spouse or partner physical abuse	1.64†	1.80*	1.56†
20. Spouse, partner, or child substance addiction	3.97***	4.56***	3.51***

[a] Substance disorder includes diagnosis of alcohol abuse or dependence or drug abuse or dependence.
[b] Partial controls include gender, parental education, and family psychiatric history.
[c] Full controls include partial controls and prior cumulative trauma exposure.
†$p \leq .10.$ *$p \leq .05.$ **$p \leq .01.$ ***$p \leq .001.$

to the overwhelming pervasiveness of such an experience, so that coping skills from prior more circumscribed stressors may not be relevant. Also, with increasing prior stress exposure, the individual may be more likely to perceive his or her personal environment as uncontrollable. In the context of depleted resources, the detrimental effects of war or political uprising are magnified.

In Tables 5, 6, and 7 we turn to effects on substance disorder. Table 5 presents the odds for first onset of any substance disorder due to stressors that are not involved in interactions with age or prior stress. Physical abuse by a parent dramatically increases odds of substance disorder by a factor of 5. Personal marital separation or divorce and spouse, partner, or child substance addiction both increase these odds by about 4, and repeating a year of school and parental divorce each increase the odds by 3.5. Parental alcohol or drug use and personal accident, injury, or illness approximately triple the odds; death of a spouse, child, or other loved one, witnessing violence or murder, and spouse or partner physical abuse approximately double the odds of substance disorder. Stressors having no statistically significant effect here include hospitalization, parental death, child near-fatal accident or illness, and war or political uprising. Again, risk estimates vary widely and are often substantial. As before, losses and victimization experiences figure prominently. In addition, we see that the addictions of others also play a large role, especially spouse, partner, or child addictions. We believe that this effect, since it does not depend on age and is separate from the effect of parental substance abuse, largely reflects the effects of partners in relationships.

The implications of background characteristics for the risk effects of individual stressors range from no reduction in effect to partial explanation to even suppressor effects in a few cases. The notable reductions in magnitude of risk effects are observed for parental physical abuse and parental divorce. We suggest that this pattern makes more plausible the interpretation that a family history of psychiatric problems plays a role in these cases. This is because men have a higher risk of substance disorders whereas women have a higher risk of psychological disorders. Since gender is related to these outcomes in opposite ways, it is unlikely that it plays a common role in reducing the effects of abuse or divorce.

Conversely, the risk effects of personal marital separation or divorce, spouse or partner physical abuse, and spouse, partner, or child addiction increase when background controls are introduced. These suppression effects could in part be due to gender. For example, partner addictions are more likely to happen to females, since men have a higher rate of these addictions. Together with the lower risk of substance disorder among women, the implication is that controlling for gender yields a larger net difference in risk due to partner or child addictions.

Table 6 presents the age-specific effects observed for parental unemployment and sexual abuse/assault on the onset of substance disorder. The effect of chronic parental unemployment increases through childhood and reaches peak levels during adolescence at age 15 and declines thereafter. This pattern certainly reflects differences in the salience of parental unemployment across stages of childhood and adolescence, but it is not clear why the effect is worst at mid-adolescence. The implication is either increased economic pressure on the child at that point, or increased symbolic and material strain at a time when adolescents are becoming aware of social position and are sensitive to peer evaluations. The experience of sexual abuse or assault increases the odds for onset of substance disorder, particularly during childhood and again in later adulthood. Minimal risk estimates for sexual abuse or assault are observed at age 16.

The differential effects of nonmarital relationship loss, spouse or partner infidelity, and natural disaster contingent upon prior cumulative stress exposure are depicted in Table 7. The increased odds of substance disorder following nonmarital relationship loss are linearly attenuated as prior stress increases. The experiences of spouse or partner infidelity and exposure to natural disaster appear to be particularly problematic in the context of both low and high levels

Table 6. *Age-varying odds[a] for onset of any substance disorder[b] by trauma exposure, Toronto metropolitan area, 1990–92*

Trauma	Age-specific effect	Partial controls[c]	Full controls[d]
3. Parental unemployment			
−1 SD (7 years)	0.00	0.00	0.00
Mean (12 years)	0.87	0.66	0.32
Maximum (15 years)	12.53	10.91	9.44
+1 SD (18 years)	0.64	0.77	0.79
18. Sexual abuse			
−1 SD (6 years)	5.48	5.16	3.86
Mean (14 years)	2.36	2.95	2.21
Minimum (16 years)	2.25	2.90	2.17
+1 SD (23 years)	3.10	3.98	3.04

[a] Odds estimated at the mean age of trauma exposure, one standard deviation below, and one standard deviation above mean age.
[b] Substance disorder includes diagnosis of alcohol abuse or dependence or drug abuse or dependence.
[c] Partial controls include gender, parental education, and family psychiatric history.
[d] Full controls include partial controls and prior cumulative trauma exposure.

of prior cumulative stress exposure. This finding is consistent with the hypothesis that both very low and very high levels of prior stress create greater vulnerability to the impacts of further stress, while middle levels optimize prior learning effects and are still within the realm of most individuals' coping potential (Wheaton & Roszell 1992).

The effect of being sent away from home in childhood on onset of substance disorder is conditioned both by age at occurrence and prior cumulative stress exposure. Although each effect is statistically significant, this stressor has a particularly low prevalence, and thus the results are not presented, owing to our lack of confidence in the estimates. However, consistent with expectations, this event is particularly stressful when experienced at younger ages or in the absence of other prior stress experiences. As age increases or as the number of prior traumatic events increases, the effect of being sent away from home attenuates.

Because of the limited number of available cases in the event history data set, it was not possible to test for three-way interactions involving age and prior cumulative stress exposure. Similarly, three-way gender interactions could not be assessed. However, gender-specific effects are observed for parental physical abuse, nonmarital relationship loss, and for spouse or partner infidelity. Rela-

Table 7. *Prior stress-varying odds[a] for onset of any substance disorder[b] by trauma exposure, Toronto metropolitan area, 1990–92*

Trauma	Trauma-specific effect	Full controls[c]
8. Nonmarital relationship ended		
0	6.39	5.69
−1 SD	1.93	1.83
Mean	0.32	0.33
+1 SD	0.10	0.10
17. Spouse or partner infidelity		
0	3.63	3.36
−1 SD	2.13	2.27
Mean	1.63	1.91
+1 SD	1.96	2.21
13. Natural disaster		
0	1.67	1.74
−1 SD	0.22	0.23
Mean	0.25	0.25
+1 SD	2.14	2.07

[a] Odds estimated at the mean of cumulative trauma exposure ($n = 5$) and one standard deviation below ($n = 2$) and one standard deviation above ($n = 7$).
[b] Substance disorder includes diagnosis of alcohol abuse or dependence or drug abuse or dependence.
[c] Full controls include partial controls and prior cumulative trauma exposure.

tive to females, the experience of parental physical abuse further increases the odds of any psychological disorder for males by a factor of 5.76; the experience of nonmarital relationship loss further increases men's odds of these disorders by 1.61. The experience of spouse or partner infidelity increases the risk of onset of substance disorder for females by a factor of 1.69 relative to males.

Conclusions

Certain stressors are prominent in our analyses of risk. Parental death is a central predictor of the onset of psychological disorder, showing risk estimates even greater than those for physical and sexual abuse when controls are considered. It is important to see that controls play an essential role in our analysis. Without controls, we might conclude that partner physical abuse has more serious consequences; with controls, it appears that parental death is a more important predictor. This pattern reflects the fact that stressors such as parental death do not occur as part of a "matrix of disadvantage" but rather exist on their own and occur relatively randomly in lives. However, abuse – precisely because the extent of its effects changes in the presence of controls – is more likely to be part of a cluster of background problems and an extension of those problems. Coming from a background of abuse probably does not describe sufficiently the array of stressors at issue in these cases. This reasoning suggests that it is important in future research that we consider the risk implications of clusters of co-occurring stressors, that is, the "matrix of disadvantage." Indeed, we need to study which co-occurring sequences tend to be prevalent first.

Our analyses suggest substantial effects of an array of traumatic experiences. Unfortunately, as reported by Kessler et al. in Chapter 2, it is very difficult to get useful estimates when all stressors are considered in one model. Thus, the study of clusters may be even more crucial to understanding the combined effect of traumas over time.

Our data do sometimes verify that these stressors have age-specific effects. As expected, in both the stress and life-course literatures, these effects are often larger at younger ages. However, what is more striking in these data is the degree to which the effects of specific stressors depend on the prior accumulated level of stress exposure. In general, we find that prior stress has an ironic benefit in that it induces relative immunity to the effects of further stressors.

We noted in our results the general importance of two types of stressors: losses and personal victimizations (Roszell 1996). Effects for abuse, infidelity, deaths, and the termination of relationships reveal substantial effects on the risk of DSM-III-R disorders. These stressors form a core of issues to focus on in understanding long-term differences in life trajectories. Specifically, it is important to explain these effects by specifying essential features in loss and victimization experiences that determine the increased risk for mental health problems.

In this chapter we step back to a more fundamental point. Obviously, there is overlap in the risk estimates of many of these stressors, since they are not independent of each other. Until further study of typical sequences reveals which stressors tend to set off chains of adversity, we will not know which stressors are the core starting points of divergence in future trajectories. Still, the data are sufficiently clear on one basic point: traumatic stressors, because of their typical timing in the life course (early) and the size of their impact on psychiatric risk (substantial), are crucial in the determination of mental health trajectories throughout life.

References

Amato, P. R., & Booth, A. (1991). Consequences of parental divorce and marital unhappiness for adult well-being. *Social Forces* 69: 895–914.

Amato, P. R., & Keith, B. (1991). Parental divorce and the well-being of children: a meta-analysis. *Psychological Bulletin* 110: 26–46.

American Psychiatric Association [APA] (1987). *Diagnostic and Statistical Manual of the American Psychiatric Association* (DSM-III-R), rev. 3rd ed. Washington, DC: American Psychiatric Association.

Aro, H. M., & Palosaari, U. K. (1992). Parental divorce, adolescence, and transition to young adulthood: a follow-up study. *American Journal of Orthopsychiatry* 62: 421–9.

Brown, G. W., Harris, T., & Bifulco, A. (1986). Long-term effects of early loss of parent. In M. Rutter, G. E. Izard, and P. B. Read (eds.), *Depression in Young People*. New York: Guilford, pp. 251–96.

Browne, A., & Finkelhor, D. (1986). Impact of child sexual abuse: a review of the research. *Psychological Bulletin* 99: 66–77.

Bryer, J. B., Nelson, B. A., Milller, J. B., & Krol, P. A. (1987). Childhood sexual and physical abuse as factors in adult psychiatric illness. *American Journal of Psychiatry* 144: 1426–30.

Burnam, M. A., Stein, J. A., Golding, J. M., Siegel, J. M., Sorenson, S. B., Forsythe, A. B., & Telles, C. A. (1988). Sexual assault and mental disorders in a community population. *Journal of Consulting and Clinical Psychology* 56: 843–50.

Cadoret, R. J., Troughton, E., Merchant, L. M., & Whitters, A. (1990). Early life psychosocial events and adult affective symptoms. In L. Robins & M. Rutter (eds.), *Straight and Devious Pathways from Childhood to Adulthood*. Cambridge University Press, pp. 300–13.

Crook, T., & Eliot, J. (1980). Parental death during childhood and adult depression: a critical review of the literature. *Psychological Bulletin* 87: 252–9.

Dooley, D., & Catalano, R. (1984). Why the ecomony predicts help-seeking: a test of competing explanations. *Journal of Health and Social Behavior* 25: 160–75.

Garmezy, N. (1983). Stressors of childhood. In Garmezy & Rutter (1983).

Garmezy, N., & Rutter, M. (eds.) (1983). *Stress, Coping, and Development in Children*. Baltimore, MD: Johns Hopkins University Press.

Gelles, R. J., & Conte, J. R. (1990). Domestic violence and sexual abuse of children: a review of research in the eighties. *Journal of Marriage and the Family* 52: 1045–58.

Gersten, J. C., Langner, T. S., Eisenberg, J. G., & Orzeck, L. (1974). Child behavior and life events: undesirable change or change per se? In B. S. Dohrenwend & B. P. Dohrenwend (eds.), *Stressful Life Events: Their Nature and Effects*. New York: Wiley, pp. 159–70.

Glenn, N., & Kramer, K. (1985). The psychological well-being of adult children of divorce. *Journal of Marriage and the Family* 47: 905–11.

Green, A. (1993). Child sexual abuse: immediate and long-term effects and interventions. *Journal of the American Academy of Child and Adolescent Psychiatry* 32: 890–902.

Holmes, S., & Robins, L. (1988). The role of parental disciplinary practices in the development of depression and alcoholism. *Psychiatry* 51: 24–36.

Kanner, A. D., Coyne, J. C., Schaefer, C., & Lazarus, R. S. (1981). Comparison of two modes of stress measurement: daily hassles and uplifts versus major life events. *Journal of Behavioral Medicine* 4: 1–39.

Kendall-Tackett, K. A., Williams, L. M., & Finkelhor, D. (1993). Impact of sexual abuse on children: a review and synthesis of recent and empirical studies. *Psychological Bulletin* 113: 164–80.

Kessler, R. C., Gillis-Light, J., Magee, W. J., Kendler, K. S., & Eaves, L. J. (1995). Childhood adversity and adult psychopathology. [Chapter 2 in this volume]

Kessler, R. C., & Magee, W. (1994). Childhood family violence and adult recurrent depression. *Journal of Health and Social Behavior* 35: 13-27.

Kessler, R. C., McGonagle, K. A., Zhao, S., Nelson, C. B., Hughes, M., Eshleman, S., Wittchen, H., & Kendler, K. S. (1994). Lifetime and 12-month prevalence of DSM-III-R psychiatric disorders in the United States. *Archives of General Psychiatry* 51: 8–19.

Maccoby, E. (1983). Social-emotional development and response to stressors. In Garmezy & Rutter (1983), pp. 217–34.

McLeod, J. (1991). Childhood parental loss and adult depression. *The Journal of Health and Social Behavior* 32: 205-20.

Mullen, P. E., Martin, J. L., Anderson, J. C., Romans, S. E., & Herbison, G. P. (1993). Childhood sexual abuse and mental health in later life. *British Journal of Psychiatry* 163: 721-32.

Norris, F. H. (1992). Epidemiology of trauma: frequency and impact of different potentially traumatic events on different demographic groups. *Journal of Consulting and Clinical Psychology* 60: 409-18.

Pearlin, L. I. (1989). The sociological study of stress. *Journal of Health and Social Behavior* 30: 241-57.

Roszell, P. (1996). A life course perspective on the implications of stress exposure. Ph.D. dissertation, Department of Sociology, University of Toronto.

Rutter, M. (1983). Stress, coping, and development: some issues and some questions. In Garmezy & Rutter (1983), pp. 1-41.

Rutter, M., & Quinton, D. (1977). Psychiatric disorder: ecological factors and concepts of causation. In H. McGurk (ed.), *Ecological Factors in Human Development*. Amsterdam: North-Holland, pp. 173-87.

Saler, L. (1992). Childhood parental death and depression in adulthood: roles of surviving parent and family environment. *American Journal of Orthopsychiatry* 62: 504-16.

Tennant, C. (1988). Parental loss in childhood. *Archives of General Psychiatry* 45: 1045-50.

Terr, L. C. (1991). Childhood traumas: an outline and overview. *American Journal of Psychiatry* 148: 10-20.

Turner, R. J., & Wheaton, B. (1991). Psychiatric distress and the use and abuse of alcohol and drugs. Grant no. 6606-4354-DA, National Health Research Development Program, Health and Welfare Canada, Ottawa.

Umberson, D., & Chen, M. (1994). Effects of a parent's death on adult children: relationship salience and reaction to loss. *American Sociological Review* 59: 152-68.

Wallerstein, J. S. (1983). Children of divorce: stress and developmental tasks. In Garmezy & Rutter (1983), pp. 265-302.

Wheaton, B. (1983). Stress, personal coping resources, and psychiatric symptoms: an investigation of interactive models. *Journal of Health and Social Behavior* 24: 208-29.

Wheaton, B. (1990). Life transitions, role histories, and mental health. *American Sociological Review* 55: 209-24.

Wheaton, B. (1994). Sampling the stress universe. In W. R. Avison & I. H. Gotlib (eds.), *Stress and Mental Health: Contemporary Issues and Prospects for the Future*. New York: Plenum, pp. 77-113.

Wheaton, B., & Roszell, P. (1992). Lifetime models of stress exposure. Paper presented at the American Sociological Association meetings (August 1992, Pittsburgh).

Wittchen, U., Robins, L., Cottler, L., Sartorius, N., Burke, J. D., & Regier, D. (1991). Participants in the multicentre WHO-ADAMHA files trials 1991: cross-cultural feasibility, reliability, and sources of variance of the Composite International Diagnostic Interview (CIDI). *British Journal of Psychiatry* 159: 645-53.

4 Intergenerational sanction sequences and trajectories of street-crime amplification

John Hagan & Bill McCarthy

Crime sometimes runs in families, and the re-appearance of crime among the sons of convicted fathers is especially well documented (e.g., Burt 1925). Yet there is little certainty about how and why this recurrence occurs. In this chapter we conceive of the arrests of sons whose fathers have been arrested as forming turning points in life histories that often increase involvement in crime. In this sense, sons' arrests become galvanizing events that, as part of intergenerational sanction sequences, culminate in turning points and amplify crime trajectories.

Of course, our conceptualization is not the first attempt to account for the re-appearance of crime across generations, and it is important to locate our effort in relation to earlier approaches to this issue. The original positivist criminologists saw the recurrence of crime across generations as evidence of a genetic link (e.g., Lombroso 1918). In contrast, early Marxist criminologists interpreted the re-appearance of crime as a result of economic necessity (e.g., Bonger 1916). Of the two hypotheses, the genetic one has proven more popular with lay and policy audiences (e.g., Wilson & Herrnstein 1985).

Research on the heritability of crime focuses on several populations, including intact biological families and twins, particularly those separated at birth. However, as noted by Walters and White (1989), many of these studies are compromised by sampling bias, inadequate control groups, differential mortality, and specification errors. The best-designed and most influential studies of the genetic transmission of crime are those that explore the association between the criminal convictions of children adopted shortly after birth and those of their biological parents (e.g., Bohman et al. 1982; Cloninger et al. 1982; Crowe 1972; Mednick, Gabrielli, & Hutchings 1984). Yet, regardless of the population studied and notwithstanding their greater popular appeal, genetic studies uncover only modestly significant statistical associations. Moreover, Walters's (1992) meta-analysis of the gene–crime relationship reveals that recent and better-designed studies provide less support for the gene–crime hypothesis than earlier research. Thus, despite the proliferation of genetic studies, this research has not significantly advanced the unraveling of the causal processes, genetic or otherwise, that lead to the reproduction of criminal behavior.

73

In his review of research on genetics and crime, Jencks (1992) emphasizes the primitive state of our knowledge of the heritability of crime. Noting that nearly all these studies are of males, he concludes as follows:

> While adoption studies certainly suggest that a man's genes have some influence on the number of crimes he will commit, they do not tell us why this is the case. In this respect they are logically analogous to studies showing that gender or skin color influences criminal behavior. The existence of such a statistical association is intriguing, but it does not have any practical meaning unless we know why it arises. At present, we don't. (p. 102)

Jencks makes the further point that to whatever extent (if any) genetic predispositions influence the causation of crime, they likely do so in combination with the societal responses crime elicits, including the state's resort to penal sanctions. So, regardless of whether assumptions of nature or nurture form the background of concerns about crime among parents and children, there is a recognition that understanding the role of legal sanctions in this association is vital.

The new sanction theories

Increasingly, theorists and researchers have sought to understand how the family and the state are linked together in using informal and formal sanctions to respond to threats of delinquency and crime. For example, Black's (1976) theory of the behavior of law asserts that the family and the state are interconnected systems of social control. Parental sanctioning is social control, even when it includes arbitrary, excessive, or brutal punishment of children (Black 1983). Black reasons that variation in family processes of social control is often associated with the nature and timing of legal sanctioning. This underlines the point that family contexts can shape or condition the influence of legal sanctions.

Hagan and Palloni (1990) argue that two distinct processes of social reproduction linked to the family could be involved in the intergenerational recurrence of crime. The first is a cultural or characterological process by which parents, through child-raising conditions and practices, reproduce in their children the characteristics that lead to crime. The second is a structural or imputational process in which crime-control agents reproduce criminal behavior through their official treatment of the children of criminal parents.

The former process is at the heart of the more traditional theories of criminogenesis, whereas the latter process is more consistent with a labeling theory of deviance. Becker's (1963) development of labeling theory includes references to contingencies and careers of criminal involvement that anticipate the attention that we give in this paper to turning points and trajectories. However, little attention has been given to intergenerational influences on crime trajectories in labeling theory, and – so far as we can determine – no attention has been given to the role of gender in specifying intergenerational crime processes. This paper is an initial step toward addressing these oversights, and has three objectives: (1) to develop insights implicit in labeling theory about turning points and trajectories along intergenerational and gender lines; (2) to examine this extension of labeling theory with data collected in a summer-long panel study of street youth in two Canadian cities; and (3) to consider the research and policy implications of this structural and imputational perspective.

Intergenerational labeling

Labeling theories of crime primarily focus on intragenerational processes that parallel a life-course interest in the development of individual lives (Elder 1994). In the most popular version of this theory, Becker (1963) describes state sanctions as "contingencies" that can forge connections between isolated acts and establish delinquent and criminal careers. According to Lemert (1967), these career contingencies mark a transition between primary and secondary deviance. Lemert argues that acts of *primary deviance* occur at random and arise from myriad causes; moreover, these initial acts have only marginal implications for subsequent deviant behavior and for an individual's self-concept. In contrast, *secondary deviance* is unique; it consists of proscribed behaviors that follow the labeling responses of others and reflects the internalization or acceptance of these definitions.

Notwithstanding these contributions, modern formulations of labeling theory are oddly silent on a further contingency: the occurrence and consequences of labeling across generations. This silence is surprising because Mead (1918) anticipated a focus on intergenerational labeling as early as 1918. In "The Psychology of Punitive Justice" (Mead 1918), the father of symbolic interactionism called attention to the inconsistencies between what today we call labeling and deterrence theories and to the potential consequences of the indiscriminate use of legal sanctions. According to Mead, "a system of punishments assessed with reference to their deterrent powers not only works very inadequately in repressing crime but also preserves a criminal class" (p. 583). Mead's structural perspective recognized the intergenerational effects of legal sanctioning, and he noted that our system of legal sanctions provides few if any mechanisms for the revocation of the stigma involved in criminal proceedings. The implication of Mead's analysis is that intergenerational labeling can induce turning points that concentrate crime across generations and lead to the formation of a permanent class of criminals.

Mead's concern about a criminal class focuses attention on the process of intergenerational labeling by suggesting that behaviors that meet labeling responses will most likely lead to subsequent deviant behavior when the recipient is the child of parents who are also labeled deviant. Said more simply, labels may have the greatest affect on the illegal behavior of adolescents when they are imposed in the context of a family that previously has been labeled deviant. We use this intergenerational interaction effect of parent and child labeling as a focal point in the test of labeling theory presented here. Before discussing this test, we further develop the idea of intergenerational labeling as a turning point in the life course, and consider the role of gender in specifying the turning point that intergenerational labeling can induce in the form of involvement in secondary deviance.

Intergenerational labeling as a turning point

Intergenerational labeling can be seen as a specific kind of chain reaction in what Rutter (1989) identifies as a "chain of adversity" in the life course. A unique feature of this conceptualization is that it does not see a single event in the life course as constituting a turning point, in the popular sense of this term. Rather, it is combinations of linked events, in a multiplicative fashion, that are more likely to establish trajectories in individuals' lives. According to Rutter (1989, p. 27), "the impact of some factor in childhood may lie less in the immediate behavioral change it brings about than in the fact that it sets in motion a chain reaction in which one 'bad' thing leads to another." With more specific reference to labeling experiences, Rutter observes that "antisocial behavior . . . will influence later environments through the societal responses it induces – such as custodial or correctional actions that may serve both to 'label' and to strengthen antisocial peer group influences" (p. 42). Intergenerational experiences that link parent and child together may be even more consequential, establishing a continuity of generations (see also Caspi & Elder 1988). The overriding implication is that, as the metaphor of a chain reaction implies, chains of adversity can have multiplier effects that create distinct turns in life-course trajectories.

Thoits (1983) makes the multiplicative effects of life events even more explicit in her discussion of the literature on social and psychological stress. Thoits observes that

> a person who has experienced one event may react with even more distress to a second . . .; to the person, life might seem to be spiralling out of control. This would produce . . . [an] interaction between event occurrences; two or more events would result in more distress than would be expected from the simple sum of their singular effects. (p. 69)

Thoits describes a vulnerability model of interaction in which early stressful events set the foundation for adverse reactions to subsequent events. In this model, "predispositions are remote, enduring physiological and psychological characteristics that . . . enhance . . . the impacts of current life experiences" (p. 80). Our premise is that the criminal labeling of parents can establish a kind of remote predisposition that, in combination with the subsequent stigmatization of their adolescent children, can form a turning point that leads to a trajectory of secondary deviance.

Stigma, shame, and sex

In a recent extension of labeling theory, Braithwaite (1989) draws a further important distinction between reintegrative shaming and stigmatization, two very different kinds of social sanctions. Reintegrative shaming is characteristic of more benign family and state sanctions (e.g., in Japan), where expressions of reacceptance follow disapproval of deviant behavior. In contrast, stigmatization is more typical of violent punishment used in abusive families and the system of official criminal sanctions that characterize North American judicial systems. In these approaches the person is punished as much or more than the behavior, in the sense that the person is degraded by humiliating familial abuse or by the official legal ceremony of criminal stigmatization (Garfinkel 1956); as well, there is usually little or no provision for reintegration, and the shame of being sanctioned is unabated. The key to Braithwaite's distinction is that reintegrative shaming includes rituals of reacceptance and reabsorption, whereas stigmatization is unremitting and exclusive.

Braithwaite extends his argument, linking gender differences to reintegrative shaming and stigmatization. Drawing on power control theory (Hagan et al. 1989), Braithwaite (1989, p. 92) reasons that, in a patriarchal society, women are socialized to be more interdependent while men are socialized to be independent, especially during adolescence.

> In a patriarchal culture, men are expected to break away from dependency on the family of procreation, to become "men of the world," even to "sow their oats," and then to "settle down" to create their own family of procreation. Women, on the other hand, are expected to swap one form of dependency (on the family of orientation) for another (on the family of procreation). Women are under no imperative to "cut free from their mother's apron strings" and certainly not to "sow their oats." In summary, in patriarchal cultures, the sanctioned sequence for males is one set of interdependencies, followed by a period as a free agent, followed by the man building a new set of interdependencies. For females, to the extent that society is patriarchal, it is one set of dependencies, followed by accepting the terms of another set of dependencies established by a male partner. The female is thus always more socially integrated, always more susceptible to shaming by those on whom she is dependent, and never quite as free to make deviant choices as the male.

Braithwaite clearly sees men and women as having very different socialized "missions" in patriarchal society, making women distinct in their response to social situations and how others respond to them. This has significant implications for involvement in delinquency and crime. As Braithwaite (1989, p. 94) argues, "to understand the lower crime rates of women, we need to understand the structurally differentiated mission of women to secure social integration in the family. It is much more difficult for women than for men to have a period in their life cycle where they make a break with that mission by cutting ties of interdependency." Women's greater integration and dependence on others has several implications. First, women are less likely to offend than males and thus are less likely to be stigmatized. Second, women who break the law and are stigmatized will be more adaptive to this sanction and more successfully re-integrated into conforming circles of behavior. On the other hand, men are more likely to strike out on a path of persistent independence and defiance of authority.

Braithwaite's linkage of a power control theory of delinquency to labeling theory clearly suggests a gender specification of the intergenerational labeling hypothesis. Specifically, intergenerational labeling (i.e., stigmatization) is a kind of turning point that is more likely among males than females to produce a defiant transition into a persistent trajectory of secondary deviance. That is, males are more likely to break free into trajectories of independent and defiant forms of secondary deviance. Or, put the other way around and in terms closer to Braithwaite's formulation, intergenerational labeling is less likely to break the interdependencies that lead females to deviate less frequently and persis-tently than males. This gender specification of intergenerational interactions in sanction sequences is a central part of the empirical analysis we present next.

Exploring sanction sequences

A meaningful exploration of intergenerational sanction sequences leading to trajectories of secondary deviance presupposes the availability of rather unique data. First, the conception proposed is developmental and therefore requires data that locate variation over time. In particular, we require data that allow temporal separation between parental and adolescent experiences with legal sanctions and primary and secondary deviant acts. A cross-sectional representa-tion of these events would not provide a convincing test of this dynamic model.

Second, a meaningful representation of the secondary deviance model re-quires extensive control for background variables that may cause both crime and sanctioning, so that putative effects of the latter can be separated from com-mon causes of the former. These background variables are potentially wide-ranging, including disadvantaging family resources and socialization capaci-ties, parental abuse and chemical dependencies, as well as subject differences in age, gender, life experiences, and prior involvement in crime. A model of secon-dary deviance that does not control for such background differences risks seri-ous misspecification.

Third, the model of involvement in secondary deviance suggested in our con-ceptualization implies more serious acts of crime than samples of high-school or college students are likely to reveal. Our model focuses on criminal acts that come to the attention of and are frequently sanctioned by the criminal justice system, but that are uncommon in random samples of the population. A sam-pling strategy that does not include serious offenders would provide an inade-quate representation of this model of secondary deviance.

In sum, a convincing exploration of our model requires panel data that are sensitive to variation in temporal sequence, with extensive measurement of background variation among subjects who are at high risk for sanctioning and serious criminal involvement. Such data are of increasing importance in tests of crime theories (e.g., Piliavin et al. 1986).

A summer panel study of street youth

Longitudinal studies of delinquency and crime typically concentrate on relatively stable populations of students that are encountered in school and tracked through adolescence, sometimes well into adulthood. In contrast, the research described here involves a panel study of 16- to 24-year-old youth living on the streets of Toronto and Vancouver during the summer of 1992. The operational definition of a *street youth* is a person between these ages without a permanent place to live. We developed this sample because past research (e.g., McCarthy & Hagan 1992) has demonstrated that these youth form a population that is at high risk of conflict with the law. More than half of the youth in our sample had been picked up and charged by the police since leaving home, and nearly one third had a father who had been arrested for a criminal offense. These levels of criminal sanctioning are far higher than in school samples, providing an important opportunity to analyze the criminogenic effects of intergenerational labeling.

Our sample originally included 482 street youth, 330 in Toronto and 152 in Vancouver, who were interviewed in 21 agencies serving homeless youth as well as in nonagency settings such as parks, street corners, and shopping malls. A team of 14 interviewers saturated these locations for first-wave interviews with street youth in both cities during June 1992. Second-wave interviews were scheduled three weeks after the first, and third-wave interviews three weeks later. Youth were paid $20 for each interview.

We used a variety of techniques to maintain connections with youth throughout the data collection period. Contact information provided by youth in their first interviews was sometimes useful in restoring connections, but many respondents either provided telephone numbers that were no longer in service or had terminated their associations with agencies. By maintaining a high visibility in the agencies and on the street, interviewers were able to develop valuable contacts and collect information about hard-to-locate youth from agency staff and other homeless youth. Perseverance in following new leads and recycling old leads, as well as repeating steps in the tracing operation, was essential in retaining respondents for subsequent interviews. Over the course of the research we were able to retain 80% of the sample for two waves, and more than half for three waves. Youth who were first contacted on the street and those who had little agency contact were the most difficult to reinterview.

The analysis that follows is based on survey data collected during the first two waves and on qualitative material gathered in third-wave semistructured interviews. To assess the impact of attrition across the first and second waves, our analysis incorporates a correction for sample selection bias. The correction for selection uses a selection hazard equation based on retention in the second-wave interviews. This selection hazard combines measures of being on the street in the first-wave interview, the reported number of nights (since leaving home) of staying on the street in nonagency settings, and the city in which the youth was interviewed. This selection hazard is significantly related to self-reported delinquency in some of our estimated reduced-form equations; however, when additional variables are included in the structural equations, the selection hazard variable becomes nonsignificant. This supports our view that sample selection bias is not a serious problem in the analysis.

Despite the high retention across the first two waves and the correction for sample selection, we cannot be sure of the precise relationship between our sample and larger populations of substantive interest, such as all street youth who come into conflict with the law. Even though our sample has the advantage of amply incorporating many such youth and is uniquely useful for purposes of testing the proposed model of secondary deviance, it is a nonprobability sample; this limits generalizations based on statistical inference.[1]

Definitions and measures

Each youth in our sample was asked to report in the first-wave interview if their father or mother had ever been arrested. These youth were also asked to report if they had themselves been charged by the police, either while living at home or since being on the street (but prior to the first-wave interview).

The street youth sampled for this research characteristically have family problems that go beyond conflict with the law, often involving multiple problems of parental mistreatment and chemical dependency. We use the terms sexual abuse and physical violence to describe the forms of mistreatment involved. We are not concerned here with the legal meanings of these terms, which are variable and uncertain. Our operationalizations are neither exhaustive nor definitive, but they include a range of possibilities, as indicated in the top part of Table 1.

Our measure of sexual abuse is referenced retrospectively to when the respondent was living at home. It consists of two items: the first asks about suggested and attempted sexual acts (including touching) by family members; the second about sexual acts perpetrated by family members (alpha = 0.887). We did not think it ethically or practically possible in a one-hour interview to ask which family members engaged in these acts or to ask in greater detail about the form these acts took. Prior work and our qualitative data indicate that sexual abuse

Table 1. *Inventory of variables* ($N = 376$)

Concepts	Indicators	X	SD
Sexual abuse	When you were at home, did one of your parents or other family members ever have or try to have/ suggest having sex with you (including touching or attempting to touch you sexually)?[a] (alpha = .887)	0.651	1.784
Physical violence	While living at home, were you every struck so hard by a parent/stepparent/guardian that it caused a bruise or bleeding?[b]	1.237	1.261
Violent father	Threatened to hit or throw something Threw something Slapped, kicked, bit, or hit with fist Hit with something Beat up[c] (alpha = .847)	4.912	5.626
Violent mother	Above items directed at respondent[c] (alpha = .896)	4.987	5.518
Maternal alcoholism	Mother had a drinking problem[d]	0.399	0.874
Maternal addiction	Mother had a drug problem[d]	0.210	0.666
Paternal alcoholism	Father had a drinking problem[d]	0.641	1.074
Paternal addiction	Father had a drug problem[d]	0.144	0.562
Father arrested	Father arrested for criminal offense (Yes = 1)	0.301	0.459
Mother arrested	Mother arrested for criminal offense (Yes = 1)	0.053	0.225
Paternal education	Level of education achieved[e]	2.803	1.788
Maternal education	Level of education achieved[e]	3.082	1.693
Family disruption	One of biological parents absent at age 10 (Yes = 1)	0.710	0.454
Paternal unemployment	Father's unemployment experience[f]	1.582	1.078
Maternal unemployment	Mother's unemployment experience[f]	1.521	0.955
Parental control	Father/mother knew where you were/who you were with when you were out[g] (alpha = .702)	12.439	4.102
Parental support	Father/mother talked about your thoughts and feelings/did things you wanted to do[g] (alpha = .545)	10.218	3.351
Time on the street	Year left home	86.652	5.440
Age	Reported years of age	19.540	3.569
Gender	Reported sex (Male = 1)	0.662	0.474
Home delinquency	Stolen food Stolen clothes Stolen things worth between $10 and $50 from store Stolen things worth more than $50 from store Sold something had stolen Broken into a house, store, school or other building and taken money, or things like stero equipment	15.434	16.686

Table 1 *(cont.)*

Concepts	Indicators	X	SD
	Broken into a locked car to get something like a tape deck or radio Beaten someone up so badly they probably needed bandages or a doctor Used a knife or other weapon in a fight Attacked someone with the idea of seriously hurting or killing that person Used or tried to use credit or banking cards without owner's permission or passed bad checks Smoked marijuana, hashish, etc. Taken LSD, PCP, angel dust, etc. Taken coke, crack, etc. Sold marijuana or hashish Sold coke, crack, or LSD[h] (alpha = .835)		
Street delinquency (Wave 1)	Home delinquency items + had sex for money[h] (alpha = .874)	35.471	26.609
Charges while home	When lived at home, how often charged by the police for a crime[h]	0.878	1.548
Charges on street (Wave 1)	Since leaving home, how often charged by the police for a crime[h]	1.694	2.091
Street delinquency (Weeks ½, Wave 2)	Street delinquency measures, days acts committed, drug use omitted[i]	3.519	7.049

Notes: X denotes mean; SD, standard deviation.
[a] Never = 0, once or twice = 1, a few times = 2, often = 3, a lot of time = 4.
[b] Never = 0, once or twice = 1, sometimes = 2, often = 3, always = 4.
[c] Never = 0, rarely = 1, sometimes = 2, often = 3, most of the time = 4.
[d] Not a problem = 0, somewhat of a problem = 1, a serious problem = 2, a very serious problem = 3.
[e] Grade school = 1, high school = 2, high-school graduation = 3, apprenticeship = 4, college = 5, university = 6.
[f] Always employed/housewife/deceased = 1, unemployed once = 2, unemployed several times = 3, unemployed most of the time = 4, unemployed all the time = 5.
[g] Never = 1, rarely = 2, sometimes = 3, usually = 4, always = 5.
[h] Never = 0, 1 = 1, 2 = 2, 3-4 = 3, 5-9 = 4, 10-19 = 5, 20-29 = 6, 30-59 = 7, 60+ = 8.
[i] Number of days specific acts committed.

overwhelmingly is perpetrated in families by stepfathers and fathers (Badgley et al. 1984; Browne & Finkelhor 1986; Finkelhor 1993). Moreover, both male and female respondents identified fathers and stepfathers as perpetrators in their open-ended interviews. For example, when asked why he left home, one young man reported as follows:

> When I left home, I was 16 years old. And I left home because I was sexually abused and physically abused by my stepfather . . . . It was really kind of hard

> to deal with, or tell anybody. . . . When I did come out [and tell] nothing was done, and we were supposed to get some help and stuff, because it happened to my sister as well.

Recalling why she left home, another respondent also described being the victim of paternal sexual abuse: "Well, my father . . . I guess he figured that whatever he did at home would not, would not have any bearing on me . . . so, he used to sexually assault me. And uh, I got very fed up with it, and actually once I turned 13, I started running away."

We inquired in greater detail about physical violence involving parents and children. We asked in a general way how often a parent/stepparent/guardian struck the youth so hard that it caused a bruise or bleeding. We also used a more detailed and specially adapted form of the Conflict Tactics Scale developed by Straus (1979, 1990). This scale contains multiple measures of physical violence by fathers and mothers and includes the following: threats to hit or throw something; throwing something; slapping, kicking, biting, or hitting with a fist; hitting with something; and beatings. As noted in Table 1, each of these scales has a reliability score of between 0.8 and 0.9.[2]

Our scale scores reveal that mothers and fathers were about equally violent in their treatment of children.[3] Moreover, although less serious forms of violence such as throwing and slapping were most common, our general physical violence measure indicates that, on average, the youth surveyed had been bruised or bloodied on at least one occasion. The extent of more severe violence was particularly notable in our interviews, and suggests that incidents similar to the following were not rare events:

> My dad was hitting me in my bedroom and I tried to run past him to get out of the bedroom, and I pushed him, and he caught me, and he laid me down on my stomach and he put his knees on my back, grabbed my neck and twisted it and he said "If you ever do that again [push him], I'll kill you." And uh, he was hitting me with a broomstick that night, and I was full of bruises just after that. I'd planned to run away like, numerous times before that, but finally this is it, you know. I thought I'm not going to put up with it anymore, and I just packed stuff and left.

We also add measures of chronic parental problems with alcoholism and drug addiction. Several youth noted that one or both parents abused alcohol or drugs or both, and many saw it as a problem. Explaining why his parents "threw him out," one respondent stated: "Uhm, we'd fight cause I'd go, 'quit drugs' and he [his father] would go, 'no.' I'd go, 'quit drinking.' He'd say, 'no.' So we just argued about that most of the time." Measures of parental mistreatment and chemical dependency are doubly important because these problems are often connected. As was evident in our interviews, chronic problems or difficulties such as addiction and alcoholism may often cause – as well as mediate – the effects of specific stressful events such as physical and sexual abuse.

Consider one youth's description of his family: "My dad was an alcoholic so he always abused me. Physically. Just punch me and stuff like that, throw me up against the wall, you know."

Thoits (1983, p. 81) emphasizes the interconnections between chronic problems and stressful incidents, noting that "events may have effects on disturbance through difficulties; that is, ongoing strains may intervene in the events-disturbance relationship." She further cites Pearlin and Lieberman (1979, p. 240), who report that "to an appreciable extent the impact of events is channelled through relatively durable problems impinging on the lives of people." Because these problems and difficulties are ongoing, they likely both cause and mediate the effects of more specific stressful events. We also control for paternal and maternal education and unemployment, parental control and support, and family disruption. Controls are also included for time on the street (i.e., since leaving home) and age. Gender, of course, is introduced as a source of both main and interaction effects.

Because there is considerable continuity over time in criminal behavior, we add extensive controls for past crime and delinquency. We incorporate detailed retrospective self-report measures of delinquency at two points in time: (1) before leaving home, and (2) since leaving home but prior to the first-wave interview. Included are self-reports of 16 kinds of crime and delinquency, such as stealing food and clothing, breaking and entering, simple and aggravated assault, larceny and fraud, drug use and dealing, and (since leaving home) having sex for money.

The outcome variable for this analysis measures delinquency reported in the second-wave interviews. Three weeks after their first interview, youth were asked to again self-report whether they had engaged in any of the same 16 criminal acts day by day (i.e., starting with yesterday, two days ago, . . .). Each act could be reported to have occurred up to twelve days. This provides a measure that parallels the notion of a crime spree (Katz 1988), which – in discussions of secondary deviance – are reputed to follow the imposition of sanctions.

The analysis

Our analysis begins in Table 2 by examining simple bivariate ordinary least squares (OLS) relationships between background characteristics and experiences, including our measures of self-reported crime in the second-wave interviews, parental mistreatment and chemical dependency, and prior delinquency. The equations used to estimate these relationships include the selection hazard term described in note 2. The most significant correlates of second-wave crime are maternal alcoholism and drug addiction, prior delinquency at home and on the street at time 1, and being charged on the street at time 1. Less significant correlates of second-wave offending include the general measure of parental physical violence, as well as the more specific and detailed measure of violence

Table 2. *Unstandardized bivariate and multivariate OLS coefficients for main and interaction effects on second-wave self-reported delinquency* ($N = 376$)

Independent variables	Bivariate relationships		Multivariate relationships			
	B	t-ratio	B	t-ratio	B	t-ratio
Sexual abuse	0.182	0.671	0.139	0.728	0.142	0.762
Physical violence	0.853	2.341*	−0.001	−0.004	0.062	0.188
Violent father	0.045	0.518	0.027	0.386	0.015	0.222
Violent mother	0.175	2.038*	0.088	1.296	0.106	1.588
Maternal alcoholism	1.706	3.309***	0.783	1.912*	0.657	1.637*
Maternal addiction	2.456	3.737***	1.621	2.955**	1.542	2.864**
Paternal alcoholism	0.238	0.524	0.249	0.761	0.361	1.129
Paternal addiction	−0.145	−0.160	−0.879	−1.500	−0.825	−1.420
Father arrested	1.515	1.420	−0.078	−0.105	−0.409	−0.277
Mother arrested	0.890	1.264	−0.538	−0.359	3.049	1.037
Paternal education	−0.540	−2.028*	−0.255	−1.299	−0.255	−1.340
Maternal education	−0.414	−1.459	−0.091	−0.477	−0.119	−0.596
Family disruption	0.709	0.658	−0.009	−0.014	0.158	0.224
Paternal unemployment	0.229	0.497	0.109	0.354	0.168	0.555
Maternal unemployment	0.582	1.133	0.468	1.370	0.494	1.476
Paternal control	−0.205	−1.784	−0.006	−0.075	−0.222	−0.257
Paternal support	−0.052	−0.351	0.008	0.693	0.139	1.314
Time on the street	−0.053	−0.593	0.032	0.060	0.032	0.550
Age	−0.009	−0.066	−0.105	−1.112	−0.061	−0.664
Gender	2.158	1.987*	1.684	2.278**	1.641	1.577
Home delinquency	0.101	3.941***	0.052	2.231*	0.051	2.208***
Street delinquency	0.103	7.574***	0.056	3.245***	0.056	3.340***
Charges while home	0.525	1.680*	−0.258	−1.095	−0.327	−1.403
Charged on street	1.083	5.688***	0.626	3.262***	0.742	1.490
Father arrested × street charges					−1.032	−1.556
Mother arrested × street charges					−2.989	−1.330
Father arrested × gender					−1.258	0.681
Mother arrested × gender					−7.140	−1.946*
Gender × street charges					−0.457	−0.876
Father arrested × street charges × gender					2.176	2.873**
Mother arrested × street charges × gender					4.386	1.856*
Selection hazard			2.969	0.763	3.998	1.033
Intercept			−4.908		−6.413	
Adjusted R^2			0.240		0.270	

*$p < .05$, one-tailed.   **$p < .01$, one-tailed.   ***$p < .001$, one-tailed.

Table 3. *Unstandardized OLS interaction effects of parental arrest and charges on street on self-reported delinquency, decomposed by gender*

Interaction terms	β	t ratio
A. Sons ($n = 249$)		
Father arrested × street charges	1.157	2.909**
Mother arrested × street charges	1.101	1.358[+]
B. Daughters ($n = 127$)		
Father arrested × street charges	−1.013	−2.422*
Mother arrested × street charges	−4.222	−3.081***

Note: All equations include selection hazard and all main effects of independent variables in Table 2.
[+]$p < .10$, one-tailed.   *$p < .05$, one-tailed.
**$p < .01$, one-tailed.   ***$p < .001$, one-tailed.

perpetrated by mothers. Gender, parental education, and being charged while living at home also are less significantly related to second-wave crime.

The next pair of columns in Table 2 reports results from an OLS regression equation that simultaneously considers the main effects of all the explanatory variables introduced in Table 1.[4] The most notable change between the bivariate and multivariate results is the reduction below statistical significance of the measured effects of physical and maternal violence, as well as parental education. Systematic introduction of selected variables into equations with the abuse items reveals that only maternal chemical dependency eliminates the effects of abuse. These results support Thoits's (1983) suggestion that chronic stressors such as addiction and alcoholism often cause and mediate the effects of stressful events such as child abuse. Meanwhile, with all other variables held constant in the middle columns of Table 2, being charged on the street at time 1 retains a strongly significant influence on second-wave self-reported crime. This highly significant effect of being charged at time 1 on self-reported offending at time 2, net of a wide array of background variables that include comprehensive measures of prior delinquency, provides compelling evidence that these sanctions play a notable role in the causation of secondary deviance.

However, the hypotheses presented earlier in this paper go beyond postulating this main effect of police sanctions on the secondary deviance of street youth. The following columns of Table 2 report the OLS coefficients from an equation that includes two- and three-way intergenerational interaction effects involving parent and child labeling and gender. Two three-way interactions are of paramount interest, reflecting the separate interactions of father and mother arrests with street youth charges and gender on involvement in secondary deviance. Both of these interactions are statistically significant.

To further clarify these results, we re-estimate separately for males and females the two-way interactions of father and mother arrests with street youth charges for second-wave offenses. As initially hypothesized, the results for males reported in panel A of Table 3 indicate that street youth with fathers or mothers who have been arrested, but especially fathers who have been arrested, are significantly more likely to be involved in secondary crime sprees. This effect of fathers' sanctioning on sons replicates earlier findings about intergenerational labeling (Hagan & Palloni 1990). In contrast, girls who are charged and whose mothers or fathers were arrested are less likely to engage in secondary deviance. These results are consistent with the linkage Braithwaite draws between power control theories and labeling theories of delinquency and crime; following sanction experiences, these girls seem more likely to be reabsorbed or reintegrated into conforming patterns of behaviors.

Discussion and conclusions

The results of the analysis presented in this paper are unique in their attention to the effects of legal sanctions across generations and genders. Prior research on legal sanctioning has focused primarily within generations and almost exclusively on males. Yet when attention is extended across generations and to females, potentially important patterns emerge in terms of turning points in the life course, gender, and legal sanctioning policies.

First, these results encourage a growing trend in human development and life-course research to extend the concept of turning points to include multiple experiences that occur across time. Although the commonsensical notion of turning points may suggest instantaneous shifts in life trajectories, findings such as those reported in this paper suggest this view is nearsighted in missing the longer-term, interacting influences that occur over time and across events and experiences. In this case, the imposition of legal sanctions compounds across generations of families, with the subsequent arrest of the child becoming the final transformative event that galvanizes the longer-term process into a turning point. The full significance of this particular kind of interactive turning point may involve the creation of an intergenerational criminal class spanning fathers and sons.

The gender-specific nature of this intergenerational process is a second important aspect of our results. Our finding of an intergenerational transference among males replicates previous work (Hagan & Palloni 1990), but the suggestion that this pattern is unique to males has not previously been considered. Rather, research on intergenerational sanctioning has followed a pattern common in other areas of research in implicitly suggesting that what is found for males generalizes to females. Yet we have not only found a different pattern among females, but indeed an opposite pattern: females who experience intergenerational sanctions in our analysis are apparently deterred and not spurred into subsequent involvement in crime. Braithwaite's linkage of power control and labeling theories suggests that females' greater integration and dependency increases the likelihood that sanctioning and responses to it will be more reintegrative than stigmatizing. We do not know how this distinction might actually be played out in our data. That is, we do not know if the legal sanctions experienced by the female street youth in our study were imposed and experienced differently than when imposed on males. Differences both of imposition and experience may be involved. In particular, we wonder whether the social support of others might play a role in muting the effects of the criminal stigmatization process for females, both during and after the sanctioning process. This is an important topic for further research.

Finally, our findings raise important policy questions. These questions involve the possibility reflected in our findings that there are systematic variations in the ways in which individuals respond to legal sanctions. Official theories of criminal sanctioning have been slow to acknowledge and incorporate such findings, probably because the observation that offenders vary in their reactions to criminal sanctions complicates the norms of uniformity that are central to classical principles of punishment. The gender-specific patterning we observe in response to the intergenerational experience of legal sanctioning suggests that the assumption of uniformity is dubious.

Notes

1. Piliavin et al. (1986, p. 105n) point out that the issue of external validity is ultimately substantive and turns on the question of whether selection procedures make the sample systematically different in influential ways from the intended population. We introduced many measures to avoid this, including use of two cities, multiple agency and street sites, varied scheduling of days and times for interviews, and a diverse and stable team of interviewers. As Piliavin et al. further note, the risks of sample selection and external validity are more severe in many previous studies that consider single schools and communities.

2. The scales developed by Straus have been used in several hundred studies with results that suggest they are both reliable and valid (see Straus 1979, 1990). As indicated by the reliability scores reported in the text, these measures also performed well in our study. Regardless of method of extraction or rotation, exploratory factor analyses consistently reduced our data to the four perpetrator-specific factors used in this analysis (results available on request).

3. An alternative to treating the items in the Conflict Tactics Scale as a single index is to separate more severe forms of violence (i.e., hitting and beating) from those that may be less severe (e.g., slapping). Although parents were reportedly much more likely to have slapped (about two thirds) than hit or beaten (about one third and one fifth respectively) their children, mothers and fathers were nearly identical in their reported likelihood of doing so. Furthermore, although mothers were slightly more likely to report having threatened violence or thrown something, overall the similarities in reported violent acts were more striking than dissimilarities. There is a Gutman-like hierarchy to the items, moving from threats to beatings, that we decided to treat as a one-dimensional scale.

4. We measure self-reported crime in the second wave in a count form that could make the use of Poisson estimations preferable to ordinary least squares regression (see Hagan & Palloni 1990). However, estimation of Poisson models revealed little variation from the OLS regression results. These results are available on request.

References

Badgley, Robin, et al. (1984). *Sexual Offenses Against Children: Report of the Committee on Sexual Offenses Against Children and Youths.* Ottawa: Canadian Government Publishing.

Becker, Howard (1963). *Outsiders: Studies in the Sociology of Deviance.* New York: Free Press.

Black, Donald (1976). *The Behaviour of Law.* New York: Academic Press.

Black, Donald (1983). Crime as social control. *American Sociological Review* 48: 34–45.

Bohman, Michael, Cloninger, C. Robert, Sigvardsson, Soren, & von Knorring, Anne-Liis (1982). Predisposition to petty criminality in Swedish adoptees: 1. Genetic and environmental heterogeneity. *Archives of General Psychiatry* 39: 1233–41.

Bonger, William (1916). *Criminality and Economic Conditions.* Boston: Little, Brown.

Braithwaite, John (1989). *Crime, Shame and Reintegration.* Cambridge University Press.

Browne, Angela, & Finkelhor, David (1986). Impact of child sexual abuse: a review of the research. *Psychological Bulletin* 99: 66–77.

Burt, Sir Cyril (1925). *The Young Delinquent.* University of London Press.

Caspi, Avshalom, & Elder, Glen, Jr. (1988). Emergent family patterns: the intergenerational construction of problem behaviors and relationships In R. A. Hinde & J. Stevenson-Hinde (eds.), *Relationship within Families: Mutual Influences.* Oxford: Clarendon.

Cloninger, C. Robert, Sigvardsson, Soren, Bohman, Michael, & von Knorring, Anne-Liis (1982). Predisposition to petty criminality in Swedish adoptees: II. Cross-fostering analysis of gene-environment interaction. *Archives of General Psychiatry* 39: 1233–41.

Crowe, Raymond (1972). The adopted offspring of women criminal offenders: a study of their arrest records. *Archives of General Psychiatry* 27: 600–3.

Elder, Glen, Jr. (1994). Time, human agency, and social change: perspectives on the life course. *Social Psychology Quarterly* 57: 4–15.

Finkelhor, David (1993). Epidemiological factors in the clinical identification of child sexual abuse. *Child Abuse and Neglect* 17: 67–70.

Garfinkel, Harold (1956). Conditions of successful degradation ceremonies. *American Journal of Sociology* 61: 420–4.

Hagan, John, & Palloni, Alberto (1990). The social reproduction of a criminal class in working-class London, circa 1950–1980. *American Journal of Sociology* 96: 265–99.

Hagan, John, et al. (1989). *Structural Criminology.* New Brunswick, NJ: Rutgers University Press.

Jencks, Christopher (1992). *Rethinking Social Policy: Race, Poverty and the Underclass.* Cambridge, MA: Harvard University Press.

Katz, Jack (1988). *Seductions of Crime: Moral and Sensual Attractions in Doing Evil.* New York: Basic Books.

Lemert, Edwin (1967). *Human Deviance, Social Problems and Social Control.* Englewood Cliffs, NJ: Prentice-Hall.

Lombroso, Cesare (1918). *Crime, Its Causes and Remedies.* Boston: Little, Brown.

McCarthy, Bill, & Hagan, John (1992). Mean streets: the theoretical significance of situational delinquency among homeless youths. *American Journal of Sociology* 98: 597–627.

Mead, George Herbert (1918). The psychology of punitive justice. *American Journal of Sociology* 23: 577–602.

Mednick, Sarnoff, Gabrielli, William, & Hutchings, Barry (1984). Genetic influence in criminal convictions. *Science* 224: 891–4.

Pearlin, Leonard, & Lieberman, Morton (1979). Social sources of emotional distress. In Roberta Simmons (ed.), *Research in Community and Mental Health.* Greenwich, CT: JAI Press.

Piliavin, Irving, Thornton, Craig, Gartner, Rosemary, & Matsueda, Ross (1986). Crime, deterrence, and rational choice. *American Sociological Review* 51: 101-19.

Rutter, Michael (1989). Pathways from childhood to adult life. *Journal of Child Psychology and Psychiatry and Allied Disciplines* 30: 23-51.

Straus, Murray (1979). Measuring intrafamily conflict and violence: the Conflict Tactics (CT) scale. *Journal of Marriage and the Family* 41: 75-88.

Straus, Murray (1990). The Conflict Tactics scale and its critics: an evaluation and new data on validity and reliability. In Murray Straus & Richard Gelles (eds.), *Physical Violence in American Families: Risk Factors and Adaptations to Violence in 8,145 Families*. New Brunswick, NJ: Transaction.

Thoits, Peggy (1983). Dimensions of life events that influence psychological distress: an evaluation and synthesis of the literature. In Howard Kaplan (ed.), *Psychosocial Stress: Trends in Theory and Research*. New York: Academic Press.

Walters, Glenn (1992). A meta-analysis of the gene–crime relationship. *Criminology* 30: 595–613.

Walters, Glenn, & White, Thomas (1989). Heredity and crime: bad genes or bad research? *Criminology* 27: 455-85.

Wilson, James Q., & Herrnstein, Richard (1985). *Crime and Human Nature*. New York: Simon & Schuster.

5 School-leavers' self-esteem and unemployment: turning point or a station on a trajectory?

David Dooley & JoAnn Prause

Background

Introduction

What happens to young people who leave high school, not for college but for the job market? Unemployment or underemployment may operate as a turning point in the way young adults view themselves, or it may culminate a life trajectory for which high school self-esteem serves as a marker. This chapter explores the relationship between employment status and psychological well-being in recent school-leavers in two ways. The first part reviews the literature on school-leaver unemployment and psychological status and locates this work in the context of studies on adult unemployment. The second part presents some preliminary empirical findings from an ongoing study of the National Longitudinal Survey of Youth (NLSY).

Developmental and economic context. The transition to adulthood includes the adjustment from being a student in high school to being a college student or a worker and from living with parents to beginning the process of living on one's own and starting a family. Of these transitions, entering the work force may be especially formative (Mortimer & Borman 1988). For young people who go from high school to college and then graduate to high-status careers, this transition may be generally agreeable. Unfortunately, many young people drop out of high school, and three out of four high school seniors either do not go to college or do not complete college (Borman 1991).

School-leavers who enter the job market cannot begin their adjustment to work until they find a job, and many have difficulty doing this. In September 1993, near the end of the most recent recession, U.S. unemployment rates were 13.5% for those aged 16 to 24 versus 5.6% for those 25 to 54 and 4.5% for those

The authors appreciate the support of this research by a grant from the William T. Grant Foundation, as well as the helpful advice of Dr. Ellen Greenberger and of members of the Consortium for Research in Stress Processes supported by the William T. Grant Foundation.

55 and over (U.S. Department of Labor 1993). Many young people become discouraged, give up on working, and may fail to "mature into young men and women able to face their futures with a sense of confidence and security," according to the William T. Grant Foundation Commission on Work, Family, and Citizenship (1988, p. 1).

Perspectives on the school-to-work transition. The experiences of school-leavers entering the work force have stimulated research from different perspectives. Economic analyses reveal that although most unemployment spells are of short duration, most unemployment in young workers is concentrated in a smaller number of long spells and in minority workers (Freeman & Wise 1982). Sociologists have conceptualized schools and the job market as filters that sort young people into work careers that parallel their parents' (Borman 1991). From this perspective, unemployment is an outcome of unjust social structures.

From a psychological perspective, the young person has a need to achieve a meaningful occupational identity within the prevailing cultural definitions. According to Erikson's (1959) developmental approach, every young person has the task of "shaping up to an occupational (or unemployed) role" (Hendry 1987, p. 196). In this view, the problem of youth unemployment is one of individual psychological well-being (Mortimer & Borman 1988). Those young people who successfully negotiate the school-to-work transition should acquire positive personal traits such as a sense of identity, autonomy, self-efficacy, and self-liking. Young people who are delayed in this transition may become disposed to self-doubt, dependency, and a self-fulfilling expectancy of failure. On the other hand, school may itself function as a kind of job, one that is more palatable to some than to others. For students with little inclination to study, schooling may seem a sentence that must be served before real life begins (Hendry 1987). In this case, leaving school may offer relief from a toxic environment regardless of whether the young person finds a job.

Although researchers have emphasized the effect of work on psychological well-being, the reverse process warrants consideration. Perhaps personality traits in adolescence predispose young people for later success or failure in employment. In this view, satisfactory employment in early adulthood follows from confidence, ambition, and competence established before leaving high school. This psychological understanding of work-force selection complements the earlier mentioned sociological view of economic sorting by social class. Both perspectives trace a continuous, even inevitable, trajectory from adolescence to adult engagement in the work force.

The transition from school to work is complex. Many high school students hold part-time jobs, a practice that does not appear uniformly beneficial (Greenberger & Steinberg 1986). After leaving high school, young people may continue to combine education and work experiences. The young who aspire to college degrees may have to drop out of school to earn their tuition, and young people who want only to work may find themselves forced, by the lack of jobs, back to school for additional credentialing or retraining.

Although having a job may be a prerequisite for reaching the next developmental stage, not all jobs are equal. Viewed as ill-equipped to function in high-level jobs, youth may find themselves marginalized, devalued, and exploited in unappealing, dead-end jobs. Although young people may be eager to work and especially malleable to their initial job experience, they may find it more stressful than beneficial (Borman 1991).

The literature reviewed here focuses less on the impact of different types of work and more on the psychological costs of unemployment. The next section deals with a portion of the large body of literature on adult unemployment, and the subsequent section presents the relatively small body of literature on school-leaver unemployment.

Unemployment and psychological well-being in adults

Most of the individual-level research on unemployment has developed conceptually within the stressful life events model. The job loss event is thought to be so impactful because employment has both manifest and latent functions. The manifest function includes income, the loss of which exposes the unemployed person to a host of threats associated with declining style of life. But as Jahoda (1982) has articulated, employment also provides such latent functions as time structure, activity, social contacts, status, and collective purpose, and research has documented the association among unemployment, stress, and these latent functions (Isaksson 1989).

Levels of analysis and types of outcomes. Unemployment stress has been studied in relation to a wide range of outcomes, but here we will focus on psychological well-being. Adult unemployment studies of mental health have most commonly used one or another of three different measures: surveys of psychological symptoms, admissions to psychiatric care, and suicide. However, these measures appear not to be highly intercorrelated and may very well respond differently to economic change (Dooley & Catalano 1986).

Because suicides and psychiatric admissions are relatively rare, they are typically studied in the aggregate as rates based on archival records. Such studies also measure unemployment in the aggregate and correlate unemployment rates over spatial or temporal units with either suicide or hospitalization rates. Analyses of suicide and unemployment rates generally find them positively associated (Platt 1984), but aggregate studies of unemployment and admission rates show less convergence (Dooley & Catalano 1986).

Aggregate studies of mental health and unemployment rates risk the "ecological" fallacy, that is, drawing incorrect individual-level interpretations from aggregated data (Robinson 1950). For example, a positive correlation of unemployment and suicide rates would not demonstrate that individuals who lose jobs are at greater risk of committing suicide. To avoid the ecological fallacy, researchers must collect measures of personal unemployment and psychological distress at the individual level. Because of the low rates of suicide and psychiatric hospitalization, most individual-level studies of unemployment and mental health rely on surveys of psychological symptoms. Such studies typically find elevated symptoms in the unemployed.

Although most economic stress and mental health studies use either the aggregate-level or the individual-level operationalization of unemployment, there exists a hybrid type that combines both. With the appropriate data it is possible to measure the separate effects of personal and aggregate unemployment, but this cross-level approach requires a large sample of respondents from varying economic conditions (e.g., Dooley, Catalano, & Rook 1988). Such cross-level studies can also test the interaction between personal and aggregate unemployment, for example, that the unemployed are relatively less adversely affected when the unemployment rate in their locality is high rather than low (Cohn 1978).

Designs to contrast trajectory and turning points. Studies that correlate economic and mental health variables at one point in time fail to control for prior psychological symptoms that may predict later job loss. For example, one study of 70 unemployed adult patients who were admitted to a psychiatric emergency unit found that all but three had suffered from a mental disorder requiring treatment prior to their unemployment (Fruensgaard et al. 1983). The view that mental disorder causes dysfunction at work, resulting in job loss and poverty, has been termed the "drift" hypothesis (Dohrenwend & Dohrenwend 1969). In contrast, the "social causation" hypothesis regards unemployment as a cause of mental distress. In the present context, drift corresponds to the continuity of a trajectory, while social causation corresponds to a turning point or change in trajectory.

Only the panel design (longitudinal, individual-level) can convincingly pit the social causation and drift hypotheses against each other. The panel approach, although used infrequently, has taken two forms in studies of working adults. One follows a group of employees who work at a plant about to close (e.g., Cobb & Kasl 1977). The other follows a large general population sample, waiting to reinterview those few who lose their jobs (e.g., Linn, Sandifer, & Stein 1985). In both approaches, time-1 symptoms often prove the best predictor of time-2 symptoms, and unemployment between interviews accounts for statistically significant but modest portions of the change in symptoms.

The historical tendency to pit drift against social causation has obscured the possibility that both processes are operating. Support for the reciprocal effects of job loss and disorder comes from an analysis of the Epidemiologic Catchment Area data on alcohol abuse (Dooley, Catalano, & Hough 1992). Consistent with social causation and controlling for time-1 alcohol abuse, those losing their jobs were over nine times more likely to become alcohol disordered within a year than those not becoming unemployed. Consistent with drift, employed people who had ever been diagnosed as having an alcohol disorder at time 1 were twice as likely to become unemployed by time 2 as those never so diagnosed.

Effects of unemployment on school-leavers

This section reviews studies on the relationship between youth unemployment and well-being (also see Feather 1990; Furnham 1994; Mortimer 1994; Winefield et al. 1993). A search of *Psychological Abstracts* for English-language publications in the past 15 years reveals few methodologically convincing studies in this area. Conclusions about youth unemployment must be based on studies of youth and not extrapolated from the adult literature.

Differences between adult and school-leaver unemployment. The school-leaver's failure to find work differs in at least three respects from that of an adult worker's job loss. First, the adult literature addresses the stressful life event of job loss, but the challenge for the school-leaver is to find a first job. One of the few studies to address this distinction compared two groups of young people, those who had been unemployed since leaving school and those of similar age who had been employed but who had recently lost work (Winefield & Tiggemann 1989a). The results indicated no difference in psychological well-being, suggesting that "job loss, as opposed to failure to find a job, is not in itself a traumatic experience for the young person" (p. 79).

The second difference between most job-loss studies and failure-to-find-first-job studies is that the former usually involves mature adults whereas the latter usually concerns young people. Even if the effects of job loss and failure to find work have similar magnitudes, the developmental phases in which they typically occur may affect their impact. Mature adults may have accumulated obligations and dependencies such as mortgages and college tuition payments that amplify the effect of their job loss. On the other hand, young people may stand at a critical juncture in their identity formation and may therefore be more sensitive to their initial failures to find work (Hendry 1987). Moreover, young people will have less experience coping with job setbacks and, if recent school-leavers, will have fewer coping skills for managing their affairs in the absence of the time structure of school or work. In cross-sectional analysis, the longer young people were out of work, the more likely they were to see their unemployment as due to their own inadequacies (Breakwell 1986). In another study, unemployed young people appeared to cope by engaging in such activities as drinking alone (Halford & Learner 1984).

Third, the economic environment offers markedly different opportunities to adult than to young job seekers. Young people are much more likely to be unemployed than older workers. In most developed countries, young people have two to three times the unemployment rate of adults (Winefield et al. 1993).

Types of school-leavers studies. Some studies of the effects of unemployment on the well-being of school-leavers have employed a qualitative approach based on intensive interviews and observations (e.g., Ullah 1987). A more quantitative cross-sectional approach surveys young people in the work force at some point after leaving school and measures the association between employment status and psychological status using standard symptom scales. For example, Stafford, Jackson, and Banks (1980) surveyed 647 young British people seven months after they left school. Those who were unemployed reported more symptoms on a brief measure of mental health (General Health Questionnaire, GHQ). This study also found that those with higher work involvement had fewer symptoms if they worked but more symptoms if they were unemployed. Findings from such cross-sectional designs, however, cannot distinguish between drift and social causation.

Variations on the cross-sectional approach have not resolved this inferential problem. For example, Rowley and Feather (1987) surveyed two groups of unemployed Australian males, one aged 15 to 24 and the other aged 30 to 49. The older group reported more psychological symptoms, and the younger group reported lower self-esteem; in both groups combined, longer unemployment was associated with lower self-esteem and higher psychological symptoms. Unfortunately, the duration-of-unemployment variable may itself be an effect – rather than the cause – of diminished self-esteem or elevated distress.

Stronger evidence comes from a longitudinal study that followed two British cohorts of young people, one leaving school in 1978 and the other in 1979 (Jackson et al. 1983). Young people moving from employment to unemployment revealed large increases in distress, and those moving from unemployment to employment revealed substantial decreases. A similar design was used with Norwegian young people, again finding adverse effects of unemployment but not measuring the school-to-work transition (Hammer 1993). Not clear from these studies is the extent to which personal characteristics that existed before leaving school might have disposed some students to have greater success at finding jobs.

Longitudinal studies beginning in high school. English-language studies of mental health have been found for only nine panels that begin before the adolescents left high school and follow them into the work force (not counting the new studies reported here and in Chapters 6 and 10 of this volume). The data for the nine former studies were collected from the late 1960s through the 1980s, largely in Australia. Table 1 summarizes the findings from these studies in chronological order of the publication on each panel. Some of these studies also tracked school-leavers who continued into tertiary schooling, and these typically found that school-continuers resembled school-leavers with satisfactory jobs more than they resembled unemployed school-leavers. Because of our focus on youths entering the labor force, the results on school-continuers were excluded from Table 1. Most studies followed school-leavers for only a year or two, but one study is represented by a series of reports reflecting follow-ups of the same panel over nearly a decade (summarized in Winefield et al. 1993).

These studies do not agree on the drift hypothesis or on the nature of the social causation hypothesis. Five studies find no support for drift (i.e., no differences in high school between later employed and unemployed workers), and another finds a reverse drift effect in which less positive self-image predicts future employment. Of these six studies, four had small sample sizes and another involved only males. One study that did find evidence for drift reported that its prediction of future unemployment status by psychological measures disappeared when such background variables as socioeconomic status were controlled (Tiggemann & Winefield 1989). Another study found "only weak support" for drift with few significant predictions among the many tested, and those few varied by gender (Spenner & Otto 1985, p. 217). In sum, the evidence inclines against drift, at least when other background characteristics are statistically controlled.

All of the studies provide some support for social causation in that, controlling for high-school well-being, the unemployed were psychologically less well-off than the employed. However, there are at least two different mechanisms by which such social causation might occur, and both appeared in different studies. One view, the stress perspective, regards unemployment in the young much as it is studied among adults – as an undesirable stressful life event (or, in this case, as non-occurrence of a desirable event) which causes harm. Consistent with this view, the earliest Tiggemann and Winefield report (1980), both small-sample Patton and Noller studies (1984, 1990), and the large-sample Banks and Jackson (1982) and Feather and O'Brien (1986) studies found that the unemployed showed declines in measures of their psychological functioning.

In contrast, the developmental perspective regards unemployment as a hindrance to accomplishing the next level of maturation. For the young person who has left the role of student, finding employment may be crucial for progression to the next social role of adult (Marini 1987). School-leavers who find work should display significant improvement in measures such as self-esteem, but those who become unemployed should be inhibited from making this role transition and stalled in a kind of moratorium, neither better nor worse off, until

Table 1. *Studies of school-leavers' employment and well-being: drift versus social causation*

Report	Sample [lag]	Measure	Drift?	Social causation?
1. Bachman, O'Malley, & Johnston (United States)				
Bachman, O'Malley, & Johnston (1978)	1,205 employed, 111 unemployed (males only) [5 years]	Self-esteem	No	Yes: employed showed more gains
2. Gurney (Australia)				
Gurney (1980a,b)	220 employed, 53 unemployed [4 months]	Psychological development scales, self-esteem	No	Yes:[a] employed showed gains
3. Winefield & Tiggemann (Australia)				
Tiggemann & Winefield (1980)	55 employed, 26 unemployed [7 months]	Satisfaction with self, happy	No	Yes:[a] unemployed showed losses
Tiggemann & Winefield (1984)	617 employed, 144 unemployed [1 year]	Mood, self-esteem, locus of control, depression	Yes	Yes: employed showed more gains
Winefield & Tiggemann (1985)	803 employed, 121 unemployed [2 years]	Mood, self-esteem, locus of control, need for achievement	Yes	Yes: employed showed more gains
Winefield, Tiggemann, & Goldney (1988)	484 satisfied employed, 76 dissatisfied employed, 77 unemployed [4 years]	Self-esteem, locus of control, depression, GHQ[b]	No	Yes: employed showed more gains
Tiggemann & Winefield (1989)	1st year: 613 employed, 139 unemployed; 3rd year: 806 employed, 137 unemployed; 5th year: 531 employed, 37 unemployed	Self-esteem, locus of control, depression, need for achievement	Not after controlling for background variables such as SES[c]	Not tested
Winefield, Tiggemann, & Winefield (1991)	417 satisfied employed, 45 dissatisfied employed, 40 unemployed [7 years]	Self-esteem, depression, locus of control, negative affect	No	Mixed: no for self-esteem; yes for negative affect; employed showed more gains
Winefield, Winefield, Tiggemann, & Goldney (1991)	353 satisfied employed, 31 dissatisfied employed, 22 unemployed [8 years]	Self-esteem, depression, locus of control, negative affect	No	Mixed: no for self-esteem; yes for negative affect and depression; employed showed more gains

Table 1 *(cont.)*

Report	Sample [lag]	Measure	Drift?	Social causation?
Winefield, Tiggemann, Winefield, & Goldney (1993)	292 satisfied employed, 32 dissatisfied employed, 8 unemployed [9 years]	Depression	No	Yes:[a] satisfied employed showed more gains
4. Banks & Jackson (United Kingdom)				
Banks & Jackson (1982)	1st year: 683 employed, 64 unemployed; 2nd year: 397 employed, 74 unemployed	GHQ	No	Yes:[a] employed showed gains and unemployed showed losses
5. Patton & Noller (Australia)				
Patton & Noller (1984)	24 employed, 21 unemployed [5 months]	Self-esteem, locus of control, depression	No	Yes: unemployed showed losses
6. Spenner & Otto (United States)				
Spenner & Otto (1985)	4,916 (unemployment duration rather than status) [13 years]	Self-esteem, locus of control	Weak; gender interaction	Yes[a]
7. Donovan et al. (United Kingdom)				
Donovan, Oddy, Pardoe, & Ades (1986)	45 employed, 43 unemployed [6–12 months]	Self-esteem, GHQ, depression, anxiety	No	Yes: employed showed more gains
8. Feather & O'Brien (Australia)				
Feather & O'Brien (1986)	1st year: 469 employed, 110 unemployed; 2nd year: 910 employed, 199 unemployed	Self-concept, locus of control, stress, life satisfaction	Yes	Yes: unemployed showed losses
9. Patton & Noller (Australia)				
Patton & Noller (1990)	1st & 2nd year: 47 employed, 40 unemployed	Self-image, depression	Reverse	Yes: employed showed gains and unemployed showed losses

[a] Analysis did not test the time-by-group interaction to see if the test–retest change in the unemployed group differed from that in the employed group.

[b] General Health Questionnaire.

[c] Socioeconomic status.

they gain employment. Support for this view was first reported by Bachman, O'Malley, and Johnston (1978) and by Gurney (1980a,b), although the latter study found this effect for self-esteem only in females. Further support came from the later, large-sample analyses by Tiggemann and Winefield (e.g. 1984) and from one of the smallest samples (Donovan et al. 1986).

Need for further research

Nature of drift and social causation effects. Although there is little evidence to date for selection by high-school self-esteem into employment, the drift hypothesis remains intuitively plausible, and school-leaver studies must routinely check it. Any new evidence for drift would warrant reconsideration of the way adolescent personality might sustain the trajectory of work-force engagement in adulthood.

Some interesting questions remain unanswered about the turning-point process of social causation. A social causation effect appears likely from the present literature, but whether it takes the stress or the developmental form remains unclear. Additional research should identify the conditions under which one or the other form appears. Perhaps the shape or magnitude of the social causation effect is affected by such subject traits as gender or psychological commitment to work (e.g., Jackson et al. 1983). Moreover, the association between unemployment and well-being may vary depending on the operationalization of unemployment. As one example, Winefield and Tiggemann (1989b) found a curvilinear relationship in which school-leavers with the shortest and the longest periods of unemployment appeared better off than those out of work for intermediate periods.

Generalizability. Little is known about recent school-leavers in the United States. The most recent large-scale studies come from Australia, and the only two from the United States both began with students in the 1960s. Of these, one excluded females (Bachman et al. 1978) and the other used a Washington state sample with few blacks or Hispanics (Spenner & Otto 1985). Another kind of generalizability pertains to the period of time since leaving school. School-leaver studies that have followed subjects for more than a few years typically experience severe attrition, which limits conclusions about long-term effects. For instance, by the ninth follow-up, òne study found only eight unemployed subjects (Winefield et al. 1993).

A third type of generalization involves the nature of the economic context in which adolescents enter the work force. None of the studies summarized in Table 1 included the aggregate unemployment rate as an independent or moderating variable, even though the opportunities given by the job market must affect the likelihood of success or failure of new workers in obtaining and holding jobs. Unfortunately, when a panel of school-leavers is drawn from the same community, all the respondents experience the same economic climate, thus limiting the variability of an aggregate economic indicator in most studies.

Design and measures. What is needed is a longitudinal design that measures – both in high school and later in early adulthood – the psychological well-being of young people along with the school-leaver's experience in the work force. The sample should represent both genders and the whole range of socioeconomic statuses and ethnic subgroups in the United States and include enough respondents to provide adequate statistical power even after a long follow-up. The data necessary for such a test have been collected as part of the National Longitudinal Survey of Youth.

Most panel studies of school-leavers' unemployment incorporated self-esteem or some other indicator of psychological well-being, such as negative affect, depression, self-image, or locus of control. Such constructs are relevant from the lifespan perspective, as it is the adolescent's satisfaction with his or her identity that must be achieved in the transition to adulthood. Consistent with this past research, the following analyses will measure the link between unemployment and self-esteem in the school-leaver.

Hypotheses. The drift hypothesis holds that self-esteem before graduating from high school will predict unemployment and underemployment after leaving school, controlling for characteristics such as ethnicity, academic ability, and aggregate unemployment rate. The social causation hypothesis holds that, controlling for individual characteristics such as gender and high-school self-esteem, later unemployment and underemployment will be associated with later self-esteem. This test will check for the shape of any social causation effect, specifically for the appearance of the stress pattern (unemployed show declining self-esteem) or the developmental pattern (employed show rising self-esteem). The tests will be cross-level in that aggregate unemployment as well as the interaction of aggregate unemployment and personal unemployment will be included in the analyses.

Study

Method

NLSY survey. The National Longitudinal Survey of Youth (NLSY) began in 1979 and is currently ongoing. The NLSY is a multistage, stratified area probability sample consisting of three separate random samples designed to represent the population of individuals born between 1957 and 1964 in the United States (see also Chapter 6 for additional details about the NLSY, particularly the child–mother data set that partially overlaps the sample studied here). One sample ($n = 6,812$) was designed to represent the noninstitutionalized civilian segment of American young people aged 14–21 as of January 1, 1979. The second sample ($n = 5,969$) was designed to oversample Hispanic, black, and economically disadvantaged non-Hispanic, non-black youth. The third sample is a military sample and will not be utilized in this project. The samples have been reinterviewed in annual follow-up studies, producing panels that extend from early high school to early adulthood with a retention rate of over 90% for the combined samples.

The NLSY provides sample case weights to be applied to each respondent during a given survey year to make population estimates. These weights correct for differential probability of selection at the initial stage of household selection and for differential completion rates at the initial screening phase of data collection, and they also allow for combination of cases obtained in the cross-section and supplemental samples. The case weights were revised in subsequent waves to allow for decline in numbers of population cohorts over time due to death, migration, or other attrition (Frankel, McWilliams, & Spencer 1983). The NLSY does not recommend using the weights when performing regression analyses; the preferred procedure is stratifying and performing regressions within groups and then comparing the regression coefficients among groups (CHRR 1990). The present research will employ case weights to perform weighted analyses and also will use interaction terms to test differential relationships in different sampling groups (Cochran 1977; Potthoff, Woodbury, & Mantou 1992).

The present study begins with the 5,241 NLSY respondents who were interviewed in 1980, who were in high school in that year, and who were (at that time) less than 20 years of age and not in the military. Of these, 390 were not reinterviewed in 1987, leaving 4,851 (a reinterview rate of 93%). This sample is further reduced to 3,403 by excluding those respondents who had completed one or more years of college as of 1987 ($n = 1,448$). Another 34 were lost because of missing data on variables that were needed to determine graduation status and years of education, leaving 3,369. Finally, 681 were eliminated as being "out of the labor force" in 1987, a broad category that describes individuals who are not working and not wanting employment – including students, homemakers, and the disabled. The present analyses are based on the remaining sample of 2,688 (less those cases that have missing values on the variables used in each cross-tabulation or regression). Although our NLSY sample overlaps somewhat the one studied by Menaghan (see Chapter 6), there are some important differences. Unlike Menaghan's, the present sample includes men and all women regardless of whether they have children, but it excludes individuals who have one or more years of education beyond high school.

Measures. The NLSY collects a variety of data reflecting early formative influences, academic ability, attitudes toward education and work, educational and occupational aspirations or expectations, and psychological measures such as self-esteem. The NLSY also collects extensive labor-force participation data that, in most cases, are directly comparable to those collected by the Current Population Survey (CPS). These data make it possible to characterize the labor-force participation of the respondents during each survey year.

Characterizations of employment status will include both "unemployment" and "underemployment" (Clogg, Sullivan, & Mutcher 1986; Sullivan 1978). Unemployment is defined here as wanting work but not working in the week prior to the survey week, and includes two subcategories: those who have tried to get a job in recent weeks, and the discouraged unemployed who have given up trying. Underemployment consists of any of the following three conditions, hierarchically defined as: involuntary part-time employment, intermittent unemployment, or low income. The "involuntary part-time employment" category includes those working fewer than 35 hours during the survey week for economic reasons (e.g., slack work, material shortages, or inability to find full-time work); voluntary part-time workers would be included within the employed category unless they fall into the last underemployment category of inadequate income. The "intermittent unemployment" category includes people who worked during the past week but reported being unemployed 15 or more weeks during the past calendar year. The "inadequate income" category includes people whose individual annual income fell below 1.25 times the poverty wage based on at least 45 weeks of employment in the past calendar year.

Each employed and underemployed respondent was characterized as either satisfied or dissatisfied with his or her job, based on one item with four responses about the respondent's current job: like very much, like fairly much, dislike somewhat, or dislike very much. Those giving either of the two "dislike" responses were coded as unsatisfied with their jobs. The 1987 employment variable is divided (for purposes of dummy variable analyses) into five groups, using the satisfied employed respondents as the reference group: satisfied employed, unsatisfied employed, unemployed, satisfied underemployed, and unsatisfied underemployed. In other cases, a simple dichotomy is used where 0 = unemployed or underemployed and 1 = employed, without regard for job satisfaction.

The NLSY also provides the local unemployment rate for respondents, reflecting the prevailing economic condition in the area of each respondent's residence in the year of the survey. A person's unemployment rate is that reported by the Department of Labor for the respondent's metropolitan statistical area in the month of March of each survey year. For a person not living in a metropolitan statistical area, this variable is derived from the unemployment rate of the respondent's state of residence.

Self-esteem was measured in 1980 and 1987 using the Rosenberg (1965) ten-item scale. This scale has been shown to reflect global as opposed to situation-specific self-esteem (O'Brien 1985). Each item has four responses, and the additive scoring method gives a possible range of 10 to 40; high scores represent higher self-esteem. When a dichotomous version of this score was appropriate, the cut point was one standard deviation below the mean (score of 27). This resulted in a split between low self-esteem (score less than or equal to 27, less than 20% of the sample) and average to high self-esteem (score more than 27, more than 80% of the sample).

Numerous control variables were used in these analyses: ethnicity (black, Hispanic, and non-black, non-Hispanic), high-school graduation status, gender, either parent's highest educational level (measured as completed years of education, as a surrogate for family socioeconomic status), age, and academic achievement (measured in 1980 using the Armed Services Vocational Aptitude Battery, ASVAB). In addition to these substantive control variables, two other variables were studied for their potential effect on the analyses. A dummy variable was used to reflect different sample origins (random sample vs. oversample of ethnic minority and poor respondents), and analyses were checked for both the main effect of sample and possible interactions between the sample of origin and the presumed causal variable. Another sampling issue pertains to the fact that the NLSY includes respondents in different stages of high school in 1980. Analytically, the subgroups that left school in different years could have been treated as separate panels to determine whether years since leaving school differentially affects the relation between unemployment/underemployment and self-esteem. More simply, such subgroup effects were studied together by representing them by dummy variables. In addition to the main effects of these subgroups, these analyses were checked for possible interactions between year left school and the variables of substantive interest.

Tests. To describe the possible drift effect, we first cross-tabulated self-esteem in 1980 with employment status in 1987. Then, dichotomous employment status in 1987 was regressed on self-esteem (measured in 1980) as well as on various control variables. For this analysis, employment status was expressed as a dichotomous variable (employed vs. unemployed or underemployed), and the analysis proceeded as a logistic regression with the effects expressed as odds ratios (Hosmer & Lemeshow 1989). To describe the possible social causation effect, we first give the 1980 and 1987 self-esteem means for the various 1987 employment groups. Then self-esteem (measured in 1987) was regressed on dummy variables representing unemployment and underemployment in 1987, controlling for self-esteem and other indicators collected in 1980.

Results

Drift. The upper portion of Table 2 presents a 2×5 cross-tabulation of self-esteem in 1980 and employment status in 1987 (Pearson chi-square $= 25.81$, $df = 4$, $p < .0001$), along with an odds ratio for each employment group. This

Table 2. *1987 employment status by 1980 self-esteem and by 1980 and 1987 self-esteem means: cross-tabulation, odds ratios, means, and standard deviations*

1980 self-esteem	1987 employment status					
	Satisfied employed	Unsatisfied employed	Unemployed	Satisfied underemployed	Unsatisfied underemployed	Total
Low esteem (≤27) n	225	19	72	83	13	412
(weighted n)	(208)	(26)	(62)	(69)	(10)	(375)
Average–high esteem (>27) n	1,314	123	253	316	25	2,031
(weighted n)	(1,436)	(130)	(191)	(282)	(28)	(2,067)
Total n	1,539	142	325	399	38	2,443
(weighted n)	(1,644)	(156)	(253)	(351)	(38)	(2,442)
Odds ratio relative to satisfied employed		0.98	1.72	1.55	3.02	
(95% confidence limits)		(0.59, 1.63)	(1.30, 2.29)	(1.18, 2.03)	(1.51, 6.01)	
Weighted odds ratio relative to satisfied employed		1.57	2.26	1.66	2.49	
(95% confidence limits)		(1.01, 2.47)	(1.66, 3.08)	(1.24, 2.23)	(1.20, 5.16)	
1980 mean self-esteem	31.2	30.7	30.2	30.4	29.6	30.9
(standard deviation)	(3.7)	(3.5)	(3.8)	(3.7)	(4.2)	(3.7)
1980 weighted mean	31.3	30.4	30.1	30.6	30.2	31.0
(standard deviation)	(3.6)	(3.5)	(3.8)	(3.7)	(3.8)	(3.7)
1987 mean self-esteem	33.1	32.1	31.7	31.8	32.2	32.6
(standard deviation)	(3.9)	(4.2)	(3.8)	(4.0)	(3.8)	(4.0)
1987 weighted mean	33.4	31.9	31.7	31.9	31.9	32.9
(standard deviation)	(3.9)	(4.2)	(4.0)	(4.0)	(3.8)	(4.0)

Table 3. *Predicting 1987 employment status: logistic regression analysis* ($N = 2,430$)

Predictor	B	SE	R	$\exp(B)$
1980 self-esteem (0 = low, 1 = average to high)	0.11	0.18	0.00	1.11
Academic achievement	0.01***	0.003	0.09	1.01
Race (0 = non-black, 1 = black)	−0.77***	0.14	−0.09	0.46
High-school graduate (0 = no, 1 = yes)	0.43***	0.11	0.07	1.54
Gender (0 = female, 1 = male)	−0.41	0.23	−0.02	0.66
Unemployment rate, 1987	−0.14***	0.02	−0.14	0.87
Sample (0 = random, 1 = oversample)	−0.33	0.18	−0.02	0.72
Sample × gender	0.49*	0.22	0.03	1.64
Self-esteem × gender	0.79**	0.24	0.05	2.20
Constant	1.22***	0.23		

Notes: Model chi-square = 246.86, $df = 9$, $p < .001$; 0 = unemployed or underemployed, 1 = employed. SE denotes standard error.
*$p < .05$. **$p < .01$. ***$p < .001$.

term (rows 4 and 5) expresses the odds of being in a particular group relative to the satisfactory employment group given low 1980 self-esteem, *divided by* the odds of being in this group relative to the satisfactory employment group given average or higher self-esteem (Fienberg 1980). Table 2 suggests a pattern of economic drift based on 1980 self-esteem. For example, the risk of being underemployed and unsatisfied relative to being satisfactorily employed is over three times greater if one had low self-esteem in 1980 (rather than average or higher self-esteem). Partitioning this table differently, we can combine the employed people into one group and the underemployed and unemployed into another. In this case, the overall odds ratio of being unemployed or underemployed relative to being employed is 1.67 for those with low (rather than average to high) self-esteem. However, this apparent relationship might be spurious, and a more elaborate analysis is needed to control for potentially confounding variables.

Table 3 gives the results of a logistic regression analysis in which the key predictor is dichotomous 1980 self-esteem (split at 27, as in Table 2) and the dependent variable is the dichotomy 0 = underemployment or unemployment versus 1 = employment. In analyses without interactions, 1980 self-esteem proved to be a significant predictor. However, the gender × 1980 self-esteem interaction reached significance, indicating that prediction of 1987 employment status by 1980 self-esteem holds primarily for males. Although females with low self-esteem in 1980 appear slightly (9%) more likely to be unemployed or underemployed in 1987, low self-esteem males were much (2.3 times) more likely than were average or high self-esteem males to be unemployed or underemployed in 1987. The same pattern of drift in male respondents appeared when the analysis

Table 4. *1987 self-esteem as a function of 1987 employment status: ordinary least squares analysis[a]* ($N = 2,443$)

Predictor	B	SE of B	Beta	t
Employed, unsatisfied	−1.01	0.30	−0.06	−3.35***
Unemployed	−0.88	0.25	−0.07	−3.56***
Underemployed, satisfied	−0.97	0.21	−0.09	−4.56***
Underemployed, unsatisfied	−0.86	0.59	−0.03	−1.47
Self-esteem, 1980[b]	0.35	0.02	0.32	16.29***
Age at reinterview (1987)	−0.26	0.06	−0.08	−4.24***
Parent's education (years)	0.06	0.03	0.04	1.88[+]
High-school graduate (0 = no, 1 = yes)	−0.34	0.21	−0.04	−1.62
Academic achievement	0.03	0.004	0.14	6.46***
Race (0 = non-black, 1 = black)	−0.38	0.33	−0.03	−1.16
Sample (0 = random, 1 = oversample)	−0.56	0.32	−0.06	−1.75[+]
Self-esteem × unsatisfied employed	0.26	0.08	0.06	3.12**
Race × academic achievement	0.04	0.01	0.08	2.81**
Sample × graduated	1.03	0.38	0.09	2.69**
Constant	38.07	1.52		24.96***

Notes: $R = 0.45$, adjusted $R^2 = 0.20$; $F = 45.26$, $dfs = 14$ and 2,428, $p < .001$.
[a] Weighted with NLSY-supplied case weights to adjust for different sampling rates and differential completion rates among various design cohorts.
[b] 1980 self-esteem is expressed as deviations from the mean to reduce multicollinearity between the main and interaction effects (Cohen & Cohen 1983; Neter, Wasserman, & Kutner 1990).
[+]$p < .10$.   **$p < .01$.   ***$p < .001$.

excluded the underemployed and contrasted the employed versus the unemployed. With or without the underemployed group, this relationship was highly significant despite controls for other predictors including ethnicity, the unemployment rate, and academic ability. Neither sample nor year of leaving school interacted with 1980 self-esteem in predicting employment status.

Social causation. The lower portion of Table 2 presents the self-esteem means in 1980 and 1987 for the five different 1987 employment groups. Although all of these groups showed an increase in self-esteem, the employed satisfied group enjoyed the greatest increase. This analysis fails to control for possible confounding variables. A repeated-measures analysis of variance or covariance, as typically used to test the effect of employment on self-esteem, cannot accommodate all of the categorical variables and interactions found to predict 1987 self-esteem. As a result, a multiple regression analysis (using ordinary least squares) was employed.

Table 4 presents a multiple regression analysis in which 1987 self-esteem is the dependent variable predicted by dummy variables for the various employment groups (with the employed satisfied group serving as the reference), controlling for self-esteem in 1980 and for various other measures and interactions. Even with all of these controls, being unemployed or satisfied underemployed or unsatisfied employed was each significantly related to 1987 self-esteem. Only the dummy for the small ($n = 38$) unsatisfied underemployed group was not significantly related to 1987 self-esteem adjusted for 1980 self-esteem. As with the drift analysis, neither sample of origin nor year of leaving school interacted with any of the employment dummy variables. However, there was one interaction involving these dummy variables: self-esteem in 1980 appeared to buffer the adverse effect of being unsatisfied with one's employment.

Discussion

Summary. As evidence of continuity in developmental trajectory, high-school students (particularly boys) with lower self-esteem in 1980 ran a greater risk of being unemployed or underemployed in 1987. As evidence of an economic event operating as a turning point, unemployment, underemployment, and unsatisfactory employment are all associated negatively with 1987 self-esteem adjusted for 1980 self-esteem. These data describe a pattern of delayed development in that all employment subgroups show increased self-esteem but none so great as the satisfied employed group.

This reciprocal relationship between self-esteem and employment is echoed in the parallel findings by Menaghan (see Chapter 6) between self-esteem and more complex, autonomous, and higher-paying occupations. In addition, the tendency of all school-leavers to increase their sense of well-being over time – with those who become fully employed outgaining the unemployed or partially employed – is also echoed in the findings of Gore and associates (see Chapter 10) for measures of depressed mood and mastery.

However, the present findings must be interpreted with some caution. Because the sample size is so large, rather small effects can reach statistical significance. In addition, this correlational design cannot support inferences of causation. Although numerous likely confounding variables were included to control for spuriousness, it is possible that some unmeasured factor accounts for the observed associations.

These findings derive from one of the few studies of school-leavers' unemployment and well-being in the United States and help to underscore the predicament of many non–college-bound youth entering the labor force. Because of the unusually long-term nature of the NLSY study and its high retention rate, it provides evidence of the lasting importance of adolescent personality characteristics for later unemployment and psychological well-being. Finally, this study offers a model for cross-level analysis by operationalizing aggregate-level as well as individual-level unemployment. As one example, the effect of 1980 self-esteem on 1987 employment status was adjusted for and compared with the significant effect of the 1987 unemployment rate prevailing in each respondent's locality. For another, the potential moderating effect of prevailing economic climate on the effect of personal employment status on well-being could be checked and ruled out in this study.

Policy and research implications. To the extent that future unemployment is predicted by high school self-esteem (drift), school interventions might be designed to raise self-esteem in order to influence future employability and labor force engagement. To the extent that unemployment harms self-esteem (social causation), accounting this social cost could be used to motivate economic policies to enhance job creation and youth employment. As a result, the comparison of these different policy choices may hinge both on the cost-effectiveness of efforts to modify the presumed cause and on the relative strength of the drift and social causation effects.

Although previous studies found support for social causation, few had looked for and none had found such a strong selection effect of early self-esteem on employment success. The present data imply that low self-esteem in high school puts all adolescents (significant main effect of 1980 self-esteem), but especially boys (significant interaction of gender × self-esteem), on a trajectory to unemployment or underemployment up to seven years later. Using a different NLSY subsample that excluded males and women without children, Menaghan reports in Chapter 6 that early low self-esteem also appears to have both direct and indirect (via education) adverse effects on girls' future occupational complexity and hourly wages. How much earlier than high school such low self-esteem is established, why boys appear to experience this drift effect more than girls (at least in the present sample), and how this selection operates are all questions requiring further investigation.

The present research also allowed for the comparison of two variants of the social causation model (stress versus development). We would expect that unemployment in school-leavers would be a doubly powerful stressor because young people are subject to the damaging effects of joblessness while undergoing a major developmental transition. Interestingly, none of the groups showed a decrease in average self-esteem over time. Self-esteem rose for all groups but appeared restrained in those who were experiencing unemployment, underemployment, or unsatisfactory employment. One surprise finding was the apparent buffering by 1980 self-esteem of the adverse effect of unsatisfactory employment on 1987 self-esteem. Why self-esteem moderated the effects of this employment status and not others such as being unemployed or underemployed invites further exploration.

Later analyses could extend the current findings in several ways. Future research might explore the work-force experience at initial attempt (e.g., time to first job or first enduring job) using different statistical approaches (e.g., event history analysis; Allison 1984). Another measure of work-force experience could reflect not just the initial attempt upon leaving school nor the final experience as measured at outcome, but rather the proportion of time in the labor force spent employed. Future studies should also attend to the different subtypes of underemployment (intermittent, low pay, involuntary part-time) and unemployment (looking for work vs. discouraged worker). As the economy is being restructured, workers appear to be at increasing risk of occupying such undesirable employment statuses, and it is possible that some of these subtypes of inadequate employment will give more evidence for continuity of trajectory while others will serve as critical turning points in psychological well-being.

Finally, future research on the experience of school-leavers needs to explore other indicators of functioning besides self-esteem. For example, Menaghan (see Chapter 6) has demonstrated the impact of employment experience of young mothers on family environments. In addition, the NLSY data set includes measures of substance abuse and depression, both of which have been linked to unemployment in adults (Dooley et al. 1992; Dooley, Catalano, & Wilson 1994). Several other school-leaver studies (including that by Gore and collaborators in Chapter 10) have found evidence for an adverse effect of becoming unemployed on depressed mood (see also Table 1 for other studies of depression in school-leavers), but only one study has reported an adverse effect on alcohol consumption (Janlert & Hammarström 1992). To determine whether such outcomes are socially significant or just statistically significant would require more epidemiologic types of measures.

References

Allison, P. (1984). *Event History Analysis: Regression for Longitudinal Event Data*. Beverly Hills, CA: Sage.

Bachman, J. G., O'Malley, P. M., & Johnston, J. (1978). *Youth in Transition, vol. VI. Adolescence to Adulthood – Change and Stability in the Lives of Young Men*. Ann Arbor, MI: Institute for Social Research.

Banks, M. H., & Jackson, P. R. (1982). Unemployment and risk of minor psychiatric disorder in young people: cross-sectional and longitudinal evidence. *Psychological Medicine* 12: 789–98.

Borman, K. M. (1991). *The First Real Job: A Study of Young Workers*. Albany: State University of New York Press.

Breakwell, G. M. (1986). Political and attributional responses of the young short-term unemployed. *Political Psychology* 7: 575–86.

Center for Human Resource Research [CHRR] (1990). *NLS Handbook, 1990*. Columbus: Ohio State University Press.

Clogg, C., Sullivan, T., & Mutchler, J. (1986). Measuring underemployment and inequality in the work force. *Social Indicators Research* 18: 375–93.

Cobb, S., & Kasl, S. V. (1977). Termination: the consequences of job loss. Report no. 76-1261, National Institute for Occupational Safety and Health, Cincinnati, OH.

Cochran, W. (1977). *Sampling Techniques*. New York: Wiley.

Cohen, J., & Cohen, P. (1983). *Applied Multiple Regression/Correlation Analysis for the Behavioral Sciences*. Hillsdale, NJ: Erlbaum.

Cohn, R. M. (1978). The effect of employment status change on self attitudes. *Social Psychology* 41: 81-93.

Dohrenwend, B. P., & Dohrenwend, B. S. (1969). *Social Status and Psychological Disorder: A Causal Inquiry*. New York: Wiley.

Donovan, A., Oddy, M., Pardoe, R., & Ades, A. (1986). Employment status and psychological well-being: a longitudinal study of 16-year-old school-leavers. *Journal of Child Psychology and Psychiatry* 27: 65-76.

Dooley, D., & Catalano, R. (1986). Do economic variables generate psychological problems: different methods, different answers. In A. J. MacFadyen & H. W. MacFadyen (eds.), *Economic Psychology: Intersections in Theory and Practice*. Amsterdam: Elsevier North-Holland, pp. 503-46.

Dooley, D., Catalano, R., & Hough, R. (1992). Unemployment and alcohol disorder in 1910 and 1990: drift versus social causation. *Journal of Occupational and Organisational Psychology* 65: 277-90.

Dooley, D., Catalano, R., & Rook, K. (1988). Personal and aggregate unemployment and psychological symptoms. *Journal of Social Issues* 44: 107-23.

Dooley, D., Catalano, R., & Wilson, G. (1994). Depression and unemployment: panel findings from the Epidemiologic Catchment Area study. *American Journal of Community Psychology* 22: 745-65.

Erikson, E. H. (1959). The problem of ego identity. *Psychological Issues* 1: 101-64.

Feather, N. T. (1990). *The Psychological Impact of Unemployment*. New York: Springer-Verlag.

Feather, N. T., & O'Brien, G. E. (1986). A longitudinal study of the effects of employment and unemployment on school-leavers. *Journal of Occupational Psychology* 59: 121-44.

Fienberg, S. E. (1980). *The Analysis of Cross-Classified Categorical Data*. Cambridge, MA: MIT Press.

Frankel, M., McWilliams, H., & Spencer, B. (1983). National longitudinal survey of labor force behavior, youth survey (NLS). Technical sampling report, NORC, University of Chicago.

Freeman, R. B., & Wise, B. A. (eds.) (1982). *The Youth Labor Market Problem: Its Nature, Causes, and Consequences*. University of Chicago Press.

Fruensgaard, K., Benjaminsen, S., Joensen, S., & Helstrup, K. (1983). Psychosocial characteristics of a group of unemployed patients consecutively admitted to a psychiatric emergency department. *Social Psychiatry* 18: 137-44.

Furnham, A. (1994). The psychosocial consequences of youth unemployment. In A. C. Petersen & J. T. Mortimer (eds.), *Youth Unemployment and Society*. New York: Cambridge University Press, pp. 199-223.

Greenberger, E., & Steinberg, L. D. (1986). *When Teenagers Work: The Psychological and Social Costs of Adolescent Employment*. New York: Basic Books.

Gurney, R. M. (1980a). The effects of unemployment on the psycho-social development of school-leavers. *Journal of Occupational Psychology* 53: 205-13.

Gurney, R. M. (1980b). Does unemployment affect the self-esteem of school-leavers? *Australian Journal of Psychology* 32: 175-82.

Halford, W. K., & Learner, E. (1984). Correlates of coping with unemployment in young Australians. *Australian Psychologist* 19: 333-44.

Hammer, T. (1993). Unemployment and mental health among young people: a longitudinal study. *Journal of Adolescence* 16: 407-20.

Hendry, L. B. (1987). Young people: from school to unemployment. In S. Fineman (ed.), *Unemployment: Personal and Social Consequences*. London: Tavistock, pp. 195-218.

Hosmer, D., & Lemeshow, S. (1989). *Applied Logistic Regression*. New York: Wiley.

Isaksson, K. (1989). Unemployment, mental health and the psychological functions of work in male welfare clients in Stockholm. *Scandinavian Journal of Social Medicine* 17: 165-9.

Jackson, P. R., Stafford, E. M., Banks, M. H., & Warr, P. B. (1983). Unemployment and psychological distress in young people: the moderating role of employment commitment. *Journal of Abnormal Psychology* 68: 525–35.

Jahoda, M. (1982). *Employment and Unemployment: A Socio-psychological Analysis.* Cambridge University Press.

Janlert, U., & Hammarström, A. (1992). Alcohol consumption among unemployed youths: results from a prospective study. *British Journal of Addiction* 87: 703–14.

Linn, M. W., Sandifer, R., & Stein, S. (1985). Effects of unemployment on mental and physical health. *American Journal of Public Health* 75: 502–6.

Marini, M. M. (1987). Measuring the process of role change during the transition to adulthood. *Social Science Research* 16: 1–38.

Mortimer, J. T. (1994). Individual differences as precursors of youth unemployment. In A. C. Petersen & J. T. Mortimer (eds.), *Youth Unemployment and Society.* New York: Cambridge University Press, pp. 172–98.

Mortimer, J. T., & Borman, K. M. (eds.) (1988). *Work Experience and Psychological Development through the Life Span.* Boulder, CO: Westview.

Neter, J., Wasserman, W., & Kutner, M. (1990). *Applied Linear Statistical Models.* Boston: Irwin.

O'Brien, E. J. (1985). Global self-esteem scales: unidimensional or multidimensional? *Psychological Reports* 57: 383–9.

Patton, W., & Noller, P. (1984). Unemployment and youth: a longitudinal study. *Australian Journal of Psychology* 36: 399–413.

Patton, W., & Noller, P. (1990). Adolescent self-concept: effects of being employed, unemployed or returning to school. *Australian Journal of Psychology* 42: 247–59.

Platt, S. (1984). Unemployment and suicidal behavior: a review of the literature. *Social Science and Medicine* 19: 93–115.

Potthoff, R, Woodbury, M., & Mantou, K. (1992). "Equivalent sample size" and "equivalent degrees of freedom": refinements for inference using survey weights under superpopulation models. *Journal of the American Statistical Association* 87: 383–96.

Robinson, W. S. (1950). Ecological correlations and the behavior of individuals. *American Sociological Review* 15: 352–7.

Rosenberg, M. (1965). *Society and the Adolescent Self-image.* Princeton, NJ: Princeton University Press.

Rowley, K. M., & Feather, N. T. (1987). The impact of unemployment in relation to age and length of unemployment. *Journal of Occupational Psychology* 60: 323–32.

Spenner, K. I., & Otto, L. B. (1985). Work and self-concept: selection and socialization in the early career. *Research in Sociology of Education and Socialization* 5: 197–235.

Stafford, E. M., Jackson, P. R., & Banks, M. H. (1980). Employment, work involvement and mental health in less qualified young people. *Journal of Occupational Psychology* 53: 291–304.

Sullivan, T. (1978). *Marginal Workers, Marginal Jobs.* Austin: University of Texas Press.

Tiggemann, M., & Winefield, A. H. (1980). Some psychological effects of unemployment in school-leavers. *Australian Journal of Social Issues* 15: 269–76.

Tiggemann, M., & Winefield, A. H. (1984). The effects of unemployment on the mood, self-esteem, locus of control, and depressive affect of school-leavers. *Journal of Occupational Psychology* 57: 33–42.

Tiggemann, M., & Winefield, A. H. (1989). Predictors of employment, unemployment and further study among school-leavers. *Journal of Occupational Psychology* 62: 213–21.

Ullah, P. (1987). Unemployed black youths in a northern city. In D. Fryer & P. Ullah (eds.), *Unemployed People: Social and Psychological Perspectives.* Philadelphia: Open University Press, pp. 111–47.

U.S. Department of Labor (1993). *Household Data. Employment and Earnings* 40(10): 15, 65.

William T. Grant Foundation Commission on Work, Family, and Citizenship (1988). *The Forgotten Half: Pathways to Success for America's Youth and Young Families.* Washington, DC: Youth and America's Future.

Winefield, A. H., & Tiggemann, M. (1985). Psychological correlates of employment and unemployment: effects, predisposing factors, and sex differences. *Journal of Occupational Psychology* 58: 229-42.

Winefield, A. H., & Tiggemann, M. (1989a). Job loss vs. failure to find work as psychological stressors in the young unemployed. *Journal of Occupational Psychology* 62: 79-85.

Winefield, A. H., & Tiggemann, M. (1989b). Unemployment duration and affective well-being in the young. *Journal of Occupational Psychology* 62: 327-36.

Winefield, A. H., Tiggemann, M., & Goldney, R. D. (1988). Psychological concomitants of satisfactory employment and unemployment in young people. *Social Psychiatry and Psychiatric Epidemiology* 23: 149-57.

Winefield, A. H., Tiggemann, M., & Winefield, H. R. (1991). The psychological impact of unemployment and unsatisfactory employment in young men and women: longitudinal and cross-sectional data. *British Journal of Psychology* 82: 473-86.

Winefield, A. H., Tiggemann, M., Winefield, H. R., & Goldney, R. D. (1993). *Growing Up with Unemployment: A Longitudinal Study of Its Psychological Impact*. London: Routledge.

Winefield, A. H., Winefield, H. R., Tiggemann, M., & Goldney, R. D. (1991). A longitudinal study of the psychological effects of unemployment and unsatisfactory employment on young adults. *Journal of Applied Psychology* 76: 424-31.

6 Intergenerational consequences of social stressors: effects of occupational and family conditions on young mothers and their children

Elizabeth G. Menaghan

The notion of a trajectory involves some patterned movement of a single object across space and time, and evokes images of inanimate objects, propelled by powerful forces, streaking across the night sky in a dramatic and predictable arc. In the sociology of the life course, we are more concerned with animate human actors whose trajectories are more subtle and who are more readily "bumped" off-course; but we nevertheless typically maintain that they are indeed propelled by powerful social forces that constrain, even if they do not completely determine, the shape of their lives. It is precisely because continuing in the same direction in which one is already headed is so much expected, in fact, that we find the exceptions interesting. We are fascinated, as social scientists and as fellow travelers from cradle to grave, when people appear to dramatically shift course, get "derailed" or "jump off the track," reinvent themselves and their daily lives, and reshape their future prospects. In comparison, we tend to be less interested in that which makes these exceptions remarkable – the strong persistence over time, for most people, of their current circumstances. Thus, dramatic turning points are foregrounded while trajectories are backgrounded. In the social stress literature, a similar emphasis can be seen in the preoccupation with life events to the relative neglect of chronic, persistent social conditions.

Yet, like the cumulative effects of a steady, day-after-day drip of water on a rock, persistent social circumstances exert a compelling impact on individual lives, even though one sees little that is dramatic or powerful when observing their impact on any given day. Previous chapters in this volume have focused on how dramatic instances of childhood adversity and trauma – often marked

This paper draws in part on several earlier papers and presentations, particularly Menaghan and Parcel (1991, 1995); Parcel and Menaghan (1994a,b); and Menaghan, Kowaleski-Jones, and Mott (1995). I acknowledge the research assistance of Lori Kowaleski-Jones and Laurie McCool. Preparation of this chapter was supported in part by research grants from NIH (HD23467, APR0961, and MH54371). I also acknowledge support from the Department of Sociology and the Center for Human Resource Research at The Ohio State University.

114

by events that are severe and unexpected, such as a parent's death or an episode of sexual abuse – may alter subsequent risk for emotional distress or disorder. Here, I focus on how variation in much more ordinary but persistent social variables – particularly parental occupational circumstances – are likely to have effects on both parents' and children's life chances. Barring major societal dislocations or reorganizations, individuals' occupational and economic locations within a society tend to be relatively stable. Changes in one's occupation tend to be relatively circumscribed: I may move from being a waitress to a cashier, or from being an elementary to a high-school teacher, but it is not likely that I will move from one to another of these two groups unless I suspend employment and seek additional education or training. Thus, the cumulating consequences of unremarkable variations in occupational conditions can be powerful forces for continuity in individual lives.

In linking social circumstances and adult well-being, there has been increasing attention to the roles that adults hold: whether or not they are married, whether or not they are employed, whether or not they have children. As Moen (Chapter 7) and Dooley and Prause (Chapter 5) review in this volume, a larger repertoire of roles (see Thoits 1986) as well as specific combinations of roles (Menaghan 1989) have been linked to greater emotional well-being of adults. Moen suggests that a more complex role repertoire has lifelong implications: in her panel studies of women who were married mothers in the 1950s and who were subsequently studied 30 years later, the number of roles in the earlier period predicted the number of roles held later in life; moreover, in both time periods, greater role involvement was linked to greater life satisfaction and a greater sense of self-worth. Dooley and Prause's studies of young men and women much earlier in the life course suggest the critical importance of the employment role: for the large majority of young Americans who do not persist in college, obtaining employment seems to support a trajectory toward a greater sense of self-worth, with self-worth in the mid-twenties significantly higher than in the high-school years. In contrast, for those who have been unable to find employment, this trajectory is dampened, and adolescent doubts about self-worth tend to persist.

Studies of family interaction and child outcomes have also focused on parental role repertoires. These studies tend to vary depending on parent gender. Studies of fathers' effects typically focus on married fathers and trace the deleterious effects of employment loss and associated economic pressures on marital interaction, father–child interaction, and both parent and child emotional well-being (Conger & Elder 1994; Elder 1974). Those focusing on mothers more often explore possible adverse effects of being employed as well as adverse impacts of family composition other than married mother–father families (for reviews of some of this extensive literature, see Menaghan & Parcel 1990 and Seltzer 1994).

But the possession of roles and statuses in themselves may have varying effects depending on the quality of those roles. Viewed longitudinally, effects of gains and losses in employment and marriage roles are also likely to vary depending on the quality of roles lost and gained (Wheaton 1990). More generally, I argue that the socially structured conditions that parents face have intergenerational consequences as well: adults buffeted by poor job conditions, difficulties in obtaining secure employment, and economic pressures are less able to provide their children with the kinds of support, structure, and warmth that would enhance the life chances of this next generation. In addition to these economic and occupational stressors, and likely to be linked to them, adults' family circumstances may also be sources of discouragement or failure – for example, the absence of a partner, the presence of a partner with whom one's relationship is marred by conflicts and disagreements, or the demands of large numbers of or closely spaced children.

These work and family social stressors, in part by undermining parents' emotional well-being, are linked to the quality and appropriateness of parent–child interaction; in turn, these patterns are linked to child outcomes. To the extent that beleaguered parents are more distant, preoccupied, or impatient with their children, stress *on* the family will be reflected in more stressful environments *within* the family. Such stress-linked shortfalls in parental attention, support, and supervision can impair their children's life chances by affecting children's school performance and their social and emotional functioning. Such effects may be particularly powerful influences on the later life course of the next generation, in part because academic success or failure and the development of social and emotional competencies during childhood and adolescence become the resources or vulnerabilities that individuals possess in dealing with the social circumstances of their own adult lives. Indeed, recent work suggesting that many mental health problems are discernible relatively early in life implies that we need to pay greater attention to factors shaping such vulnerability or resilience.

The study of family influences on children has a long history and provides strong support for the general argument that what parents do with and for their children – the materials they provide, the attention and warmth they display, and the investments of time and energy they make in their children – have real consequences (see e.g. Belsky 1984; Bradley & Caldwell 1979; Crouter et al. 1989; Moore & Snyder 1991; Parcel & Menaghan 1994b; Patterson & Bank 1989). Yet optimal family interaction is an elusive goal for many parents. It is important to view family patterns themselves as phenomena that need to be explained, and to seek the social sources of problematic interaction. In my own work on the quality of family interaction for young children, I have focused in particular on mothers, and have paid attention less to employment status and more to how the occupational conditions that employed mothers experience affect both their interaction with children and their children's emotional and cognitive development. These studies have taken advantage of the rich information on both mothers and children available in the child–mother data sets of the National Longitudinal Surveys of Youth (NLSY).

This data collection effort began in 1979 with a nationally representative sample of young men and women (aged 14 to 21 on January 1, 1979), with oversamples of ethnic minorities and economically disadvantaged groups. Beginning in 1986, there have been biennial assessments of the children born to the female NLSY respondents. Thus, the data contain an unusual wealth of background data on these mothers, collected on an annual basis, as well as detailed information about their children.

Toby Parcel and I have collaborated on a series of studies focused on employed mothers with children aged 3–6 at the time of the first child assessments in 1986 (Menaghan & Parcel 1990, 1991, 1995; Parcel & Menaghan 1990, 1993, 1994a,b; Rogers, Parcel, & Menaghan 1991). Our basic conceptual model reflects three major influences: social stress theories, socialization arguments, and human capital/resources frameworks. Following social stress arguments, we assume that the connection between economic or occupational experiences and mental health outcomes involves three key links. First, societal factors affect individual emotional well-being; difficulties in roles that are highly salient to the self or threatening to prized identities are particularly painful. Second, individual well-being affects interaction. Individuals struggling with emotional turmoil or depression are less available for satisfying interaction and are more prone to either withdraw from interaction or become aggressive and argumentative. Such adults find it difficult to be responsive and consistent in interactions with spouses or children. Third, distressing patterns of interaction constitute an additional stressor, further undermining individuals' emotional equilibrium. Precisely because individual family actors find it difficult to discern the social and economic roots of problematic interaction, they can be bewildered by interpersonal difficulties and hence prone to attribute problems to personality flaws or moral failings. Thus, social contexts that adversely affect adult emotional well-being have implications for the mental health of other family members, including children.

Socialization arguments such as those proposed by Kohn and Schooler (1983) put less emphasis on the workers' emotional state and more on their values and attitudes about themselves and the world. At the most general level, these arguments suggest that what one does on the job is critical in shaping adult attitudes and parent–child interaction. When parents' work is more substantively complex and offers greater opportunities for self-direction, parents place greater value on their children's developing self-direction and are less concerned with behavioral conformity per se. Thus, work conditions that increase the adult's sense of mastery and competence and permit greater autonomy will affect how parents treat their children.

These two strands of theory are not entirely independent: since attitudes about self and society shape emotions, work that enhances certain attitudes is apt to be linked to greater emotional well-being as well. Conversely, work that is routinized, heavily supervised, or low in autonomy and substantive complexity produces a sense of powerlessness and alienation that both colors beliefs about the possibility of control in other aspects of life and arouses psychological distress (see Mirowsky and Ross 1986, 1989).

Finally, human capital arguments draw attention to the differences in intelligence, initiative, educational attainment, physical health, and social competencies that shape individuals' prospects in the labor force and in family life. Individuals are not randomly assigned to occupations or to marital statuses. The unobserved variables that lead to a premature exit from high school, an early marriage or pregnancy, or an unfortunate partner choice may be as important in explaining later outcomes as the subsequent marital status or occupational conditions that we observe. Although it is highly unlikely that selection into more or less stressful contexts "explains" outcomes independent of the social stressors themselves, we *are* likely to overestimate the effects of social stressors if we do not take selection factors into account. In addition, variations in individual and family vulnerability are likely to interact with social stressors, reinforcing aversive consequences for many and buffering them for some. We therefore emphasize the importance of controlling for individual characteristics and resources when trying to assess the effects of occupational and economic factors on families and individual lives.

In evaluating the linkages between adult social stressors, family patterns, and children's outcomes, it is easiest to envision a rather straightforward mediational model such as that depicted in Figure 1: parental characteristics affect their occupational and economic circumstances, and those stressful circumstances help to predict greater problems in parent–child interaction and in the overall quality of the home environments that parents provide. Explicit consideration of family interaction helps to account for much of the previously observed effects of social stressors on the intellectual, social, and emotional well-being of children. In pursuing this general idea across a series of samples and analyses, I have been increasingly struck by the need to add numerous contingencies and qualifications to this overall model. Here I review what these findings suggest about the linkages between social circumstances and children's home environments, and supplement them with some additional analyses.

Social influences on young children's home environments

In our early study of employed mothers and their children, we considered the effects of both occupational and family circumstances on the quality of children's home environments (Menaghan & Parcel 1991; Parcel & Menaghan 1994b,

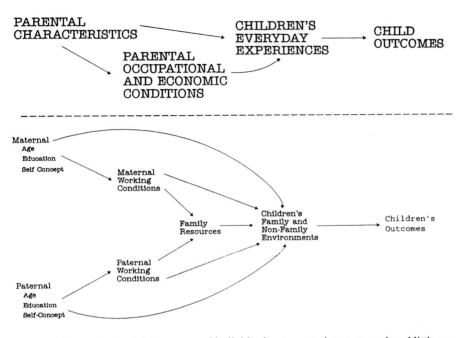

Figure 1. Social stressors and individual outcomes: intergenerational linkages.

chap. 3). The measures of social stressors included both the quality of employment, as tapped by variations in the substantive complexity of the occupation, level of wages, and usual work hours, as well as the number of children with whom parents are coping and variations in the number and relationships of other adults in the family household – in particular, whether the mother had a spouse, a male partner, or a female relative also in the household (all of the children studied lived with their mothers). Home environments were assessed using an abridged version of the age-specific HOME scales developed by Bradley and Caldwell (Bradley & Caldwell 1977, 1979, 1984; Bradley et al. 1988). The items include both maternal report and interviewer observations; they tap both maternal contributions to family home environments and the contributions of other family members, but they give greater emphasis to actions of the mother. The measure used assesses three major dimensions: cognitive stimulation, maternal responsiveness, and good physical environment (for additional measurement detail, see Menaghan & Parcel 1991).

To measure occupational complexity, we matched the 1970 and 1980 detailed U.S. Census occupational codes for parents' jobs to information on occupational content by Census occupational code contained in the Dictionary of Occupational Titles, or DOT (U.S. Department of Labor 1977). This information includes 42 items tapping the extent of involvement with data, people, and things in the occupation; temperament needed to perform work activities; physical demands of the job; and environmental working conditions (see also Parcel 1989). The scale of substantive complexity used here (Cronbach's alpha = 0.94) includes 19 items describing occupational content in terms of such features as dimensions of direction, control, and planning; influencing people; preference for abstract versus routine activities; complexity of working with data and people; preference for scientific and technical versus business activities; numerical and verbal aptitudes required; and low extent of repetitive or continuous processes.

For preschool children with employed mothers, maternal work quality (as assessed by higher occupational complexity) and lower family stress (as assessed by smaller family size) predict higher scores on a global measure of the overall quality of home environments. Neither being married nor, among those married, variations in spouses' occupational conditions has significant effects.

When I expand this sample to include 3- to 6-year-old children's mothers who were not working in 1986, a somewhat more complicated picture emerges that highlights the nonadditive effects of various work–family situations on children's family environments. The effects of mothers being employed and of mothers being married interact, with employment having a more powerful effect when mothers are not married, and marriage having a larger positive effect when mothers are not employed. We continue to see that, for the employed mothers, occupational complexity has a positive effect; this does not vary by mother's marital status or other characteristics. In addition, maternal wages have a more positive effect for unmarried mothers. Combining these effects, we can contrast predicted differences in effects as a function of mother's marital status and employment at differing levels of complexity and wages (Figure 2). All of these contrasts control for differences in maternal background (including early self-esteem, cognitive ability, and educational attainment) and in child characteristics (including ethnicity, gender, age, health problems, and birth weight). Compared to those who are both unmarried and not employed (set to zero for these comparisons), unmarried mothers employed at average jobs provide significantly more positive home environments ($B = 0.28$), while those who are employed at jobs high in complexity and wages are still higher ($B = 0.44$). In contrast, those unmarried and employed at jobs low in occupational complexity and wages are only marginally higher in home environments than unmarried mothers without any jobs at all. Thus, while employment has a positive effect for unmarried mothers, the strength of that effect varies depending on the quality of employment. For married mothers, differences by employment status and quality are dampened: married mothers who are not employed are similar to married mothers employed at average jobs (Bs are 0.42 and 0.41, respectively) and also similar to unmarried mothers employed at good jobs (i.e., jobs high in wages and complexity). Variations in maternal wages produce a less steep gradient in home environments than they do for unmarried mothers.

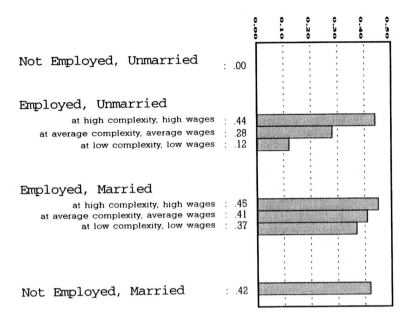

Figure 2. Home environments: predicted values by maternal employment, occupational conditions, and marital status. *Note:* Analyses based on sample of NLSY mothers and children aged 3–6 in 1986; unstandardized regression coefficients shown; value for children of unmarried not employed mothers set to zero. Models control for parents' education and ethnicity, number of other siblings present, and child characteristics (age, gender, low birth weight, and health problems).

We did not find significant effects of spouses' occupational conditions on children's home environments, even where mothers were not themselves employed. However, in a related study of children aged 5–8 living with married parents (Menaghan 1994) that also included children of both working and nonworking mothers, fathers' occupational complexity predicted better home environments, and this effect was stronger in families where mothers were not employed. This pattern suggests that the benefits for young children of fathers' more complex occupations may vary depending on the total configuration of work and family roles of both parents.

More recent studies of older children (aged 10–14) also find effects of work and family circumstances on the quality of family interaction (Menaghan, Kowaleski-Jones, & Mott 1997). In these analyses, we distinguished parental efforts to provide cognitive stimulation from overall maternal warmth. For these older children, we found that the quality of *both* mothers' and fathers' (or stepfathers') employment – as tapped by greater occupational complexity – had significant effects on the quality of cognitive stimulation and on the maternal warmth available. For these older children, the benefits of greater paternal job complexity for cognitive stimulation hold regardless of the employment status of mothers. Thus, this series of analyses suggest that fathers' occupational conditions become increasingly important as children grow older.

Social sources of change in children's home environments

Recent analyses of how changes in work and family circumstances affect changes in home environments also contribute to this emerging picture, and suggest additional contingencies. These analyses use the larger and more heterogeneous sample of preschool-aged children with both initially employed and not employed mothers, following them over a two-year window from 1986 to 1988 (Menaghan & Parcel 1995).

We find that recent changes in occupational conditions - complexity, wages, and hours - have little impact on changes in home environments. In part, this reflects the continuities over time in occupational conditions; consistency was more apparent than were dramatic changes. In contrast, recent changes in family composition - both the birth of an additional child and the termination of a marriage - did negatively change family environments. Family changes seem to have more immediate impacts on the warmth and nature of parent-child interaction, whereas occupational conditions, which remain relatively stable, may have more slowly accumulating effects via gradual alterations in parental attitudes and values.

Because our study of change included mothers who were not initially employed, we were also able to observe effects of mothers just beginning employment. This had significant adverse effects in our additive models, compared to mothers who remained employed at both time points; but the effects depended on the quality of the mothers' employment. When the mothers' new employment was in an occupation with an average level of complexity, beginning employment had a significant negative impact; this effect was significantly more severe when mothers began working in jobs low in complexity, with the quality of home environments dropping nearly a third of a standard deviation. In contrast, when mothers began work in occupations that were above average in substantive complexity, we observed no negative effect; indeed, the sign of the effect under these conditions was positive (although not statistically significant).

Remaining without employment across the two-year study period also had negative overall effects on the quality of family interaction. Again, however, this effect depended on other factors - in this case, the mother's marital trajectory. The negative effects of persistent non-employment that were observed in the additive model are restricted to the subset of mothers who also remain unmarried. Mothers who were both persistently unmarried and persistently non-employed over the two-year period experienced a decline in home environments that was more than three times that experienced on average by other persistently unmarried mothers, and more than nine times larger than that produced by persistent non-employment alone.

Among unmarried mothers who *were* employed, effects varied depending on the wages they were able to obtain. For mothers whose wage levels were high (implying annual maternal earnings in this sample of $19,760 in 1988), remaining unmarried had no significant negative impact on the quality of their children's home environments. However, for other unmarried mothers working at lower-wage jobs, home environments declined.

Thus, mothers rearing children alone seem to face a special dilemma. If they remain out of the labor force, the persistence of low interpersonal and economic resources in the family takes a toll that damages the quality of children's home environments during their critical early school years. On the other hand, if they can find employment only at a low-wage job (a likely scenario), these mothers may gain relatively little. Thus, work and family circumstances combine in nonadditive ways to shape the quality of family interaction, both cross-sectionally and over time.

Effects of current work and family circumstances on child outcomes

In focusing attention on how both maternal resources and later occupational and current circumstances affect family interaction and the quality of children's home environments, I have asserted that home environments in turn have important consequences for children's outcomes. Let me briefly provide some additional texture to that assertion, and suggest how attention to family interaction patterns help us to understand the effects of social stressors on children's cognitive and emotional outcomes. I emphasize likely interactive effects that have been relatively neglected in recent literature but which suggest that linkages between parental social stressors and children's outcomes are stronger under some circumstances than others.

In both Parcel's and my studies of employed parents and their young children, and in more recent studies of older children in collaboration with Mott and Kowaleski-Jones, we find that better family environments and parental efforts to provide support for cognitive skills predicts better academic outcomes and fewer behavior problems. Maternal warmth also makes a difference in reducing behavior problems, and for the older children it interacts with parental structuring efforts to reduce academic problems. Such parental efforts have significant effects even when earlier levels of problems are controlled. These strong effects support the need for greater research efforts to understand the social conditions that make such parental actions easier or more difficult.

In some cases, family interaction patterns appear to interact with social stressors to modify their effects. For example, in our study of older children, the adverse effects of being in a mother–stepfather family on both academic and behavior problems are minimized when parental structuring is higher, suggesting that this family interaction measure can buffer the potential negative effects of the family form. Other contingencies suggest some amplification of adverse impacts. For example, parental relationship problems were associated with lower maternal warmth, and the adverse effects of parental relationship problems on children's school performance were also especially great when maternal warmth was low. Moreover, we find that social stressors themselves interact, with nonadditive implications for intergenerational outcomes. Although the interactions noted here need to be replicated in other samples and other analyses before we can be confident about their precise form, our findings suggest several emerging generalizations that could serve as guiding hypotheses for future work on stress and families.

First, *greater parental resources can dampen the negative impact of difficult occupational and family circumstances on family interaction patterns and on child outcomes;* conversely, parental resources are particularly critical when work and family conditions are more difficult. For example, for young children's behavior problems we find that the adverse impacts of mothers' having recently ended their marriage or having had another baby are less powerful for mothers with more positive self-concepts, yet more powerful for those with lower psychosocial resources. It is important that future research consider such potential interactions in assessing the impacts of current social stressors on families, and not simply treat parental resources as additive controls.

Second, *the effects of employment status, and changes in employment status, vary with occupational quality, at least for mothers.* Our findings suggest that maternal entrances to and exits from the labor force have differing consequences depending on the quality of maternal employment entered or left: employment entry is more positive when the mother enters a more substantively complex occupation or one with higher wages; likewise, exit from a job characterized by low wages, long hours, and less complex conditions is more beneficial than other exits. For example, the effect of mothers' stopping work on young children's behavior problems was more beneficial for mothers whose jobs had been lower in challenge and complexity and had involved extensive overtime hours. And as we have noted earlier, beginning employment in a job offering little complexity was associated with declining home environments.

Similarly, mothers' employment is likely to be more or less advantageous depending on the quality of employment she is likely to find. For example, in our analysis of the effects of mothers' employment and working conditions – both currently and during the first three years of their children's lives – on child verbal skills and behavior patterns, we found that mothers' being employed during the child's first few years had more positive impacts for those who obtained employment in complex occupational settings than for those whose later employment was less complex or challenging (Parcel & Menaghan 1994).

Third, *work and family conditions, and changes in those conditions, may interact in their effects,* and these interactions tend to take two forms. First, *combinations that increase the total set of family demands will be more negative than other combinations.* An example is the observed interaction between mothers' occupational complexity and the birth of an additional child in our analyses of children's reading skills, where increases in mothers' occupational complexity – which we would expect to be generally positive – had less positive effects when mothers had also recently had a new baby than when they had not. Similarly, fathers' working overtime hours had more adverse implications for children's behavior problems when the family had recently added another child. These examples point to the dilemmas confronting adults trying to "get ahead" at work as they also face new demands at home.

The second form of work and family interaction suggests that *work and family conditions may interact in an offsetting or compensatory way;* specifically, we find that *more positive occupational circumstances may buffer the effects of some difficult family conditions.* For children's behavior problems, the quality of the mother's current employment buffered the adverse effects of ending the marriage, with effects more benign for mothers whose current occupations were higher in complexity and more adverse for mothers working in less complex occupations. As noted earlier, having a high-wage job reduced the negative effects of remaining unpartnered on the quality of children's family environments.

Fourth, when two parents are present, *the effects of one parent's working conditions vary depending on the working conditions of the other parent.* Again, as with interactions between work and family conditions, these contingencies may take two forms. On the one hand, *combinations that increase the overall demands of employment for the family will have more negative effects.* For example, the combination of two parents being on overtime work schedules was associated with significantly more behavior problems than when only one parent worked overtime hours. Similarly, benefits of mothers' occupational complexity for children's verbal skills were significantly lower when fathers were working overtime schedules, and benefits of *either* parent's occupational complexity for math and reading scores were reduced when the other parent's occupation was also high in complexity. Indeed, among two-parent families, maternal employment status itself may have differing effects depending on the spouse's occupational conditions.

On the other hand, *the effects of one parent's stressful occupational conditions may be offset by positive features of the other's.* For example, fathers having only part-time work had less negative impacts on the quality of children's home environments when mothers were employed, especially if more than part-time – a case where maternal employment was a clear benefit to children.

These numerous contingencies suggest that the intergenerational costs of adult social stressors vary in complex ways; these diverse interactions may be interpreted optimistically or pessimistically. Emphasizing the positive, we may note that resource-rich parents can resist the negative effects of some difficult work and family conditions, that good parental working conditions can offset some family difficulties, that one parent's difficulties can be offset by the other's efforts, and that parental efforts to provide optimal family environments can protect their children even under adverse circumstances. More pessimistically, we may note that it is precisely those parents who are in the worst circumstances who are also likely to be lower in personal psychosocial and intellectual resources, making it more difficult for them to sustain positive family interaction; that many families have a single adult grappling with work and family demands; and that husbands and wives may be too similar in the occupational problems they face to compensate for one another's difficulties. In any case, research that is sensitive to such interactive effects will be better able to contribute to our developing understanding of the processes linking social stressors and their effects across generations, and the conditions under which such links may be broken.

The cumulative impacts of maternal resources: an exploration

In discussing the effects of ongoing occupational and family circumstances, I have emphasized that children's home environments and their patterns of interaction with parents are influenced by parental employment status and occupational conditions. To the extent that conditions tend to persist over time, occupational conditions in particular are powerful shapers of continuity in children's life chances. I have also noted that a major difficulty in efforts to attribute causal status to current social stressors impinging on parents and children is the competing hypothesis that such linkages may be largely spurious. It is reasonable to expect that the psychological and social characteristics that mothers bring to their current situations affect their adult choices (see Clausen 1991). A positive self-regard, and an optimistic expectation that one's own efforts can yield positive effects, are psychological resources on which individuals can draw in adulthood (Rosenberg & Pearlin 1978; Rosenberg, Schooler, & Schoenbach 1989). Thus, mothers' initial levels of esteem in early adulthood should affect their later circumstances, and these underlying social competencies or vulnerabilities may be partially responsible for the "effects" of occupational conditions or family composition on children's experiences and outcomes. These relatively stable parental attributes will make for greater continuity in children's life chances as well.

To establish the explanatory power of social stressors, it is crucial to control for the intellectual and psychosocial resources that parents bring to the current situation. In the studies summarized here, we were able to take advantage of the longitudinal background data collected in earlier years from these children's mothers to control for key maternal background factors and resources – for example, her cognitive skills, sense of mastery, and self-esteem. In the discussion so far, I have emphasized the effects of current work and family conditions on the quality of the home environments that mothers provide their children. It is striking, however, that mothers' early level of self-esteem is consistently positively correlated with more favorable current occupational and family circumstances; early self-esteem also has significant direct effects on family interaction and child outcomes even when indirect effects operating through current circumstances are statistically controlled. These findings prompt questions about how much of a role early attitudes about self play in shaping current circumstances, and to what extent social circumstances may alter self-concept, including self-esteem. Self-esteem has been described as both a social force influencing the present and future and as a social product influenced by past experience (see Rosenberg et al. 1989); it is important to explore these possible dual impacts in shaping the lives of mothers and their children. In Chapter 5 of this volume, Dooley and Prause, using a partially overlapping sample of NLSY women as well as NLSY men, suggest that initial levels of self-esteem are predictive of later employment for young men but less so for young women. They also find that obtaining satisfactory employment improves later self-esteem for both men and women. My analysis focuses on the subset of women who have become mothers after 1980, are employed in 1986, and completed the reassessment of esteem included in the 1987 round of the NLSY. This sample is somewhat larger than the sample of 1986 employed mothers used in other analyses by Menaghan and Parcel, since it does not exclude those whose children were under age 3 (and therefore ineligible for the child assessments).

Self-esteem as a social force: effects of initial self-esteem on occupational and family conditions

To what extent does initial self-esteem affect later circumstances? Figure 3 highlights the major findings. Because educational attainment is a powerful potential mediator of these effects, I first estimated the effects of initial self-esteem and other maternal characteristics on educational attainment. Even with controls for family composition at age 14, her parents' education, and her own cognitive skill, young women with higher self-esteem in 1980 obtained more years of schooling by 1986. If one also controls for initial level of education in 1980 (not shown), early esteem also predicts increases in educational attainment between 1980 and 1986.

I next estimated a series of regression equations predicting current work and family circumstances from early self-esteem and subsequent educational attainment; these models include demographic controls. Controlling only for background, mothers with higher initial esteem were more likely to be living with a husband (not shown). However, as shown in Figure 3, this effect is nonsignificant when educational attainment is also included in the model, indicating that early esteem affects marital status only indirectly through higher educational

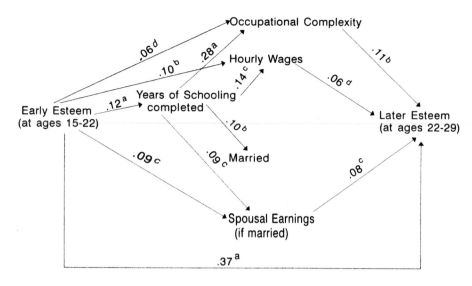

Figure 3. Effects of early self-esteem on occupational and family conditions, and consequences of conditions on later self-esteem. *Note:* Analyses based on sample of NLSY mothers employed in 1986 and interviewed in 1987; standardized regression coefficients shown. All models control for mothers' parents' education, mothers' family composition at age 14, ethnicity, and cognitive skills. Models predicting later self-esteem also control for mothers' family size, mothers' work hours, and spouses' occupational complexity and work hours.

attainment. Esteem also has a direct positive effect on the level of spousal earnings among married mothers. Even after controlling for both background and intervening educational attainment, mothers with higher early levels of self-esteem are married to men earning higher annual incomes. In addition, mothers with more education are married to men earning higher incomes, supporting an additional indirect effect of early self-esteem on spousal earnings via higher educational attainment. These findings suggest that self-confident women are later more apt to experience more advantaged marital circumstances.

Similar effects are apparent for occupational conditions, as indexed by the substantive complexity of the 1986 job and by hourly wages. Educational attainment has a strong positive impact on the quality of mothers' employment, suggesting an indirect effect for early self-esteem. Even after controlling for these indirect effects via educational attainment, initial esteem has significant positive direct effects on occupational complexity and hourly wages. Thus, in partial contrast to Dooley's findings that higher early self-esteem does not have a powerful effect in selecting young women into employment per se, these data suggest that self-esteem does predict better occupational and family circumstances among mothers who are employed.

Self-esteem as a social product: predicting change in mothers'
self-esteem over time

The right-hand side of Figure 3 displays estimated effects of current occupational and family circumstances on change in self-esteem over time. Controlling for the time-1 level of self-esteem in the equation, better occupational circumstances (i.e., more complex and autonomous occupations and higher wages) predict increased esteem in 1987. Family conditions also shape changes in self-esteem, with higher spousal earnings associated with improvements in esteem. Thus, as social causation arguments would emphasize, difficult work and family circumstances erode adult self-esteem over time, whereas more advantaged circumstances shore up one's sense of self-worth.

It is noteworthy that, like Dooley and Prause, we find evidence of reciprocal effects of adult self-concept. In other words, there is evidence both for social selection – of less confident women into more disadvantaged family and occupational circumstances – as well as for social causation, since these circumstances play a role in reducing esteem still further. Stated positively, more initially self-confident mothers obtain more education and can obtain more substantively complex employment, which further enhances their sense of self-worth. They are more likely to marry and, if married, to have spouses earning higher incomes. These findings suggest that the personal resources that mothers bring to young adulthood help to propel them onto a trajectory that may produce widening differences in young adulthood and diverging life chances for their children.

Conclusions

We began by noting that social circumstances exert a compelling impact on individual lives, tending to maintain them on a predictable trajectory. The extension of this argument across generations suggests that parental social circumstances affect children's family environments and shape their cognitive skills and socioemotional behavior. But social circumstances themselves reflect in part the resources and competencies that have been developed earlier in the life course. The study of young NLSY mothers suggests that young women's early self-esteem influences how much education they complete, the men they marry, and the jobs they obtain. These variant initial circumstances affect both mother and child: a mother's subsequent sense of her own self-worth is altered depending on her circumstances, as is the cognitive stimulation and warmth that she provides for her children.

However, these trajectories are not inescapable. In studying changes in family environments, even over the very short time period of two years, two things are striking. First, the absence of change, as reflected in remaining unmarried and remaining not employed, is linked to a further deterioration in family environments. This is consistent with a worsening spiral of effects over time that maintains a downward trajectory in the next generation. On the other hand, there are indications of recovery from difficult circumstances: some mothers who are rearing children alone, a group at high risk for difficulties, have obtained employment of sufficient quality and wage levels that the environments they provide for their children are little different from those of married mothers.

What factors make such recovery more likely? Clearly, individual resources – both intellectual and psychological – play a role. So, too, do broader social circumstances. An obvious example is the distribution of occupational opportunities and rewards in the United States today. Dooley and Prause have described the "unwelcoming economy" that greets young high-school graduates; others have described the uncertainty and overload that plagues workers in industries that are reducing the number of their employees and increasing the responsibilities of those that remain. This economic climate affects individual men and women and their relationships with one another: marital formation is less likely, and marital disruption more common, as economic pressures increase. More positively, decreasing cultural and legal acceptance of gender discrimination and gender segregation in the workplace mean that women have greater life chances today than in the past or in other societies, especially when marriages end. Thus, societal circumstances, and improvement or deterioration in those circumstances over time, constrain individual patterns of stability and change, and are themselves an understudied influence on individual and intergenerational trajectories.

References

Belsky, J. (1984). The determinants of parenting: a process model. *Child Development* 555: 83–96.
Bradley, Robert H., & Caldwell, Bettye M. (1977). Home observation for measurement of the environment: a validation study of screening efficiency. *American Journal of Mental Deficiency* 81: 417–20.
Bradley, Robert H., & Caldwell, Bettye M. (1979). Home observation for measurement of the environment: a revision of the preschool scale. *American Journal of Mental Deficiency* 84: 235–44.
Bradley, Robert H., & Caldwell, Bettye M. (1984). The relation of infants' home environments to achievement test performance in first grade: a follow-up study. *Child Development* 55: 803–9.
Bradley, Robert H., Caldwell, Bettye M., Rock, Stephen L., Hamrick, Holly M., & Harris, Pandia (1988). Home observation for measurement of the environment: development of a home inventory for use with families having children 6 to 10 years old. *Contemporary Educational Psychology* 13: 58–71.
Clausen, John (1991). Adolescent competence and the shaping of the life course. *American Journal of Sociology* 96: 805–42.
Conger, Rand, & Elder, Glen H., Jr. (1994). *Families in Troubled Times: Adapting to Change in Rural America.* New York: de Gruyter.

Crouter, A. C., Perry-Jenkins, M., Huston, T. L., & Crawford, D. W. (1989). The influence of work-induced psychological states on behavior at home. *Basic and Applied Social Psychology* 10: 273–92.

Elder, Glen H., Jr. (1974). *Children of the Great Depression*. University of Chicago Press.

Kohn, Melvin L., & Schooler, Carmi (1983). *Work and Personality: An Inquiry into the Impact of Social Stratification*. Norwood, NJ: Ablex.

Menaghan, Elizabeth G. (1989). Role changes and psychological well-being: variations in effects by gender and role repertoire. *Social Forces* 67: 693–714.

Menaghan, Elizabeth G. (1994). The daily grind: work stressors, family patterns, and intergenerational outcomes. In William Avison & Ian H. Gotlib (eds.), *Stress and Mental Health: Contemporary Issues and Future Prospects*. New York: Plenum.

Menaghan, Elizabeth G., Kowaleski-Jones, Lori, & Mott, Frank L. (1997). The intergenerational costs of parental social stressors. *Journal of Health and Social Behavior* 38.

Menaghan, Elizabeth G., & Parcel, Toby L. (1990). Parental employment and family life: research in the 1980s. *Journal of Marriage and the Family* 52: 1079–98.

Menaghan, Elizabeth G., & Parcel, Toby L. (1991). Determining children's home environments: the impact of maternal characteristics and current occupational and family conditions. *Journal of Marriage and the Family* 53: 417–31.

Menaghan, Elizabeth G., & Parcel, Toby L. (1995). Social sources of change in children's home environments: effects of parental occupational experiences and family conditions over time. *Journal of Marriage and the Family* 57: 69–84.

Mirowsky, John, & Ross, Catherine E. (1986). Social patterns of distress. *Annual Review of Sociology* 12: 23–45.

Mirowsky, John, & Ross, Catherine E. (1989). *Social Causes of Psychological Distress*. New York: de Gruyter.

Moore, Kristin A., & Snyder, Nancy O. (1991). Cognitive attainment among firstborn children of adolescent mothers. *American Sociological Review* 56: 612–24.

Parcel, Toby L. (1989). Comparable worth, occupational labor markets and occupational earnings: results from the 1980 census. In Robert Michael, Heidi Hartmann, & Brigid O'Farrell (eds.), *Pay Equity: Empirical Inquiries*. Washington, DC: National Academy Press.

Parcel, Toby L., & Menaghan, Elizabeth G. (1990). Maternal working conditions and child verbal ability: studying the transmission of intergenerational inequality from mothers to young children. *Social Psychology Quarterly* 53: 132–47.

Parcel, Toby L., & Menaghan, Elizabeth G. (1993). Family social capital and children's behavior problems. *Social Psychology Quarterly* 56: 120–35.

Parcel, Toby L., & Menaghan, Elizabeth G. (1994a). Early parental work, family social capital, and early childhood outcomes. *American Journal of Sociology* 99: 972–1009.

Parcel, Toby L., & Menaghan, Elizabeth G. (1994b). *Parents' Jobs and Children's Lives*. New York: de Gruyter.

Patterson, Gerald, & Bank, L. (1989). Some amplifying mechanisms for pathologic processes in families. In Megan R. Gunnar & Esther Thelen (eds.), *Systems and Development*. Hillsdale, NJ: Erlbaum.

Rogers, Stacy J., Parcel, Toby L., & Menaghan, Elizabeth G. (1991). The effects of maternal working conditions and mastery on child behavior problems: studying the intergenerational transmission of social control. *Journal of Health and Social Behavior* 32: 145–64.

Rosenberg, Morris, & Pearlin, Leonard I. (1978). Social class and self esteem among children and adults. *American Journal of Sociology* 84: 53–77.

Rosenberg, Morris, Schooler, Carmi, & Schoenbach, Carrie (1989). Self-esteem and adolescents: modeling reciprocal effects. *American Sociological Review* 54: 1004–18.

Seltzer, Judith (1994). Consequences of marital dissolution for children. *Annual Review of Sociology* 20: 235–66.

Thoits, Peggy (1986). Multiple identities and psychological well-being: a reformulation and test of the social isolation hypothesis. *American Sociological Review* 48: 174–87.

U.S. Department of Labor (1977). *Dictionary of Occupational Titles,* 4th ed. Washington, DC: U.S. Government Printing Office.

Wheaton, Blair (1990). Life transitions, role histories, and mental health. *American Sociological Review* 55: 209–23.

7 Women's roles and resilience: trajectories of advantage or turning points?

Phyllis Moen

A key component of healthy development over the life course is the cultivation and maintenance of psychosocial resilience. In this chapter I draw on a life-course approach to consider pathways to resilience in the later years of adulthood, in terms of a sense of competency and esteem on the one hand and of connectedness to the broader community on the other. As an illustrative empirical example of life-course analysis I examine women's lives, drawing on panel data collected at two points in time, 30 years apart.

The nature of resilience

"Resilience" and "protective factors" are the counterparts to "vulnerability" and "risk factors," connoting successful adaptation to challenges and adversity (Werner 1990). Although resilience has typically been used to refer to psychological attributes of the individual, the protective factors promoting such resilience encompass social as well as psychological elements. Research and theory in the areas of stress and developmental psychopathology depict two sets of protective factors promoting resilience in the face of life's adversities: social resources and personal resources (Rutter 1987; Schaefer & Moos 1992). *Social* resources pertain to social integration or connectedness in the form of occupying multiple roles, the presence of a confidant relationship, good relationships with family and friends, and access to support networks. *Personal* resources encompass subjective dispositions such as self-esteem, mastery, a positive outlook, self-understanding, empathy, altruism, maturity, and basic values and priorities. Both personal and social resources can be termed *psychosocial* resources or, alternatively, *coping* resources.

Research has documented the importance of these psychosocial resources in moderating the negative psychological effects of stressful events and ongoing strains (e.g., Bandura 1989; Betz & Hackett 1987; Lazarus & Folkman 1984).

This research was supported by Grants #R01-A605450 and #1P0-A611711-01 from the National Institute on Aging.

For example, studies have shown that the effects of stress on depressive symptomatology are lessened in the face of such personal coping resources as self-esteem and mastery (Pearlin et al. 1981; Pearlin & Schooler 1978; Thoits 1987). Similarly, social integration in the form of multiple role involvements has been negatively associated with depressive symptomatology (see Forest, Moen, & Dempster-McClain 1996; Thoits 1983, 1986). Thus, individuals with high levels of personal and social resources are typically more effective in coping with life's stressors and strains than are those lacking such assets. In this chapter, individuals with high levels of personal and social coping resources are characterized as *resilient*.

Resilience in the later years

Both elements of psychosocial resources – positive psychological dispositions and social integration – are important components to successful aging, serving as protective factors that promote both physical and emotional health in the face of the biological and social dislocations and turning points associated with growing old. But there is no broad consensus as to what contributes to resilience in the later years of adulthood. Investigators have neither charted continuity or change in trajectories of resources over the life course nor documented how social and personal resources are connected to one another over the lifespan.

Existing research findings suggest a certain consistency in self-conception and well-being concomitant with aging (Veroff, Douvan, & Kulka 1981), with older individuals as likely as younger ones to report high levels of self-esteem and general life satisfaction (Baltes & Baltes 1990). However, most studies are based on cross-sectional designs; little is known about the processes by which adults retain, lose, or achieve multiple role involvements and positive views of themselves and their lives as they age. A more dynamic, life-course perspective would suggest that both earlier psychosocial resources and the timing and trajectories of adult roles might affect subsequent resilience in later adulthood.

Pathways to resilience

Is there continuity across the lifespan in resilience? Specifically, do individuals' feelings of well-being (such as optimism, self-esteem, and mastery) or their social integration (such as multiple role involvements) in earlier adulthood persevere as they move into and through midlife? Other chapters in this volume emphasize the importance of childhood experiences for subsequent development; in this chapter I examine continuity and change throughout adulthood, focusing not on stress and adversity per se but rather on the tools with which individuals cope with stress and adversity – the psychosocial resources facilitating resilience at every life stage.

Other scholars are incorporating just such a temporal perspective. Elder and colleagues (Elder 1974; Caspi, Elder, & Bem 1987, 1988), for example, have looked at continuity and change in personality characteristics from childhood to adulthood. Quinton and Rutter (1988) have examined the pathways perpetuating continuity in family dysfunction. Brown and Harris (1978) have charted the long-term effects of early life events on women's subsequent depression. Menaghan (1989) and Wheaton (1990) have investigated the impacts of adult role transitions on well-being. Clausen (1991, 1993) has documented the importance of feelings of competence during adolescence in shaping the adult life course. The notion of hardiness (Maddi & Kobassa 1984) submits that psychological resources acquired earlier in life (such as a sense of control and self-worth) serve to promote a fulfilling life and as a buffer to stress. A focus on continuity in resilience suggests a certain cumulativeness in advantage over time (Merton 1968); those who are better off in their early years of adulthood are also better off in their later years.

A life-course formulation considers the temporality of peoples' lives, the links between life biography and social history, and the settings that shape and are shaped by individual choices (Elder 1992, 1995). It provides an analytic approach to resilience that emphasizes both continuity and change across the lifespan as well as the dynamic interplay between historical time and individual lives (Moen, Dempster-McClain, & Williams 1995; Moen & Erickson 1995). This perspective features consideration of (1) lives over time, including the trajectories and turning points that are the focus of this volume; (2) lives in the context of prior and ongoing resources and experiences; and (3) lives in historical time, with different cohorts confronting different forms of stress, constraint, and opportunity. The remainder of this chapter draws on my own research (the Women's Roles and Well-Being Project) to focus specifically on women's resilience as they move into their later years. I consider continuity and change in the protective mechanisms of social integration and psychological dispositions, as well as the links between the two.

Lives over time

One key theme in life-course analysis is that early experiences have long-term consequences, suggesting the possibility of accentuation of personal and social resources over time. A second theme is that *development persists throughout adulthood,* shaped both by individual choices and social forces, including the situational imperatives accompanying various role transitions, turning points, and trajectories (Elder 1995; Elder & Caspi 1990).

What are the impacts of various life paths on psychosocial protective mechanisms? Significant life events can reshape not only the direction of one's life course but also one's psychosocial resources, fostering (or inhibiting) the development of resilience. For example, Bandura (1982) counsels that self-conceptions of competence or mastery are drawn from personal experience as well as from socialization processes. Thus, adult transitions can affect attitudes and beliefs about one's self. For example, research has shown that the feelings of efficacy of single-parent women change concomitant with changes in their lives. Downey and Moon (1987) found that two major life changes – getting married and obtaining higher income – enhanced single-parent women's subsequent sense of efficacy.

Magnusson (1995) points out that some events are in effect "chance" occurrences, such as widowhood, a health crisis, war, or economic downturns. Other events are "purposive," as individuals choose for example to marry or divorce, move, buy a new house, take on or leave a job, or return to school. He also notes that the effects of these changes may either be immediately visible, constituting a key "turning point" (Clausen 1995) in life, or develop slowly over time.

Thus, both turning points and trajectories can affect resilience. Yet life's transitions, turning points, and trajectories are themselves shaped by prior experiences and dispositions (Kohn 1995; Rutter et al. 1995). Hence, an important proposition of the life-course paradigm is that *earlier resources affect life pathways as well as psychosocial resources later in life*. Examining continuity and change in psychological and social resources throughout the lifespan therefore requires a dynamic, life-course view (e.g., Lachman 1986). What is the impact of moving out of family, occupational, or community roles in middle and later adulthood, or of taking on new roles at this time? Roles may have different impacts at different stages of the life course and in different contexts. This is especially true regarding role transitions in later life, since so little is known about the import of family and nonfamily roles beyond the normative years of retirement. We do know that there is typically a decline in family and nonfamily roles in later years, as children leave home, marriages frequently dissolve, and individuals move out of the labor force (Menaghan 1989; Moen, Dempster-McClain, & Williams 1992; Smith & Moen 1988).

Because earlier experiences shape well-being later in life, there should be a certain "cumulativeness" to resilience, with women high in psychological resources or social integration in earlier adulthood being most likely to possess these same resources in their later years.

Lives in context

A life-course, role-context approach (Moen, Dempster-McClain, & Williams 1989, 1992; Spitze et al. 1994) draws on role theory and temporal considerations to suggest that the *contexts* of life transitions, trajectories, and turning points also matter. Resources, such as previous levels of emotional well-being and social integration, could well serve as moderators of life transitions and turning points, tempering the outcomes of negative events (Brown & Harris 1978) and enhancing the outcomes of positive events.

Particular family stresses and situational contingencies can either promote or hamper women's resilience in old age. For example, Gove and Hughes (1979) and Veroff et al. (1981) suggest that women's responsibility for the welfare of children, husbands, and ailing relatives may have deleterious consequences for their own well-being. Because these nurturant role obligations are of an ongoing nature, such caregiving may have a negative effect on self-care and one's own health. Despite these potential deleterious effects, women (and men) living alone are likely to be more vulnerable than those who share life with a child or a spouse. Becoming divorced or widowed may serve to reduce both social and psychological resources, but this may vary in terms of the timing of these transitions. For example, marital dissolution relatively early in life may foster a better accommodation to singlehood in later years.

A life-course perspective holds that the impacts of earlier resources and life pathways cannot be understood without reference to issues of timing, trajectory, and transitions. Are particular roles and life experiences more conducive (or detrimental) to well-being and social integration later in life than others? How does the patterning of women's role involvements throughout adulthood affect their resilience in the later years of adulthood?

One can envision three routes by which early resources could shape subsequent resilience. First, there could be stability and continuity over time in these resources, a life pattern of ongoing well-being and social connectedness (see A, Figure 1). Second, these resources can shape the life chances and choices of individuals, creating life styles and pathways that in turn shape future psychosocial resources (see B, Figure 1). Third, early psychosocial resources can also moderate the impacts of stress and adversity on subsequent resilience (see C, Figure 1). These three pathways can operate simultaneously or in parallel over the life course to promote or reduce resilience. Clearly, earlier psychosocial resources – or their absence – can affect subsequent life choices and changes over the life course, perpetuating the cumulation of advantage or disadvantage. Distinctive turning points in the form of life stresses and adversity can likewise affect resilience for better or for worse.

Lives in historical time

A life-course approach also considers lives in historical time, focusing on how societal changes may influence both the nature of the life course and the resources individuals bring to each life stage (Elder 1995). For example, Elder has

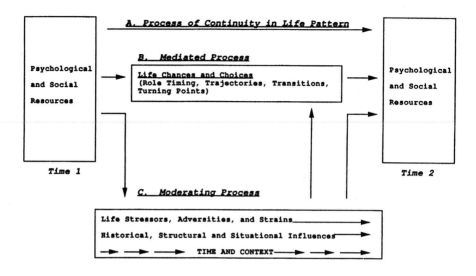

Figure 1. Pathways to resilience: three processes linking resilience over time.

shown how the Great Depression and the Second World War transformed the life course of individuals (Elder 1974; Elder & Liker 1982). Thus, key situational imperatives and experiences may be historically specific. The social changes in women's roles in the second half of the twentieth century point to the ways that risks, roles, and resilience are shaped by the times in which one lives (Forest et al. 1995; Moen 1992, 1994). Historical changes in the structural imperatives shaping lives and the situational imperatives embodied in chance occurrences can each break the cycle of cumulative advantage or disadvantage, producing turning points that affect both life paths and resilience.

An illustrative example: the Women's Roles and Well-Being Project

To illustrate a life-course approach to women's resilience, I draw on findings from a two-wave panel study of women who were interviewed in 1956 in a medium-sized city in upstate New York and reinterviewed 30 years later. A random sample of 427 women who were both wives and mothers were interviewed in 1956 (Dean & Williams 1956). This same group was located and reinterviewed in 1986. We were able to locate 408 (95.6%) of the 427 original respondents; 82 (19.2%) were deceased and 326 (96.3%) were contacted for an interview. We were left with only 19 (4.4%) who could not be found (Dempster-McClain & Moen, in press; Moen et al. 1989). Of the 326 who were alive and contacted in 1986, only 3% (13 women) refused to be interviewed. In analyzing the life trajectories of these female subjects, we have drawn on information from the initial interview in 1956 as well as from the second interview in 1986, when extensive life history material was collected in addition to responses to more structured questions. This "catch-up" design (Kessler & Greenberg 1981) of our study of women's roles and well-being offers a rare opportunity to examine the pathways to resilience in old age.

The sample consists of four cohorts: cohort 1 was born between 1905 and 1917, cohort 2 between 1918 and 1922; cohort 3 between 1923 and 1926; and cohort 4 between 1927 and 1933. Life history data on these women were collected in 1986 when members of the oldest cohort were in their seventies and early eighties and those of the youngest cohort in their mid- to late fifties (see Table 1). The sample consists of 313 women, with complete life history data available to age 55 on all but three of them (for further information see Moen et al. 1989, 1992). We draw on data on these women from ages 18 to 55, so that age is not confounded with cohort.

Women in cohort 1 (born between 1905 and 1917) reached adulthood during the Great Depression of the 1930s. Their lives were touched by the dislocations stemming from this economic crisis and from World War II. They were moving into their later years of adulthood by the time of the women's movement in the 1970s. The second cohort (born between 1918 and 1922) became adults during World War II, when they were exposed to the unprecedented employment opportunities open to women in war-related industries. Their thirties and forties were spent in the family-oriented 1950s and early 1960s. Women who reached adulthood after World War II (cohort 3, born between 1923 and 1926) were touched by the expanding postwar economy and the prevailing atmosphere of optimism, as well as by the nation's preoccupation with traditional gender roles. They were already in their forties when the women's movement began to flourish in the 1970s. The fourth and most recent cohort (born between 1927 and 1933) reached maturity during the 1950s, becoming wives and mothers at a time when marriage and motherhood were seen as the singular calling for women who could afford to devote their time to them. But they also were the most apt to be influenced by the changing opportunity structure accompanying the women's movement in the 1970s.

Dividing our sample into four cohorts is a convenient way to assess possible historical changes in the interplay between psychological resources and social roles in women's lives. However, it is important also to recognize the similarities across cohorts. All of the women in our sample were wives and mothers in the family-oriented 1950s, and the preponderance of women were in their childbearing years at that time. All lived through the remarkable drama of the social transformations in gender roles during the second half of this century. What is different is the timing of this historic shift in the life course of women born in different times, providing distinctive experiences shaping the life pathways and expectations of each cohort (see e.g. Elder 1981, 1992, 1995).

Table 1. *Cohorts in Women's Roles and Well-Being Project*

	Range of birth dates	Year turned age 23	Year turned age 65	Age at start of WWII (1941)	Age at end of WWII (1945)	Age at time of 1956 interview	Age when Kennedy died (1963)	Age at time of 1986 interview
Cohort 1 (n = 97)	1905 through 1916	1928 to 1939	1970 to 1981	36 25	40 29	51 40	58 47	81 70
Cohort 2 (n = 91)	1917 through 1922	1940 to 1945	1982 to 1987	24 19	28 23	39 34	46 41	69 64
Cohort 3 (n = 54)	1923 through 1926	1946 to 1949	1988 to 1991	18 15	22 19	33 30	40 37	63 60
Cohort 4 (n = 71)	1927 through 1932	1950 to 1955	1992 to 1997	14 8	18 12	29 23	36 30	59 53

A key issue of this volume concerns continuity and change in stress, adversity, and the protective mechanisms associated with resiliency. In the program of research associated with our study on women's roles and well-being, we have focused on psychological well-being and multiple role involvement across the lifespan (Moen et al. 1989, 1992, 1995) as well as across generations (Forest et al. 1996; Moen & Erickson 1995).

Continuity and change in psychological resources

In order to examine continuity in emotional resources over time, we employ two measures of psychological well-being at two different time points (1956 and 1986). The first, a measure of general life satisfaction, was based on a three-item scale developed by Robin M. Williams, Jr. (Dean & Williams 1956). It is similar to those used in national surveys by Campbell, Converse, and Rogers (1976) and Veroff et al. (1981). It has a standardized alpha of 0.62 and ranges from low life satisfaction (1) to high life satisfaction (3).

The second measure is one of self-esteem, also constructed by Williams in 1956 from eight questions concerning general self-appraisal as well as factors related to the traditional feminine self-image. This measure has a standardized alpha of 0.61 and ranges from low (1) to high (3) self-esteem. These two measures were highly correlated in 1956 ($R^2 = 0.371$), when women in the survey ranged in age from 24 to 50, but less so by 1986 ($R^2 = 0.297$), when they ranged in age from 54 to 81 (Moen, Dempster-McClain, & Williams 1995).

Because there may be maturational and/or cohort differences in the stability of well-being, it is important to consider the means and standard deviations of the two measures of well-being in 1956 and 1986 for women in different cohorts (see Tables 2 and 3). There are no statistically significant cohort differences in women's ratings of their general life satisfaction in either 1956 or 1986. However, women in all cohorts report a decline in their life satisfaction from 1956 to 1986. By contrast, there is an increase in ratings of self-esteem over the 30-year period, with the youngest cohort (those 53–59 in 1986) experiencing the greatest improvement in self-esteem. In both 1956 and 1986, the third cohort (those 60–63 in 1986) report the highest levels of self-esteem.

Education is also typically associated with psychological resources (Elder & Liker 1982; Gecas & Seff 1990; Langner & Michael 1963), and there are differences in our sample by educational level in 1956 ratings of both general life satisfaction and self-esteem. Respondents with more than a high school education reported significantly higher levels of well-being in 1956. Those with at least some college, as compared to those with a high-school diploma or less, also reported higher levels of life satisfaction in 1986. However, general life satisfaction scores for both educational groups declined between 1956 and 1986. As

Table 2. *Average ratings of women's reported general life satisfaction, 1956 and 1986, by age cohort*

Cohort	Age (1956)	Age (1986)	GSAT56 (range: 1–3)			GSAT86 (range: 1–3)			GSATDIFF (range: −1.67–1.0)		
			Mean	SD	n	Mean	SD	n	Mean	SD	n
1	40–51	70–81	2.67	0.36	97	2.48	0.49	93	−0.19	0.52	93
2	34–39	64–69	2.67	0.35	91	2.51	0.41	90	−0.16	0.43	90
3	30–33	60–63	2.79	0.26	54	2.60	0.43	54	−0.19	0.44	54
4	23–29	53–59	2.68	0.37	71	2.54	0.45	70	−0.13	0.47	70
Total sample	23–51	53–81	2.69	0.34	313	2.52	0.45	307	−0.17	0.47	307
Difference by cohort											
F value (p)			1.89 ($p=0.131$)			0.85 ($p=0.47$)			0.28 ($p=0.84$)		
Significance			No signif. difference by cohort			No signif. difference by cohort			No signif. difference by cohort		

Note: SD denotes standard deviation.
Source: 1956 Cornell Study of Women's Roles, National Institute of Mental Health M-902 (principal co-investigators John P. Dean and Robin M. Williams, Jr.); 1986 Women's Roles and Well-Being Project, National Institute of Aging R01-AG0-5450 (principal co-investigators Phyllis Moen and Robin M. Williams, Jr.).

Table 3. *Average ratings of women's reported self-esteem, 1956 and 1986, by age cohort*

Cohort	Age (1956)	Age (1986)	SELF56 (range: 1–3)			SELF86 (range: 1–3)			SELFDIFF (range: −1.75–1.61)		
			Mean	SD	n	Mean	SD	n	Mean	SD	n
1	40–51	70–81	2.33	0.47	97	2.33	0.44	91	−0.01	0.48	91
2	34–39	64–69	2.36	0.41	91	2.40	0.40	91	−0.04	0.42	91
3	30–33	60–63	2.50	0.40	54	2.62	0.37	54	0.12	0.48	54
4	23–29	53–59	2.21	0.49	71	2.50	0.39	71	0.30	0.48	71
Total sample	23–51	53–81	2.34	0.45	313	2.44	0.41	307	0.098	0.47	307
Difference by cohort											
F value (p)			4.53 ($p=0.004$)			6.71 ($p=0.000$)			6.55 ($p=0.0003$)		
Significance			Signif. difference: Cohort 3 vs. 4			Signif. differences: Cohort 2 vs. 3 and Cohort 1 vs. 3, 4			Signif. differences: Cohort 4 vs. 1, 2		

Note: SD denotes standard deviation.
Source: Same as Table 2.

Table 4. *Average ratings of women's reported general life satisfaction, 1956 and 1986, by educational level*

Educational level in 1956	GSAT56 (range: 1-3)			GSAT86 (range: 1-3)			GSATDIFF (range: -1.67-1.0)		
	Mean	SD	*n*	Mean	SD	*n*	Mean	SD	*n*
High-school graduate or less	2.65	0.35	202	2.49	0.48	197	-0.16	0.48	197
More than high school	2.77	0.31	111	2.59	0.38	110	-0.19	0.45	110
Total sample	2.69	0.34	313	2.52	0.45	307	-0.17	0.47	307
Difference by educational level									
F value (*p*)	9.61 (*p* = 0.002)			4.10 (*p* = 0.04)			N.S.		

Note: SD denotes standard deviation; N.S., not significant.
Source: Same as Table 2.

Table 5. *Average ratings of women's reported self-esteem, 1956 and 1986, by educational level*

Educational level	SELF56 (range: 1-3)			SELF86 (range: 1-3)			SELFDIFF (range: -1.75-1.61)		
	Mean	SD	*n*	Mean	SD	*n*	Mean	SD	*n*
In 1956									
High-school graduate or less	2.27	0.46	202	2.45	0.39	196	0.18	0.46	196
More than high school	2.47	0.42	111	2.43	0.45	110	-0.04	0.47	111
Additional education after motherhood									
No	2.34	0.45	229	2.42	0.43	223	0.07	0.49	223
Yes	2.35	0.46	84	2.51	0.37	84	0.17	0.42	84
Total sample	2.34	0.45	313	2.44	0.41	307	0.10	0.47	307
Difference by educational level									
F value (*p*)	14.51 (*p* = 0.002)			N.S.			15.77 (*p* = 0.0001)		
Difference by additional education									
F value (*p*)	N.S.			N.S.			N.S.		

Note: SD denotes standard deviation; N.S., not significant.
Source: Same as Table 2.

seen in Table 4, the difference scores are both negative and similar in magnitude. A different picture emerges when looking at the change in self-esteem by educational level (see Table 5). The more educated group experiences a slight drop in

Table 6. *Average number of roles in 1956 and 1986 and change by cohort*

Cohort	Age (1956)	Age (1986)	ROLES(1956) (range: 0–6)			ROLES(1986) (range: 0–6)			Change in number of roles, 1956–86 (range: −5–+3)		
			Mean	SD	*n*	Mean	SD	*n*	Mean	SD	*n*
1	40–51	70–81	4.19	1.01	97	3.20	1.26	89	−1.07	1.41	89
2	34–39	64–69	4.35	0.88	91	3.69	1.54	87	−0.68	1.21	87
3	30–33	60–63	4.22	0.98	54	3.85	1.10	53	−0.42	1.12	53
4	23–29	53–59	4.01	1.06	71	3.61	1.31	69	−0.41	1.66	69
Total sample	23–51	53–81	4.20	0.99	313	3.55	1.23	298	−0.69	1.39	298
Difference by cohort											
	F value (*p*)		1.58 (*p* = 0.20)			3.93 (*p* = 0.009)			3.94 (*p* = 0.009)		
	Significance		No signif. difference by cohort			Signif. differences: Cohort 1 vs. 2, 3			Signif. differences: Cohort 1 vs. 3, 4		

Note: SD denotes standard deviation.
Source: Same as Table 2.

self-esteem, whereas the less educated group reports an increase, resulting in significant difference scores. This suggests that more psychologically resilient women stay resilient as they age. But it also offers the possibility for change, as women with little self-esteem improve their self-evaluations in tandem with growing older (see Moen, Dempster-McClain, & Williams 1995).

Continuity and change in social integration

We also examined continuity and change in the protective mechanism of social integration in the form of women's multiple role involvements (Moen et al. 1992). In order to gauge stability and change in such social integration, we used a measure of multiple roles – taken at two points in time (1956 and 1986) – that is the sum of the roles of each individual woman at the time of the 1956 and 1986 interviews. Six roles are incorporated in this measure: worker, church member, friend, neighbor, relative, and club or organization member. The measures of social integration, ROLES'56 and ROLES'86, are operationalized as the number of such positions *actively* occupied by women. Thus, for example, it is their enactment of religious affiliation – by attending services on a regular basis rather than mere church membership – that matters. However, we use membership in clubs or organizations (rather than attendance) since our analysis shows that such membership, unlike church membership, is virtually synonymous with attendance. These ROLES measures are similar to those employed by Thoits (1986), except that in this sample there is no variance in marriage and motherhood since all the respondents are married and had children present in the home in 1956. Various measures of marital and empty-nest status in 1986 are, however, incorporated in the analysis. Table 6 shows the average number of roles occupied in 1956 and 1986 for the four cohorts of women. In 1956 there are no significant differences between cohorts in number of roles, but 30 years later the oldest cohort – those in their seventies and eighties – occupy fewer roles than do their younger peers. All cohorts show a decline in number of roles from 1956 to 1986, but the oldest experience the greatest role reduction. Still, women in their seventies in 1986 occupy on average more than three roles (see Table 6).

The biggest difference in 1986 between the 64–91 and the 53–63 age groups is in employment: only 12% of the older women are working in 1986, compared to 53% of the younger group. But the older women are slightly more likely than those in their fifties and sixties to be active churchgoers (67% to 61%) and neighbors (68% to 60%). Only 55% of the older women remain married (mostly due to widowhood) by 1986, compared to 80% of the younger women.

Pathways to women's resilience

Also considered were the effects of women's role biographies (the timing and duration of role occupancy throughout adulthood) on their subsequent well-being (Moen, Dempster-McClain, & Williams 1995). Specifically, we include six measures of role involvement. First is *current role involvement,* measured by the sum of multiple roles (described previously) these older women occupied at the time they were interviewed. Second is the number of roles occupied 30 years earlier. This measure reflects not so much women's lives in this particular year (1956) as the degree of their *integration in earlier adulthood.* Third, we look at *role change* from 1956 to 1986 in terms of whether individuals moved up or down in number of roles, from above the median to below, or vice versa. (The reference category is "consistently low," that is, those women who were below the median in number of roles in both 1956 and 1986.) Fourth is *duration* of involvement from age 18 to 55; this is assessed using a group of variables that capture the total number of years, during the prime of adulthood, that the respondent was employed outside the home, volunteered, provided care for preschool children, and remained married. The fifth set of measures – role trajectories or patterns – is based on the *timing* of these role involvements between marriage and age 55. These mutually exclusive categories include never involved, continuously involved, intermittent involvement, late entrance (starting the role after age 40), and early exit (leaving by age 40). Sixth, *last role occupancy* measures the number of years since the respondent was last involved in a role.

Psychological resources

Looking just at the links between social and psychological resources in earlier adulthood, we found that women occupying multiple roles in 1956 had higher levels of psychological well-being (Miller, Moen, & Dempster-McClain 1991). Thirty years later, the same positive relationship holds; women occupying multiple roles in 1986 are still likely to report high levels of psychological well-being (Moen, Dempster-McClain, & Williams 1995). But this tells us little about the stability or dynamics of the links between these two resources. Accordingly, we drew on various measures of role biography to assess their association with women's sense of self-esteem and general life satisfaction in their later years. A number of aspects of their social integration throughout adulthood were related to women's successful aging.

Specifically, we found that women's multiple role occupancy as younger adults (in the 1950s) was positively related to their subsequent longevity, physical health, and psychological well-being (Moen, Dempster-McClain, & Williams 1989, 1992, 1995). This gauge of earlier social integration was linked as well to earlier (1956) feelings of self-esteem and general life satisfaction (Miller et al. 1991), which in turn were strongly connected to esteem and life satisfaction in later life (Moen, Dempster-McClain, & Williams 1995).

Looking at data from both 1956 and 1986, we found that having been highly integrated (in terms of being above the median in number of roles) at either time is positively related to women's later life self-esteem and life satisfaction, suggesting that older women incorporate their past experiences in shaping their current assessment of themselves and their lives.

Other manifestations of role biography involve the duration and timing of roles. For example, trajectories of continuous or intermittent volunteering, the duration of time spent volunteering throughout adulthood, and/or the length of time since one last volunteered are more closely related to self-esteem than are current involvements in these roles in women's later years. Stopping volunteer activities before age 40 reduces general life satisfaction to a degree that more than offsets the positive effects of currently occupying multiple roles (Moen, Dempster-McClain, & Williams 1995).

Differences by educational level

Because educational level has been shown to be so important for psychological well-being in broader populations (Kessler 1982), we considered whether the pathways to women's well-being in later adulthood may differ for women with higher and lower levels of education. We have seen that women with at least some college education experience little net change in self-esteem from 1956 to 1986, but report higher levels of general life satisfaction in both 1956 and 1986 than do those with only a high-school diploma or less (see Tables 4 and 5). How are these differences by educational level played out in women's lives?

We found some similarities as well as a number of differences between college-educated women and those with only a high-school diploma or less (Moen, Dempster-McClain, & Williams 1995). Specifically, women with less education appeared to benefit from having multiple roles either contemporaneously or earlier in adulthood (1986 or 1956), whereas college-educated women's sense of esteem and life satisfaction were related to their current (1986) level of integration. Moreover, their previous (1956) level of general life satisfaction is positively related to the life satisfaction of high-school–educated older women, but not to that of those with some college education.

It is important to remember that the respondents with at least some college education had relatively high self-esteem scores in 1956 and remained at approximately the same level in 1986. By contrast, those with only a high-school diploma or less reported lower self-esteem scores in 1956 – yet by 1986, their self-esteem ratings were on par with those of the more educated women. These findings point to the importance of context (in this case, education) in shaping continuity and change in resilience.

Social integration

Although data from our study (as well as research by Thoits and others) show that such resources as social integration into multiple roles promote psychological well-being, it is not clear what promotes social integration in the later years of adulthood. It appears from our data that some women do in fact develop a *life pattern* of continuity in their social role involvements, while others adopt a pattern of few such involvements (Figure 1, segment A). Using multiple regression analyses, we found that women occupying multiple roles in 1956 are the most likely to be occupying multiple roles in 1986, after controlling for health and other background factors (Moen et al. 1992). Duration of work and volunteer roles are also related to multiple roles in 1986, suggesting that extended involvement in roles throughout adulthood promotes role occupancy later in life. Indeed, women who had worked continuously from age 18 to 55 are more likely to have multiple roles in 1986.

However, some roles may be more integrative than others, promoting future connectedness in old age. For example, we found that any involvement as a volunteer, regardless of when it occurred, is positively related to women occupying multiple roles in later adulthood. These findings are not simply a case of those who are psychologically resilient becoming more connected to the broader society, since psychological well-being in 1956 was unrelated to multiple role occupancy 30 years later. Some situational imperatives, such as health problems, also matter. For instance, having had a serious illness is negatively related to

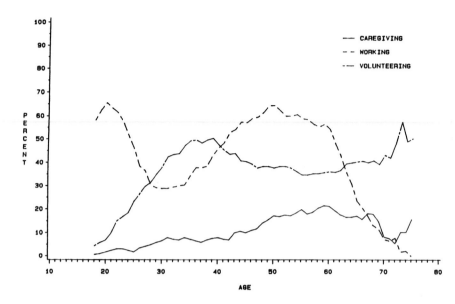

Figure 2. Percentage of women working, caregiving, and volunteering, by age (entire sample).

multiple role occupancy in 1986, whereas women with larger families are *more* likely to occupy multiple roles in their later adult years.

We also examined in detail the social integration of the two oldest cohorts of women (Moen et al. 1992). These women ranged from age 64 to 81 in 1986, past the typical retirement age for women in the United States. For this group, the duration of paid work and volunteer work in the years from ages 18 to 55 remain important predictors of social integration in later years, as do the number of roles held in 1956. Even for these older women, any involvement – early, late, intermittent, or continuous – as a volunteer serves to promote multiple role occupancy in old age. This is an important consideration, given that volunteering is a role that continues into the later years (see Figure 2).

Early resiliency and subsequent life pathways

Earlier in this chapter I drew on Merton's (1968) notion of the cumulation of advantage to suggest that protective mechanisms early in the life course may serve to facilitate life chances and choices that build on these existing resources, and (conversely) that those without resilience-promoting resources can experience a life course of cumulative disadvantage. In the Women's Roles and Well-Being Project we have conducted a number of investigations assessing how women's psychosocial resources in the 1950s shape their subsequent life course (Figure 1, segment B). We consider four important adult role trajectories and potential turning points: volunteering, caregiving, returning to school, and divorce. Each of these affects the psychological and social resources promoting resilience.

Volunteering

From our analyses of longevity, health, and psychological well-being (Moen, Dempster-McClain, & Williams 1989, 1992, 1995), we know that social participation (in the form of memberships in clubs and volunteering more generally) has salutary effects. But what accounts for whether or not women become volunteers? Using event history analytic techniques to examine the movement of women into and out of volunteer roles, we find that women who had a strong sense of self-esteem in the 1950s have a lower rate of volunteer exit, and those who have a previous spell of volunteering have a higher rate of becoming volunteers and a lower rate of leaving volunteer roles (Moen & Dempster-McClain 1996). Thus, volunteering both promotes and is a consequence of psychological well-being and social integration.

How does volunteer participation mesh with women's shifting family obligations over the life course? Event history analyses suggest that having young children in the home may be particularly conducive to volunteering; women with preschoolers are both more likely to become volunteers and less likely to exit the volunteer role than are those whose children are school-aged or older. Moreover, having the last child leave home actually reduces the rate of volunteer entry. Several of our respondents explicitly commented on the link between raising children and volunteering, with one making the point that "my kids volunteered me" for school-, church-, and other community-related activities. However, our finding that having more children reduces the rate of entry suggests that, although volunteering may well be compatible with the early child-rearing phase of women's lives, having many children at home strains that compatibility.

Do women located differently in the social structure evidence different pathways to or from volunteer participation? Our analyses of the rates of entry and exit by educational level suggest that the paths are more similar than different, and that there are not distinct dynamics affecting volunteer transitions of women with more or less education. Nonetheless, there do appear to be different dynamics operating to propel women into (as opposed to out of) the volunteer role. For example, being employed reduces the rate of entry into, but not exit from, volunteering. Similarly, educational level promotes the rate of entry but not of exit. Having a strong sense of self-esteem inhibits the rate of volunteer role exit, but has no significant effect on entry into the volunteer role. On the other hand, some variables seem to promote volunteer participation more generally. For example, having previously volunteered increases the rate of entry and decreases the rate of exit. The same is also the case for having preschoolers in the house, which likewise enhances the rate of volunteer entry and reduces the rate of volunteer exit.

What we see, then, is that less educated women are less likely to take on volunteering than are college-educated women, which is in line with Merton's (1968) notion of the cumulation of advantage. Women with a high sense of self-esteem are likely to remain as volunteers longer, maintaining social as well as psychological resilience. It should be noted that, for those with less education, volunteering can be an important turning point in the pathway to resilience. Those women who do become volunteers experience the same beneficial effects (in terms of health and psychological well-being) regardless of their educational level.

Caregiving

As women move into midlife they tend to become caregivers of sick or infirm husbands or aging relatives; 53% of the women in our sample were caregivers at some point in their lives, with most episodes of care involving an older relative (Moen, Robison, & Dempster-McClain 1995; Moen, Robison, & Fields 1994; Robison, Moen, & Dempster-McClain 1995). Event history analysis suggests that a more traditional lifestyle – having large families, marrying at an early age, and being active as a volunteer – increases the rate of women being caregivers (Robison et al. 1995). We found distinctive pathways for women born in different historical times, with the incidence of caregiving actually increasing for women in more recent cohorts (born 1923–33, compared to those born 1905–22). Family composition and family involvements are much more important in promoting caregiving for women born between 1905 and 1922 than for those born between 1923 and 1933. In spite of their greater involvement in paid employment, women in more recent cohorts take on caregiving in addition to employment. Women in the older cohorts and women with at least some college education who expressed a sense of general life satisfaction in the 1950s are more apt to become caregivers as they age. Thus, psychological resources such as life satisfaction seem to pave the way for women to become caregivers. It could be that emotional strengths equip women with the resilience necessary to be caregivers.

However, does caregiving promote or rather detract from psychological health? Our analysis of possible moderators of the impacts of caregiving suggests that the answer is: "it depends" (Moen, Robison, & Dempster-McClain 1995). We found that the timing and duration of role occupancy are important considerations, with the duration of caregiving first promoting and then diminishing three of five measures of well-being. Caregiving for one or two years may well enhance women's sense of purpose, whereas for longer durations the strains accompanying this role may come to outweigh its benefits.

In terms of the age of those currently involved in caregiving, we found that occupying the caregiving role is positively related to a sense of mastery for women in their fifties and early sixties but not in their late sixties and beyond. Older caregivers, especially those in their seventies, are moving into the years when they may themselves require care, and may be worried about their own health and their future abilities – in particular, how long they can anticipate continuing caregiving.

How do the various roles of employment, caregiving, and volunteering interrelate in terms of psychological resources? Our results are unambiguous regarding the meshing of employment and caregiving: older women who are currently working and have been caregivers are better off in terms of their sense of mastery, self-esteem, and life satisfaction than are those who are not employed (Moen, Robison, & Dempster-McClain 1995). The findings on volunteering in conjunction with caregiving are just the opposite, with volunteering and caregiving combined promoting more depressive symptomatology and less mastery. Why the combination of volunteering and caregiving should produce negative outcomes is not clear, but suggests the possibility that the volunteering activities of caregivers could be connected to their caregiving role, producing even more strains.

Returning to school

We also assessed the likelihood that women would return to the formal educational system after becoming wives and mothers (Bradburn, Moen, & Dempster-McClain 1995). School re-entry can be an important turning point, altering subsequent life chances and reshaping women's life pathways. For example, it can improve their paid labor-force rewards, affect their marital duration (Esterberg, Moen, & Dempster-McClain 1994), and open up new options and identities. We found that 22% of the respondents in our sample returned to school at some point, with women going back to school in their thirties, forties, fifties, and even sixties (Bradburn et al. 1995). Here, too, we see a certain cumulativeness of advantage: more-educated women (especially those with some college) are more likely to seek additional education following marriage and motherhood, whereas those with less education are less likely to obtain the additional training that could benefit them the most.

Returning to school can itself set in motion subsequent transitions, such as divorce (Esterberg et al. 1994). We have also seen that women who return to school are more likely to have an adult child return home following an empty-nest period (Munsch, Moen, & Dempster-McClain 1995). (Almost 60% of the women in this sample had an adult child return home at some point.) For those with more than a high-school education, returning to school is positively and significantly related to self-esteem in later adulthood (Moen, Dempster-McClain,

& Williams 1995), suggesting an interplay between life experience and subsequent resilience.

Divorce

All of the women in this sample were wives and mothers at the time of the 1956 interview, permitting an analysis of the factors affecting the likelihood of their subsequent divorce over the next 30 years (Esterberg et al. 1994). We found that extensive employment in early adulthood, as well as returning to school following marriage and motherhood, increased the rate of marital dissolution. But so also did positive feelings of self-esteem in the 1956 interview. That women with higher self-concepts opt out of marriage at a faster rate suggests that these women may view marriage as more optional than do women with lower self-esteem, possibly recognizing more alternatives outside of marriage.

We did not find either divorce or widowhood to have a significant impact on social integration (multiple role occupancy); widowhood but not divorce did affect psychological resources (Moen, Dempster-McClain, & Williams 1995).

Conclusions

Both social resources, in the form of social integration into multiple roles, and psychological resources, in the form of a sense of self-esteem and satisfaction, constitute protective factors enhancing the resilience of women as they approach and move through their later years of adulthood. Those possessing such resources can best weather life's exigencies. Social resources (in the form of role identities held) provide social contacts, social identity, and social status, thus giving purpose, meaning, and guidance to life (Pearlin et al. 1981; Thoits 1986). However, few studies have sought to explicate the pathways by which role biographies may affect psychological resources – and vice versa – over the life course. How do earlier psychological dispositions affect subsequent connectedness through multiple role occupancy? How do the shape and configuration of role identities throughout adulthood affect subsequent well-being? The program of research in the Women's Roles and Well-Being Project sheds some light on this dynamic process.

Our findings suggest that investigators need to focus on the *trajectory of resilience* over the life course and in shifting situational and sociocultural contexts. The findings summarized here confirm not only that contemporaneous roles and resources are related to women's psychosocial resources in later life, but further that life experiences throughout adulthood are also important. Thus, a life-course approach to continuities and changes in social and psychological resources appears to be a useful strategy; an understanding of resilience at any life stage inevitably involves an investigation of contingencies and pathways.

One pathway is a life pattern of continuity, suggesting stability in both psychological and social resources throughout adulthood (Figure 1, A). In our study, the best predictors of psychological resources in later adulthood are previous psychological resources, and the best predictor of social resources (in the form of multiple role occupancy) is prior multiple role occupancy. But we also saw changes in these resources between 1956 and 1986, suggesting that contextual considerations – in the form of social forces and experiences throughout adulthood – also shape resilience in the later years. For example, the number of roles women occupy in 1986 is in fact positively related to general life satisfaction and self-esteem in 1986. Moreover, time spent volunteering throughout adulthood and the length of time since one last volunteered are also consequential for self-esteem, whereas stopping volunteer activities before age 40 reduces general life satisfaction.

We also showed that the psychological effects of the potentially negative experience of caregiving are contingent on the roles and resources that women bring to the caregiving transition. This points to the moderating role of prior psychosocial resources.

What is missing in this body of work is attention to the *meanings* of life changes and their timing. Wheaton (1990) has made the important point that exiting negative roles can have salutary consequences. Thus, whether leaving or remaining in particular roles is beneficial or detrimental to later resilience depends at least in part on how these roles are defined, and when they occur. For example, becoming divorced may or may not be seen as a crisis (Wheaton 1990). One of our respondents, after providing the date of her divorce, paused and said, "best day of my life!"

Greater understanding of how the structure and meaning of roles throughout the life course encourages or hinders psychological health suggests multiple pathways to resilience. We find in our study a process best described as a "cumulation of advantage"; women with social and psychological resources in the 1950s are the most apt to possess these same resources 30 years later. Still, our findings point to the variability in personal and social resources over the life course in tandem with distinctive life experiences (Dannefer 1984). Life choices and contingencies – in the form of resources, role trajectories, transitions, and turning points – shape both behavior and outlook in complex and evolving processes that involve cumulation *and* change.

References

Bandura, A. (1982). The self and mechanisms of agency. In J. Suls (ed.), *Psychological Perspectives on the Self*, vol. 1. Hillsdale, NJ: Erlbaum, pp. 3–39.

Bandura, A. (1989). Regulation of cognitive process through perceived self-efficacy. *Developmental Psychology* 25: 729–35.

Baltes, P. S., & Baltes, M. (1990). *Successful Aging: Perspectives from the Behavioral Sciences.* Cambridge University Press.

Betz, N. E., & Hackett, G. (1987). Concept of agency in educational and career development. *Journal of Counseling Psychology* 34: 299–308.

Bradburn, K. B., Moen, P., & Dempster-McClain, D. (1995). Women's return to school following the transition to motherhood. *Social Forces* 73: 1517–51.

Brown, G. W., & Harris, T. (1978). *Social Origins of Depression: A Study of Psychiatric Disorder in Women.* London: Tavistock.

Campbell, A., Converse, P. E., & Rodgers, W. L. (1976). *The Quality of American Life.* New York: Sage.

Caspi, A., Elder, G. H., Jr., & Bem, D. J. (1987). Moving against the world: life-course patterns of explosive children. *Developmental Psychology* 23: 308–13.

Caspi, A., Elder, G. H., Jr., & Bem, D. J. (1988). Moving away from the world: life-course patterns of shy children. *Developmental Psychology* 24: 824–31.

Clausen, J. A. (1991). Adolescent competence and the shaping of the life course. *American Journal of Sociology* 96: 805–42.

Clausen, J. A. (1993). *American Lives: Looking Back at the Children of the Great Depression.* New York: Free Press.

Clausen, J. A. (1995). Gender, contexts, and turning points in adult lives. In Moen, Elder, & Lüscher (1995), pp. 365–89.

Dannefer, D. (1984). Adult development and social theory: a paradigmatic reappraisal. *American Sociological Review* 49: 100–16.

Dean, J. P., & Williams, R. W., Jr. (1956). Social and cultural factors affecting role-conflict and adjustment among American women: a pilot's investigation. Progress report submitted to the National Institute of Mental Health, Bethesda, MD.

Dempster-McClain, D., & Moen, P. (in press). Finding respondents in a follow up study. In J. Giele and G. H. Elder, Jr. (eds.), *Crafting Life Studies: Intersection of Personal and Social History.* New York: Cambridge University Press.

Downey, G., & Moen, P. (1987). Personal efficacy, income, and family transitions: a study of women heading households. *Journal of Health and Social Behavior* 28: 320–33.

Elder, G. H., Jr. (1974). *Children of the Great Depression: Social Change in Life Experience.* University of Chicago Press.

Elder, G. H., Jr. (1981). History and the life course. In D. Bertaux (ed.), *Biography and Society.* Beverly Hills, CA: Sage, pp. 77–115.

Elder, G. H., Jr. (1992). The life course. In E. F. Borgatta & M. L. Borgatta (eds.), *The Encyclopedia of Sociology.* New York: MacMillan, pp. 1120–30.

Elder, G. H., Jr. (1995). The life course paradigm: social change and individual development. In Moen, Elder, & Lüscher (1995), pp. 101–39.

Elder, G. H., Jr., & Caspi, A. (1990). Studying lives in a changing society: sociological and psychological explorations. In A. I. Rabin, R. A. Zucker, R. A. Emmons, & S. Frank (eds.), *Studying Persons and Lives.* New York: Springer, pp. 201–47.

Elder, G. H., Jr., & Liker, J. K. (1982). Hard times in women's lives: historical influences across 40 years. *American Journal of Sociology* 88: 241–69.

Esterberg, K. G., Moen, P., & Dempster-McClain, D. (1994). Transition to divorce: a life-course approach to women's marital duration and dissolution. *Sociological Quarterly* 35: 289–307.

Forest, K. B., Moen, P., & Dempster-McClain, D. (1995). Cohort differences in the transitions to motherhood: the variable effects of education and employment before marriage. *Sociological Quarterly* 36: 315–36.

Forest, K. B., Moen, P., & Dempster-McClain, D. (1996). The effects of childhood family stress on women's depressive symptoms: a life course approach. *Psychology of Women Quarterly* 20: 81–100.

Gecas, V., & Seff, M. (1990). Social class and self-esteem: psychological centrality, compensation, and the relative effects of work and home. *Social Psychology Quarterly* 53: 165–73.

Gove, W. R., & Hughes, M. (1979). Possible causes of the apparent sex differences in physical health: an empirical investigation. *American Sociological Review* 44: 126–46.

Kessler, R. C. (1982). A disaggregation of the relationship between socioeconomic status and psychological distress. *American Sociological Review* 47: 752–64.

Kessler, R. C., & Greenberg, D. F. (1981). *Linear Panel Analysis: Models of Quantitative Change.* New York: Academic Press.

Kohn, M. L. (1995). Social structure and personality through time and space. In Moen, Elder, & Lüscher (1995), pp. 141–68.

Lachman, M. (1986). Personal control in later life: stability, change, and cognitive correlates. In M. M. Baltes & P. M. Baltes (eds.), *Psychology of Control of Aging.* Hillsdale, NJ: Erlbaum, pp. 207–36.

Langner, T. S., & Michael, S. T. (1963). *Life Stress and Mental Health.* New York: Free Press of Glencoe.

Lazarus, R. S., & Folkman, S. (1984). *Stress, Appraisal, and Coping.* New York: Springer.

Maddi, S. R., & Kobassa, S. C. (1984). *The Hardy Executive: Health under Stress.* Homewood, IL: Dow Jones–Irwin.

Magnusson, D. (1995). Individual development: a holistic integrated model. In Moen, Elder, & Lüscher (1995), pp. 19–60.

Menaghan, E. G. (1989). Role changes and psychological well-being: variations in effects by gender and role repertoire. *Social Forces* 67: 693–714.

Merton, R. K. (1968). The Matthew effect in science. *Science* 159: 56–63.

Miller, M., Moen, P., & Dempster-McClain, D. (1991). Motherhood, multiple roles and maternal well-being: women of the 1950s. *Gender & Society* 5: 565–82.

Moen, P. (1992). *Women's Two Roles: A Contemporary Dilemma.* Westport, CT: Greenwood.

Moen, P. (1994). Women, work, and family: a sociological perspective on changing roles. In M. W. Riley, R. L. Kahn, & A. Foner (eds.), *Age and Structural Lag: Society's Failure to Provide Meaningful Opportunities in Work, Family, and Leisure.* New York: Wiley, pp. 151–70.

Moen, P., & Dempster-McClain, D. (1996). The dynamics of women's volunteer roles. Unpublished manuscript.

Moen, P., Dempster-McClain, D., & Williams, R. W., Jr. (1989). Social integration and longevity: an event history analysis of women's roles and resilience. *American Sociological Review* 54: 635–47.

Moen, P., Dempster-McClain, D., & Williams, R. W., Jr. (1992). Successful aging: a life course perspective on women's roles and health. *American Journal of Sociology* 97: 1612–38.

Moen, P., Dempster-McClain, D., & Williams, R. W., Jr. (1995). Women's roles and well-being in later adulthood: a life course perspective. Paper presented at ISA World Congress (July, Bielefeld, Germany).

Moen, P., Elder, G. H., Jr., & Lüscher, K. (eds.) (1995). *Examining Lives in Context: Perspectives on the Ecology of Human Development.* Washington, DC: American Psychological Association.

Moen, P., & Erickson, M. (1995). Linked lives: a transgenerational approach to resiliency. In Moen, Elder, & Lüscher (1995), pp. 169–210.

Moen, P., Robison, J., & Dempster-McClain, D. (1995). Caregiving and women's well-being: a life course approach. *Journal of Health and Social Behavior* 36: 259–73.

Moen, P., Robison, J., & Fields, V. (1994). Women's work and caregiving roles: a life course approach. *Journal of Gerontology: Social Sciences* 49: S176–S186.

Munsch, J., Moen, P., & Dempster-McClain, D. (1995). Refilling the empty nest: are maternal characteristics related to the likelihood of their adult children returning home? Unpublished manuscript.

Pearlin, L. I., Lieberman, M., Menaghan, E., & Mullan, J. (1981). The stress process. *Journal of Health and Social Behavior* 22: 337–56.

Pearlin, L. I., & Schooler, C. (1978). The structure of coping. *Journal of Health and Social Behavior* 19: 2–21.

Quinton, D., & Rutter, M. (1988). *Parenting Breakdown: The Making and Breaking of Intergenerational Links.* Averbury, UK: Gower.

Robison, J., Moen, P., & Dempster-McClain, D. (1995). Women's caregiving: changing profiles and pathways. *Journal of Gerontology: Social Sciences* 50: S362-S373.

Rutter, M. (1987). Psychosocial resilience and protective mechanisms. *American Journal of Orthopsychiatry* 57: 315-31.

Rutter, M., Champion, L., Quinton, D., Maughan, B., & Pickles, A. (1995). Origins of individual differences in environmental risk exposure. In Moen, Elder, & Lüscher (1995), pp. 61-93.

Schaefer, J. A., & Moos, R. H. (1992). Life crises and personal growth. In B. N. Carpenter (ed.), *Personal Coping: Theory, Research, and Application*. Westport, CT: Praeger, pp. 149-70.

Smith, K. R., & Moen, P. (1988). Passage through midlife: women's changing family roles and economic well-being. *Sociological Quarterly* 29: 503-24.

Spitze, G., Logan, J. R., Joseph, G., & Lee, E. (1994). Middle generation roles and the well-being of men and women. *Journal of Gerontology: Social Sciences* 49: S107-S116.

Thoits, P. A. (1983). Multiple identities and psychological well-being: a reformulation and test of the social isolation hypothesis. *American Sociological Review* 48: 174-87.

Thoits, P. A. (1986). Multiple identities: examining gender and marital status differences in distress. *American Sociological Review* 51: 259-72.

Thoits, P. A. (1987). Gender and marital status differences in control and distress: common stress versus unique stress explanations. *Journal of Health and Social Behavior* 28: 7-22.

Veroff, J., Douvan, E., & Kulka, R. A. (1981). *The Inner American*. New York: Basic Books.

Werner, E. E. (1990). Protective factors and individual resilience. In S. J. Meisels & J. P. Shonkoff (eds.), *Handbook of Early Childhood Intervention*. Cambridge University Press, pp. 97-116.

Wheaton, B. (1990). Life transitions, role histories, and mental health. *American Sociological Review* 55: 209-23.

II   Turning points: changes in life trajectories

8 Becoming unsupervised: children's transitions from adult-care to self-care in the afterschool hours

Deborah Belle, Sara Norell, & Anthony Lewis

In many American families today, no parent returns home from work until hours after the school day has ended. Some children attend formal afterschool programs during these hours or return home to a grandparent or other adult caregiver. During the elementary school years, however, children often begin to spend time after school on their own. Cain and Hofferth (1989) report that 2.4 million children in the United States regularly spend time unsupervised by adults or older teenagers, and that the percentage of children who are unsupervised increases steadily with age.

Children without adult supervision often arouse concern. During World War II, Zucker (1944) saw maladjustment and delinquency looming for "latchkey" children whose mothers sought wartime employment. "The house key tied around the neck is the symbol of cold meals, of a child neglected and shorn of the security of a mother's love and affection" (Zucker 1944, p. 43). As Medrich et al. (1982) observe:

> Many feel that children this age should be within safe distance, if not under the actual supervision of adults most of the time. They should move each day from one sphere of adult influence, the school, to another, the home, as rapidly as possible. When this ideal goes unrealized, as it often does, a "problem" is readily inferred, either in parenting or in the social provision of child care. (p. 63)

Although unsupervised children clearly violate the sensibilities of many observers, from a historical or cross-cultural perspective children's freedom from adult supervision is hardly new. In nineteenth-century American cities, children spent much of their time on the streets with other children, unsupervised by adults (Hareven 1989). In many non-Western cultures, young children are supervised more often by siblings than by parents (Weisner & Gallimore 1977) and are required to exhibit far more independence and responsibility than are generally expected from American children (Whiting & Whiting 1975).

This research was supported by the William T. Grant Foundation, the National Institute of Mental Health, and by an Evelyn Green Davis fellowship to the Bunting Institute of Radcliffe College for the first author. We are grateful for this support, and for the generosity of the research participants in sharing their insights and experiences. Names of all research participants are pseudonyms.

Developmental considerations

Developmentally, middle childhood is a time in which parents continue to exercise supervisory control over their children but in which children "begin to exercise moment-to-moment self-regulation" (Maccoby 1984, p. 191). Often this self-regulation occurs away from the visual scrutiny of adults. While access to parents may be advantageous, during middle childhood and early adolescence children are also thought to benefit from appropriate opportunities for independence and responsibility, particularly in the context of supportive relationships with parents and other adults (Bryant 1989; Hoffman 1979). As Hoffman (1979, p. 862) argues, school-age children still need "love, guidance, a boost in confidence, [and] a home base," but they also need "independence, a chance to cope on their own, [and] an opportunity to develop a sense of responsibility and a feeling of competence."

However, the premature granting of independence also can be problematic, as can independence without parental care. Antisocial and risky behaviors such as drug use are more common in young people when their parents do not monitor their behavior, even at a distance, and when parents are uninvolved and uninformed about their children's lives (Feiring & Lewis 1993; Maccoby 1984; Sampson 1992).

Do children who are unsupervised in the afterschool hours experience beneficial chances "to cope on their own," or malign experiences of premature independence? Do they experience their lack of supervision as parental neglect, or as evidence of parental approval and trust? Should the movement from adult supervision to self-care be viewed as a turning point in development, leading to significant consequences for children, or should this movement be seen as part of an inevitable trajectory from dependence toward maturity? Does lack of supervision lead to consequences for children, or is lack of supervision itself the consequence of the child's demonstrated readiness for autonomy? Is lack of supervision a stressor to children? And if it is, what factors potentially buffer the stressful nature of this experience?

This chapter attempts to answer these questions and considers the consequences to children of becoming unsupervised in the afterschool hours. The first part of the chapter critically reviews the existing research on lack of adult supervision as a risk factor for children, pointing both to the methodological limitations of the studies and to their underlying assumptions about the role of adult supervision in children's lives. We then turn to qualitative data from an intensive longitudinal study of employed parents and their children to explore the significance to children of self-care. This section of the chapter considers how the implications of self-care may vary depending on the reasons children become unsupervised, the specific challenges they face in the afterschool setting, and the constructions they place on being unsupervised after school.

Research on unsupervised children

Zucker (1944) was the first to publish concerns about unsupervised children, but the earliest systematic research to assess the well-being of such children is probably Woods's 1972 study, "The unsupervised child of the working mother." Since this pioneering effort there have been fewer studies of unsupervised children than might have been expected, given the extent of popular concern with this issue. Published empirical studies are shown in Table 1. As can be seen, the methodological characteristics of these studies limit our ability to draw clear conclusions from the research.

Most of the studies use cross-sectional designs, which makes it impossible to be certain that the presumed "outcome variables" have not led to the child's assignment to a particular afterschool arrangement, rather than the other way around. Certainly children are not randomly assigned to afterschool arrangements, and several authors interpret at least some of their findings as illuminating the forces that contribute to the child's assignment. Steinberg (1986), for instance, found parental permissiveness associated with self-care (among boys) and with distance from home (among girls). Galambos and Maggs (1991) found that parental acceptance was lower and conflict with parents higher among self-care girls away from home than among other girls. These patterns did not hold for boys, however. In fact, self-care boys away from home actually had *more* accepting parents than did other boys.

Studies also define supervision in different ways, so that a child characterized as "supervised" in one study would appear as "unsupervised" in another. Lovko and Ullman (1989), for instance, consider a child unsupervised if he or she regularly spends as little as 30 minutes per week without supervision, while to be considered unsupervised in Messer, Wuensch, and Diamond's study (1989) one would have to be unsupervised two hours each day for a year. Potential providers of supervision are limited to adults in some studies, but may include children or adolescents of various ages in other studies. As Riley and Steinberg (1993, p. 2) note: "A 10-year-old in the care of a 12-year-old sibling is considered 'supervised' by both Steinberg (1986) and Cole & Rodman (1987), but 'latchkey' by Cain & Hofferth (1989) and Vandell & Ramanan (1991)." Some studies define the unsupervised child as one who returns home to an empty house, while others include children who are unsupervised at other locations in the community.

Most studies do not limit the research population to those young people whose parents are employed and away from home during the afterschool hours. Thus, children can be considered "unsupervised" if they spend afterschool time at the local shopping mall or park, even if their mothers or fathers are at home all the time. Rodman, Pratto, & Nelson (1988) question this research practice, arguing that it confounds the issue of parental control style with the issue of parental absence as necessitated by employment.

Table 1. *Empirical studies contrasting the well-being of self-care and supervised children*

Study	Time frame	Method	Sample	Excludes non-employed parents?
Woods (1972)	Cross-sectional	Questionnaires and interviews	108 5th-graders; black, urban, low-income	Yes
Long & Long (1982)	Cross-sectional	Semistructured interviews	85 1–6th-graders; black, urban	No
Galambos & Garbarino (1985)	Cross-sectional	Questionnaires	39 5th-graders and 38 7th-graders; lower middle-class, white, rural	Yes
Rodman, Pratto, & Nelson (1985)	Cross-sectional	Interviews and questionnaires	52 4th-graders and 44 7th-graders; racially and socio-economically diverse	No
Toenniessen, Little, & Rosen (1985)	Cross-sectional	Questionnaires	38 6th-graders; middle-class, suburban	No
Steinberg (1986)	Cross-sectional	Questionnaires	865 5–9th-graders; racially and socio-economically diverse	No

Definition of self-care	Who describes arrangement	Reliability assessed?	Variables	Negative consequences for self-care children compared to supervised children?
Unsupervised by an adult over 18 years old	Child and mother	Yes	Personal and social adjustment, intelligence, school achievement, health, family relationships, school behavior, community behaviors	Yes, but for girls only
Alone routinely during afterschool hours, with or without siblings	Child	No	Self-help skills, personal responsibility, fear development (coping, nightmares, expressed fears), family relationships, socializing play	Yes
Alone without adult supervision before or after school	Parents	No	School adjustment, classroom orientation, fear of outdoors, academic achievement	No
No one (or only younger sibling) present after school	Child	No	Self-esteem, locus of control, social adjustment, interpersonal relations	No
Without adult supervision for part of each school day; child typically returns from school to an empty house	Parents	No	5 most/least experienced feelings	Yes
Unsupervised or with a younger sibling or peers after school in various settings	Child	No	Susceptibility to peer pressure	Yes, but only for those away from home and without adult monitoring

Table 1 *(cont.)*

Study	Time frame	Method	Sample	Excludes non-employed parents?
Vandell & Corasaniti (1988)	Cross-sectional	Questionnaires	150 white 3rd-graders; predominantly middle-class	No
Diamond, Kataria, & Messer (1989)	Cross-sectional	Questionnaires	44 5th- and 6th-graders; rural	No
Lovko & Ullman (1989)	Cross-sectional	Questionnaires	116 3rd–5th-graders; predominantly white, middle-class	No
Messer, Wuensch, & Diamond (1989)	Retrospective	Questionnaires	188 college students; predominantly Caucasian	No
Richardson, Dwyer, McGuigan, Hansen, Dent, Johnson, Sussman, Brannon, & Flay (1989)	Cross-sectional	Questionnaires	4,932 8th-graders; socioeconomically and racially diverse	No
Dwyer, Richardson, Danley, Hansen, Sussman, Brannon, Dent, Johnson, & Flay (1990)	Cross-sectional	Questionnaires	4,852 8th-graders; socioeconomically and racially diverse, urban	No

Definition of self-care	Who describes arrangement	Reliability assessed?	Variables	Negative consequences for self-care children compared to supervised children?
At home without adult supervision	Parents	No	Standard test scores, academic grades, conduct grades, classroom sociometric ratings, work/study skills, emotional well-being, adult–child relationships, self-competence	No
Left to care for oneself after school	Child	Yes	Academic achievement, behavior problems, school adjustment	Yes
Child regularly spends at least 30 minutes per week without direct supervision of someone in the 7th grade or older	Parents	No	Anxiety, self-perceived social ability, behavior problems	No
Unsupervised by an adult after school during elementary or middle-school years	Student	No	Academic aptitude, personality	No
Caring for self during out-of-school hours	Child	Yes	Substance use: cigarettes, marijuana, alcohol	Yes
Care of self at least one afternoon or evening per week	Child	Yes	Self-report of grades, substance use (cigarettes, marijuana, alcohol), truancy, risk taking, peer influences, anger, stress, fear of being along, family conflict	Yes

Table 1 *(cont.)*

Study	Time frame	Method	Sample	Excludes non-employed parents?
Galambos & Maggs (1991)	Longitudinal	Questionnaires	112 6th-graders; suburban	Yes
Vandell & Ramanan (1991)	Cross-sectional	Questionnaires	390 3rd–5th-graders; low-income, urban, ethnically diverse	No
Woodard & Fine (1991)	Retrospective	Questionnaires	248 college students; white, middle/upper socio-economic status	No
Berman, Winkleby, Chesterman, & Boyce (1992)	Cross-sectional	Questionnaires	297 4th- and 6th-graders; ethnically and racially diverse	No
Richardson, Radziszewska, Dent, & Flay (1993)	Cross-sectional	Questionnaires	3,993 9th-graders; racially diverse	No
Posner & Vandell (1994)	Cross-sectional	Questionnaires and interviews	216 3rd-graders; urban, low-income	No

Steinberg (1986), for instance, studied susceptibility to peer pressure among adolescents in grades 5–9. Young people were categorized as either adult-supervised at home or elsewhere, or as unsupervised at home or elsewhere, on the basis of their "usual" situation after school. Although the children of unemployed mothers were more likely than the children of employed mothers to spend afterschool time at home with a parent or other adult, more than 60% of the children with unemployed mothers were not to be found in this situation.

Definition of self-care	Who describes arrangement	Reliability assessed?	Variables	Negative consequences for self-care children compared to supervised children?
Regularly cares for oneself after school	Child	No	Peer experiences, self-image, parent–child relations	Yes, but only for girls away from home
Care for self after school or by a sibling under 15 years old	Mother	No	Cognitive ability, self-perception, behavior problems	Yes, but not when family income and emotional support are controlled
Caring for self or with younger siblings regularly during out-of-school hours	Student	No	Cognitive adjustment, emotional adjustment, personality development	No
Without adult supervision after school on more than three days a week	Child	Yes	Self-esteem	No
Unsupervised care after school	Child	No	Cigarette use, alcohol use, marijuana use, depressed mood, academic grades, risk taking	Yes
Unsupervised after school for 3 days a week or more	Parents	Yes	Reading performance, academic achievement, conduct grades, peer relations, emotional adjustment, adult relations, work habits, behavior problems	Yes

This means that 60% of the children of unemployed parents potentially appeared in this study as "unsupervised" children. Similarly, Richardson et al. (1989) examined alcohol, tobacco, and marijuana use among eighth-grade students who spent differing amounts of unsupervised time after school. The employment status of parents is never assessed by these researchers, and once again it is possible that the children of unemployed parents appear in this study as "unsupervised" young people.

Furthermore, most studies ask only one family member to describe the child's afterschool arrangement and do not attempt to assess the reliability of this description. The reliability issue is not a trivial one, as is shown in the few studies that have assessed agreement between independent reports of the child's afterschool arrangements. Only Berman et al. (1992) had strongly encouraging results, finding perfect agreement in a sample of eleven families. However, Richardson et al. (1989) found that while adolescent and parent reports of supervision were significantly correlated, the Pearson r values ranged only between 0.31 and 0.42. Interestingly, children were four times more likely than parents to report the higher number of hours spent in self-care, suggesting a substantial bias in reporting as a function of the informant chosen.

Weisner and Gallimore (1977) conducted an observational study of children after school in their homes and neighborhoods, and compared children's self-reports of their supervision status to those of trained observers. After each observation period, the child was asked, "Is anyone taking care of you?" Substantial disagreement was found between the children's responses and the judgments of the observers. Weisner and Gallimore (1977, p. 187) offer possible explanations for these discrepancies, but refuse to label one set of reporters accurate and the other biased: "Girls seem to underreport times when they are not being cared for, while boys overreport. Or are our criteria for inferring caretaking structure wrong, so that it is the observers who are (differentially) over- and under-reporting?" The authors speculate that girls may be more sensitive to caretaking relationships and that boys may prefer to think of themselves – and present themselves to others – as autonomous and independent.

Findings of the empirical research

Given the methodological diversity and limitations of the studies, it is not surprising that they have produced no clear consensus about the significance of afterschool supervision. Some studies report problems for unsupervised children, others find no differences between supervised and unsupervised children, and credible studies have reported poorer outcomes for children who spend afterschool time with older siblings, babysitters, afterschool teachers, and their own mothers than for children who spend afterschool time on their own.

Several of the negative outcomes have been found for adolescent rather than younger children, and in studies that include young people with unemployed parents. Richardson et al. (1989), for instance, found that eighth-graders who spent more than eleven hours per week in self-care were at twice the risk of using alcohol, tobacco, and marijuana as young people who were never unsupervised. Steinberg (1986) found that unsupervised fifth- through ninth-graders who spent afterschool time at home were no more susceptible to peer pressure than those who were supervised by parents at home. However, adolescents who spent unsupervised afterschool time at a friend's house or "hanging out" were more susceptible to peer pressure than either of the at-home groups.

Several studies of younger children have not found deficits among those who are unsupervised. In a particularly comprehensive investigation, Vandell and Corasaniti (1988) compared third-grade self-care children with children who spent afterschool time at home with their mothers, at home with sitters, or in formal afterschool programs. Reports from parents, teachers, children's peers and the children themselves revealed no differences between self-care and mother-care children in the large array of variables studied. However, children who attended afterschool programs were viewed more negatively by peers, made lower academic grades, and had lower standardized test scores than mother-care or self-care children; likewise, children who stayed with sitters after school were viewed less favorably by their peers than the self-care or mother-care children. The authors speculate that these findings may reflect the poor quality of many afterschool programs, stigma attending their use, or a self-selection factor in which only those children viewed by parents as needing adult supervision are assigned to center care.

In another well-designed study with an unexpected outcome, Berman et al. (1992) found no deficits in self-competence scores among the fourth- and sixth-graders who cared for themselves after school. The authors did find, however, that children cared for after school by older siblings reported significantly lower self-competence scores in the domains of global self-worth, social acceptance, and physical appearance when compared with children cared for after school by adults and with children in self-care.

Perhaps the most counterintuitive finding was produced by Vandell and Ramanan (1991), who studied supervision arrangements among third-, fourth-, and fifth-graders from the National Longitudinal Survey of Youth. Most of these children were born to teen-aged mothers, and almost half lived in households with incomes below the poverty line, making this an economically stressed research sample. The authors found the lowest levels of adjustment and well-being among children cared for by their own mothers after school. This group also experienced more poverty and less emotional support than did other groups of children in the study. Latchkey arrangements were associated with some negative effects, but these disappeared when controls were introduced for family income and emotional support.

Research suggests that the nature of afterschool supervision may not be the most crucial variable to consider. Instead, the location at which children spend unsupervised time and "distal" supervision by parents who monitor afterschool activities may be more critical aspects of the child's afterschool experience, as suggested by Steinberg's (1986) research. Galambos and Maggs (1991) replicated and extended Steinberg's work by showing that sixth-grade girls without adult supervision who spent afterschool hours away from their homes engaged in more problem behaviors than did at-home or adult-supervised girls. Boys showed no effects of self-care in any situation. Similarly, when Howard, Broquet, and Farrell (1991) examined the impact of afterschool arrangements on over a thousand predominantly black and low-income seventh-grade students, they found that whether or not students spent afterschool hours with an adult failed to predict any of their behavioral outcomes. But students who spent afterschool hours away from home, *whether supervised by an adult or not,* reported lower school grades and poorer school attendance records and were more likely to engage in drug use, minor and major delinquency, and sexual intercourse than children at home after school. Adult supervision was important, however, in predicting emotional and personality variables. When away from adults after school, students reported more distress and depression and lower levels of self-esteem and self-reliance.

The research on "latchkey" and supervised children has thus suggested some fascinating complexities. It has not yet produced a coherent picture of the implications of self-care for children, probably because it has not provided a sufficiently rich account of what children actually do after school and why.

The Children's Afterschool Experiences Project

The remainder of this chapter therefore turns to data from an intensive study of 53 children and their employed parents who were interviewed annually for four years about the children's afterschool arrangements and their emotional, behavioral, and academic well-being. Participation in the study was limited to urban families with parents employed full-time and with at least one child in elementary school at the start of the study. Single-parent families and low-income families were purposively overrepresented in the study, as it was anticipated that these families would face constraints in arranging satisfactory afterschool situations for their children that were not shared by two-parent and higher-income households. Families were recruited using a variety of methods, including the distribution of leaflets through the public schools, in-person recruitment at parents' meetings, and solicited referrals from community workers.

One third of the families had annual incomes of less than $20,000 per year, a third had incomes in the $20,000–$30,000 range, and a third had incomes of more than $30,000. Fifteen of the families were African–American, one was Hispanic, one was Asian, and 36 of the families were non-Hispanic white. All but three mothers had high-school diplomas, over half of the mothers had completed a college education, and four mothers had advanced degrees. We focused on the youngest child in each family who was attending elementary school. These children (31 girls; 22 boys) ranged from 7 to 12 years of age at the start of the study, and 33 of the children lived in single-parent families.

After informed consent was obtained from parents and children, family members were interviewed separately and privately about the child's afterschool routine, social support network, emotional well-being, and behavioral adjustment. Interviews included both forced-choice questionnaires and open-ended questions, lasted between one and two hours, and were generally conducted in the family home. Families were reinterviewed annually for four years. Attrition from the study was minimal, with all but one family finishing the study.

Becoming unsupervised

At the beginning of the study, adult supervision was the norm for most of the children, most of the time. Some children spent their afterschool time in formal afterschool programs, others in specialized activities such as team practices and music lessons, and others at home with an adult caretaker such as a relative or paid babysitter. Over the course of the study, more and more children ventured into unsupervised settings, until by the end of the study all but three of the children were regularly spending some unsupervised time each week. Children typically began spending unsupervised time at age 10 or 11, although a fourth of the children in the study were unsupervised at a younger age. These figures are in accord with those of a survey study of midwestern families (Steinberg & Riley, n.d.) which found that three quarters of the surveyed parents believed that most children were ready for regular self-care between the ages of 10 and 12. Furthermore, these were the ages at which the parents first typically allowed their children to spend unsupervised time after school on a regular basis.

Whereas some children spent only a few hours a week without adult supervision, others were unsupervised for considerably longer. Several parents either had professional jobs that required frequent work away from home on evenings and weekends, or held multiple jobs or jobs with evening shifts. One 12-year-old child, whose single-parent mother sometimes worked as many as 100 hours a week, rarely saw her mother during waking hours. Although the child spent some of her afterschool hours in a local drop-in program, she spent most of her evening time with her 14-year-old brother or alone.

Children often became unsupervised because situational constraints made adult supervision difficult or impossible. In many cases children lost their eligibility for afterschool programs when they reached a certain age, and no reliable substitute could be found. (In the communities where the research was conducted, as in most communities nationwide, virtually no formal afterschool programs extended beyond the fifth grade.) Sometimes an adult who supervised the child in earlier years moved out of the household. Parents in some cases found the cost of afterschool supervision unacceptably high. Otherwise appealing afterschool programs were sometimes made unattractive by the logistics involved in attending them, such as the long walk that children would have returning home.

Although contextual factors seem to have been powerful in moving many children into self-care, children themselves often precipitated the change, preferring the independence of self-care to what were perceived as "babyish" or unappealing afterschool programs. Several children were described as "day-cared out" or "burnt out" on formal afterschool programs. Other children needed more time for homework than their afterschool programs allowed, or wanted to pursue specialized lessons or activities that were incompatible with attendance at a regular afterschool program. Some children wanted time to "veg out" after the demands of the school day. Steinberg and Riley (n.d., pp. 5–6) have discussed such concerns as representing "developmental press for self care."

When Stacey Moore began working full time again after years of part time work, her daughters refused to go to afterschool programs. "Barbara felt and Bonita agreed that, having been in programs since they were little, . . . they were tired of a structured program that they had to follow." And, as Mark (their father) pointed out, they were used to coming home. They developed their own schedule of activities within the neighborhood, and have been on their own after school ever since.

Children sometimes appeared to slip into unsupervised arrangements without the active awareness of their parents. When Valerie Murphy was 10 years old, she was described by her mother as spending her afterschool time with a close family friend who lived a few doors away. Yet Valerie told the interviewer that she went home alone to play, watch television, and do homework after school. Perhaps the disagreement is partially a semantic one, since supervision can be an elastic concept. Ms. Murphy may consider Valerie supervised if their family friend is available to Valerie in the afternoons, while Valerie may prefer to think of herself as unsupervised.

Whereas in the Murphy family it seems that the child is slipping away from adult supervision, in the Berger family it appears that the parent is elusive. Carol Berger tells the interviewer that she is usually home when her daughter, Marguerite, returns from school each day, and this is reasonable since Carol works as an assistant teacher and completes work at about the same time Marguerite finishes school. Marguerite tells her interviewer, however, that her mother is home in the afternoon only "occasionally," and that she really does not know where her mother is after school.

These discrepancies between the reports of parents and children are reminiscent of the low rates of agreement found by Richardson et al. (1989). What is particularly striking in this study is that these discrepant pictures of afterschool supervision were given by parents and children interviewed simultaneously and in adjacent rooms.

Moving from unsupervised to supervised settings

While most children moved from supervised to unsupervised settings over the course of the study, several children moved against the current, from unsupervised settings to supervised ones. This movement back to adult supervision generally came about because of a change in family circumstance – such as a mother spending time at home on maternity leave, a parent losing a job, or an adult relative moving into the house – and it often had little impact on the previously unsupervised child. In some cases children were provided greater adult supervision in response to a specific crisis. When Eric Holden was caught playing hooky and stealing from cars, his mother responded by bringing Eric to work with her after school and during most days of the school vacation week. Her boss was "really marvelous" and truly supportive of Eric's being there, but this arrangement was only temporary and, after several weeks, Eric returned to spending his afternoons alone.

The challenges of afterschool arrangements

One child's afterschool situation may pose very different challenges and demand very different sorts of coping responses than another child's afterschool situation. The stressful challenges children experience in the afterschool hours, and the ways in which children respond to these challenges, will be considered in this section.

Moment-to-moment self-regulation (Maccoby 1984) is required of many children during the afterschool hours. Children need to comply with appropriate rules and guidelines for behavior, avoid undue risks, and complete required tasks, often without the prodding of adults. This proved a particularly difficult challenge for some.

As 11-year-old Zach Monroe expresses it, "I'm having a serious problem with discipline." Zach's single mother has a professional job that often requires her to work evenings, and on these days "Zach has to be totally responsible for himself." Peggy describes Zach's afterschool arrangement as "more like no arrangement at all." After school Zach is supposed to do his homework in the library, go home, or go to a friend's house. However, Zach rarely gets his homework done. "Most kids go to the library and get their homework done, but I go there and fool around," he says. Peggy frequently arrives home to discover that Zach has eaten nothing, has left his homework undone, and has failed to straighten up the apartment as he was asked to do.

Whereas Zach often fails to regulate his own behavior, 11-year-old Layla Williams generally succeeds. Her single-parent mother works two and sometimes three jobs to provide the family with an approximation of a middle-class lifestyle, and Layla and her brother rarely see their mother during the week. Jocelyn may be physically absent, but her rules govern and organize the time her children spend without her. As she says, "I know how to run my home, even when I'm not there." The children must call her when they get home from school. They must do their homework, with the television off, before they can go outside to play. If they have no homework, they must spend some time studying. Jocelyn finds it reassuring to know that when she works she doesn't have to worry about her children. Layla says, "I know what are the things that need to be done, so I do it."

In addition to regulating their behavior, children in many afterschool arrangements were challenged by the need to *regulate their emotions.* Children fended off fear, loneliness, and boredom, or coped with them as best they could. Zach Monroe fears burglaries and sometimes keeps a golf club handy near his bed. His mother confirms that they live in a high-burglary neighborhood, and their apartment actually was robbed once during the course of the study.

For many children, the afterschool hours present the challenge of *self-development,* the opportunity to learn new skills or acquire new knowledge. When their mother went back to work full-time, Barbara and Bonita Moore developed a full schedule of activities that included their own Olympics (both girls are serious athletes), a fair (for which they did their own baking), picnics, trips to the local park, and swimming at a nearby pool. They also wrote, produced, and performed their own play, making their own costumes.

Whereas the afterschool hours offer the Moore girls freedom to pursue their own agendas, for others these hours require increased *attention to the needs of others.* Four days a week, Doreen Morrison (a single parent) doesn't get home from her job until 7:00 in the evening. Her 12-year-old daughter Chantel takes responsibility for her own schoolwork, for the housework, and for 5-year-old sister Nikki, all without waiting for her mother to direct her. According to Ms. Morrison, Chantel has no rules about chores. She is good about doing things around the house on her own. Chantel likes the fact that her mother works. "I feel almost like my mother." Ms. Morrison sees the two of them as "more like a team than mother and daughter."

When Omar Jones was younger he regularly attended the afterschool program in his housing project, or waited in the hallway for a parent to come home from work. These days, his mother is sometimes with him until his father comes home, but several times a week she must leave for work about an hour before Mr. Jones returns from his job. On these occasions, 8-year-old Omar is responsible for his 4-year-old brother, Christopher, and his sister of only 14 months, Jamila. According to Ms. Jones, the rules are clear. "I don't allow the kids to touch the appliances. They have to stay in one room. The rest of the house is closed off. If Christopher has to go to the bathroom, Omar has to take him. Jamila is supposed to stay in the playpen."

Ms. Jones is very unhappy about the arrangement. Omar "doesn't have the freedom he should after school. School can be a pressure and then he has the added responsibility of watching his siblings. I'm surprised he's not doing badly in school." But Ms. Jones adds, "He's hurt by it. He cries, 'Mommy, when are you going to stop so I can go out and play?' It's only normal to feel bad when your mother lays so much responsibility on you." Shortly before our next interview with the Jones family, Omar's mother left her job to spend more time with her children.

The absence of others gives rise to many stressful challenges in the afterschool hours, yet stress also arises from the *unwanted presence of others*. Rebecca Myers spends two afternoons a week at home, and her stepfather is generally there as well. Rebecca and Sam do not have a good relationship, and when Sam is in the house Rebecca often retreats to her own room. This, in turn, limits her options during the afternoon hours and contributes to her experience of boredom. Later in the study, Rebecca's mother says that Rebecca and Sam are "slowly working on their relationship." She attributes this change to Sam's stopping his drinking and to the meetings of Alcoholics Anonymous he now attends.

Peers can also constitute a stressful unwanted presence. Julie Samuels was promoted from second grade directly to fourth grade, and in her afterschool program she does not fit in comfortably with either the third-graders or the fourth-graders. Her mother complains that the afterschool teachers do little to help Julie find a supportive set of friends. Later in the study she leaves the afterschool program with her mother's blessing, and begins spending afternoons at home or exchanging visits with two unsupervised girls who are her close friends. In this new situation she spends more time alone, but feels less lonely than she did in the midst of her peers.

A final challenge many children face is to *find meaning* in the way they spend their afterschool time. The children in low-income families generally know very well that their mother's employment is necessary for their own subsistence, and they understand her absence from the home as crucial to their own economic well-being. When 10-year-old George Lee was asked how he felt about his mother working, he said he liked it better, "so we have a roof over our heads and food." In contrast, Carl Peters has difficulty understanding why his mother cannot spend afterschool time with him. A school teacher, her workday coincides with his own. However, she stays on at the school to grade papers and plan the next day's lessons, tasks she accomplishes more efficiently at the school than at home. Carl experiences her absence each afternoon as a puzzling rejection. Weiss (1974) argues that those who take responsibility for the well-being of a child find meaning in their own lives through the sense of being needed, the opportunity to nurture another. Many of the sibling caretakers in our study appeared to derive such meaning, even when their responsibilities imposed sacrifices.

Meiguei Chen began taking care of her younger sister, Lian, when Meiguei was 9 years old and Lian was 5. Lian can be an obstacle to Meiguei's social life. "Sometimes my friends ask me to go to their house after school, but I have to say no, because who would take care of my sister?" Despite this, and despite the girls arguing "all the time," Ms. Chen believes that they are developing a closer relationship because of the time they spend together after school. Meiguei agrees. "We always play games, and during the games she'll say, 'Oh, do you know what happened today?'"

Conclusion

Examining the experiences of specific children and their afterschool arrangements throws some light on the complex findings of previous quantitative research. This study found frequent discrepancies between the descriptions of afterschool arrangements provided by parents and children. Apparently, afterschool arrangements exist "in the eye of the beholder," not simply as objective realities. Children are not randomly assigned to afterschool arrangements. Many children become unsupervised because they wish to be so, while others become unsupervised despite their wishes. Children appraise and respond to their afterschool arrangements in diverse ways. Absent parents are sometimes experienced as psychologically present, and those who are present can be experienced as psychologically absent. Unsupervised time leaves one child painfully adrift, liberates the creative energies of another, and seems irrelevant to a third.

Clearly, some children are unready for the challenges they face in the afterschool hours when adults are not with them. Accessible, affordable, and age-appropriate supervised programs would make a great difference to many children and their parents. Yet other children do seem ready for the considerable independence and responsibility they experience after school. They and their parents should not be stigmatized because the children are unsupervised after school. It is not contradictory to argue that some children suffer without adult supervision while others thrive in unsupervised situations.

Sooner or later, virtually all of the school-aged children in this study spent unsupervised time after school, suggesting that the movement to self-care may be a more nearly universal turning point in children's lives than is sometimes recognized. Longitudinal research that attends to the specific challenges children face in the afterschool hours, and to the child's role in appraising and responding to these challenges, is necessary in order to enhance our understanding of this turning point in the lives of children.

References

Berman, B. D., Winkleby, M., Chesterman, E., & Boyce, W. T. (1992). After-school child care and self-esteem in school-age children. *Pediatrics* 89: 654–9.

Bryant, B. (1989). The need for support in relation to the need for autonomy. In D. Belle (ed.), *Children's Social Networks and Social Supports.* New York: Wiley, pp. 332–51.

Cain, V. S., & Hofferth, S. L. (1989). Parental choice of self-care for school-age children. *Journal of Marriage and the Family* 51: 65–77.

Cole, C., & Rodman, H. (1987). When school-age children care for themselves: issues for family life educators and parents. *Family Relations* 36: 92–6.

Diamond, J. M., Kataria, S., & Messer, S. C. (1989). Latchkey children: a pilot study investigating behavior and academic achievement. *Child and Youth Care Quarterly* 18: 131–41.

Dwyer, K. M., Richardson, J. L., Danley, K. L., Hansen, W., Sussman, S., Brannon, B., Dent, C., Johnson, C. A., & Flay, B. (1990). Characteristics of eighth-grade students who initiate self-care in elementary and junior high school. *Pediatrics* 86: 448–54.

Feiring, C., & Lewis, M. (1993). Do mothers know their teenagers' friends? Implications for individuation in early adolescence. *Journal of Youth and Adolescence* 22: 337–54.

Galambos, N. L., & Garbarino, J. (1985). Adjustment of unsupervised children in a rural setting. *Journal of Genetic Psychology* 146: 227–31.

Galambos, N. L., & Maggs, J. L. (1991). Out-of-school care of young adolescents and self-reported behavior. *Developmental Psychology* 27: 644–55.

Hareven, T. (1989). Historical changes in children's networks in the family and community. In D. Belle (ed.), *Children's Social Networks and Social Supports.* New York: Wiley, pp. 15–36.

Hoffman, L. (1979). Maternal employment. *American Psychologist* 34: 859–65.

Howard, C. W., Broquet, A. J., & Farrell, A. D. (1991). The impact of after-school context and supervision on urban middle school youth's prosocial and problem behaviors. Paper presented at the biennial meetings of the Society for Research in Child Development (April, Seattle).

Long, T., & Long, L. (1982). Latchkey children: the child's view of self care. ED no. 211-229, ERIC Document Reproduction Service.

Lovko, A. M., & Ullman, D. G. (1989). Research on the adjustment of latchkey children: role of background/demographic and latchkey situation variables. *Journal of Clinical Child Psychology* 18: 16–24.

Maccoby, E. (1984). Middle childhood in the context of the family. In W. A. Collins (ed.), *Development during Middle Childhood: The Years from Six to Twelve.* Washington, DC: National Academy, pp. 184–239.

Medrich, E., Roizen, J., Rubin, V., & Buckley, S. (1982). *The Serious Business of Growing Up: A Study of Children's Lives Outside School.* Berkeley: University of California Press.

Messer, S. C., Wuensch, K. L., & Diamond, J. M. (1989). Former latchkey children: personality and academic correlates. *Journal of Genetic Psychology* 150: 301–9.

Posner, J. K., & Vandell, D. C. (1994). Low-income children's after-school care: are there beneficial effects of after-school programs? *Child Development* 65: 440–56.

Richardson, J., Dwyer, K., McGuigan, K., Hansen, W., Dent, C., Johnson, C. A., Sussman, S., Brannon, B., & Flay, B. (1989). Substance use among eighth-grade students who take care of themselves after school. *Pediatrics* 84: 556–66.

Richardson, J., Radziszewska, B., Dent, C. W., & Flay, B. R. (1993). Relationship between after-school care of adolescents and substance use, risk taking, depressed mood, and academic achievement. *Pediatrics* 92: 32–8.

Riley, D., & Steinberg, J. (1993). How should we define latchkey children? Contrasts of children in exclusive self-care, partial self-care, and sibling care. Paper presented at the biennial meetings of the Society for Research in Child Development (March, New Orleans).

Rodman, H., Pratto, D. J., & Nelson, R. S. (1985). Child care arrangements and children's functioning: a comparison of self-care and adult-care children. *Developmental Psychology* 21: 413–18.

Rodman, H., Pratto, D. J., & Nelson, R. S. (1988). Toward a definition of self-care children: a commentary on Steinberg. *Developmental Psychology* 24: 292–4.

Sampson, R. J. (1992). Family management and child development: insights from social disorganization theory. In J. McCord (ed.), *Facts, Frameworks, and Forecasts* (Advances in Criminological Theory, vol. 3). New Brunswick, NJ: Transaction, pp. 63–93.

Steinberg, J., & Riley, D. (n.d.). Parents' decisions about after-school care: the role of children's developmental press. Unpublished paper, Child and Family Studies, University of Wisconsin, Madison.

Steinberg, L. (1986). Latchkey children and susceptibility to peer pressure: an ecological analysis. *Developmental Psychology* 22: 433-9.

Toenniessen, C. S., Little, L. F., & Rosen, K. H. (1985). Anybody home? Evaluation and intervention techniques with latchkey children. *Elementary School Guidance and Counselling* 20: 105-13.

Vandell, D. L., & Corasaniti, M. A. (1988). The relation between third graders' after-school care and social, academic, and emotional functioning. *Child Development* 59: 868-75.

Vandell, D. L. & Ramanan, J. (1991). Children of the National Longitudinal Survey of Youth: choices in after-school care and child development. *Developmental Psychology* 27: 637-43.

Weisner, T., & Gallimore, R. (1977). My brother's keeper: child and sibling caretaking. *Current Anthropology* 18: 169-90.

Weiss, R. (1974). The provisions of social relationships. In Z. Rubin (ed.), *Doing unto Others.* Englewood Cliffs, NJ: Prentice-Hall.

Whiting, B., & Whiting, J. (1975). *Children of Six Cultures.* Cambridge, MA: Harvard University Press.

Woodard, J. L., & Fine, M. A. (1991). Long-term effects of self-supervised and adult-supervised child care arrangements on personality traits, emotional adjustment, and cognitive development. *Journal of Applied Developmental Psychology* 12: 73-85.

Woods, M. (1972). The unsupervised child of the working mother. *Developmental Psychology* 6: 14-25.

Zucker, H. L. (1944). Working parents and latchkey children. *Annals of the American Academy of Political and Social Science* 236: 43-50.

9 Children whose parents divorce: life trajectories and turning points

Donald Wertlieb

The divorce of one's parents can be a crucial and formative experience with powerful impact on the rest of one's life. Time and time again, retrospective reports focus on divorce as a "turning point" in the life of a family and its individual members (Clausen 1990). The experience of parental divorce is part of the fabric of life for significant numbers of U.S. children, with estimates suggesting that 30% to 50% will see their parents' marriages end. The divorce rate for remarried couples (49%) is slightly higher than the divorce rate for first marriages (47%); thus, many children experience divorce repeatedly (Crosbie-Burnett 1994). In addition, there is mixed evidence concerning the beneficial or ameliorative effects of parental remarriage for children (Zill, Morrison, & Coiro 1993) and ample evidence that – whether in a single-parent home or a remarried/stepparent home – children whose parents have divorced exhibit more behavior problems and lower levels of social competency than children from "intact" homes (Hetherington & Clingempeel 1992).

"Demographers who try to portray the family experiences of children are scratching their heads, wondering how to capture the complex life courses that many children born in the 1980s and 1990s will follow" (Furstenberg & Cherlin 1991, p. 12). Although there is some suggestion of a stabilization or even a decline in the rate of divorce in the 1990s, the influences of divorce experiences pervade contemporary life and figure centrally in most analyses of child and adult health and well-being. Clinicians, researchers, and public policy professionals struggle to comprehend the effects of divorce and to construct means for its now well-documented untoward sequelae. This chapter is a contribution to that enterprise, as it seeks to take stock of recent divorce research and related work in human development. Having committed to a stress-and-coping model that postulates a range of alternative developmental pathways as trajectories for "children of divorce"[1] (Wertlieb 1991), I seek to identify key variables and processes that might be considered turning points – factors associated with the variation in these trajectories and destinations (see Chapter 1 in this volume).

179

I begin with a brief, selective review of recent divorce research. Among the challenges posed by this task is linking sets of literatures with their own traditions and so encountering clashes between clinical and empirical approaches, quantitative and qualitative analyses, and sociological and psychological perspectives. In addition, some of the work can be considered "adult" literature, often distinct from the "child literature"; a very few studies include longitudinal analyses providing a bridge between these two (e.g., Wallerstein & Blakeslee 1989; Werner & Smith 1992). Among the most interesting links is the process of intergenerational transmission of divorce, which is well established (e.g., Belsky & Pensky 1988; McGue & Lykken 1992; White 1990) yet to date insufficiently analyzed. As will be elaborated further, this notion of transmission is "perhaps more appropriately and even less felicitously, 'intergenerational transmission of behaviorally, socially, and psychologically troubled relationships'" (Kitson 1992, p. 357). These foci will allow consideration of some of the key trajectory and turning-point factors in the process of adaptation to divorce.

An additional challenge inherent in grasping the literature on divorce is navigating the rapids of associated political rhetoric and controversy, above and beyond the heuristic clashes just noted. At times, these controversies point to significant factors relevant to the present effort to map diverse developmental trajectories. For instance, the unfortunate early habit of basing target study groups on "father absence" renders unintelligible the effort to distinguish correlates of experiences as diverse as death, divorce, and abandonment. Similarly, whether in politics or in research, the notion of a single-parent family seriously confounds the diverse experiences of children growing up in homes without married parents, whether the stereotypical "welfare mom" or the 1990s middle- and professional-class phenomenon of "Murphy Brown" single mothers. In another vein, in a subcultural context where a particular religious commitment figures centrally in the life of a family, divorce as experienced and constructed can take on meaning and impact far different from a context where religiosity is not a part of defining experiences, meaning-making, and coping. An historical perspective becomes especially important in describing and explaining cohort differences associated with the processes of adjustment to divorce.

The scientific, policy, and lay literatures refer to the "divorce revolution" of the 1960s and 1970s. In 1995, *Marriage in America* (CFA 1995) proclaims its end: "The divorce revolution – the steady displacement of a marriage culture by a culture of divorce and unwed parenthood – has failed" (p. 1). How divorce is experienced and studied is influenced by the sociohistorical context. The benefits of the life-course developmental perspective assumed in this volume, the focus on the study of lives in a changing society, achieve particular salience (Elder 1991; Elder, Modell, & Parke 1993).

The effects of divorce on children (circa 1996)

As the "divorce revolution" subsides, transforms, or shifts direction, analyses and reviews by key scholars permit a state-of-the-art account of the effects of divorce on children (Cherlin et al. 1991; Emery & Forehand 1994; Furstenberg & Cherlin 1991; Hetherington & Clingempeel 1992). Both salutary and harmful effects are documented (Amato 1993; Barber & Eccles 1992; Zill et al. 1993). Among the salutary effects are the greater sense of responsibility and self-esteem that may emerge for some children in single-parent, female-headed homes. Children "may develop less gender-role stereotyped occupational aspirations and family values, which could lead to their increased success in the labor market" (Barber & Eccles 1992, p. 122).

Amato and Booth (1991) applied three conceptual models to data on long-term divorce adjustment and generated partial support for each: a *socialization* model, emphasizing dysfunctional learning experiences inherent in conflicted or single-parent families as well as impaired parental attention and supervision; an *economic deprivation* model, capturing the frequently dramatic decline in socioeconomic status and resources; and a *family stress* model that includes consideration of the variety of traumatic or challenging events and experiences faced by a child as parents divorce – conflict, moving residences, loss of contact with immediate or extended family members, remarriage, and so forth. In their national survey of over 1,200 people, 152 of whom experienced the divorce of their parents before the age of 18 years, a range of outcomes and group differences were evident. Those who experienced divorce showed lower levels of well-being than those who grew up in continuously intact happy families. Those who grew up in unhappy intact homes also had lower levels of well-being. If parental divorce was not associated with decline in quality of relationship with parents and a subsequent divorce was not encountered – a so-called low-stress divorce trajectory – then adult well-being matched that of the nondivorced group and surpassed that of the unhappy intact group.

In terms of group data on children whose parents divorce, negative effects are evident but not for all children, and the overall effect sizes are statistically significant but relatively small: anywhere from 0.08 to 0.23 standard deviations (Emery & Forehand 1994). The emergence or re-emergence of negative effects in adolescence or adulthood seems quite evident in the data from the current or recent adult populations (Amato and Keith 1991a; Kiernan 1992; Zill et al. 1993). How today's children will look as adults remains unclear (Amato 1994); the mission to map trajectories and turning points based on existing data and theory is launched under considerable limitations. As noted, the changing context, prevalence, and meaning of divorce are likely to influence future presentations. Kiernan (1992) is not sanguine in her assessment of cohort and cross-cultural differences noted in her study of divorce effects in Great Britain. The conceptual frameworks for these findings emphasize complex, multifactorial stress-and-coping adjustment processes associated with a range of outcomes. These constitute the diverse developmental pathways taken by children whose parents divorce, and ultimately require comprehensive longitudinal research (Amato 1993; Amato & Kieth 1991a,b; Emery & Forehand 1994; Hetherington & Clingempeel 1992; Wertlieb 1991).

An emerging consensus sees divorce as a marker for a period of upheaval, distress, and decline in well-being for most children. Preceding, during, and up to three years subsequent to the marital dissolution, most children experience new challenges and exhibit a range of symptoms and psychosocial problems. A complex web of protective and risk factors shapes the form and longevity of these difficulties. These include individual factors (gender, age, race, temperament, attitudes, and coping style), family factors (supportive parent–child relations, siblings, pre- and postdivorce interparental conflict, quality and quantity of contact with noncustodial parent, parenting styles, economic decline) and extrafamilial or community support factors (contact with adult caretakers, social support, group therapy) (Emery & Forehand 1994).

Though there are certainly instances where divorce is a harbinger of relief or happiness – especially in cases of emotional or physical abuse, severe parental psychopathology, or substance abuse – most children are affected negatively when their parents divorce. Still, Wheaton (1990) has demonstrated some dimensions of the chronic stress *relief* that follows even "stressful" divorce transitions, at least for adults represented in a Canadian national survey.

Consensus is less extant when considering the longer-term aftermath of divorce. Amato and Keith (1991a), in a meta-analysis of 37 studies involving over 81,000 people and conducted between 1952 and 1991, conclude that "the long-term consequences of parental divorce for adult attainment and quality-of-life may prove to be more serious than the short-term emotional and social problems in children" (p. 40). Furstenberg and Teitler (1994), examining the selective occurrence of divorce as well as the well-documented destructive processes in both divorcing and nondivorcing problem marriages, suggest that this assessment could be premature. Certainly the same dynamic web of risk and protective factors noted earlier influences the longer-term outcomes, constituting at times the turning points we seek to describe. All recent analyses and reviews acknowledge the considerable methodological and theoretical limitations under which data are generated as we pursue the question of the psychosocial costs of divorce for children and map the trajectories of their multiple, alternative developmental pathways.

Controversy has focused on two particular concepts central to this task. Some researchers have proposed a *sleeper* effect, suggesting that such challenges as adolescence, adulthood, single-parent family life, or parental remarriage and/or redivorce may trigger a delayed effect of parental divorce. Other researchers have focused on an *intergenerational transmission* of divorce to portray some crucial dimensions of how lives are affected by parental divorce. Each of these debates informs the effort to identify trajectories and turning points.

Sleeper effects

Among the more intriguing and controversial findings of the high-profile longitudinal clinical investigation of 60 families adjusting to divorce (reported by Wallerstein & Blakeslee 1989) is the so-called sleeper effect. They found that more than half of their female adolescent subjects considered to be coping well at the time of their parents' divorce exhibited a clinically significant (even "dangerous") decline in adjustment in early adulthood, at the ten-year follow-up. A few boys showed a similar pattern. The authors map a set of life-course trajectories in this way:

> The cumulative effect of [their parents'] failing marriage and divorce rose to a crescendo as each child entered young adulthood. It was here, as these young men and women faced the developmental tasks of establishing love and intimacy, that they most felt the lack of a template for a loving, enduring and moral relationship between a man and a woman. It was here that anxiety carried over from the divorced family relationships threatened to bar the young people's ability to create new, enduring families of their own. (pp. 299–300)

> A significant number of young women are living with an intolerable anxiety about betrayal. (p. 62)

Such findings, and such dramatic exposition, stirred great emotion in both the public and the scientific community, some of it well-captured in Dunlop and Burns' (1995) paper, "The sleeper effect – myth or reality?" Calling upon data from a ten-year longitudinal study including 80 adolescents from 37 divorcing families and 41 intact families, Dunlop and Burns could generate "no convincing support" (p. 375) for a sleeper effect. Their analysis addressed some (but certainly not all) of the weaknesses of the Wallerstein study. They conclude their report with attention to the problem of reconciling cross-national and cross-cultural data.

A study considered to be more rigorous than the report of Wallerstein and Blakeslee is the Kauai (Hawaii) longitudinal study, which followed an entire 1955 birth cohort of 505 children through adulthood (Werner & Smith 1992). Those individuals who experienced the dissolution of their own marriages by the age-32 follow-up had a "vulnerability" most potently defined by having experienced a parental divorce or remarriage in childhood. Werner and Smith do not commit themselves to a sleeper-effect explanation, but they profess to

> share a common concern with Wallerstein and Blakeslee (1989) . . . [who] find in a clinical sample what we find in an entire birth cohort: The psychological

effects of parental divorce extend into adulthood and can interfere with the establishment of a strong bond of commitment and intimacy for a significant minority of men and women. Because parental divorce is currently the most prevalent risk factor for children in our society, its long-term consequences for the children need more attention. (p. 198)

Though not a major focus in their analysis of extensive data from over 1,000 children in the National Survey of Children, Zill et al. (1993) document a "marginally reliable" longitudinal gender interaction effect as a sleeper effect, whereby young women whose parents had divorced were more apt to have problematic relationships with their mothers, despite positive relations in adolescence. The Zill et al. (1993) study is not cited by Dunlop and Burns (1995). The notion of a sleeper effect remains a challenge for those seeking to map the life courses of children whose parents divorce.

Intergenerational transmission of divorce

The developmental trajectory reflecting a sleeper effect would portray a period of well-being on particular outcomes near the time of parental divorce and a subsequent decline, implicating a turning point as a deflector of the curve (see Chapter 1). As noted, this pattern is evident for some young people. A related but not fully overlapping trajectory, perhaps a more general case, can be sketched from the notion of an intergenerational transmission of divorce. Though a more general trajectory, it involves a narrower specification: the divorced subset of the significant number of adults who experienced the divorce of their own parents. The metaphor of intergenerational transmission is suggestive of both biogenetic and psychosocial hypotheses. The greater likelihood of divorce in one's early life experience repeating itself in a subsequent adult phase is substantiated by numerous studies, but the causal explanations and associated depictions of trajectories and turning points are far from clear (Belsky & Pensky 1988; Kitson 1992; McGue 1994; McGue & Lykken 1992; White 1990).

The genetics of divorce is a relatively new research domain. Yet findings are both robust and replicated, requiring the developmentalist and developmental psychopathologist to reflect upon this explanatory level, especially when committed to multifactorial stress-and-coping models or to frameworks of resiliency and vulnerability. Using the traditional twin study design of behavioral genetics, McGue and Lykken (1992) examined the claim that divorce runs in families by comparing 722 monozygotic twin pairs with 794 dizygotic twin pairs in the Minnesota Twin Registry. As expected, and consistent with previous literature, over 20% of these individuals had been divorced at least once; consistent with other estimates of the rate at which divorce runs in families, about 30% of the marriages of individuals with a divorced first-degree relative also ended in divorce. A substantially high risk of divorce (45%) was evident when that relative was a monozygotic twin. A calculation using logistic regression weights for parental and twin divorce status yields a 77.5% predicted rate in the presence of divorce and a much smaller 5.3% rate in the absence of twin and parent divorce. These findings have been replicated (Turkheimer et al. 1992). Like most findings in behavioral genetics, the implication is *not* that parental divorce or other developmental risks are "predestined" by virtue of the significant genetic component: "Any genetic influence on divorce is likely to be highly indirect, mediated by multiple physiological, neurochemical and behavioral systems" (McGue 1994, p. 110). Rather than as a trait that will inevitably unfold, this genetic evidence should be considered as specifying certain ranges of preprogrammed pathways of change and development. For those committed to mapping trajectories for children whose parents divorce, "a behavioral genetic perspective may help explain why the effect of divorce on offspring functioning appears to be manifested prior to parental separation" (Block, Block, & Gjerde 1986; an early expression of inherited factors that are associated with divorce in adulthood?), or why "only a *small minority* [sic] of children appear to bear any long-term consequence as a result of parental divorce (heterogeneity due to genotype–environment interaction?)" (McGue 1994, p. 111).

The microscopy of a genetic perspective prompts the telescopy of an evolutionary perspective, an elegant dialectic only recently being considered by family researchers as they embrace developmental and developmental–psychopathological frames of reference. Relevant theory and data are marshaled by Wright (1994) in *The Moral Animal: Evolutionary Psychology and Everyday Life*. A dramatic *Time* magazine cover heralded publication of the book with a bold headline: "Infidelity: It may be in our genes"; an inside subtitle read "Devotion and betrayal, marriage and divorce; how evolution shaped human love." Drawing heavily from genetics, primatology, anthropology, and sexology, Wright describes evolutionary psychology and crafts a convincing set of scenarios documenting gender differences, courtship and marital behaviors, and other biopsychosocial processes central to analysis of divorce – its causes, and its effects on society and on individual children and adults. For instance, he cites work explaining the negative impact on children of serial monogamy in terms of an "obvious" Darwinian prediction that stepparents will "tend to care less profoundly for children than natural parents." Given that parental investment is a precious resource and a basic buffer against stress, natural selection would "favor those parental psyches that do not squander it on nonrelatives – who after all, do not carry the parent's genes." A child is at considerably greater risk of parental abuse when living with a stepparent and a biological parent than when living with two biological parents.

This invocation of genetic, evolutionary, or constitutional factors as crucial elements of an explanatory framework is especially compelling in light of the power of the recent "cascade" theory of marital dissolution and stability proposed by Gottman (1993). According to this theory, psychophysiological processes that are measurable in the laboratory can predict not only divorce but also responsiveness to an explicit, cost-effective form of psychotherapy, "minimal marital therapy." Data on children or life-course data have yet to be presented.

Acknowledging the influence of heritability and evolution, and integrating the more distal elements of the sleeper effect, a psychosocial framework for the intergenerational transmission of divorce has empirical support across several domains of theory and data. Again, we have available the well-executed meta-analysis alluded to previously (Amato & Keith 1991a) as well as much subsequent debate (Amato 1993; Demo 1993; Furstenberg & Teitler 1994; Kurdek 1993) implicating a variety of social psychological processes in the increased prevalence of divorce among adults whose own parents divorced. Effect sizes are generally weak but appear in terms of lower educational attainment, earlier entry into marriage, earlier childbearing, lower income, and lower socioeconomic well-being – all potential experiences, even turning-point markers, associated with divorce. Cherlin (1992) cautions us wisely, noting that in a key study (McLanahan & Sandefur 1994), low income accounts for about half of the intergenerational effect and most divorces do not transmit. Nonetheless, if ours is the divorce generation by virtue of its statistical profile – each child growing up now stands a better than 50-50 chance of experiencing his or her parents' divorce – then what of the next generation, given the cross-generational transmission of divorce?

Trajectories, turning points, and destinations

Implicit in the notions of trajectories and turning points as proposed by Clausen (1990) and Elder (1991) and as elaborated here by Wheaton and Gotlib (1995) is the notion of a *destination*. One of the better studies of children's adaptation to divorce invokes such destinations in terms of "winners, losers and survivors" (Hetherington 1989, p. 1). In her presidential address to the Society for Research in Child Development, Hetherington summarized the Virginia Longitudinal Study of Divorce and Remarriage, a model at the time for multimethod multisource developmental research, with an answer to this question: "What enduring effects do divorce and remarriage have on children?" Her response reflected the complexity alluded to earlier in arguing for a view of a *range* of alternative developmental pathways for these children: "Depending on the characteristics of the child – particularly the age and gender of the child, available resources, subsequent life experiences, and especially interpersonal relationships – children in the long run may be survivors, losers, or winners of their parents' divorce or remarriage" (p. 13).

These "destination" characterizations, derived through empirical cluster analyses of observational, interview, and standardized test data (collected at two months and at one, two, and six years), are a useful starting point for painting trajectories and turning points for children of divorce. In the short term, virtually all children experience a period of distress, dysfunction, and recovery in the first two to three years. Some children (the losers) continue with compromised functioning over the course of childhood and, presumably, adolescence. They are characterized as "aggressive and insecure" children, and their difficulties are presented at home, in school, and with peers. There were many more boys than girls in this group. Unavailable fathers or rejecting fathers or stepfathers were prevalent.

The legacy follows them into adulthood. Among the more poignant portraits of the experiences of these "damaged" children are those described by Wallerstein and Blakeslee (1989). How large or small a proportion these "few" losers represent remains a topic of controversy in the field (Emery & Forehand 1994; Hetherington & Furstenberg 1989; Kelly & Emery 1989). Emery and Forehand (1994) are probably correct in their proposition that there are fewer casualties of divorce than estimated by clinical investigators but more than estimated by large sociological surveys. In addition, they introduce the notion of "children's underlying unhappiness despite successful coping" (p. 77) as an outcome category, akin perhaps to the "survivors" described by Hetherington (1989).

Who are these survivors? Six years after their parents' divorce, a group of children (then about 10 years of age) in the Virginia study were characterized as "opportunistic-competent." They appeared to be doing very well in many respects: low in behavior problems, high in self-esteem, and well engaged at school both academically and socially. They were adept at managing stressful situations and were strategic, even manipulative, in relating to peers and adults. They had close and supportive relationships with one parent but often had one parent who was disturbed, neglectful, or rejecting. These youngsters had less depth or longevity in their friendships and were especially tuned into the power and status dimensions of children and adults.

In contrast to these survivors was a group of "winners" described as "caring-competent." They, too, were faring well at middle childhood. They were less concerned with power and prestige in relationships, and rated higher in helping and sharing than any other group in the study. There were many more girls (18) than boys (5) in this group, and none of the boys' mothers had remarried. The single background factor noted to distinguish the caring-competent from the opportunistic-competent individuals was that, even at this early age, the former held responsibilities for caring for others – either a younger sibling or an ill or dysfunctional family member. This finding was consistent with the divorce adjustment process identified much earlier by Weiss (1979), "growing up a little faster." These children are now adolescent. Whether "winners, losers, or survivors" characterizes their functioning now or in adulthood is yet to be reported, though a glimpse at some of the adult literature helps articulate the diverse range of trajectories.

Social or psychological *survival* is the kernel of Hetherington's (1989) metaphor. Some recent data address survival in more concrete terms. Again, it is longitudinal research that provides pieces of the trajectories; this time, the destination is death. Yes, all developmental trajectories end there eventually, and a now-classic review (Bloom, Asher, & White 1978) documented the increased morbidity and mortality associated with marital separation and divorce. However, only recently has there been an intriguing lifelong longitudinal analysis that can contribute to the effort to map multiple alternative developmental trajectories for children whose parents divorce. In an archival prospective cohort design, Friedman and his colleagues (1995) followed up a sample of gifted children studied since their preadolescence in 1921, participants in the Terman Life-Cycle Study (a.k.a. "the Termites"). Using hazard regression analysis (survival analysis) to predict longevity, Friedman and associates found that in this group of more than 1,000, those children whose parents divorced faced a 33% greater mortality risk than those whose parents remained married, at least until the child reached 21 years. Death of a parent had little effect. "Only 13% of the people in the Terman sample had faced the divorce of their parents during childhood, a situation different from that faced by children today. . . . In the Terman sample, our analyses suggested that parental divorce was the key early social predictor of premature mortality, throughout the life-span" (p. 71).

Discussion

The preceding consideration of the correlates and effects of divorce in the lives of children, including the intergenerational transmission of divorce, confirms the heuristic value of the life-course approach and its emphasis on the "fundamental interplay of life trajectories (continuity) and turning points (change)" (Wheaton & Gotlib 1995). The following examination of some features of the approach highlighted by the divorce example will help to identify important challenges for researchers and for those who seek to use the approach to improve the quality of life for children – at the levels of clinical intervention and public policy both.

A turning point is, in most general terms, a change in the direction in the life course with respect to a prior established trajectory, a change that has the long-term impact of altering the probability of life destinations (see Chapter 1). Certainly, then, divorce is a turning point for many individuals. We reiterate our earlier clarification that divorce must be conceptualized not as a singular, time-delimited event but rather as a complex sequence of experiences. These experiences include, for example, the traumatic event of overhearing one's parents fight and finding one of them gone from the family home; legal proceedings; moving to new quarters or school; adapting to life in a single-parent household; reconstituting family life with a remarriage; and so on (Wertlieb 1991). Especially in this extended definition of the divorce experience, we agree with Wheaton and Gotlib's (1995) observation that many life trajectories include multiple turning points, with no easy distinction among them.

As a typology of turning points emerges, divorce is best acknowledged as a conditional turning point. It is pervasive, but not universal. Whereas early theory and research failed to distinguish among parental loss due to death, abandonment, or divorce – and tended to view single parenthood in a similarly undifferentiated fashion – more recent work documents numerous distinctions and implies specific ranges of alternative developmental pathways for children whose parents divorce. Some of these children will cope with remarriage, some will survive a subsequent divorce, and some will be among those who divorce in their adult lives.

Furstenberg and Cherlin (1991) begin their excellent review of divorce effects on children by noting that "divorce is only a transitional event" (p. 12). In the life-course approach adopted here, we take their implication as reference to the event as part of a complex set of experiences, rather than as a preclusion of its consideration as a turning point. Divorce is certainly a transition and sometimes merely a transition in a child's developmental trajectory. When divorce is best viewed as a "way station" and when it is best viewed as a turning point can be conceptualized. In many instances the most accurate or useful view, as articulated by Wheaton and Gotlib (1995), recognizes divorce as a "conditional turning point." Among the conceptual and empirical questions now worth asking is what are the variables and processes involved in a transition such as divorce reaching the threshold of becoming a (transformational) turning point? As one considers the complex and dynamic web of risk-and-resiliency factors that have been noted to influence the process of adaptation to divorce, which are most significant in specifying this "conditionality"? Which are generic, and which (if any) are "divorce-specific"? Sequence, timing, and context are key elements of any effort to address these questions, central as they are to the twin concepts of life trajectories and turning points. Caspi and Moffitt's (1993) "Paradoxical theory of personality coherence" provides a provocative framework for examining individual differences in light of the contextual ambiguity inherent in differentiating transitions and turning points.

Among the tensions experienced in conceptualizing and describing divorce as a conditional turning point is the interplay of nomothetic and idiographic specifications. We noted complex discrepancies between the findings of clinical research (e.g., Wallerstein & Blakeslee 1989), quasiexperimental investigation (Hetherington & Clingempeel 1992), and large-scale surveys (e.g., Cherlin et al. 1991). For the moment, the resolution posed by Emery and Forehand (1994) will suffice: clinical studies may exaggerate pathological outcomes; surveys may underestimate such outcomes; and notions of survival or coping despite underlying unhappiness need to enter our multidimensional repertoire of outcome indices. In the further articulation of the trajectory and turning-point approach, we will need to capitalize on the integration of clinical and qualitative investigation with experimental, quasiexperimental, and survey methods. The mutual interest in (and, indeed, reliance upon) longitudinal data can serve as an important integrative focus.

The powerful and poignant retrospective reports of "turning points" have prompted attention to this vehicle for the study of developmental continuities and changes (Clausen 1990). However, utility of the approach requires progress in specification and quantification of the processes and destinations so easily and matter-of-factly conveyed in personal narratives and interviews. The dilemmas are neither unfamiliar nor insufferable. Brewin, Andrews, and Gotlib (1993) confirm that the rich resources of retrospective narratives can be cultivated to address the task of mapping trajectories and turning points in individual's lives.

To date, we have a few long-term longitudinal data sets and a number of cross-sectional and longitudinal studies of children and of adults, with some linkage suggested across the schism between them. Among these links is the notion of intergenerational transmission discussed previously. Moreover, we have interesting reports from a cross-sectional prospective study of 258 children whose parents divorced within the prior two years (Sandler, Tein, & West 1994). This work, though currently at only a six-month follow-up, already shows the promise of contemporary inquiry that acknowledges and describes alternative developmental pathways for children whose parents divorce; it also demonstrates the utility of multifactorial stress-and-coping or risk-and-resiliency frameworks. Though not executed within an explicit perspective of life-course trajectories and turning points, this study provides some initial clues about individual differences in coping as well as the contexts that influence trajectories and mental health destinations for children whose parents divorce.

Developmental psychopathology, though relatively new in its emergence as a discipline, actually has a deep tradition of theory and longitudinal data relevant to the general questions of trajectories and turning points. Volumes edited by Robins and Rutter (1990), Rolf et al. (1990), and Haggerty et al. (1994), as well as the journal *Development and Psychopathology,* document numerous investigations that can be translated into understandings about trajectories and turning points. These studies involve personality traits and styles; delinquent, antisocial, and criminal behavior; and mild to severe psychopathology. Conspicuous in its absence from this literature is an explicit focus upon divorce as a variable, though it certainly is a recurrent (mostly negative) correlate. Previously, we have warned against the "psychopathologizing" of the divorce experience and have attributed this tendency to the focus of clinical and psychiatric research. It seems warranted and useful to revisit extant developmental psychopathology databases in order to consider analyses that use the focus of divorce as a turning point. The more recent balance in considering both salutary and negative effects, resiliency or buffering factors in addition to risk factors, and normative-objective frames (Barber & Eccles 1992) could facilitate this task.

Whether in reconsideration of extant data or in designing a prospective longitudinal study, one encounters the dilemma of our conceptual sophistication having outrun our methodological expertise. In the areas of measurement and statistical analysis, the elegance of our multifactorial models outpaces our resources and tools. On the horizon in family research – and well underway in a number of other domains and fields – are a number of promising methods that might benefit researchers who plan to pursue description of alternative trajectories and turning points for children whose parents divorce. Some of the methods provide an avenue for addressing the nomothetic–idiographic tension noted earlier. Magnusson and Bergman (1990) employ a "pattern" approach that facilitates operationalization of notions of sequences and aggregations as turning points. Of particular interest are recent uses of growth curve analysis in the study of learning disabilities (Francis et al. 1994; Shaywitz & Shaywitz 1994) and chronic illness (Clay et al. 1995). Such methods were used by Friedman and associates (1995) in their "Termite" study associating divorce with decreased longevity. Willet, Ayoub, and Robinson (1991) demonstrate the use of growth curve analysis to assess effectiveness of intervention for families at risk for child abuse or neglect. In this volume, Willet and Singer (Chapter 14) consider the use of these methods for studying turning points and life trajectories.

Motivating many researchers who map life trajectories of children of divorced parents is the desire to inform or craft appropriate interventions aimed at facilitating their adaptation in both childhood and adulthood (Sandler et al. 1994). Descriptions of turning points and trajectories in naturalistic terms is a step toward altering those trajectories and inserting positive turning points. In the clinical world there is no shortage of generic or specific interventions focused on the ills of divorce (Hodges 1986; Wolchik & Karoly 1988). To date, however, only a handful have empirical support (Alpert-Gillis, Pedro-Carroll, & Cowan 1989; Gottman 1993).

An interesting paradox or "catch-22" is evident in the literature reviewed here documenting divorce effects, reflecting both the complexity and confusion in our thinking as well as the influence of values upon our interpretations of data. In their comprehensive review of the risk-and-resiliency factors in adaptation to divorce, Emery and Forehand (1994) are explicit in noting group psychotherapy as a protective factor, albeit resting their conclusion upon a single study. Among school-age children whose parents divorced, the study demonstrated increased assertiveness and self-esteem as well as decreased anxiety for those who participated in a short-term psychoeducational intervention (Alpert-Gillis et al. 1989). In contrast, for Zill et al. (1993), the negative outcomes or "developmental problem areas" they assessed included "ever received psychological help." Indeed, 40% of their children from divorced families did receive such help, about twice the proportion in the nondivorced National Survey of Children sample. Furstenberg and Cherlin (1991) are appropriately circumspect in their assessment of extant mental health services: "Should these limited mental health interventions prove to be beneficial to a wide range of parents and children, they could become a valuable tool for managing the emotional upset of divorce" (p. 111).

Among the potential advantages of articulating trajectories and turning points in children's lives is the fit with the current agenda in developmental psychopathology that emphasizes targeting interventions in coherent and cost-effective ways (Kazdin 1992). Basic research (e.g., mapping trajectories) and evaluation of interventions (potential turning points) are both part of the enterprise. It remains unclear whether divorce – even in the broadened definition of experience (vs. event) adopted here – constitutes a "best practice" target, or whether some other element of the dynamic web of individual (e.g., age, temperament), familial (degree of conflict, access to each parent, etc.) or extra-familial (social support, etc.) risk-and-resiliency processes should be the focus. Among alternative foci are conflict resolution skills for parents and children and coping with poverty. Also inherent in the developmental psychopathology agenda is a shift of emphasis toward prevention. This shift also enables a public health and public policy perspective on addressing the needs of all children and families, including those who divorce.

We have applauded advances in appreciating and documenting the complexity of a life-course analysis of trajectories and turning points for children whose parents divorce, but we have also noted significant gaps and morasses in the available data. Nonetheless, the literature is replete with recommendations derived from these limited data to reform and craft relevant public policy. Sources are as diverse as the scientific literature (e.g., McLanahan & Sandefur 1994), "white papers" issued by such as the Institute for American Values (CFA 1995), and nonpartisan, nonprofit research organizations (e.g., Zill 1995). A rich and varied menu of policy recommendations aims at reducing economic insecurities, sharing responsibilities among parents and government agencies, and improving our basic and applied research technology. Each of the policy goals is to be applauded, though inherent conflicts and limitations constrain both clarity of position and enthusiasm for specific directions.

Winett (1995) has proposed a compelling generic framework for health promotion and disease prevention, a public health approach well-matched with the exigencies faced by children whose parents divorce (and by those who seek to understand and help them). Especially attractive is its developmental–ecological perspective, consistent with the trajectory and turning-point approach of this volume:

> A developmental perspective suggests other means of segmenting populations and better positioning, targeting and distributing interventions, including considering the cognitive and social abilities of children, planning product offerings to fit needs at important milestones (e.g., a move to a new school, the birth

of a child, or retirement), and assessing how products can be redesigned and offered at appropriate times and settings for people at different developmental points. . . . A developmental perspective also involves a careful examination of how settings can be modified through the consideration of public health measures and through ecological theory to benefit particular population segments. (p. 348)

These milestones, points, and settings are the markers of trajectories and turning points in the lives of children whose parents divorce. It is our hope that the next decade of research on these markers, and on the processes of risk and resiliency that anchor and energize them, will not only provide a fuller description of the needs and strengths of these children but also the means of reducing their risks and promoting their resiliency.

Note

1. Allen (1993) protests our tendency to label children whose parents divorce as "children of divorce," as if there were a single defining "social category" or feature of their lives. I concur that the label can be misleading or even damaging. Indeed, the highly contextual stress-and-coping and turning-point notions help describe the rich and complex variation in children's lives. See also Miller (1993) for an exposition on the influence of values on a related substantive literature: adolescent pregnancy and parenthood.

References

Allen, K. R. (1993). The dispassionate discourse of children's adjustment to divorce. *Journal of Marriage and the Family* 55: 46–50.

Alpert-Gillis, L., Pedro-Carroll, J., & Cowan, E. (1989). The children of divorce intervention program: development, implementation and evaluation of a program for young urban children. *Journal of Consulting and Clinical Psychology* 57: 583–9.

Amato, P. R. (1993). Children's adjustment to divorce: theories, hypotheses, and empirical support. *Journal of Marriage and the Family* 55: 23–38.

Amato, P. R. (1994). Life-span adjustment of children to their parents' divorce. *The Future of Children* 4: 143–64.

Amato, P. R., & Booth, A. (1991). Consequences of parental divorce and marital unhappiness for adult well-being. *Social Forces* 69: 895–914.

Amato, P. R., & Keith, B. (1991a). Parental divorce and adult well-being: a meta-analysis. *Journal of Marriage and the Family* 53: 43–58.

Amato, P. R., & Keith, B. (1991b). Parental divorce and the well-being of children: a meta-analysis. *Psychological Bulletin* 110: 26–46.

Barber, B. L., & Eccles, J. S. (1992). Long-term influence of divorce and single parenting on adolescent family- and work-related values, behaviors, and aspirations. *Psychological Bulletin* 111: 108–26.

Belsky, J., & Pensky, E. (1988). Developmental history, personality, and family relationships: toward an emergent family system. In R. A. Hinde & J. Stevenson-Hinde (eds.), *Relationships within Families: Mutual Influences*. Oxford University Press, pp. 193–217.

Block, J., Block, J., & Gjerde, P. (1986). The personality of children prior to divorce: a prospective study. *Child Development* 57: 827–40.

Bloom, B., Asher, S., & White, S. (1978). Marital disruption as a stressor: a review and analysis. *Psychological Bulletin* 85: 867–94.

Brewin, C. R., Andrews, B., & Gotlib, I. H. (1993). Psychopathology and early experience: a reappraisal of retrospective reports. *Psychological Bulletin* 113: 82–98.

Caspi, A., & Moffitt, T. E. (1993). When do individual differences matter? A paradoxical theory of personality coherence. *Psychological Inquiry* 4: 247–71.

Cherlin, A. J. (1992). *Marriage, Divorce, Remarriage,* rev. ed. Cambridge, MA: Harvard University Press.

Cherlin, A. J., Furstenberg, F. F., Chase-Lansdale, P. L., Kiernan, K. E., Robins, P. K., Morrison, D. R., & Teitler, J. O. (1991). Longitudinal studies of effects of divorce on children in Great Britain and the United States. *Science* 252: 1386–9.

Clausen, J. (1990). Turning point as a life-course concept. Paper presented to the American Sociological Association (August, Washington, DC).

Clay, D., Wood, P., Frank, R., Hagglund, K., & Johnson, J. (1995). Examining systematic differences in adaptation to chronic illness: a growth modeling approach. *Rehabilitation Psychology* 40: 61–70.

Council on Families in America [CFA] (1995). *Marriage in America: A Report to the Nation.* New York: Institute for American Values.

Crosbie-Burnett, M. (1994). Remarriage and recoupling. In P. C. McKenry & S. J. Price (eds.), *Families and Change: Coping with Stressful Events.* London: Sage, pp. 219–41.

Demo, D. H. (1993). The relentless search for effects of divorce: forging new trails or tumbling down the beaten path? *Journal of Marriage and the Family* 55: 42–5.

Dunlop, R., & Burns, A. (1995). The sleeper effect – myth or reality? *Journal of Marriage and the Family* 57: 375–86.

Elder, G. H. (1991). Life course. In *Encyclopedia of Sociology,* vol. 3. New York: Macmillan, pp. 1120–30.

Elder, G. H., Jr., Modell, J., & Parke, R. D. (1993). Studying children in a changing world. In G. H. Elder, Jr., J. Modell, & R. D. Parke (eds.), *Children in Time and Place: Developmental and Historical Insights.* Cambridge University Press, pp. 3–21.

Emery, R., & Forehand, R. (1994). Parental divorce and children's well-being: a focus on resilience. In Haggerty et al. (1994), pp. 64–99.

Francis, D., Shaywitz, S., Steubing, K., Shaywitz, B., & Fletcher, J. (1994). The measurement of change: assessing behavior over time and within a developmental context. In Lyon (1994), pp. 29–58.

Friedman, H., Tucker, J., Schwartz, J., Tomlinson-Keasy, C., Martin, L., Wingard, D., & Criqui, M. (1995). Psychosocial and behavioral predictors of longevity: the aging and death of the "Termites." *American Psychologist* 50: 69–78.

Furstenberg, F. F., & Cherlin, A. J. (1991). *Divided Families: What Happens to Children When Parents Part.* Cambridge, MA: Harvard University Press.

Furstenberg, F. F., & Teitler, J. O. (1994). Reconsidering the effects of marital disruption: what happens to children of divorce in early adulthood? *Journal of Family Issues* 15: 173–90.

Gottman, J .M. (1993). A theory of marital dissolution and stability. *Journal of Family Psychology* 7: 57–75.

Haggerty, R. J., Sherrod, L. R., Garmezy, N., & Rutter, M. (eds.) (1994). *Stress, Risk and Resilience in Children and Adolescents: Processes, Mechanisms and Interventions.* Cambridge University Press.

Hetherington, E. M. (1989). Coping with family transitions: winners, losers, and survivors. *Child Development* 60: 1–14.

Hetherington, E. M., & Clingempeel, W. G. (1992). Coping with marital transitions. *Monographs of the Society for Research in Child Development,* vol. 57.

Hetherington, E. M., & Furstenberg, F. (1989). Sounding the alarm. *Readings: A Journal of Reviews and Commentary in Mental Health* 4: 4–8.

Hodges, W. (1986). *Interventions for Children of Divorce*. New York: Wiley.

Kazdin, A. E. (1992). Child and adolescent dysfunction and paths toward maladjustment: targets for intervention. *Clinical Psychology Review* 12: 795–817.

Kelly, J., & Emery, R. (1989). Review of second chances: men, women and children a decade after divorce. *Family and Conciliation Courts Review* 27: 81–3.

Kiernan, K. (1992). The impact of family disruption in childhood on transitions made in young adulthood. *Population Studies* 46: 213–34.

Kitson, G. C. (1992). *Portrait of Divorce: Adjustment to Marital Breakdown*. New York: Guilford.

Kurdek, L. A. (1993). Issues in proposing a general model of the effects of divorce on children. *Journal of Marriage and the Family* 55: 39–41.

Lyon, G. R. (ed.) (1994). *Frames of Reference for the Assessment of Learning Disabilities: New Views on Measurement Issues*. New York: Brookes.

Magnusson, D., & Bergman, L. (1990). A pattern approach to the study of pathways from childhood to adulthood. In Robins & Rutter (1990), pp. 101–15.

McGue, M. (1994). Why developmental psychology should find room for behavioral genetics. In C. Nelson (ed.), *Threats to Optimal Development: Integrating Biological, Psychological and Social Risk Factors* (Minnesota Symposia on Child Psychology, vol. 27). Hillsdale, NJ: Erlbaum, pp. 105–19.

McGue, M., & Lykken, D. T. (1992). Genetic influence on risk of divorce. *Psychological Science* 3: 368–73.

McLanahan, S., & Sandefur, G. (1994). *Growing Up with a Single Parent: What Hurts, What Helps*. Cambridge, MA: Harvard University Press.

Miller, B. C. (1993). Families, science, and values: alternative views of parenting effects and adolescent pregnancy. *Journal of Marriage and the Family* 55: 7–21.

Robins, L., & Rutter, M. (eds.) (1990). *Straight and Devious Pathways from Childhood to Adulthood*. Cambridge University Press.

Rolf, J., Masten, A. S., Cicchetti, D., Nuechterlein, K. H., & Weintraub, S. (eds.) (1990). *Risk and Protective Factors in the Development of Psychopathology*. Cambridge University Press.

Sandler, I. N., Tein, J., & West, S. G. (1994). Coping, stress, and the psychological symptoms of children of divorce: a cross-sectional and longitudinal study. *Child Development* 65: 1744–63.

Shaywitz, B., & Shaywitz, S. (1994). Measuring and analyzing change. In Lyon (1994), pp. 59–68.

Turkheimer, E., Lovett, G., Robinette, C., & Gottesman, I. (1992). The heritability of divorce: new data and theoretical implications. *Behavior Genetics* 22: 757 (abstract).

Wallerstein, J., & Blakeslee, S. (1989). *Second Chances: Men, Women and Children a Decade after Divorce*. New York: Ticknor and Fields.

Weiss, R. (1979). Growing up a little faster: the experience of growing up in a single-parent household. *Journal of Social Issues* 35: 97–111.

Werner, E. E., & Smith, R. S. (1992). *Overcoming the Odds: High Risk Children from Birth to Adulthood*. Ithaca, NY: Cornell University Press.

Wertlieb, D. (1991). Children and divorce: stress and coping in developmental perspective. In J. Eckenrode (ed.), *The Social Context of Coping*. New York: Plenum, pp. 31–54.

Wheaton, B. (1990). Life transitions, role histories and mental health. *American Sociological Review* 55: 209–23.

Wheaton, B., & Gotlib, I. (1995). Trajectories and turning points over the life course: concepts and themes. [Chapter 1 in this volume]

White, L. K. (1990). Determinants of divorce: a review of research in the eighties. *Journal of Marriage and the Family* 52: 904–12.

Willett, J., Ayoub, C., & Robinson, D. (1991). Using growth modeling to examine systematic differences in growth: an example of change in functioning of families at risk of maladaptive parenting, child abuse, or neglect. *Journal of Consulting and Clinical Psychology* 59: 38–47.

Winett, R. A. (1995). A framework for health promotion and disease prevention programs. *American Psychologist* 50: 341–50.

Wolchik, S., & Karoly, P. (eds.) (1988). *Children of Divorce: Empirical Perspectives on Adjustment*. New York: Gardner.

Wright, R. (1994). *The Moral Animal: Evolutionary Psychology in Everyday Life*. New York: Pantheon.

Zill, N. (1995). Family change and student achievement: what we have learned, what it means for schools. In A. Booth & J. Dunn (eds.), *Family-School Links: How Do They Affect Educational Outcome?* Hillsdale, NJ: Erlbaum.

Zill, N., Morrison, D. R., & Coiro, M. J. (1993). Long-term effects of parental divorce on parent-child relationships, adjustment, and achievement in young adulthood. *Journal of Family Psychology* 7: 91–103.

10 Life after high school: development, stress, and well-being

Susan Gore, Robert Aseltine, Jr.,
Mary Ellen Colten, & Bin Lin

Introduction

Despite demographic studies indicating that a significant number of stressful role transitions occur during the early adult period (Hogan & Astone 1986), few studies have sought to investigate their impact on early adult adjustment (cf. Roberts & Bengston 1993). Moreover, taking a life-course perspective, early adulthood is an important transitional period during which development may continue on the trajectory established in adolescence or be altered in significant ways. Thus, mental health studies of young adults are important not only for describing functioning at this time of life, but also for advancing new lines of investigation that explore the patterning of psychological functioning over the life course.

In this chapter we report on a sample of young adults whom we have been studying since they were in high school. Using data obtained during the high-school years and from a post–high-school interview in 1992, we examine mental health and social functioning during this period and consider whether there are particular subgroups for whom post–high-school roles and experiences constitute a significant change or "turning point" in psychosocial functioning. We take graduation from high school as a focal transition event because it signals cultural expectations to find or explore a direction or set of goals involving economic independence and socioemotional attachments beyond the family of origin. Specifically, the roles and structure of daily life change considerably for most graduates and, as Jessor (1993) has underscored, there is a developmental reorganization of the principal ecological contexts: family, peers, work, and education. This degree of change and the required adjustment, in addition to the normative emphasis placed on the individual's independent efforts to shape the subsequent life course, can be expected to affect young adult mental health.

Support for this project was provided by the National Institute of Mental Health, Grant #R01-MH42909. We extend our thanks to Carol Cosenza for her research assistance and to members of CRISP for their helpful critique.

In addition, because transition from high school signals these important maturational challenges, we believe there is considerable turning-point potential inherent in this transition period, at least for some classes of individuals. Some evidence for this view is also available from interviews of our study participants when they were somewhat younger. Using these data, we were able to contrast a recently graduated cohort with the bulk of our study population who were still in high school with respect to depressed mood and other indicators of social functioning (Aseltine & Gore 1993). We found that earlier mental health and behavioral problems were less predictive of functioning one year later for the graduates than for the others. In other words, there was more continuity in the mental health trajectory of the youngsters still in high school, in contrast with discontinuity for those whose lives had changed in major ways. These findings suggested to us the opportunities for "turnarounds" and significant growth during the years immediately after the transition from high school. Now that our entire study population is beyond the high-school years, we can investigate the sources of change and whether the mental health of particular subgroups is more likely to change during the post–high-school years.

Postgraduation roles and psychological health

We have divided our sample into several groups reflecting some basic differences in direction or "tracks" that might shape post–high-school experience in both the short and long term. Our analyses involve group contrasts among individuals in three different role situations: working full time (nonstudent), being in college full time, and being unemployed or underemployed (nonstudent). In addition, we consider one variation in the full-time student situation: being enrolled in a four-year residential college versus commuting from the parents' home to a two- or four-year college. Guided by research on early adult development (Erikson 1986; Grotevant & Cooper 1988) and by Thoits's (1986, 1992) conceptualization of identity-relevant stress, we have assumed that identity issues express themselves in positive and negative experiences in roles involving school and work, as well as in social relations both in these settings and beyond: in the family, in friendships, and in intimate ties. Thus, different school and work situations can be expected to structure different types of problems in new roles and in social relationships, with these identity-relevant experiences in turn shaping mental health and well-being during this period.

The transition from high school to the world of work is a life event that brings about perhaps the most significant change from previous achievement-related roles, carrying with it distinctively new instrumental responsibilities and the expectation that economic independence will soon be attained. When the transition is successful, the young adult has found the niche that has been sought. Conversely, the absence of a work role may jeopardize relationships with significant others; in particular, it may deprive young adults of the economic means and a setting in which achievement and socialization needs can be met, with implications for mental health and development. Thus, in contrasting full-time workers with workers who are unemployed or underemployed, we expect that the unemployed/underemployed subgroup will evidence worse mental health; this may be accounted for by their having more deficits in relationships, more financial stress, and lower sense of satisfaction in their current and previous work life.

The contrast between residential and nonresidential college students interests us because it may illuminate how family and peer relations and postgraduation adjustment are affected by variation in the context of the college role. We expect that one advantage of residential schooling is the opportunity it provides to establish greater autonomy from parents without the degree of conflict that might ensue from living together. That is, young adult exploration of identity options tends to occur within a context of gradual and mutual redefinition of parent–child bonds (Steinberg, Elmen, & Mounts 1989). By virtue of its home-away-from-home quality, residential college offers room for exploration and change to take place, yet does not jeopardize family connectedness or bring with it risk of loss. In contrast, we might expect the commuting college student to be disadvantaged in this respect, because the close proximity of family provides more opportunity for parent–child disagreement and conflict concerning issues of identity exploration and commitment. Hence, for the young adult who commutes to college, there may be a poorer fit between the needs of the individual and the suitability of the environment to those needs. Commuting students may also find integration into peer networks to be more problematic. Although commuting students may have the benefit of maintaining some of their close friends from high school and the community, there is no assurance that this existing network will continue to be a useful arena for identity development; conversely, the relatively more homogenous nature of the residential college environment, which offers easy access to social opportunities, may better facilitate the choice of friends and dating partners.

Trajectories and turning points

In making this set of contrasts, we are emphasizing the ways in which postgraduation roles may structure social experience for different subgroups, with the varying experiences in turn affecting mental health. A different question is whether the qualities of the transition experience and observed changes in mental health should be interpreted as reflecting a trend in the ongoing psychosocial trajectory or, alternatively, as reflecting a turning-point experience. Our analytic focus on subgroups rather than individual case data necessarily dictates the possibilities we will uncover. For example, residential college students as a whole can be expected to experience a modest improvement in mental health and role functioning from high school to college, consistent with the position taken by Clausen (1991) that the family, through its resources and socialization environment, helps bring about this type of situation for its "planfully competent" offspring. In other words, the young adults whom we find in a relatively successful residential college situation at our postgraduation interview will have selected into that role, with these background forces and their personal capabilities continuing to make a positive impact on their functioning. According to Clausen (1991), it is this mutually reinforcing interaction of person and environment that shapes a stable life course (in his example, a successful life course) – a process of continuity that seems at odds with the notion of a turning point.

In contrast, to detect a turning point it must be possible for us to observe a discontinuity in functioning over time, with either a significantly better or worse developmental trend accompanying the role changes made with graduation. There is some reason to believe that this potential is inherent in the situation of young adults who become full-time workers. Although this relatively less advantaged subsample faces a potentially difficult transition, previous research on the poor fit between the high-school structure and curriculum and the developmental needs of nonacademically oriented students (Hamilton 1990) suggests that the full-time workers may use graduation as an opportunity to find an environment for which their instrumental goals and talents are better suited. This possibility for a turnaround is consistent with Rutter's (1990) understanding of "resilience" as a process involving the interplay between person and environment, and with his view that one mechanism for resilience is the opening up of opportunities that may be potentiated during periods of normative transition. Thinking of turning points as involving changes in the fit between person and environment also encourages us to consider the developmentally distinctive trajectories of our various work and school subgroups. It follows from these group differences that transition from high school will not have a uniform turning-point effect because any change in psychosocial functioning must be evaluated with reference to the pre-existing differences in pathways. Thus, the changes made at the transition from high school will constitute a turning point only for individuals in some subgroups – a position analogous to the diathesis-stress perspective in risk research, where the concept of diathesis in our framework is reflected in the subgroup differences that act in concert with early adult role experiences.

Method

Sample

The data for these analyses come from a prospective study of mental health and social adaptation in late adolescence and early adulthood. The first wave of the study, conducted in the spring of 1988, was based on a systematic probability sample of 1,208 ninth-, tenth-, and eleventh-graders in three community high schools in the Boston area. Youths were reinterviewed in 1989 and 1990 at approximately one-year intervals, and then again in 1992. Retention rates exceeded 85% in all three follow-ups, resulting in a wave-4 sample of 900 youths.

The analyses for this chapter utilize the second and fourth data collections because all students were in high school at the wave-2 interview, which is used as the pretransition assessment, and all students had left high school prior to the wave-4 interview. To avoid confusion, wave 2 is called "time 1" and wave 4 "time 2" throughout. Because we initially sampled young people in the ninth, tenth, and eleventh grades, these young adults have been out of high school for varying lengths of time at the time-2 interview. At time 2, members of the oldest cohort had been out of school just over three years, and the youngest cohort for just over one year.

The wave-4 sample consists of 41% boys and 59% girls, with the bulk (68%) of these individuals 19 and 20 years of age. Also at this interview, 43% of the sample report being in attendance at a residential college, 25% as a two- or four-year student commuting to college from home, 21% working full time (and non-student), and 12% working part time or unemployed (and nonstudent). For 34% of the sample, parents' highest attained educational level is high-school graduate or less. Forty-nine percent of the sample report a parent attaining a college degree, and 17% report a parent as having some college education. The sample includes few youths from extremely disadvantaged circumstances, and is almost entirely (94%) Caucasian.

Measures

Dependent variables. We take a broad view of adjustment and adaptation that incorporates attention to psychological distress as well as to general quality of life and positive self-perceptions. The measure of *depressive symptoms* used in this analysis is the Center for Epidemiological Studies Depression (CES-D) scale (Radloff 1977). This 20-item index assesses the self-reported frequency of depressive symptoms experienced over the past week on a four-point scale. In validation studies with samples of Oregon high-school students (Lewinsohn et al. 1993; Roberts, Lewinsohn, & Seeley 1991), elevated scores on the CES-D were highly predictive of clinical depression.

Problems of adjustment may also become manifest along different dimensions. Research on younger adolescents has indicated that the transition to junior high school is associated with a number of maladaptive cognitions, perhaps jointly influenced by achievement-related stressors and the normative shifts in self-definitions of competence that occur around that time (Ruble & Frey 1991). Concerns about mastery may also become salient during early adulthood, especially for young adults who are in a developmentally more precarious trajectory (i.e., part-time and unemployed workers whose major role is work). For this reason, we also consider *self-perceptions of mastery* as a measure of adaptation.

For these two outcome measures we are using change – in depressed mood and in perceptions of mastery – as a basis for evaluating the impact of the young adults' experiences in their various roles. In contrast with this assessment strategy, Clausen (1972) has argued that subjective reconstructions of influential events provide an important perspective on an individual's life history, which in our data may be reflected in young adults' retrospective appraisal of life quality during the time following graduation. In other words, graduates' satisfaction with life over this period should reflect their degree of comfort and success in the transitions they have made and in the roles they currently occupy. In order to assess this subjective component of adaptation, we use graduates' appraisals of satisfaction with "the way your life has changed since you left high school" as a single-item *quality-of-life* measure of adaptation. The wording of this question and the seven-point response scale (ranging from "delighted" to "terrible") follow the measurement strategy for quality-of-life assessments developed by Andrews and Withey (1976).

Independent variables and controls. The independent variables in this analysis were designed to capture a set of developmentally salient experiences for young adults across the various roles or tracks. A first set of variables encompasses young adults' evaluations of their *functioning in school and work roles*. These dimensions include: having money problems, enjoying school or work, feeling pressure at school or work, performing poorly at school or work, and being socially integrated at school or work. Each of these dimensions is assessed by three or four items asking respondents how true are a number of statements about their work or school experience (e.g., "you have made some good friends at school/work," a social integration item; "you have more to do than you can handle," a work/school pressure item). Pearlin and associates (1981) have characterized these kinds of social stresses as "role strains." Because the role experience variables pertain to postgraduation experiences, these questions could not be asked at time 1.

To supplement measures of role-related experiences, analyses also include measures of positive and negative aspects of peer and family relations, capturing conflict as well as warmth and support. *Conflict with parents over autonomy* is measured by five items assessing the extent to which young adults find their parents overprotective and interfering (e.g., parent(s) "act domineering and try to tell you what to do and how to run your life"). The measure of *family relationship problems* assesses the frequency of arguments with mother and father, being let down or disappointed by parents, the start of new problems with parents, and an increase in problems with parents. *Family support,* a three-item measure of positive affect in the family, assesses the extent to which the young adult feels loved and trusted by his or her parents and enjoys being with them. In addition, to assess a more behavioral aspect of family integration, we use a five-item measure of frequency of *talking with parents* about school and work problems, future plans, relationships, and family problems.

We also examine positive and negative aspects of young adults' relations with peers with measures that roughly parallel those used to assess family relations. *Friend stress* is a three-item measure of frequency of problems with friends, involving criticism, too many demands, and friends creating tensions and arguments. Conversely, the five-item measure of peer support asks young adults how true are a number of things about their friendships, including "having a friend you talk to about your private thoughts and feelings," "your friends are good at helping you solve problems," "you have a friend to count on for feedback on how you are doing." We also use a five-item measure of frequency of *talking with friends* from questions having the same content as the parent questions. To complete our assessments of relationships, we use a one-item measure of *satisfaction with dating and intimate relationships,* and a dichotomous measure of serious *love relationship problems* during the past three years. The latter variable consists of the number of serious relationships that have ended in an upsetting way (e.g., broken engagements, marital separations or divorces, upsetting breakups) between times 1 and 2.

Five control variables measured at time 1 are included in the analyses. *Family's standard of living* was assessed through a measure usually employed in studies of adult populations to assess income adequacy (Dubnoff 1985). Respondents were asked: "What best describes your family's standard of living – would you say you are very well off, living very comfortably, living reasonably comfortably, just getting along, nearly poor, or poor?" Family's social class was measured by *parents' highest level of educational attainment,* an ordinal variable ranging from completion of fewer than eight grades of school to having reached graduate or professional school. In addition, controls for young adults' *sex, age,* and *high-school grade-point average* are included. As with all study measures, these measures are derived from the respondents' self-reports.

Results

Predictors of post–high-school adaptation

Our first goal is to obtain an overview of the major influences of early adult adjustment. For each of the dependent variables we estimated regression models containing the predictor variables in the domains of family, friendship, and dating relations, as well as the work and school role functioning variables. Except for the retrospective measure of change in quality of life and the measures of

Table 1. *Significant associations between social relations and role functioning and outcomes*

	Depressed mood	Mastery	Quality of life
Family			
Family support	−	+	+
Family relationship problems	+	N.S.	N.S.
Conflict with parents	+	−	−
Talk with parents	N.S.	N.S.	N.S.
R^2 increment	0.027*	0.028*	0.028*
Friend			
Friend support	−	+	+
Friend relationship problems	+	−	N.S.
Talk with friends	−	N.S.	N.S.
R^2 increment	0.018*	0.030*	0.006
Dating			
Satisfaction	−	+	+
Failed relations	N.S.	N.S.	N.S.
R^2 increment	0.033*	0.017*	0.036*
Work and school roles			
Pressure	+	−	N.S.
Social integration	N.S.	N.S.	+
Poor performance	+	−	−
Enjoy school/work	−	+	+
Money problems	+	−	−
R^2 increment	0.033*	0.041*	0.057*
R^2	0.390	0.389	0.272

Notes: The R^2 is for the full regression model. The R^2 increment is the arithmetic difference in R^2 between the full model and the models omiting each set of time-2 predictors. All models control for background characteristics and baseline measures of predictors and outcomes. N.S. denotes not significant.
*$p \leq .05$.

school and work adjustment, these models also included the baseline (time-1) measures of the outcomes and the variables concerning role experience and social relations, which allows us to interpret the time-2 coefficients as the effects of change on postgraduation adaptation (Kessler & Greenberg 1981).

Table 1 summarizes the significant regression results, with signs indicating the direction of each effect. Family and friendship supports and stresses, as well as dating satisfaction, are fairly consistently associated with the three outcomes in the expected direction, with some exceptions. Interestingly, friendship stresses appear not to enter into appraisals of quality of life subsequent to graduation, although they are strongly related to depressed mood and sense of mastery. The measures of interaction with parents and friends (talk with parents, talk with friends) contributed little to the equation, probably due to their correlation with the more global indicators of parental and peer support, which were significantly associated with all three outcomes. Finally, among the set of role functioning measures, concerns about role enjoyment, performance, and money evidenced the most pervasive effects.

Patterns of effects become clearer through considering variance explained by each cluster of predictors. Familial relations have fairly consistent effects across the three outcomes, with an increment of almost 3% in variance explained. Satisfaction with dating and intimate relationships also brings about a significant increment (of roughly 2–3%) in variance explained across outcomes. Friendship support and conflict variables significantly affect sense of mastery, and to a lesser extent depressed mood, but have a negligible effect on quality of life since graduation. Adding together the variance explained by the friendship and dating satisfaction variables also suggests the importance of extrafamilial relationships during this transition, particularly with respect to depression and mastery.

The role functioning variables contribute the greatest increment in variance explained for all three outcomes. Importantly, the effects of these predictors are most pronounced in the quality-of-life domain, where the increments associated with friendships are more modest. Because increases in dating satisfaction also contribute heavily to quality-of-life appraisals, it is evident that young adults' thoughts about life quality subsequent to graduation are strongly influenced by success and satisfaction in the central activities of early adulthood: dating, work roles, and school roles. It should be noted that the total amount of variance explained for quality of life is much lower than that of the other two variables primarily because it is a retrospective measure of change and thus has no baseline control.

Subgroup differences in adaptation, relationships, and role functioning

The analyses to this point offer a general perspective on the influences of early adult adaptation. Although these roles are only recently embarked upon, we expect to find subgroup variation in these experiences and in adaptation because school and work roles should structure life experience, as well as perceptions of self and others, even at this early stage.

A first issue concerns whether the school or work pathway taken shapes change in postgraduation adaptation. Inspection of the mean levels of depressed mood and mastery in Table 2 indicates a secular change in the sample as a whole,

Table 2. *Means and standard deviations of depressed mood, mastery, and quality of life, by postgraduation work and school roles*

| Postgraduation role | Depressed mood | | | | Mastery | | | | Quality of life | |
| | Time 1 | | Time 2 | | Time 1 | | Time 2 | | Time 2 | |
	Mean	SD	Mean	SD	Mean	SD	Mean	SD	Mean	SD
Residential college student	10.6	7.69	9.05	7.27	15.8	3.26	17.0	3.16	5.99	0.86
Commuter college student	11.3	8.21	10.3	7.86	15.0	3.24	16.0	3.32	5.58	1.12
Working full-time	12.8	9.16	9.56	7.00	15.3	3.38	16.6	3.22	5.44	1.05
Working part-time or unemployed	14.8	9.34	14.4	9.55	14.6	3.19	15.2	3.38	5.09	1.37

Notes: These are unadjusted group means. SD denotes standard deviation.

in which all groups of young adults are improving after graduation. However, as the data in Table 2 indicate, the improvements in well-being following graduation are not as substantial for the young adults who are nonstudents and underemployed or unemployed, and these individuals also report the lowest levels of postgraduation quality of life: their average quality-of-life score falls in the "mostly satisfied" category (5 on the 7-point scale), whereas scores of the residential college students averaged in the "pleased" (6) category. As the data suggest, the positive changes in mastery and depressed mood from time 1 to time 2 for each of the three school and work subgroups are all significantly greater than the change seen in the unemployed/underemployed subgroup, with one exception: the commuter student group does not significantly differ from the unemployed/underemployed group with respect to change in mastery.

These trends over time also indicate that both those working full time and those who are underemployed or unemployed evidenced higher levels of depressed mood and a lower sense of mastery at the baseline than students who went on to college. Young adults working full time had the greatest positive change in depressed mood of all subgroups, suggesting the role of a successful transition in "turning around" a substantially poorer picture of mental health during the high-school years.

Given these group differences in baseline psychosocial functioning, Table 3 presents group differences in postgraduation adaptation net of controls for baseline functioning. The coefficients in the first column of each panel represent the contrasts between young adults working full time and those in each of

Table 3. *Postgraduation roles and well-being: subgroup contrasts in depressed mood, mastery, and quality of life*

Postgraduation role	Depressed mood				Mastery				Quality of life			
	B	SE	B	SE	B	SE	B	SE	B	SE	B	SE
Residential college student	0.085	0.089	—		0.005	0.093	—		0.504*	0.100	—	
Commuter college student	0.207*	0.090	0.122	0.080	−0.248*	0.095	−0.252*	0.084	0.120	0.102	−0.385*	0.090
Working full-time	—		−0.085	0.089	—		−0.005	0.093	—		−0.504*	0.100
Working part-time or unemployed	0.550*	0.113	0.466*	0.110	−0.336*	0.120	−0.341*	0.116	−0.328*	0.128	−0.833*	0.124
R^2	0.245*				0.157*				0.161*			

Notes: Regression coefficients from two mathematically equivalent equations are presented for each outcome. The first model contrasts all youths with those working full-time; the second contrasts all youths with those attending residential college. All models control for baseline levels of the respective outcomes, baseline measures of family and peer relations, and controls for age, sex, family's standard of living, and parents' education. SE denotes standard error.

* $p \leq .05$.

Table 4. *Changes in social relationships and postgraduation role functioning: group differences*

	Residential vs. Commuters	Residential vs. Work full-time	Work full-time vs. work part-time or unemployed
Family relations			
Family support			+
Problems with parents	−		−
Conflict with parents	−		−
Talking with parents		+	
Friend relations			
Friend support	+		
Friend stress			
Talking with friends		+	
Role functioning			
Enjoy school/work	+		
Feel pressured		+	
Social integration	+	+	+
Poor performance	−		
Money problems			−

Note: $p \leq .05$ for all relations indicated.

the other three school and work subgroups. In the second column, the contrast is between the residential college students and individuals in the other three subgroups. Looking first at contrasts with the full-time workers, these young adults not only have significantly lower depressed mood and higher sense of mastery than the underemployed/unemployed subgroup, but also fare significantly better than the commuting college students on these variables. Residential college students report a significantly better quality of life than the full-time workers, but are otherwise similar.

Taking residential college students as the comparison group, contrasts with the commuters are most relevant. These contrasts show that the commuters have lower levels of mastery and report a poorer quality of life since graduation, although they are not significantly more depressed. Evidently the strains that are experienced in this status do not bring about increases in negative affect but are reflected more subtly in cognitive appraisals of life quality and in self-perceptions of mastery.

To further explore subgroup contrasts, Table 4 describes group differences in postgraduation role experiences and social relations. Looking first at the differences in the experiences of the residential college students versus commuters, the former do evidence both fewer problems and conflicts with parents and higher levels of friendship support than the commuters, as predicted. The greater comfort of residential students in social relations is also evidenced in the domain of role functioning, as reflected in the social integration variable and in greater enjoyment of school. The contrasts between the residential college students and full-time workers are interesting in that they highlight some positive and negative aspects of each role. Workers experience less social integration and more performance worries, but fewer feelings of pressure than do residential college students. In social relations, the only difference that emerges is frequency of talking with parents and friends. Because the groups are otherwise similar in overall sense of support from family and friends, the findings on the "talking variables" may reflect differences in the orientation to social relations, with the college culture bringing about more self-examination through interaction with others. Finally, as compared with the full-time workers, underemployed and unemployed workers evidence less support and more problems in the family domain. They also report marginally less friendship support. We would have expected this group to evidence more pervasive problems in the role functioning domain, but again it is the social deficits (i.e., lack of social integration) that are highlighted, as well as financial concerns.

At this point we have observed some group differences in postgraduation adaptation as well as differences in their role experiences and social relationships. Building on these models with controls for background characteristics and baseline measures, we re-estimated the regressions to include the postgraduation role experience and social relations variables (data not shown). From these models we determined whether the group differences in outcomes described in Table 3 might be accounted for by group variation in the postgraduation role experiences and social relations seen in Table 4. Our strongest finding was in the contrast between the part-time and underemployed workers and their closest counterpart, the full-time workers. Here we found that for the mastery and quality-of-life outcomes, group differences in the variables concerning role experiences and social relations completely account for the better adjustment of the full-time workers. Controlling for the predictor variables reduced the group difference to nonsignificance (likewise, the degree of change in the coefficient representing the group contrast was not significant). Controlling for these variables also reduced somewhat the differences between these groups in depressed mood, but only marginally.

The contrasts when taking the residential college students as the reference group were not striking. Because the commuters and residential college students differed in so many aspects of their role experiences and social relations, and since the commuters did evidence lower postgraduation mastery and quality of life, we had expected that differences in adaptation might be explained by controlling for these life experiences. This was not the case; the group differences for the three outcomes were reduced by only about one third with the controls for the role experience and social relations variables. Finally, in our earlier analyses we found that the residential college students and full-time workers both evidenced high levels of postgraduation well-being, but that the workers gave lower ratings for quality of life since graduation. Controlling for the workers' somewhat poorer evaluations of their work roles did not account for this group difference in quality of life.

Discussion

Subgroup differences in mental health and processes of adjustment

We have focused on several tracks that define early adult school and work roles, recognizing that there is considerable flux in these pathways because the study population is relatively young. It is not surprising, therefore, that the most striking contrasts involved the full-time workers and the unemployed or part-time workers. These two groups can be seen as relatively similar in goals and orientation, but have differential success in making the transition from high school to the labor force. It is significant that the problems of the unemployed and underemployed workers are not limited to their work life. The social aspects of their life situation appear to be at least as problematic for them, since they report less family and friendship support as well as more problems and conflicts with parents. Even in the role functioning domain, social integration at their current job or (for the unemployed) last job is the prominent problem in addition to financial stress. When these stresses and deficits in support are controlled, the underemployed or unemployed workers do not significantly differ from full-time workers in mastery and quality of life.

By all criteria, the full-time workers appear to have made a highly successful adaptation. In terms of family and friendships, they look very much like the healthiest subgroup – residential college students – in that they show little sign of strain in the family and friendship domains. Although the full-time workers experience predictable problems and deficits on the job, the groups are similar in depressed mood and mastery.

Our data also suggest that it is appropriate to characterize the full-time workers as experiencing a turnaround in their mental health trajectory, which is an important way of manifesting psychosocial resilience. Given the full-time workers' relatively high level of depressed mood and low sense of mastery at time 1 (see Table 2), we suspect that the turnaround occurs after high-school graduation with the opportunity for change in the social environment – in particular, finding a better fit with a work setting than was the case with high school. In further evaluating this experience as a turnaround, it is useful to return to the contrast between the full-time workers and the unemployed or underemployed individuals. Although we lack detailed data about experiences during the three-year period between time 1 and time 2, we did employ a life chart at time 2 to record negative school and work disruptions occurring subsequent to high-school graduation. A preliminary look at this data reveals that the full-time workers as a group did not have a smooth transition to work after graduation. Like the unemployed or underemployed individuals, they had both school and job disruptions, and their mean number of school disruptions was only somewhat smaller than that experienced by the unemployed workers. Thus, it is tempting to say that their improvement in mental health represents an even more impressive turnaround. It is also the case, however, that at time 1 the workers were in somewhat better mental health than were the unemployed workers at time 1. This leads us to a more complex formulation of the process, in which we see elements of both continuity and change. That is, it is perhaps most accurate to say that the somewhat better pregraduation mental health of the workers allowed them to "select into" finding a suitable job and to cope with the disruptions that occurred before this employment. At the same time, the turning-point qualities of this transition are striking, because the workers were not in the best of mental health at time 1 and in addition did not differ from unemployed or underemployed individuals in their high-school grade-point average (data not shown).

The findings with respect to commuters may also speak to the issues of autonomy and new role definition, although these data are not as clear. On a descriptive level, the contrasts with residential college students indicate more stress at home for the commuters, less friendship support, and less enjoyment in social roles. Paralleling the findings for the subgroup of part-time workers and unemployed, the commuters experience many strains in social relations in addition to less satisfaction with their school situation. In the regression analysis, however, we found that controlling for these various strains did not account for the differences between the residential and commuter students. It is possible that subgroup differences may be due to the commuter's enhanced vulnerability to negative experiences in the home or at school, which is an interactive model not examined here.

A clue to this puzzle may also lie in understanding the antecedents of becoming a commuter college student. Going to a commuter college may be the result of a clear choice, a consequence of other school disruptions and other life events, of a failure to plan, or of other personal characteristics that also affect the quality of experience once this role is assumed. Turning again to our data on post–high-school disruptions, the data do indicate that the commuters have had more job and school disruptions between time 1 and time 2 than the residential college students. It seems likely that these changes in status relate to being a commuter student at time 2, a chain of events that emphasizes the problematic elements in the developmental trajectories of some commuting students. Thus, the variability in the commuter college subgroup (in terms of how they came to occupy this status) may have interfered with our effort to explain the contrasts in adaptation between this group and the residential college students.

Some final issues concern methodology. The fact that findings were not always consistent across the set of dependent variables suggests the value of casting the net widely. A few points can be made in this respect. First, although the full-time workers are exceedingly well-off in terms of depressed mood and mastery, their quality of life is not on a par with that of the residential college students. In fact, their mean value is slightly lower than that of the commuter students. This transition should be more challenging for the full-time workers than the residential college students, and the group difference in quality of life suggests that their hardships are reflected in somewhat attenuated positive cognitions about change (or perhaps due to curtailed hopes for the future). Looking across the entire sample, another value to our focusing on quality of life in addition to mastery is that the former is where the role functioning variables seem to have their biggest impact (see Table 1). Finally, in contrasting full-time workers with the part-time and unemployed workers, we found that role experiences and social relations explained little in the depression differential but reduced to nonsignificance the group differences on the other two outcomes. Thus, were we to have limited the analysis to depressed mood alone, some important group differences in adjustment would have been overlooked.

In our analytic design, the variables pertaining to role experience and social relations, as well as the three dependent variables, are all measured concurrently through self-reports at time 2. Thus, we may be incorrect in assuming that postgraduation statuses shape social relations and role experiences, in turn affecting depressed mood, mastery, and appraisals of life quality. For example, negative changes in the family environment may influence a young person's ability to get settled in a satisfactory work or school situation. In addition, with respect to the young adults who are underemployed or unemployed, time-2 appraisals of their affect and their social environment could be seen as a syndrome, with negative affect and poor social relations reciprocally interrelated. With our research design it is impossible to be certain about processes, but there are theoretical considerations that focus our attention on the etiological role of the strains in the domain of social relations and social integration. We argued at the outset that the residential college setting makes readily available a new peer group that can meet affiliative and social developmental needs of young adults who choose this pathway. In contrast, other subgroups of graduates can be expected to have more difficulty in finding and maintaining new friendships. This view is supported by our data. It is striking that the only variable in the role functioning area that is problematic for the commuting students, the full-time workers, *and* the part-time or unemployed workers is the social integration variable. Because the developmental perspective assumes that identity development and growth occur through social relationships in family, school, and work contexts, the data would seem to support the social causation view that a lessened sense of mastery and a lower quality of life result when new roles and life situations thwart the social needs of young adults.

These analyses will be replicated and extended when our entire sample of young adults is beyond the college years, allowing us to better model these prospective longitudinal relationships. On the basis of this preliminary picture, we conclude that differences in challenge and adjustment can be seen even at this early stage, that failure to find a niche at work or school are the major pitfalls of this life period, and that early adulthood offers the opportunity for positive turning-point experiences.

References

Andrews, F. M., & Withey, S. B. (1976). *Social Indicators of Well-Being: American's Perceptions of Life Equality.* New York: Plenum.

Aseltine, R. H., Jr., & Gore, S. (1993). Mental health and social adaptation following the transition from high school. *Journal of Research on Adolescence* 3: 247–70.

Clausen, J. A. (1972). Life course of individuals. In M. W. Riley, M. Johnson, & A. Foner (eds.), *Aging and Society,* vol. 3. New York: Sage, pp. 457–514.

Clausen, J. S. (1991). Adolescent competence and the shaping of the life course. *American Journal of Sociology* 96: 805–42.

Dubnoff, S. (1985). How much income is enough? Measuring public judgements. *Public Opinion Quarterly* 19: 285–9.

Erikson, E. H. (1986). *Identity: Youth and Crisis.* New York: Norton.

Grotevant, H. D., & Cooper, C. R. (1988). The role of family experience in career exploration: a life-span perspective. In P. B. Baltes, D. Featherman, & R. M. Lerner (eds.), *Lifespan Development and Behavior,* vol. 8. Hillsdale, NJ: Erlbaum, pp. 231–57.

Hamilton, S. F. (1990). *Apprenticeship for Adulthood: Preparing Youth for the Future.* New York: Free Press.

Hogan, D. P., & Astone, N. M. (1986). The transition to adulthood. *Annual Review of Sociology* 12: 109–30.

Jessor, R. (1993). Successful adolescent development among youth in high-risk settings. *American Psychologist* 48: 117–26.

Kessler, R. C., & Greenberg, D. F. (1981). *Linear Panel Analyses: Models of Quantitative Change.* New York: Academic Press.

Lewinsohn, P. M., Hops, H., Roberts, R. E., Seeley, J. R., & Andrews, J. A. (1993). Adolescent psychopathology: I. Prevalence and incidence of depression and other DSM-III-R disorders in high school students. *Jounal of Abnormal Psychology* 102: 133–44.

Pearlin, L. I., Lieberman, M. A., Menaghan, E. G., & Mullan, J. T. (1981). The stress process. *Journal of Health and Social Behavior* 22: 337–56.

Radloff, L. S. (1977). The CES-D scale: a self-report depression scale for research in the general population. *Applied Psychological Measurement* 1: 385–401.

Roberts, R. E., & Bengtson, V. L. (1993). Relationships with parents, self-esteem, and psychological well-being in young adulthood. *Social Psychology Quarterly* 56: 263–77.

Roberts, R. E., Lewinsohn, P. M., & Seeley, J. R. (1991). Screening for adolescent depression: a comparison of depression scales. *Journal of the American Academy of Child and Adolescent Psychiatry* 30: 58–66.

Ruble, D. N., & Frey, K. S. (1991). Changing patterns of comparative behavior as skills are acquired: a functional model of self-evaluation. In J. Suls & T. A. Wills (eds.), *Social Comparison: Contemporary Theory and Research*. Hillsdale, NJ: Erlbaum, pp. 79–113.

Rutter, M. (1990). Psychosocial resilience and protective mechanisms. In J. Rolf, A. Masten, D. Cicchetti, K. Neuchterlein, & S. Weintraub (eds.), *Risk and Protective Factors in the Development of Psychopathology*. Cambridge University Press.

Steinberg, L., Elmen, J. D., & Mounts, N. S. (1989). Authoritative parenting, psychosocial maturity, and academic success among adolescents. *Child Development* 60: 1424–36.

Thoits, P. A. (1986). Multiple identities: examining gender and marital status differences in distress. *American Sociological Review* 51: 259–72.

Thoits, P. A. (1992). Identity structures and psychological well-being: gender and marital status comparisons. *Social Psychology Quarterly* 55: 236–56.

11   Turning points in midlife

Elaine Wethington, Hope Cooper, & Carolyn S. Holmes

This chapter describes three exploratory studies of psychological turning points during the middle years. A psychological *turning point* is defined as a perceived, long-lasting redirection in the path of a person's life (Clausen 1993). The initial impetus for this project was to expand empirical knowledge of human development in adulthood, exploring both continuities and discontinuities in personality, beliefs, experience, and management of life problems. Until relatively recently, theoretical speculation and research on human development in midlife has been dominated by a life or developmental stages paradigm (e.g., Gould 1978; Levinson et al. 1978; Loevinger 1976; Sinnott & Cavanaugh 1991), and more popularly by the "midlife crisis" (Sheehy 1976, 1995). According to these perspectives, midlife change is triggered by encounters with normatively expected transitions associated with social maturity, such as taking leadership of the family, launching children, and reaching the peak of one's work career. According to the life and developmental stages perspective, successful transit through midlife is characterized by a growing acceptance of responsibility toward others, a sense of maturity, and emotional and personal fulfillment in response to fulfilling social obligations (Levinson et al. 1978; Riegel 1975). The "crisis" perspective, on the other hand, tends to emphasize the struggle rather than the fulfillment: profound social and personal changes may be resisted, perceived as difficult to accomplish, or seen as symbolic of impending aging and death, rather than welcomed as indicative of accomplishment and work well-done.

Researchers have long questioned the specifics and overall utility of the age-graded stages of development perspective that underlie both the venerable research paradigm as well as the popular image of the midlife crisis. One difficulty of the stages of development perspective is that it was designed to fit the male life course (e.g., Levinson et al. 1978); women were left out (Apter 1995;

This program of research was supported by grants to Ronald C. Kessler and Elaine Wethington from the MacArthur Foundation Research Network on Successful Midlife Development and USDA grant #321-7419 to Elaine Wethington. We owe special debts to George W. Brown, Bert Brim, and members of the MacArthur Foundation Research Network on Successful Midlife Development for their suggestions at critical phases of this project.

215

Friedan 1993; Perun & Bielby 1980). Another difficulty is that studies operationalizing the perspectives on midlife development outlined by Gould (1978) and Levinson and colleagues (1978) have found that the majority of men in midlife do not report an experience resembling a midlife crisis (e.g., Farrell & Rosenberg 1981; McCrae & Costa 1990). A recent review of midlife crisis studies by Brim (1992) estimated that only about 10% of men report such experiences. More recent empirical research in population-representative samples, using standard measures of psychological adjustment, has also called into question the crisis perspective on midlife. Self-reported psychological distress is, on average, the lowest among middle-aged men and women, compared to other age groups (Kessler et al. 1992). Personality stasis, rather than change, seems to characterize both men and women through their middle years (McCrae & Costa 1990).

Yet the crisis perspective persists on several levels, the most notable being the frequent media attention that it receives. The term "midlife crisis" is a staple of the literary and popular entertainment scene. The first author reviewed headlines and feature articles in the *New York Times* Living Arts section for 15 months, beginning in late 1994. The term "midlife crisis" was used an average of twice a month to headline a review of a major book, film, or television program. For example, the insecurity and befuddlement experienced by the male lead of the movie *Sabrina* after falling in love for the first time was characterized as a midlife "meltdown." The term "midlife crisis" appeared weekly in feature stories, generally portrayed as a real entity that loomed for both women and men (although in slightly different flavors). Prestigious fictional works and commentary (e.g., *Fly-fishing through the Midlife Crisis* and *Gray's Anatomy*) interpret personal experience through this lens. (One reviewer even complained that *Fly-fishing* did not have *enough* about the midlife crisis in it.) Even the works of an author as venerable as Jane Austen have been subjected to current interpretations of how beliefs and behaviors change in middle age: much has been made of Austen's youth while writing the exuberant and sardonic *Sense and Sensibility* versus her middle age while writing the "mature" love story *Persuasion*.

The midlife crisis has also become a therapeutic and counseling theme. In response to popular interest in adjustment in the middle years, a therapeutic subindustry ("midlife crisis counseling," "preparing for the midlife crisis") has grown up to meet a number of people's expectations that a crisis during midlife is inevitable. Perhaps more likely, young men and women who in the past have sought therapy to adapt to adult life are now seeking more (but different) therapy to adapt to the responsibilities and changes of middle age.

In addition, there may be a material basis for belief in the midlife crisis among the most culturally influential age group in current American society, the Baby Boom generation. This generation – relatively highly educated, adept in the everyday language of pop psychology, and used to breaking the rules about age-appropriate behavior inherited from previous generations (Strass & Howe 1991) – may be seizing upon the media image in order to encapsulate its own unique experience with aging through the middle years. (Perhaps the *New York Times* writers and reviewers who are Baby Boomers are shaping that understanding now.) As Baby Boomers have aged, they have observed changes in their own behavior toward others and in attitudes toward themselves. Following old habits, they analyze and dissect them. These changes may not in most cases have reached what a stress researcher or other social scientist may be comfortable calling a "crisis," but people may be trying to derive personal meaning from these changes by interpreting them as indicators of the midlife crisis, a handy and culturally available label.

We know of no research that has tracked belief in the midlife crisis over time. Our own research, reported in this paper, suggests that middle-aged people (defined broadly as those age 30–70) readily see themselves as having grown wiser, "tougher," and more realistic over their lifetimes. People may not see themselves in crisis throughout their middle years, but they do perceive that they have changed and matured in response to external events. The pilot studies described in this chapter seek to understand how ordinary people perceive psychological changes occurring in themselves. The assumptions of the project are that the type, timing, and sources of these changes are highly variable across individuals but that they are more apt to occur in contexts that demand a reassessment of strengths and weaknesses, moral values, decisions made in the past, and plans and expectations for the future. Pilot data on the psychological experiences and changes we call *psychological turning points* have suggested that the sources of these reassessments are major life events, role transitions with a great deal of personal or social meaning, and periods of reflection prompted by events that symbolize the advance of aging or the finite nature of life, such as the sudden death of a middle-aged acquaintance.

The concept of a turning point has the potential for orienting systematic research in this area, as well as for replacing the term "midlife crisis." Following Clausen (1993), a turning point is defined as a period or point in time in which a person has undergone a major transformation in views about the self, commitments to important relationships, or involvement in significant life roles (e.g., job, marriage). A turning point involves a fundamental shift in the meaning, purpose, or direction of a person's life and must include a self-reflective awareness of, or insight into, the significance of the change. Major life events, chronic difficulties, normative life transitions, minor events, and such internal, subjective changes as self-realizations or reinterpretations of past experiences may bring on a turning point. These can be either positive or negative in character.

In this chapter we report preliminary findings related to four specific research issues: (1) adults' perceptions of their experience of psychological turning points; (2) experiences, role transitions, and events perceived as having triggered turning points; (3) the relation (if any) between turning points and depression, another profound psychological experience; and (4) life-course-related factors (e.g., normative expectations for age- or status-appropriate behavior and achievements) associated with experiencing a turning point.

Research perspective

This study utilizes a perspective combining two well-established theoretical approaches: the stress–crisis and life-course perspectives. The stress–crisis approach, as empirically developed by Brown and Harris (1978), asserts that the sorts of life stressors that provoke severe psychological and physical distress are those posing the most direct challenge or threat to long-held plans and intentions. After experiencing such stressors, people often report that life has lost its "meaning"; in turn, resolution comes when such meaning is restored. Often, these resolutions are experienced as new beginnings, or "fresh starts." Following Brown and Harris, this project hypothesizes that life events are the catalysts, or triggers, that bring about turning points.

The life-course perspective (Elder & Rockwell 1979; Perun & Bielby 1980) assumes that the content and timing of individual transitions are dependent on historical and social structural factors that shape the typical life course of individuals in particular social groups and at particular historical times, as well as on individual biography. For the purposes of this research, psychological turning points are defined from the point of view of people reporting them; however, it is assumed as well that normative expectations for the behavior and achievements to have been completed by a particular chronological age, for a particular social group, and at a particular historical time shape the propensity to have a psychological turning point following a specific trigger. Thus, while the research relies on the point of view of the individual who is changing, an essential assumption is that the content and timing of turning points is dependent on factors that shape the typical life course of individuals at particular historical times.

Research on psychological turning points

Clausen (1993) provided a useful and thorough description of which psychological experiences may constitute a life turning point. According to Clausen, a psychological turning point can occur when an individual has an experience or a realization that induces *reinterpretation of past experiences* in a fundamental way. A turning point is a perceptual reinterpretation or reorientation directed at the self, a close significant other, or activities in a major life role (e.g., work, marriage, parenting, self-development). Clausen's empirical research uncovered four types of turning points; essentially, these are changes in perceived *identity.*

One type of turning point involves a change or reformulation of commitment to a major life role, to activities in a major life role, or to a relationship with a close, significant other. However, not all changes or reformulations of this sort are also turning points. In order for a psychological turning point to occur, there must eventually emerge (or pre-exist) a self-reflective awareness of, or insight into, the significance of the change to one's future life.

A second type of turning point is a major change in perspective on life. This sort of experience also may or may not qualify as a turning point, depending on whether there is evidence that this new perspective involves new insight about the implications of the change. A third type of turning point is a change in important life goals. A fourth type of turning point is a major change in view of the self, defined as profound realizations about one's strengths and weaknesses. Similarly, to qualify as turning points, these experiences must also involve new insights or evidence that redirection was attempted because of this insight.

The role of stress and adversity as a trigger for turning points

In previous research (e.g., Kessler & Wethington 1991; Mattlin, Wethington, & Kessler 1990; Wethington, Brown, & Kessler 1995) we have adapted aspects of the Life Events and Difficulties Schedule (or LEDS; Brown & Harris 1978) for use in improving life event measurement in conventional surveys. To address the present issue, we were immediately attracted to the potential of LEDS interviewing techniques and its associated event rating system for extracting reports of turning points, providing an initial system for organizing and categorizing these reports, and examining (in at least an exploratory way) their causes.

Figure 1 presents the relations we hypothesize among stressful experiences and other triggers, psychological turning points, and another profound psychological experience – depression. Social role transitions can lead to psychological turning points if the role transition involves exposure to unexpected, challenging, or unforeseen changes in the self, or if the transition in and of itself marks a fateful turn in life, precluding taking other paths. The resolution of a long-term chronic difficulty can lead to a turning point if the resolution of the difficulty involves changing a significant aspect of the self, such as a self-generated and motivated reversal of something that had been bothersome for a long time (see also the "dynamic" developmental research approach described in Labouvie-Vief 1982 and in Labouvie-Vief, Hakim-Larson, & Hobart 1987). A symbolic event – defined as a minor event (such as the death of a middle-aged acquaintance) that symbolizes future change – can lead to a turning point if it prompts a period of reflection that leads to a resolution to change enduring habits of life.

Severe, negative events may also lead to a turning point. First, a severe negative event or the onset of a long-term difficulty may provoke a period of reflection that leads to a psychological turning point. This causal change might be

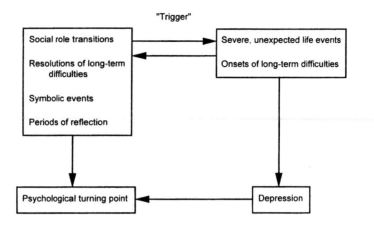

Figure 1. Hypothesized relationships among triggers, psychological turning points, and depression.

mediated by an episode of depression. Other people may have the depression without the turning point, which suggests that there are a number of personal factors impeding or facilitating the experience of a turning point.

Methods

In our studies, we have developed a series of questions tapping experiences as potential turning points. Using intensive, semistructured interviewing techniques, we ask men and women aged 30–70 if they have recently experienced changes in the way they think or feel about themselves, significant others, or their plans and dreams for the future (see Appendix). We probe respondents about what events or circumstances may have caused this experience, what else was going on in their lives at the time that could have added more stress to the experience, how the experience has affected different aspects of their lives, and whether the experience has changed their views of who they are and what they can accomplish in the future.

The three studies

The purpose of study 1 was to examine the phenomenon of psychological turning points. The purpose of study 2 was to explore the relation between psychological experiences and stressful life events. Study 3 was conducted to prepare for 1,000 telephone interviews about midlife turning points and other psychological experiences. For this larger study (sponsored by the MacArthur Foundation Research Network on Successful Midlife Development), a telephone version of the instrument had to be developed. The study Ns and populations are summarized in Table 1.

Table 1. *Study populations*

Study	N	Age range	Recruitment strategy	Method of interviewing
1	70	28–65	Volunteer	Face-to-face; semistructured
2	125	21–70	Purposive selection from volunteers	Face-to-face; semistructured
3	138	21–79	Population-representative sample	Telephone; semistructured
4[a]	1,000	30–70	Population-representative sample	Telephone; semistructured

[a] In progress.

Measures

Because the purpose of study 1 was to discover the boundaries of – and then classify a broad group of reports into a typology of – turning points, a qualitative method of discovery was used. "Stem" questions embodying Clausen's (1993) typology of psychological turning points were written. We experimented with a number of different ways of asking the turning-point stem questions and probing for information.

Based on extensive pilot work, questions were written to represent psychological turning points in three different areas of life. Respondents were asked if they had experienced a "turning point like that" in the past twelve months (see Appendix for examples); if they had not, they were asked if they had experienced a turning point in the past five years. The three areas of life and identity explored were love relationships and nurturance, work, and the self (which includes health). In addition to the psychological turning-point questions, questions about major life events and transitions (e.g., job loss, marriage, divorce) were also included in the interview, anticipating that some respondents might not initially understand the turning-point questions but could have experienced a turning-point–like change in response to a life event.

If a respondent answered "yes" to one of the turning-point or life event questions, the response was probed. A series of optional, semistructured probe questions were developed. These probes were designed to encourage respondents to report the nature of their psychological reactions to these events and turning points, as well as the implications of the event or turning point for other domains of life and feelings about the self (see Appendix).

Respondents for study 1 were recruited from several sources. Many were recruited from a subject pool of adults in southeastern Michigan maintained by the Institute of Gerontology (University of Michigan). Others were recruited through newspaper advertisements and contacts at a local community college. A total of 70 adults aged 30–65 contributed usable data to this study. All respondents were volunteers, and a large number volunteered in order to describe what they called their "midlife crisis."

Because this was a volunteer and convenience sample, no claim can be made for its representativeness. Concerted efforts were made to recruit respondents from diverse social, educational, and racial backgrounds; nevertheless, the sample does not adequately represent people of lower social status. The sample was 60% female and 89% white; the mean age of respondents was 47.

For study 2, a volunteer sample of 125 community-dwelling residents was recruited in 1992. The investigators placed advertisements in local newspapers and posted flyers at local community college billboards, welfare offices, the YMCA, and churches. Respondents were offered $25 to participate. In order to avoid overrepresentation of white, highly educated college-town dwellers in the sample, recruitment was concentrated in an industrial city with a high unemployment rate and a large minority population. Volunteers for the study were screened on the telephone, and were selected to provide a balance of sex, race, age, and educational characteristics. The sample was 25% minority.

The sample recruitment strategy resulted in an unusually high proportion of study respondents who reported an episode of depression in the previous year (45%). A number of volunteers were residents of the YMCA, long-term unemployed, or substance abusers. Given that most studies of midlife are conducted among those with advantaged backgrounds, the overrepresentation of very disadvantaged people made possible a wider canvass of self-perceived midlife change than is typically attempted.

For study 3, a national sample of telephone numbers was purchased from Survey Sampling, Inc. One hundred and thirty-eight interviews were completed in the summer of 1994. The third pilot survey met three objectives important for pursuing further research. First, the pilot study served as the means of adapting a heretofore face-to-face interview for the telephone. The adaptations included shortening questions to make them usable on the phone and developing intensive semistructured telephone probing techniques for gathering information about the experiences. The second objective of the pilot study was to examine the distribution of turning points in an unselected sample. The previous pilot studies recruited volunteers from populations more likely to report a midlife crisis or to be experiencing severe social stress. The third objective was to examine the association between self-reports of turning points and episodes of depression in the past twelve months. The response rate was 50%; this figure is low because no refusal conversion was attempted.

Analysis methods

The answers to the turning-point questions in the interviews were transcribed, as well as briefly summarized in writing by the interviewers during the interview. The transcriptions and written summaries were analyzed by the investigators and classified into categories. The classification scheme evolved over time in response to the growing variety of experiences related in the interviews as the composition of the samples changed.

Three types of classification were carried out, in sequence. The first was a classification by type of event or experience – revelation about another, fulfilling a special dream, or change in a close relationship (see Appendix). The second classification was by degree. Experiences were rated for the degree or severity of life change they seemed to entail. (The rating was done by the first author, who has been trained in the LEDS event and difficulty rating system advanced by Brown & Harris 1978.) The third classification was conducted on the reported experiences that seemed likely to be psychological turning points in Clausen's (1993) typology. In this step, experiences were classified by their self-reported causes into four categories. The categories were: triggered by a negative severe life event or chronic difficulty (as defined by Brown & Harris 1978); triggered by a positive major life event or transition; triggered by a minor event particularly symbolic to the respondent; or occurring without an event in the social environment (e.g., period of reflection, religious conversion, etc.). Because a number of the respondents described their experiences while undergoing therapy, a category representing turning points attributed to psychological treatment was added during analysis of the transcripts.

Results

Types of turning points

By definition, a turning point is a psychological process; that is, it involves changes in awareness, a new self-insight, or new reflection about the meaning of things. The new awareness, insight, or reflection can be focused on one's motivations, limitations, or talents, or it can be focused on situational factors and external circumstances that have an impact on one's life.

The reported psychological turning points indeed fall into two large categories: self-insights, which are essentially new insights and awareness into one's motives, personal limitations, and talents; and insights into situational factors, such as the behavior or motives of significant others, limits to controlling specific situations, and the need to control emotional reactions through endurance or diversion into other activities. These two classifications emerged from the semistructured probes designed to gather self-reflective data about psychological insight. The types of self-reported turning points that emerged from the study are listed in Table 2.

The most frequently reported turning point was an *awareness of growth and development*. These were almost always reported in the context of relationship, job, or other role change. The words respondents used most often to describe the turning points were "new maturity," "finally growing up," and a new "sense

Table 2. *Typology of psychological turning points (combined studies)*

A. Awareness of growth and development
Relationship(s) have/has become closer
   (a) Achieves greater intimacy in relationship(s)
   (b) Renewed commitment to relationship(s)
   (c) As a result of taking on a new role
Sense of self becoming more mature
   (a) Self-insight and new realizations about self and personality
   (b) Feeling of having "grown up"
   (c) New sense of responsibility or commitment toward relationships or work
"Mastery" experience
   (a) Feeling like a success due to hard work
   (b) Changing behavior; overcoming a bad/harmful habit
   (c) Taking on a new role and mastering unusual challenges

B. Awareness of the need to change the self
Struggling to figure out how self need(s)(ed) to change in order to accommodate to
   external changes
   (a) Process of re-evaluating commitments, values, decisions, relationships, and work life
   (b) Experiences in therapy and self-help groups

C. Asserting control over choices and direction of life
Took definite steps to shape aspects of life
Taking on a new hobby or avocation that builds self-esteem
Decisions reflecting a commitment to role, relationship, or work
Renewal of commitment to role, relationship, or work
Assertive self-reliance

D. Recognition of limitations
Learned that another person could not be controlled
Learned that a job situation could not be controlled
Learned that some other aspect of life (e.g., personality) could not be controlled
Acceptance; resignation; endurance

E. Experiences of psychological loss or relinquishment
Expresses feelings of regret about situation or person; no repair possible
Compensating for dissatisfaction – takes on a new hobby or avocation in response to
   impending loss
Relinquishes hope of fulfilling dream

F. Managing mental health problems or depression

G. Giving up completely

---

of responsibility." Feelings of new or renewed "mastery" were also reported in this context, due to hard work, facing new challenges, or changing old destructive habits.

Another frequently reported turning point was a new awareness of the *need to change the self in the future.* These were reported by people who did not perceive a great deal of change occurring in their personalities or views or habits, but who nevertheless had experiences that triggered a process of reevaluating commitments, values, past decisions, relationships, or work life. The most commonly mentioned themes were "struggle," "accommodate to change," and the use of psychological therapy and self-help groups. These could be characterized more precisely as psychological turning points in the making.

Another recurring theme of description was *asserting control over choices and direction of life*. These were actions that involved taking definite steps to shape the future, taking on new avocations, or making decisions that had an impact on commitments to work, family, or other important roles. Common respondent descriptions were "self-assertiveness," "self-reliance," and "renewal."

Many respondents also reported that their psychological turning points involved a discovery of their own limitations. They learned that another person, a job, or their own personality could not be controlled, and that they must discover how to accept and adapt. Among older respondents (older than age 55), the themes of "resignation," "acceptance," and "endurance" predominated. Younger respondents were more likely to dwell on their feelings of psychological loss and regret at these discoveries.

For about 15% of the sample, the struggle to manage depression or other serious mental health and substance abuse problems was the major "psychological experience" of the past year. (This high proportion reflects the special characteristics of the second pilot study sample.) A few reported achieving control over their symptoms as turning points. A very small proportion (less than 5%) of respondents reported, as a psychological turning point, "giving up" completely on trying to change a situation or trait of the self.

Triggers of psychological turning points

The majority of psychological turning points (65% over three studies) are associated with having experienced a severe event or long-term chronic difficulty (as defined by the criteria outlined by Brown & Harris 1978). About 15% are associated with positive life transitions, but interestingly, most of these positive transitions were determined to have caused or resolved an ongoing difficulty in the person's life. The remainder (20%) are associated with psychological therapy, events outside the study's time frame, and minor events. The transitions brought on by therapy are all accountable to therapy that was sought after experiencing severely threatening events (e.g., unexpected divorce, death of a loved one, long-term unemployment). Similarly, the events outside the study's time frame are universally severe. They include events such as divorce, which may require several years to resolve emotionally and practically.

The experience of severely threatening events, however, does not always lead to having a psychological turning point. For example, older respondents (over age 55) report just as many severe events as younger respondents, but are less likely to report a psychological turning point. (Some of the older respondents volunteered that they had experienced a psychological turning point in the distant past that had helped them deal with their current troubles.)

The most commonly reported triggers were major events and transitions related to important relationships and to work or career. The most frequently reported relationship triggers were: getting married; becoming a parent or grandparent; ending a marriage; having a serious breakdown in marriage or other close relationship; and taking over the leadership of one's extended family because of the death or illness of a parent. The most common work or career triggers were: beginning a career or new job; being laid off, particularly from a career job; retiring; and deciding to go back to school for occupational training.

Less frequent but not uncommon experiences reported to have triggered a psychological experience or turning point involved volunteer and community leadership. None of these events and situations was classified as a major event, nor were any of them clear role "transitions." These included religious experiences and conversions, taking on a leadership or sacramental role in a church, being elected to the board of a community organization, and becoming more involved in helping underprivileged children.

Finally, some people reported that new avocations or activities induced psychological turning points. Two examples are having time to develop an artistic talent into a serious career and taking up a new sport (in this case learning that one can handle very demanding physical challenges). These turning points are almost always described as processes or long transitions. Further probing revealed that they usually follow a career or family event that led the respondent to take up this activity as compensation or replacement for a lost role or dissatisfying aspect of life.

Turning points and depression

Are those disposed to depression more or less likely to experience a psychological turning point? The data from the pilot studies suggest that very few people report experiencing both depression and a turning point in response to the same severe life event, at least within the one year before the interview. Depression does not appear to facilitate a psychological turning point, although learning how to manage or control one's illness (see Table 2) was reported as a turning point. This suggests that the study of psychological turning points might be a way to systematize the positive psychological impact of undergoing major life stressors (Schaefer & Moos 1992).

Life-course factors associated with turning points

Given previous research, it seems likely that normative beliefs about age- or status-appropriate transitions, and the time at which they should occur, have an impact on how events are interpreted (Menaghan 1989). The same is likely to be true for experiencing a turning point after a life event or transition. According to the life-course perspective, people should reach statuses and age positions that make a turning point more likely.

There are hints in the three pilot studies that timing is important. On- and off-time events, social status, expectations of how one should behave in a particular role, and the general influence of popular ideas about "where one should be" may influence an individual's state of mind, which in turn affects the perception that one is undergoing a turning point in the presence of a novel stressor or new demand (Perun & Bielby 1980). A case in point from our studies relates to work events. Women who go back to work in midlife report that they experience a sense of "growth," "accomplishment," and "new mastery." Their reported reactions do not resemble the experiences reported by men of their age as much as they do the experiences reported by younger men and women who achieve their first promotion, or succeed in landing a first "career" job.

Another straightforward prediction from the life-course perspective is that the type of turning point experienced should differ by age; more specifically, that turning points (as we have defined them for people at midlife) should also be more common among the middle-aged than those who are younger or older. Psychological turning points cluster, albeit moderately, by age. For example, the highest proportion of respondents reporting *any* psychological turning point during the past year are those aged 40–54.

There is also a trend for *type* of turning point to cluster by age group. Respondents under age 40 are more likely to report major psychological experiences that involve consciousness of "growth," need to change the self in response to life experiences, and conscious redirection of their lives. (As noted earlier, the older respondents reporting such turning points are former homemakers who have entered the labor force or have continued their schooling after a long time away.) Only respondents age 55 and above report insights regarding the need for endurance, acceptance, and resignation. In addition, respondents age 40 and older also predominate among those who have learned to accept some limitations on their ability to control their situation and environments. Younger people are much less likely to discuss limits, even displaying hostility or disbelief when asked questions about ever feeling that way. Finally, it appears that those of higher social status are also somewhat more likely to report psychological turning points. In contrast, gender and race are not as predictive, at least in the data collected so far.

Discussion

The data presented here, although preliminary, have numerous implications for other studies of stress as well as for studies of midlife development. The findings suggest a number of useful amendments to the image of the midlife crisis.

First, this study suggests what people may be thinking when they say they have undergone a midlife crisis. It is fairly clear that some people mean "the crisis I had when I was middle-aged," whether it be a divorce, job loss, problem with children, or unfamiliar challenge. What makes it a midlife "crisis" is the interpretation one gives to the meaning of the event and the particular sort of coping one chooses in adapting to the event.

Second, the idea of crisis (speaking generally) seems to be confounded in most people's minds with "coping" and "effort." A number of respondents used the term "crisis" to describe relatively minor events. What they seem to have had in mind is that coping required unusual effort on their part. Perhaps this inflation of the severity of minor events is due to the lack of experience in most people's lives of such truly severe social and personal crises as war, famine, epidemic, or economic depression (Samuelson 1996). Another possibility is that people with busy lives and multiple responsibilities find that making decisions can be very challenging, requiring the continuing acquisition of new knowledge and the resolution of complex and contradictory impulses (Kegan 1995). Certainly the "newness" of the challenge – that is, a challenge that had not before been encountered – is a recurring theme as people report what prompted them to begin thinking and acting differently in a way they now perceive as a psychological turning point. After all, if coping requires little new effort, it will not be particularly remarkable or remembered.

Third, the great interest in the midlife crisis may be a product of the growing experience of a nonnormative life course, at a prevalence not observed in previous generations. Some people do everything at the "right time": marriage after starting a career; children two years after marriage; refocusing on the marital relationship after children are launched; and retirement at age 65. Their lives are normative, at least from the perspective of the World War II generation. But those now entering their forties have taken a number of different options: they married later, put off having children, bore children outside of marriage, started a career late in life, focused on career rather than traditional family pursuits, or "dropped out" of the corporate work culture to pursue more relationship-based means of personal fulfillment. A nonnormative life course may not always mean that life and roles are disorganized, but it does mean that expectations for behavior and the means available to resolve personal problems are less prescriptive than they were for the previous generation.

Fourth, although the predominant experience that people perceive as a turning point in midlife may be spurred by a severe event or undertaken to resolve a period of difficulty, the resolution itself is often perceived as positive. People describe the satisfaction they feel from taking on responsibility, not fleeing from it; indeed, this is a strong component of the popular idea of the midlife crisis. In offering an alternative for the idea of the midlife crisis, Brim (1992) suggested that the focus turn to how ordinary people begin to change their lives so that they cope with "just manageable" stresses and challenges. What people today perceive as the crisis of midlife is the adjustment they make in their goals, aspirations, interpretations of events, and views about their possibilities for achievement.

Fifth, an overarching theme from reports of turning points is that of "control." For better or worse, Americans at midlife are grappling with the discovery that they do not have control, or that they are possibly losing control. This recalls the notion (Brandstaedter & Baltes-Goetz 1980) that as people age, and presumably mature, they give up the belief that they can control everything. This realization can promote emotional health – within limits. At midlife, striving for the impossible or the unlikely seems unwise; you learn to "pick your battles," "reconcile yourself to the familiar," "live and let live." You learn to curb your tongue, keep your own counsel, stop giving advice when it is not solicited, and give up trying to force someone to love you. This process does not occur without loss and regret, but it is generally interpreted as leading to greater wisdom and a more mature kind of happiness.

To illustrate this point, it may be worthwhile to return to a literary example from the nineteenth century. In Jane Austen's *Persuasion,* the heroine is given a second chance at a full life: to rekindle a love relationship with someone whom – because of prudence – she rejected years before. This is an event not at all unlike the events and situations reported by our respondents as triggering a re-evaluation of their beliefs, past decisions, and character. Austen's description of the lovers' ultimate reunion illustrates the impact the passing of time, experience, and living with loss has had on the psychological experience of falling in love when one has passed youth:

> There they exchanged again those feelings and those promises which had once before seemed to secure every thing, but which had been followed by so many, many years of division and estrangement. There they returned again into the past more exquisitely happy, perhaps, in their reunion, than when it had been first projected; more tender, more tried, more fixed in the knowledge of each other's character, truth, and attachment; more equal to act, more justified in acting. (p. 238)

Appendix: Turning-point questions and probing strategies

A. Questions for events ("triggers") predicted to bring about psychological turning points

Loss. "In the past 12 months, were you fired or did you lose your business?"

Revelation. "During the past 12 months, did something happen to make you change your view of the *character* of a very close friend or relative – something that made you realize that they were not the person you thought they were? (How about during the past 5 years?)"

Danger/challenge. "During the past 12 months, did you have any very serious physical injury or flare-up of a major health problem?" "Thinking again about the past year and about anything that you have not already described, have you had any other situation that you would consider to be a *major life crisis*?"

Chronic difficulty. "Did you have any *serious, ongoing* tensions, conflicts, or arguments with any of your close friends or relatives during the *past 12 months*?"

B. Questions specifically about psychological turning points

Successes and dreams. "Some people have dreams for their future. Sometimes they're realistic, sometimes not, but often they are important. During the past 12 months, were you able to fulfill a *special dream* like that?" "In the past 12 months, did you give up for good on fulfilling one of your dreams?"

Revelations about the self. "During the past 12 months, has anything like that happened to you, something that let you see a side of yourself you did not want to know or that made you realize you were not the person you thought you were?" "What about the opposite side of the situation? Did you find out something about yourself in the past 12 months that made you realize that you were a much *better* person than you thought you were?"

C. Probe strategies for establishing psychological turning points

1. "Please tell me a little about that situation." – Gathers information to assess severity of threat.

2. "Was there a particular event that brought this on?" – Establishes what triggered the turning point (if present).

3. "When did that happen?" – Interviewer establishes date of turning point, and the date of its trigger.

4. Optional ("free" probes):

    (a) "How did this change your view of yourself?"
    (b) "What changed about you because of this experience?"
    (c) "What sort of impact has this had on your important relationships?"
    (d) "How has this changed your commitment to your job?"
    (e) "Has this changed the way you look at the world? Other people?"

References

Apter, T. (1995). *Secret Paths.* New York: Norton.

Austen, J. (reprinted 1992). *Persuasion.* New York: Knopf.

Brandstaedter, J., & Baltes-Goetz, B. (1980). Personal control over development and quality of life perspectives in adulthood. In P. Baltes & M. Baltes (eds.), *Successful Aging: Perspectives from the Behavioral Sciences.* Cambridge University Press, pp. 197–224.

Brim, G. (1992). *Ambition: How We Manage Success and Failure Throughout Our Lives.* New York: Basic Books.

Brown, G. W., & Harris, T. O. (1978). *Social Origins of Depression.* New York: Free Press.

Clausen, J. A. (1993). *American Lives: Looking Back at the Children of the Great Depression.* New York: Free Press.

Elder, G. H., Jr., & Rockwell, R. C. (1979). The life course and human development: an ecological perspective. *International Journal of Behavioral Development* 2: 1-21.

Farrell, M. P., & Rosenberg, S. D. (1981). *Men at Midlife.* Boston: Auburn House.

Friedan, B. (1993). *The Fountain of Age.* New York: Simon & Schuster.

Gould, R. (1978). *Transformations: Growth and Change in Adult Life.* New York: Simon & Schuster.

Gray, S. (1994). *Gray's Anatomy.* New York: Vintage.

Kegan, R. (1995). *In Over Our Heads: The Mental Demands of Modern Life.* Cambridge, MA: Harvard University Press.

Kessler, R. C., House, J. S., Herzog, A. R., & Webster, P. (1992). The relationship between age and depressive symptoms in two national surveys. *Psychology and Aging* 7: 119-26.

Kessler, R. C., & Wethington, E. (1991). The reliability of life event reports in a community sample. *Psychological Medicine* 21: 723-38.

Labouvie-Vief, G. (1982). Dynamic development and mature autonomy. *Human Development* 25: 161-91.

Labouvie-Vief, G., Hakim-Larson, J., & Hobart, C. J. (1987). Age, ego level, and the life-span development of coping and defense processes. *Psychology and Aging* 3: 286-93.

Levinson, D., Darrow, C. N., Klein, E. B., Levinson, M. H., & McKee, B. (1978). *The Seasons of a Man's Life.* New York: Knopf.

Loevinger, J. (1976). *Ego Development: Conceptions and Theories.* San Francisco: Jossey-Bass.

Mattlin, J. A., Wethington, E., & Kessler, R. C. (1990). Situational determinants of coping and coping effectiveness. *Journal of Health and Social Behavior* 31: 103-22.

McCrae, R., & Costa. P. (1990). *Personality in Adulthood.* New York: Guilford.

Menaghan, E. G. (1989). Role changes and psychological well-being: variations in effects by gender and role repertoire. *Social Forces* 67: 693-716.

Perun, P. J., & Bielby, D. (1980). Structure and dynamics of the individual life course. In K. W. Back (ed.), *Life Course: Integrative Theories and Exemplary Populations.* Boulder, CO: Westview, pp. 97-119.

Raines, H. (1993). *Fly-fishing through the Midlife Crisis.* New York: Morrow.

Riegel, K. (1975). Adult life crises: toward a dialectical theory of development. In N. Datan & L. Ginsberg (eds.), *Life Span Development and Psychology: Normative Life Crises.* New York: Academic Press, pp. 99-123.

Samuelson, R. J. (1996). *The Good Life and its Discontents: The American Dream in the Age of Entitlement, 1945-1995.* New York: Times Books.

Schaefer, J., & Moos, R. (1992). Life crises and personal growth. In B. Carpenter (ed.), *Personal Coping: Theory, Research, and Applications.* Westport, CT: Praeger, pp. 149-70.

Sheehy, G. (1976). *Passages.* New York: Dutton.

Sheehy, G. (1995). *Passages 2000: The Revolution of Second Adulthood.* New York: Random House.

Sinnott, J., & Cavanaugh, J. C. (1991). *Bridging Paradigms: Positive Development in Adulthood and Cognitive Aging.* New York: Praeger.

Strass, W., & Howe, N. (1991). *Generations: The History of America's Future, 1584-2069.* New York: Morrow.

Wethington, E., Brown, G. W., & Kessler, R. C. (1995). Interview measures of life events. In S. Cohen, R. C. Kessler, & L. U. Gordon (eds.), *Measuring Stress: A Guide for Health and Social Scientists.* New York: Oxford University Press, pp. 79-89.

12 Adaptation to retirement

Robert S. Weiss

Retirement is one of several turning points of aging. Others include health failure that leads to restrictions in activity and to dependency, deaths of contemporaries that diminish community, and the death of a spouse, from which follow grief and loneliness. Among the turning points of later life, only retirement is not unmitigated loss.

In the past 50 years there have been several large-scale and many smaller-scale studies of satisfaction with retirement. The studies suggest strongly that retirement can be either burden or boon; in every study, substantial proportions of respondents are dissatisfied with retirement and substantial proportions are satisfied. Dissatisfaction with retirement is reported to characterize from a fifth of respondents (Barfield & Morgan 1978) to a third (Shanas et al. 1968) to somewhat more than a third (Streib & Schneider 1971). Satisfaction with retirement is reported to characterize from about a third of retired men and women (Atchley 1976; Streib & Schneider 1971) to somewhat more than a third (Palmore et al. 1985).

Professionals and high-level managers may be the occupational groups for whom retirement is most sharply a turning point. It is in these occupational groups that career is best established and also that investment in work appears to be strongest. More than members of other occupational groups, professionals and managers are likely to say they would continue to work even without financial necessity (Morse & Weiss 1955). Furthermore, savings and pensions among members of these groups are likely to be adequate to ensure that financial concern will not limit retirement's freedom. The problems and possibilities of retirement as a new phase of life might therefore be expected to show themselves with particular clarity among former professionals and managers. In contrast, among those whose life work consisted of short-term jobs requiring diffferent skills, or no skills at all, retirement may be virtually without meaning. As young people they would have experienced spells of unemployment

Work reported here was supported by a grant from the National Institute of Aging, 1-R01-AG07363-01.

232

between jobs; as older people unemployment simply becomes the rule (Rubinstein 1986).

This paper is based on repeated interviews with 45 men and 27 women in managerial or professional occupations who, when first contacted, intended to retire within a year or had just recently retired. Most of those who intended to retire did indeed do so, although several maintained part-time associations with their previous firms or worked part-time as consultants. A few respondents embarked on second careers after their retirement, again usually on a part-time basis, and without the intense investment they had given to their first careers. Two respondents returned to full-time work in their previous occupations after an interval of retirement – one because his children seemed to him to be mishandling the family business, the other because he found retirement intolerable.

All but six of the men were recruited from four upper-income suburbs by use of street lists that supply the names, ages, and occupations of residents at every address. Men whose ages were given as 62 or more and whose occupations were professional or managerial were telephoned and asked if they intended to retire during the coming year. Those who said that they thought it likely or certain that they would retire within the year were asked if we could interview them within the next few weeks and then again six months after their retirement. Those who were already retired were asked if we could interview them immediately and then again in six months to a year. Thirty-nine men, about 80% of those contacted, agreed to the interviews. The additional half-dozen men were recruited by personnel managers of three large firms who asked retiring employees if they were willing to be interviewed.

Finding women about to retire from managerial and professional positions was more difficult than finding men. Eight women were found using street lists. Most of the remainder were directed to the study by cooperative personnel managers. Five volunteered to be interviewed after reading a story about the study that appeared in the local newspaper.

Of the 72 respondents who provided first interviews, four could not be contacted for second interviews and three who were contacted declined. Two respondents, although anticipating retirement, changed their minds and did not actually retire. In all, 40 men and 23 women provided postretirement interviews. Most of these respondents were interviewed a third time, a year to two after their retirement.

Retirement's benefits and burdens

A former manager's or professional's first experience of retirement – after he or she emptied the files and cleaned out the office desk, enjoyed or endured the retirement party, and completed the requisite exchange of goodbyes – was likely to be sudden awareness of a surprising freedom. No longer was there work to go to. Indeed, work's demands had entirely ended. Staying home or going out had become solely a matter of personal choice. A former engineer said: "It's ten degrees below. And you don't need to go out today. And you feel happy! And that's a marvelous feeling!"

Many respondents were pleased to recognize in themselves a diminution of stress, now that they no longer needed to mobilize themselves to deal with the challenges and crises of the workplace. One respondent said he would not have survived for much longer under the stress his work had imposed. Another respondent, a former department head, spoke of retirement as having been a salvation: "Retirement, I think, was the salvation for me as far as stress level was concerned. Now I don't have the stress and the strain and responsibility of doing the kinds of things where – 'You did that? You're fired!'" Other respondents spoke of being pleased that they were no longer beset by the problems and conflicts of the workplace. A woman who had headed public relations for a small firm felt she had much more energy now that she was retired. Before retirement she had regularly come home exhausted, desperate for a cup of tea and an hour of quiet. She felt it wonderful to be free of such depletion.

Yet many among the newly retired reported having experienced initial discomfort with retirement's freedom from the constraints and burdens of work. It didn't seem right to them that they were home when others were working, that they were able to have a lazy morning on a day others were up and out. Except for a small number of professionals and businessmen who had retired gradually by cutting back their hours of work, the event of retiring had been a sudden shift from full-time work to full-time leisure. Some felt that adaptation required more time. Six months after his retirement, a former mid-level manager said:

> What I found difficult was adjusting to the fact that I didn't have anything to do. Some mornings I'd get up and – this was when I first started – I'm getting on to it now, but I wouldn't feel just right about not having something to do and not having to be somewhere. I'm better about that now. Much better. It's time, healing. I began to realize after a while that there wasn't anything wrong with not doing anything. But it took some doing for a while.

Another former executive, a woman who had been manager of a branch bank, also experienced difficulty in adapting to a life that no longer required that she wake early.

> I had the hardest time at first. I never had to have an alarm clock. I automatically woke up at quarter to six every morning. It was my time to get up. Well, I did not have to be up and out by eight o'clock, be at my desk by nine. I said, "What am I doing still getting up at quarter of six?" That took time.

Adaptation seemed to occur for this respondent within the first six months of retirement. With adaptation to retirement, the respondent found the absence of rush and tension to be entirely gratifying.

> Now I can stay in bed until about seven or a little after. And I enjoy that. And I enjoy not having to get up and rush around getting dressed. To me, I think that is wonderful. To be relaxed. I can stay in my robe and I can have my cup of coffee. I like that. It's not the hustle bustle. The time is nice now that I do not have to rush.

Adaptation to freedom from work's demands might come slowly and unobtrusively. One respondent described being taken by surprise when, after a few months of retirement, he recognized how much he had slowed down.

> It was three or four months after retirement before I noticed the change. And then I suddenly realized that, hey, this big list that I always keep of things to do? I used to put red dots on the things that were time-sensitive, that had to be done today, or had to be done with a date. Suddenly the red dots disappeared. Everything could be done tomorrow.

However, adaptation to retirement did not always occur. Each of the benefits of retirement could be experienced as a deprivation. The freedom from need to show up at work meant that one was no longer needed and, also, made social isolation possible. The freedom from need to deal with work's challenges made possible a loss of acuity and a diminished sense of worth. The freedom to get up when one wanted or to use one's time as one wanted was, from another perspective, structurelessness. A former engineer complained that the absence of a work routine left him adrift.

> You've been in a discipline for all of those years, where Monday meant you started the week and Friday meant you ended the week. And then you have two days to do everything you would normally want to do, in terms of yard work, traveling, or anything like that. So you more or less knew exactly what day it was. If it was somewhere between Monday and Friday, you knew how many days it was to the weekend. And all of a sudden there's no discipline.

Work, by defining as its domain five days of the week and eight hours of the day, had structured respondents' time. Even divisions of the year had been given meaning by the organization of work, with summer the time for vacation and Labor Day the start of a new work year. With the ending of work, days moved seamlessly from early waking through lunch time and dinner time to evening television and bed. The division between weekday and weekend was muted. Without work to take a vacation from, it became impossible to take a vacation. (For further discussion of work as a *zeitgeber,* see Young & Schuller 1991.)

During their working years, respondents had maintained relationships based on their occupations. Throughout the workday they would encounter people who knew them in their occupational identities. Interaction with these people had reinforced those identities. After retirement, work-related relationships vanished. A former lawyer commented on the absence of the incidental contacts his work had brought him.

> After you have been in the same building for forty years you get to know the people. Like there are lawyers in the building I know to say hello to, just a brief

conversation. There are lawyers over the next street, by the courthouse. There are judges and clerks and others that I see back and forth. You don't get into detailed conversation with them, but at least you say hello, how are you, and what's doing, and this and that. If you don't come into town you don't see them any more, and you don't say hello to them, spend the time of day with them for a minute or two.

With the ending of work-related contacts, isolation became a possibility, especially for those respondents who were unmarried and lived alone. Because there was no special need to go out, remaining at home through the day was a constant temptation. Bad weather, feeling out of sorts, or just the absence of a destination could cause a respondent to spend the day alone. A widow who before retirement had helped run a small business said:

> The weather is bad - like in snow - you think, really is it worth going today or not? When you have a job, you go anyway. There is a purpose - to go to a job. If you are doing the job you always go somewhere, even in the bad weather. So you are with some people. But when you are retired, if it is stormy, you have nothing except yourself. If it is raining very hard, you say "Why should I go today?" You have no purpose to go anywheres. So you put off going. So you feel cut off more.

Another respondent, a divorced woman, fell into the habit of staying at home. A year after her retirement from a successful career in book publishing she remained in touch only with her two grown children; otherwise she had withdrawn from social contact. Most days, except for grocery shopping, she saw no one at all. She said that she did not feel unhappy, although she regretted the direction her life had taken. She said:

> I don't have depths of despair. I don't have anything. My life is, the euphemism I guess today is, "couch potato." I stay home. I try to go out as infrequently as I can. I'm afraid I'll meet someone I know. And I don't want anyone seeing me this way. I don't know how I would handle it. I've become an inept - or what I think [is] an inept - nothing.

Even among the married, the companionship of a spouse might not entirely compensate for the loss of work associations. At work, respondents had been people of importance; they weren't quite that at home. A former manager said:

> I miss work terribly. And yet the thoughts of going back to a five-day week, commuting to the city, makes me feel a lot better. But you can't lose that sense of importance, and not have it affect you. Now the only person that you can exercise any importance with is with your wife. And she long ago put you in a position, where you still are, that she's glad to listen, but I'm just a husband.
>
> At work, in my heyday, I was not a power figure, but I was relatively important, in my consideration and I think in my boss's consideration. And now I'm just a husband.

Some sense of marginality to the world of work seemed next to inescapable in retirement. Except for those few who maintained a link with their occupational world as consultants, respondents recognized that they no longer counted among those with whom they had spent their careers. For some respondents this could mean that they no longer counted at all. At the least, the identity of active participant in the world of work could no longer be maintained. A former business manager said:

> I was quite reasonably successful in what I did. And then it stops. So you no longer feel you're in the main stream of things. You're no longer doing what you were trained to do. Suddenly not doing something that I'd been doing, you know, eight hours a day for thirty-five years. It's a new feeling. Not easy to define. It's a vague feeling of discontinuity. It makes you feel uneasy.

The engagement of work activities was lost. Respondents could no longer mobilize themselves to meet the challenges of work, could no longer involve themselves in projects that might command the recognition of colleagues. Life in retirement, though free of stress, seemed flaccid, lacking in excitement. A former lawyer said:

> Even though I've been trying cases for thirty years, forty years, I never had a case that didn't worry me. I never had a case which, as trial approached, didn't concern me. Or, to put it differently, didn't cause a certain amount of tension. And I never got into court on a trial where I wasn't really uptight until it got rolling. For all that, I enjoyed the experience. I enjoyed the trials. I had reason to enjoy the outcomes, mostly. And on to the next one. I've not enjoyed the experience of the absence of tensions.

A few among the retired did try to maintain involvement with colleagues even while retired. A former businessman, who returned to work after five or six months of retirement, said about his experience in retirement:

> I was quite upset. I couldn't stand the inactivity. My mind was still going. I was on the phone, gabbing away, all day long. Talking to business acquaintances, friends of mine, people in business. Reading every bit of newspaper I could – magazines, trade journals – as they would come, keeping abreast of what was going on in the world. And, not feeling sorry for myself, but really resenting that I was out of it.

The activities available to the retired, though they could be gratifying, were rarely as engaging as their work had been. And most respondents, most of the time, did nothing special: they read the papers, prepared meals, shopped, talked with children or a few friends, watched television. In this respect our sample resembled that of Young and Schuller (1991). Only a third of a sample of retirees in East London whose occupations had been like the occupations of the retirees described here engaged in activities that Young and Schuller considered enriching, productive, or gratifying.

A few respondents did seem to have successfully replaced the activities of their work with a mix of volunteer activities, self-improvement activities, travel, and hobbies that involved them with others. A man in his early sixties, retired from a position as manager of a family business, said about his retirement:

> It's allowed me to get involved in a lot of things. I got involved in yoga and all kinds of other things. And I found a part of me which I guess was there originally but which had gotten totally lost. So I think it was the best thing that I could have done for myself.

This respondent's budget of activities included a good deal of travel; frequent visits with his grown children (he was divorced); attention to an apartment house he owned and managed; an interest in folk dancing, in which he taught a course for an adult education program; and a valued relationship with a woman who was still employed. He was no longer the effective manager he had once been – responsibility for the apartment house aside – but he remained energetically involved in the social world.

A few other respondents could also have agreed with a statement sometimes offered by the most active among the retired: "I don't know how I ever had time to work." They treated their retirement as an opportunity to maintain or develop a range of social associations, including classes they might teach or take, family they kept up with, friends whom they saw with some frequency, and travel. Their retirement was anything but an experience of withdrawal from the social world – although it was not, even with all their activity, as engaged with others as their work lives had been.

Two respondents described productive activities that approached being new occupations and that served them as central life interests. In one instance the new activity was photography, in the other, furniture making. The photographer regularly entered shows and on occasion received awards. The furniture maker had a waiting list for his beautifully designed and skillfully crafted pieces. Each of these respondents had been ungratified in his work (although the furniture maker had managed a successful business). Their retirement experience was not one of leaving fulfilling work for an empty retirement; it was, instead, the opposite one of leaving unfulfilling work for a retirement that made possible work they valued highly.

A few respondents returned in their retirement to a long-neglected interest: a musical instrument they had played as an adolescent, or a craft they had put aside to attend to the demands of work. Or they undertook a long-anticipated project: to winterize a summer home, or visit European capitals. Such projects could provide a sense of achievement and reassurance that competence had not ended. Traveling with one's spouse seemed often to provide shared experiences of heightened awareness.

But not all anticipated projects turned out to be successful retirement activities. Activities that were by their nature solitary and isolating, and so without the support of others, tended not to work as retirement projects. A former physician had anticipated involving himself in several such projects:

> Certain things that I had already decided I'd like to do when I was retired – I had a stamp collection ever since I was a kid, been buying stamps all these

years. And I got stamps stored away upstairs and some really valuable stuff in a safe deposit box. I say I have got to get this collection organized and cataloged because, if anything happens to me, someone will get rid of it for peanuts, and it's really worth something. And I don't get around to it.

I've thought of taking photography up again. I used to do a lot of photography. Somehow, I don't get to it. I've thought of taking classes. I've thought of relearning German, which I've just about forgotten. I can still read it as well – not as well as I read English, but certainly well. But I used to be able to speak it, with some effort. Now I can barely speak it. I'd like to, while I'm still capable of learning, achieve some facility. And I'd like to travel to Europe. But this inertia sets in.

A few respondents said that they had been unable to find retirement activities that engaged them. The former businessman who spent his day trying to keep up with the work world that he had left said that the one truly engaging event during his interval of retirement had been the arrival of the morning newspaper. In an interview held before his return to work, he said:

I have hours to waste. I get up the same time. We eat in the dining room, breakfast and all. I get in there in the morning. I stand in the window like a fool, waiting for the damned paper man to come. Every once in a while I tease him, I tell him, "Hey, I'll give you an extra five bucks, come early with the paper, will you?" So he brings the paper and I sit there and I read it. And this could be at six, six-thirty, in the morning. How long does it take you? An hour? So seven o'clock, seven-thirty, I'm through. The rest of the street hasn't awakened yet.

The respondent had tried coins and stamps as hobbies, but the activities of sorting and filing struck him as pointless.

I did try coins once. I bought about a thousand dollars, literally a thousand dollars, worth of pennies. I looked and looked until my fingers – I've got arthritic fingers – and they got so numb. And I got blind. And I thought, "This is ridiculous." I didn't care. So if I found a penny that was worth ten dollars – big deal. Somebody tried to get me involved in stamps. But I needed something that really physically and mentally challenged me.

Projects that lacked both challenge and social support could easily appear meaningless. Nor did it matter to anyone if they were dropped. Indeed, absence of social support alone might make an activity difficult for a retiree to maintain. Two respondents had retired with the intention of writing monographs in their fields. But no one else had cared about the monographs and, when the respondents gave them up, no one else was disappointed.

A few respondents could not reconcile themselves to the loss of the community of their work. One man, after a year of discomfort in retirement, was asked by an executive in his former firm to become a consultant to a program he had launched. We talked with him not long after he accepted the invitation. Referring to an earlier interview with us, he said:

When I talked with you, before I had this offer for the consulting, I knew that I was going to go off the deep end at the end of the year. It was a feeling of loss

and apprehension. Thirty-eight years with the same company does something
to you. And no longer to be a part of that relationship, even though you don't
commit hari kari or anything like that, it's just an uncomfortable feeling. Very
uncomfortable.

Adaptation to retirement required, for most respondents, accepting themselves as no longer active in the world of work. One respondent, a former manager, described suddenly seeing himself, in his new life, from the perspective of
his working identity, and reacting with dismay. "This morning I went out to
the square to get some coffee. I take a bus when I do that. And I was standing
at the bus stop, and all these old men were around. And I thought, my God, I'm
beginning to be part of this group."

However, only a minority of respondents reported maladaptation to retirement in the form of boredom or restlessness or feelings of isolation or of loss
of a valued identity. Most respondents described their lives as good enough,
and some seemed thoroughly pleased to be retired. Gardening, getting out for
walks, having friends in, shopping, and even doing crossword puzzles were
gratifying activities that helped make them content with life. Few felt themselves to be bored or to have time hanging heavy on their hands.

Money matters occupied a good deal of the time of several retirees and was
felt by them to be as engaging as their work had been. The management of an
investment portfolio could easily require hours each day: there could be, every
day, financial news to keep up with, financial publications to read, and stock
evaluations to calculate, as well as personal accounts to monitor. Simply keep-
ing track of household expenditures could be engaging. The energy once given
to managing work activities could now be redirected to domestic finance.

> I have everything all written down, as to what we have at the beginning of the
> year when I retired. And twelve months from now I'll go and add it up again
> and see whether we are ahead or not. Or how far behind we are. What is in the
> savings account, what is in the checking account. What is in the IRA, the 401K.
> At the end of the year add it all up again and see if we did break even, did we
> lose money, or what did happen. Until I know that, I don't know how I could
> plan ahead. I don't know what we spent when I was working. Except that we
> never had much money left over at the end of the year, apparently.
>
> We never had a budget as such. We never really needed one. And we have al-
> ways come out at least even by the end of the year. What it is going to be in
> retirement, I don't know.

Many respondents were pleased that they now had more time to be with their
families. They could make themselves available as babysitters to grandchildren. They could visit children and grandchildren who lived at a distance, and
perhaps spend holidays with them. A respondent whose difficult divorce had
separated him from his children was pleased that retirement had given him the
time to become closer to them.

> I have three children. And my relationship was distant. And with at least two of them I now have a wonderful relationship. It was because I had the time and the desire and the ability to put a lot of effort into it. Now even though none of them live near here I have an excellent relationship with two of them and at least an ongoing relationship with the third. And that is extremely gratifying to me.

A former executive who was childless valued his retirement because it made it possible for him to visit his nieces and nephews. A former minister could now be with his children at times when, in the past, he would have had to be with his congregation.

> If we want to go to see our granddaughter and see our great granddaughter, who live pretty far from here, we've done that. We were able to go on a Wednesday for Thanksgiving. I wasn't responsible for a Thanksgiving service and so we were able to stay there. And I didn't have to rush back for Sunday service.

Another man, a former sales executive, said that his work had been so consuming that he had hardly been available to his family. Even when he was at home, his work had preoccupied him. Now, with retirement, he was able to participate fully in family life.

> When I was working I was constantly on the go. Constantly. I had a tremendous amount of responsibility. And I could never release myself of this. I could be sitting in my kitchen and talking to my children or my wife or having a cup of tea with my wife, and my thoughts were always about what was going on in the company. But now I'm completely relieved of that. I feel as if a great weight has been relieved from me.

The most successful of retirement activities seemed not only gratifying in their own right but also to provide some of the engagement with others and reassurance of worth that had been provisions of work. Travel, for respondents who were married, constituted a joint undertaking in which challenges were planned for, met, and afterward described to friends and kin. The photography and furniture making referred to earlier brought with it relationships with suppliers, colleagues, and audiences or customers. Yet it was also important that stress and burden be limited. Taking on new commitments tended to be unwanted: being with children and grandchildren seemed especially valued by respondents when they could be helpful without assuming continued responsibility for care.

Important to adaptation to retirement was a redefinition of the self that made the ending of career acceptable. One former businessman said it had taken a bit of time, but he finally recognized, with pleasure, that he would never again have to put on a tie each workday morning. Being able to find pleasure in the slower pace of retirement and its absence of urgency was an expression of this changed definition of self. Those among the retired who made this shift were most likely to find retirement gratifying.

A changed definition of self could include continued contribution to a field, or involvement in a field, despite the career's end. Relationships with members of the former work community might then be maintained, although contacts would probably be less frequent. Should the retired person retain a position as a consultant to the firm he would, by everyone's definition, no longer be a full participant in the life of the workplace. Nevertheless, continued participation in what had been the retired person's community of work could sustain his or her feelings of worth. A former university professor said:

> I still teach. I have time to write. I have good health. So my retirement is not dull at all. It's beautiful. Because I still continue to share. That's what teaching means: to share. And I can still continue.

> As long as you are part of a crew of a ship or something, you fight for your own life and for everybody else's life, because a ship can sink or float. Now, there is a way of watching a ship from the shore. I don't go to faculty meetings. I don't try to influence another colleague in order to have a majority of voting. I don't vote. But I'm not only on the shore. I occasionally do step on the ship.

For respondents who were married, retirement required a restructuring of the marital relationship. There was now, as one occasionally reported quip would have it, "half as much money and twice as much husband," although in truth it could be the wife's retirement that had to be dealt with rather than the husband's. One fear expressed by some wives, in their anticipation of their own or their husband's retirement, was that they would be asked to provide service for their husbands throughout the day, or at least be available as companions – a fear that was expressed in the joking, "I agreed to 'for better or for worse'; I didn't agree to 'for lunch'." Nor was this concern entirely without foundation. A former bank official said, about the effect of his retirement on his wife:

> Well, she's a little more restricted. She hasn't admitted to it, but I don't think that she associates with her friends as much as she used to, because I'm home, and I think she feels a little guilty if she's not home for my lunch. Even though I assure her not to worry about me, because I can take care of myself, I know it's restricting her. And I just say please call so and so and go out. And she says, "Oh, yeah, I will." And she does sometimes.

Many among the retired indicated a new reliance on their husbands or wives for companionship. Without the sociability of the workplace, and with time on their hands, they turned to their spouses. A former manager said:

> I tend to be kind of a loner anyway. I'm not one who has close friends. I don't have some guy that I'll go to and tell him my troubles, some buddy somewhere. Mainly I talk to my wife.

> I think, with retirement, we're closer, because we do more things together. We have more time together. Ah, she'll throw me out of the kitchen once in a while. I'll be out there, yack, yack, yacking. And she'll say, look, I'm trying to mix this recipe or something, be still, I have to count. And I'll go away.

The greater availability of the retired person – the retired person's now constant presence in the home, together with the retired person's increased need for the companionship of the spouse – required some response from the spouse. Some among the husbands and wives of the retired were pleased at the increased opportunity for companionship; some insisted on maintaining time for themselves; and some, whose marriages had been based on a degree of separateness between the spouses, sought to maintain that separateness.

In one instance it was the wife who retired and was newly at home. She had been a marketing manager and had traveled a great deal, sometimes being away from home for weeks at a time. Now it was the husband who had to defend his domain in the home from his wife's intrusion, and to deal with his wife's new need for companionship. The wife, who was our respondent, said:

> I was not the typical housewife. I always worked out of town. He always had the house for whatever he wanted, whenever he wanted. I retired just like that, cold turkey. I did not go back to work. When I came home, retired, I was into his domain. And that was terrible. I was trespassing on his territory. On his time.

> I found myself questioning him: "Where are you going?" "What are you going out for?" He has a friend, they go walking every day. "Well I always have." I'd say, "Yeah, but I'm home now. That isn't going to happen any more, is it?" And he said, "Of course it is going to happen." And I said, "Well, I'm home now, you don't have to do that." He said, "So you are home, but I have to do what I do." So that was ironed out. And that was great. Because I couldn't respect a man that doesn't respect his own actions.

Having more time together could be a problem for couples who had learned to keep a certain distance. One businessman had been concerned with how well he and his wife would manage his being at home all the time. Before his retirement he said: "We both recognize that as you get older, you start to bicker. In any relationship. And it's bad enough when I'm only there weekends, or at nights. The thought of my being there *all* the time, you know, you start to really look at it seriously." When we spoke with this respondent six months after his retirement, he told us that he and his wife had indeed been getting on each other's nerves. He saw the answer as finding some sort of work:

> I've got to get a job. Part time. I don't care if it's packing groceries. I've got to have some routine, something I have to do. And you know, the other thing, get away from your wife. That gets a little wearing for both of you.

> Our disagreements are really picayune, minor things. I guess that happens to everyone, you know. When will you put the cap back on the toothpaste? This sort of thing. I guess the more you're around the house the more you're inclined to notice little things like that.

However, in most cases the increased time the retired person now had for companionship was seen as a benefit for the marriage. Not only did the retired person have more time for the spouse, but now – no longer preoccupied by problems of work – the retired person could interact with the spouse much more fully. A former department head said:

> I think my wife enjoys my company more, in that she'll remark on something, I'll put down what I'm doing and I'm willing to discuss that. Whereas, before, we never read the newspaper together, to begin with. Or if she said something to me in the morning, you know, geez, watch it, I'm shaving, I gotta catch the train, you know, and this sort of thing.
>
> So I have time to have that communication with my wife that I didn't have before. Because now I'm interested in things like that. The inner workings of, say, the church's board of directors are more interesting to me now because I have time to listen to them. Before, they sort of faded in importance. You're going to have more outreach? Fine. And that was the end of the conversation. Now I'll take time to hear about who's doing what, and so forth.

For most respondents, retirement seemed a turning point in their marriages almost as much as it was in their work lives. No longer were respondents' marital partnerships concerned with supporting the respondents' functioning at work. No longer did work demands compete with the demands of the family for respondents' attention. At the same time, issues of domain responsibility and of closeness and separateness had to be reconsidered. Respondents had new needs for companionship and for support. Activities that could involve the spouse, such as bridge and doubles tennis, might now be sought. Travel worked well here.

In sum, adaptation to the new way of life that began with departure from work seemed to have a number of requirements. It required that the retired person find activities that were adequately engaging. It required that the retired person accept a new definition of self based on something other than competence within an occupation. It required that the retired person find, within the life situation of retirement, support for activities and for feelings of worth. And it required that the retired person find a satisfactory reorganization of relational life. For those who were married, this last meant dealing with the opportunity for more time and more companionship with the spouse and with greater need for the spouse's support. It might also mean reconsidering the household routine and the household division of labor. Most among the retired whom we interviewed had met all these challenges, though not, ordinarily, without some discomfort along the way.

References

Atchley, Robert C. (1976). *The Sociology of Retirement*. New York: Halsted.
Barfield, Richard E., & Morgan, James N. (1978). Trends in satisfaction with retirement. *The Gerontologist* 18: 19–23.
Morse, Nancy C., & Weiss, Robert S. (1955). The function and meaning of work and the job. *American Sociological Review* 20: 191-9.

Palmore, Erdman B., Burchett, Bruce M., Fillenbaum, Gerda G., George, Linda K., & Wallman, Laurence M. (1985). *Retirement: Causes and Consequences.* New York: Springer.

Rubinstein, Robert L. (1986). *Singular Paths: Old Men Living Alone.* New York: Columbia University Press.

Shanas, Ethel, Townsend, Peter, Wedderburn, Dorothy, Friis, Henning, Milhoj, Poul, & Stehouwer, Jan (1968). *Old People in Three Industrial Societies.* New York: Atherton.

Streib, Gordon F., & Schneider, Clement J. (1971). *Retirement in American Society: Impact and Process.* Ithaca, NY: Cornell University Press.

Young, Michael D., & Schuller, Tom (1991). *Life After Work: The Arrival of the Ageless Society.* London: HarperCollins.

III   New methods for the study of the life course

13 Construction and use of the life history calendar: reliability and validity of recall data

Nan Lin, Walter M. Ensel, & Wan-foon Gina Lai

Introduction to the problem

The study of stress has made significant strides over the past two decades. A major current research thrust has been to construct the process of stress and distress over the life course, as evidenced in the various contributions to the present volume (see also the review by Elder, George, & Shanahan 1994). Time-lagged analysis of earlier stressors on later distress allows a more confident interpretation of the causal ordering between stressors and distress. Timing and duration of events and social role changes (see Chapter 7 in this volume) – such as getting married or divorced (Chapter 9); leaving school (Chapter 10); finding or leaving jobs (Chapter 5); losing parents, children, or loved ones; experiencing combat; or natural or human disasters – may have subsequent health consequences on the individuals involved (Brown & Harris 1978; Elder 1986; George 1993; Moen, Dempster-McClain, & Williams 1992; Pearlin et al. 1981; Wheaton 1990) as well as on later generations (Elder, Caspi, & Downey 1986; Rossi & Rossi 1990; see also Chapter 6 in this volume).

The life-course approach advances the conceptual argument that similar experiences during various life stages may exert differential impacts on a person's subsequent mental and physical health. A similar event that is important at one stage in life may not be so at another stage, and vice versa. A life-course analysis of the stress–distress model is a logical and essential elaboration of the differential impact model.

The ideal source of data for such a life-course analysis of stress would be a panel design in which information from the same set of respondents is gathered "on time" over the course of their lives. Such data sets are rare and costly. Often, recall data are obtained from respondents or their significant others (e.g., their mothers) regarding life experiences or stressors in earlier life stages. The retrospective design makes an important assumption: that such data are valid and

The work reported here is supported by a research grant (MH-48167) from the National Institute of Mental Health.

249

reliable. At a minimum it is assumed that if recall errors do occur then they do so in a random fashion, such that in aggregation they do not bias the estimation of the relationship between the recalled stressors and contemporaneous or later distress.

Some studies have attempted to assess the extent of recall errors in social surveys. Romney and Weller (1984), for example, found a strong correspondence between observed interaction data and recall data. Powers, Goudy, and Keith (1978), on the other hand, found great variation in the congruency of measures when they compared interview and recall data. For example, when data are used as estimates for the sample as a whole, retrospective and current items seem to produce the same results. Powers and collaborators also showed that when a study is designed to examine variable relationships, retrospective data are similar to current data. On the other hand, when data are providing descriptions of past situations on an individual level, retrospective data can be questionable. Jenkins, Hurst, and Rose (1979) examined recall of life events and found that events pertaining to one's children, relocation, deaths or losses, and legal problems tend to remain stable, whereas changes in health, work, and financial situations were not very stable. They suggest that long-term recall of life events, particularly those that are not crises, may not be reliable. Peters (1988) found that, in a study comparing retrospective and panel data on life-cycle events, both do equally well in predicting the hazard rates of first marriage.

These studies suggest that the extent of recall errors tends to be associated with (1) routine rather than dramatic or traumatic experiences; (2) psychological rather than social experiences; and (3) individual predictions rather than patterns of associations among variables. Very little is known regarding the extent and nature of recall errors associated with retrospective data on social stressors.

Currently, two major issues confront researchers interested in the use of retrospective data in the study of stress over the life course. One is the need to develop a more comprehensive coverage of life experiences. Past attempts seem to have concentrated on one or a few traumatic experiences during childhood or early adolescence (e.g., losing a parent due to death or divorce). Although a singular or a few traumatic experiences may be salient for recall purposes, the life-course perspective reminds us that a particular experience will have differential impacts on different individuals. Moreover, the timing and duration of the experience over the life course also may exert differential impacts. Likewise, one type of experience may be stressful for some individuals and during certain life stages, but not for others or at other life stages. Focusing on a single or few traumatic experiences may lead to self-fulfilling and biased conclusions. At this stage of theoretical development, a more systematic and comprehensive approach is needed. This approach seeks a representative sample of relevant experiences (events and social role changes) throughout the life course. The extent to which different configurations and combinations of experiences prove to be stressful during certain life stages and for different individuals should in fact constitute the basic research question.

A second need relates to the assessment of both the extent and the nature of recall errors incurred. The degree of recall errors informs us about the extent to which the recall data might affect reliability in the modeling of the stress–distress process. If it is determined that they do, then the next issue is whether the effect is random or systematic in nature. If it is random, then one can argue that the stress–distress model remains valid. If it is systematic, in that the extent of recall errors is related to certain social and psychological characteristics, then perhaps we may devise certain correction procedures to take into account such systematic bias.

This chapter attempts to make such contributions. We examine a panel of respondents in upstate New York who have been subjects in multiwave studies (Lin, Dean, & Ensel 1986). The first-wave data were collected in 1979; subsequent waves were collected in 1980 and 1982. In 1993 and 1995 we conducted two more waves of the survey, which include a life history calendar covering 1979 to 1994.

The construction of the life history calendar was guided by the literature of life event studies and life experiences research, as well as by findings from our own research data. It initiates the development of an inventory representing significant life history experiences for a community population. Together with the on-time information regarding the respondents' life experiences during and around 1979–82 gathered in the first three waves, we have information on portions of the recall data gathered in 1993 and 1995 that correspond to the on-time data. Comparing and matching the on-time and recall data offer the opportunity to estimate recall errors and assess their systematic bias.

Such an approach and utilization of a panel data set does constitute a methodological advance, but still has its limitations. First, we did not extend the time frame back to earlier stages of the life course – namely, the childhood and teen experiences. The original sample in 1979 was based on the population of adults (18 and older) in the sampled community. Thus, it misses stressors associated with early development stages. Second, the items in the life history calendar closely follow data gathered in the first three waves (so that the actual and recall data could be compared). These items represent two types of experiences: (1) changes in social roles such as marital status, births of children, employment, and residence; and (2) experiences of life events such as family relations, work or financial problems, health/illness/death problems, or personal problems. In other words, they reflect experiences shared by a substantial proportion of the general population from which the sample was drawn. As a result, traumatic and extreme experiences such as combat, sexual abuse, drug abuse, and extreme poverty are not measured (see Chapters 2–5 in this volume for efforts along these lines).

Finally, to some extent the on-time data are in fact also recall data, in that they were provided by the respondents to the interviewers in the face-to-face surveys. The extent to which they contained errors cannot be assessed. Thus, any differences between the 1993–95 reports of experiences for 1979–82 and the on-time data collected in the 1979–82 surveys are considered as errors. This is based on the assumption that the on-time data are valid. That is, we assume that any errors embedded in the on-time data tend to be random, and not systematically associated with psychological disposition or social position. The extent to which such an assumption is violated may reduce the validity of this methodology. The confirmation or rejection of this assumption awaits further research.

The database

The data used in the current study comes from a panel study initiated in 1979 in a metropolitan area in upstate New York (the Albany Study). To date, five waves of data have been collected. The first three were collected in the years of 1979, 1980, and 1982, and two more waves were collected in 1993 and 1995. The present chapter uses the data from the 1979, 1980, and 1993 surveys.

The first three waves, 1979–82

In the first wave of the study (T1), a multistage probability sample of 1,091 adults aged 18–70 was chosen using housing data provided by the census. The characteristics of the sample represented the total population of the area as defined by the census. The second wave of the study (T2) was conducted in 1980. In this wave, 80% ($N = 871$) of those respondents who participated in T1 agreed to participate. The third wave of the study (T3) was conducted in 1982. In this wave, 62% ($N = 677$) of the original sample were reinterviewed.

More than 95% ($N = 639$) of those respondents who participated in T3 were also interviewed in T1 and T2. Although there was a tendency to lose young and unemployed individuals in the second and third waves of the study, an examination of the key study variables showed no significant differences between those who continued in the study for all three waves and those who dropped out after the initial wave of interviewing.

The fourth wave, 1993

Before the fourth wave of data collection, rigorous attempts were made to track respondents who participated in the first wave. These attempts consisted of tracing through telephone directories, mailings to respondents, and visits by interviewers to the respondents' last known addresses. In 1993–94, the fourth wave of data collection was conducted. By this time, at least 11% ($N = 124$) of the original respondents had died. Of the surviving respondents ($N = 967$), 58% ($N = 558$) were successfully reinterviewed, 9% ($N = 85$) refused to be interviewed, and 34% ($N = 324$) could not be located. The fifth wave of data was gathered in 1995.

The current analysis is conducted for those respondents who participated in all of the first four waves (1979, 1980, 1982, and 1993) and includes a total of 419 individuals. Among these respondents, 46% are males (compared to 50% in the initial 1979 sample), the average age is 55 in 1993 (or 41 in 1979, compared to 40.7 reported in 1979), 93% are white (compared to 89% in 1979), 69% are married (compared to 64.1% in 1979), and 59% are employed (compared to 53.8% in 1979). The average extent of schooling is 12.54 years (about the same as in 1979), the average personal annual income is between $20,000 and $24,999 (compared to $7,000–$9,999 in 1979), and the average of household income is $40,000–$44,999 (compared to $10,000–$20,000 reported in 1979).

Construction of the life history calendar

The purpose of the life history calendar is to obtain information on important life experiences that occurred to respondents in the 14 to 16 years since the first wave of data was collected. Since this was a long period to cover, it was deemed important to keep the list of critical experiences concise and manageable.

As Freedman and associates (1988) have noted, there is no single standard for a life history calendar. Such a calendar should consist of two dimensions: domains and time units. Domains are areas of events of interest to the researcher; time units reflect the specific periods in which the researcher wishes to examine them. The domains cover the variables of interest, and the time units should be justified on past measurements of variables of interest.

Selection of life changes

The first decision made was to focus on *changes in life experience*. Change is the major criterion in the development of life event inventories, assuming that change induces adjustment and thus stress. Likewise, the research literature on life course and development focuses on changes and/or new experiences, as they may signal turning points, transitions, or at least new environmental stimuli. Any of these may trigger psychological and physiological responses, potentially leading to distress.

Our interest was to cover two types of life changes. The first type consists of life-course events reflecting changes in demographic and role characteristics, and includes five major categories: (1) marital status changes; (2) births of children; (3) changing education experiences; (4) employment changes; and (5) residential changes. The second type of life changes includes occurrences traditionally referred to as life events. These include events such as the death of someone close, serious accident or injury, change in financial state, changes in social activity, and so forth.

For inclusion in the life history calendar, an event or experience had to meet one of two criteria. The first criterion was that the event had a reasonable readjustment weight (Holmes & Rahe 1967). The second criterion was that the event had to be rated as undesirable. Past research has suggested that both readjustment weight (Holmes & Rahe 1967) and undesirability (see Lin et al. 1986 and Thoits 1983 for reviews) are important aspects for assessing a life event's potential impact on distress.

The current research program determined that a weight of 30 to 100 would be used as the readjustment criterion. This range reflects the top 50 percent of the original 43 life events in the social readjustment rating scale devised by Holmes and Rahe (1967). Events were considered undesirable if more than 50% of the respondents experiencing them in the first three waves of the Albany Study rated them as undesirable. We should note that some events that met either of these two criteria also happened to fall in the category of life changes that reflect changes in demographic characteristics (e.g., death of a spouse, divorce, separation, birth of a child).

Grouping of life changes

In the present study, experiences and events are grouped into ten categories:

(1) changes in marital status – married, divorced, separated, death of a spouse;
(2) birth of children – gave birth to first child, gave birth to other child;
(3) change in residence – moved within town, moved out of town;
(4) change in education – started school, graduated, ceased going to school;
(5) change in employment – started to work for the first time, started to work other than the first time, was laid off, business failed, out of work over a month, out of work less than a month, was fired, retired;
(6) deaths – death of a child, death of a close friend, death of a brother or sister, death of parent, death of other close family member;
(7) financial/legal/work-related changes – detained in jail, experienced worsened financial status, had foreclosure of mortgage or loan, made major purchase or mortgage loan, had troubles with boss, troubles with co-workers;
(8) health changes – had serious illness, had serious injury, changed health of a family member;
(9) personal changes 1 – had sexual difficulties, experienced an increase in arguments with a partner;
(10) personal changes 2 – changes in recreation and in social activities.

The first five categories deal with changes in social role statuses whereas the latter five categories deal with significant events, traditionally treated as stressors. These constructed categories will simplify our discussion.

Time units used for reporting life changes

Past research using the life history approach has used many different time units, which can be as short as a day or as long as a year. Although a variety of factors affect the time units used in a life history calendar, two were important to us: the length of time available for the interview and the burden of recall placed on the respondent.

As noted earlier, the current study covers a 16-year interval. Using weekly or monthly time units would impose too great a recall burden on the respondent. Also, since most studies using life event inventories have adopted a period covering one year prior to the interview, we decided that a one-year interval for other life experiences would maintain a certain level of consistency in time measurement. The use of a one-year time unit would allow the development of counts of life events (by types) for each of the 15 years since initiation of the study.

The constructed life history calendar was pretested and underwent modifications. The final version, used in the 1993 study, appears in Appendix A. The calendar documents the initiation and termination dates for each change experienced. The current study focuses on the initial point of each experience episode, but the calendar can be used as well to examine duration and timing (for cohort, period, and aging) effects.

Recalled experiences

The present chapter makes comparisons between 1979–80 on-time data and recall data. In the life history calendar, we asked respondents for changes since April 1979, the starting point of the panel surveys. Thus, the first full-year information is available starting in 1980. However, the 1980 survey was conducted during the spring and summer. For those respondents interviewed early in the 1979 survey, data on changes in the past twelve months (which the survey ascertained) cover a few months back into 1978 and would miss several months in the latter part of 1979. Such overlap with the previous year and omission of several months also were true for the 1980 survey. We decided to combine the data from the two waves so that at least data for the latter months of 1979 and early months of 1980 were obtained for all respondents. Nevertheless, recall errors measured in the present study represent the maximal possible extent of actual recall errors. Alternative time units (e.g., using 1979 or 1980 as the baseline) were examined, and the results were consistent with those reported here.

The analysis proceeds in several phases. We first examine the extent of recall errors for each category of experiences. To do this, we created a dummy variable of recall error for each category. If the same number of experiences or

Table 1. *Recall errors for ten categories
of life changes, 1979–80 (N = 419)*

Categories	Frequency	Percentage with recall errors
None	105	25.1
1	116	27.7
2	79	18.9
3	47	11.2
4	34	8.1
5	15	3.6
6	15	3.6
7	6	0.2
9	1	0.2

events was mentioned in both the on-time and recall data, the variable received a score of 0. If there was any discrepancy, no matter how many or in which direction (recall number either lower or higher than the on-time number), the variable received a score of 1. Table 1 shows the percentage of respondents making recall errors over the ten categories for 1980. As can be seen, about one quarter (25.15%) of the respondents made no recall errors in any of the ten categories. About another quarter (27.7%) made recall errors in only one of the ten categories. About four fifths (82.9%) of the respondents made recall errors in three or fewer categories, and only 7.6% made recall errors in five or more categories.

Next, we examined the distribution of recall errors in each of the ten categories; the results appear in Table 2. For each category of experiences, we counted the number of discrepancies between the actual reports in 1979–80 and the recalled information for 1979–80 in the 1993 survey. As can be seen in the first column, life changes reported on-time tended to concentrate in the education, employment, deaths, financial/legal/work, health, and personal 2 (recreation and social activities) categories. In contrast, recall (presented in column 2) was substantially lower in reporting changes in categories of deaths, financial/legal/work, health, and personal 2. When we summed all recall errors, whether they were due to underreporting (missing the experience reported in 1979–80) or overreporting (mentioning an experience not reported in 1979–80), they tended to concentrate on financial/legal/work, health, and personal 2 categories (see column 3 in Table 2). Recall of personal experiences was less error-prone (e.g., marital changes, births of children, residential moves, or personal changes 1 – sexual difficulties and argument with partner/spouse). This is due in part to the fact that changes in these categories were few. On the other hand, errors in re-

Table 2. *Actual (on-time) and recalled life experiences, 1979–80*

Life experiences	Actual (mean)[a]	Recall (mean)[a]	Mean recall error[b]
Marital changes	0.05	0.05	0.03
Births	0.05	0.06	0.05
Residential moves	0.14	0.08	0.07
Education	0.25	0.10	0.16
Employment	0.27	0.28	0.20
Deaths	0.29	0.13	0.23
Financial/legal/work	0.34	0.05	0.32
Health	0.42	0.09	0.37
Personal 1[c]	0.08	0.02	0.08
Personal 2[d]	0.49	0.03	0.34

[a] Mean occurrence refers to the mean number of experienced changes in each category.
[b] Mean of recall errors is based on counts of errors in each category. Since errors include both underreporting and overreporting, the mean does not necessarily equate to the difference of the means presented in the first two columns.
[c] Sexual difficulties, and arguments with partner or spouse.
[d] Changes in social activities and recreation.

calling chronic experiences or daily routines such as health, deaths, financial/legal/work changes, and recreational and social activities (personal 2) tended to be more extensive.[1]

Underreporting versus overreporting

The extent of recall errors can be further analyzed in several ways. One way is to distinguish between overreporting and underreporting. Overreporting is said to have occurred when recall indicates a particular type of experience for 1979–80 when there was no actual (on-time) experience reported in the 1979 and 1980 surveys; this may be seen as a type-II error (accepting an event when there is no such event). Underreporting occurs when recall indicates no such experience in 1979–80 even though it was reported in 1979 or 1980; this may represent a type-I error (rejecting an event when there is such an event). Of the two, overreporting may be more serious, since it represents the construction or invention of non-experiences. Table 3 shows the extent of over- and underreporting errors for each of the ten categories of experiences.

As can be seen, the recall errors are overwhelmingly due to underreporting of actual experiences. No more than 3% of respondents show overreporting in

Table 3. *Overreporting and underreporting*
errors, 1979–80[a]

| | Percentage of respondents | | |
| | Over-reporting | Under-reporting | Total[b] |
Life experiences			
Marital	0.00	0.03	0.03
Births	0.03	0.02	0.05
Residential moves	0.00	0.11	0.11
Education	0.00	0.16	0.16
Employment	0.00	0.17	0.17
Deaths	0.00	0.21	0.21
Financial/legal/work	0.00	0.25	0.25
Health	0.00	0.33	0.33
Personal 1	0.00	0.07	0.07
Personal 2	0.00	0.27	0.27

[a] Recall error is a dummy variable, with 1 = difference in actual and recall values and 0 = same actual and recall values.
[b] Total includes percentage of respondents who underreport or overreport or both.

any category. For underreporting, again, the extent of errors is concentrated in categories representative of health and death events, financial/legal/work changes, and recreational and social activities (personal 2). The fewest errors in underreporting occur for intimate and family experiences such as marital status changes, childbirths, and sexual difficulties or arguments with partner (personal 1). We conclude, therefore, that *recall errors tend to reflect underreporting* rather than overreporting life experiences *and tend to occur for chronic or routine activities* rather than intimate and family experiences. That is, recall errors should result in the underestimation of the impacts of life experiences over time. This underestimation is more severe for chronic and daily routine experiences.

Error in selective retention or in timing of experience

Recall errors may result not from forgetting the experiences, but from forgetting the exact timing of the experiences. Thus, something that actually happened 14 years ago might be remembered as something that happened 13 or 14 years ago, or vaguely remembered as something happening roughly between 10 and 15 years ago. Since the panel study contains on-time data for 1979, 1980, and 1982, it is possible to explore such timing errors. For the actual 1979–80 experiences, we vary the recall interval categories among one year (1979), two years

Table 4. *Percentage of respondents with underreporting errors at
various recall intervals when the actual interval is one year (1979–80)*

Life experiences	1979	1979–80	1979–81	1979–82	1979–83
Marital status	0.01	0.01	0.01	0.01	0.01
Married	0.01	0.01	0.01	0.01	0.01
Divorced	0.00	0.00	0.00	0.00	0.00
Separated	0.00	0.00	0.00	0.00	0.00
Widowed	0.00	0.00	0.00	0.00	0.00
Birth	0.01	0.01	0.01	0.01	0.01
Residential move	0.08	0.08	0.07	0.07	0.02
Education	0.10	0.09	0.09	0.08	0.08
Employment	0.12	0.11	0.10	0.09	0.09
Deaths	0.13	0.13	0.13	0.12	0.11
Friend	0.05	0.05	0.05	0.04	0.04
Family member	0.10	0.09	0.08	0.08	0.07
Child	0.00	0.00	0.00	0.00	0.00
Financial/legal/work	0.17	0.17	0.17	0.17	0.16
Gone to jail	0.00	0.00	0.00	0.00	0.00
Financial problems	0.08	0.08	0.08	0.08	0.08
Foreclosure	0.00	0.00	0.00	0.00	0.00
Major mortgage or loan	0.05	0.05	0.05	0.05	0.05
Trouble with boss/worker	0.06	0.06	0.06	0.06	0.06
Health	0.20	0.19	0.19	0.19	0.18
Personal injury/illness	0.10	0.10	0.09	0.09	0.09
Injury/illness in family	0.12	0.12	0.12	0.12	0.11
Personal 1	0.04	0.04	0.04	0.04	0.04
Sexual difficulties	0.02	0.02	0.02	0.02	0.02
Arguments with partner	0.02	0.02	0.02	0.02	0.02
Personal 2	0.16	0.16	0.16	0.16	0.16
Change in social activities	0.05	0.05	0.05	0.05	0.05
Change in recreation	0.15	0.15	0.15	0.14	0.14

(1979, 1980), three years (1979, 1980, 1981), four years (1979, 1980, 1981, 1982),
and five years (1979, 1980, 1981, 1982, 1983). That is, recalled experiences thought
to have occurred during 1979, 1980, ... are combined respectively to compare
with the actual experiences reported in the 1979–80 surveys. Analyses show little variation from those presented in Table 4 for the two-year (1979–80) recalls.
Thus, we conclude that *recall errors are mostly due to forgetting or selective
retention,* rather than the timing of their occurrences.

In summary, recall errors seem to reflect forgetting some of the more chronic
or routine changes and experiences in life. Further, there is little evidence to suggest that people "make up" or construct (i.e., overreport) changes and experiences. Changes and experiences that are recalled tend to reflect what actually
happened, only to a lesser extent. Thus, recall data may result in underestimating the long-term effects of life changes. Whatever lagged effects these recalled

changes may exert on subsequent distress can be considered as reliable and valid, and the estimated effects tend to err in the conservative direction.

Detecting systematic errors

The final task of this chapter is to determine the extent to which the patterns of recall errors are systematic. The recall errors found (Tables 1, 2, and 3) are moderate to minimal, and reflect underestimation. Nevertheless, to carry through this exercise, we attempt to assess whether these recall errors are related to any social or psychological characteristics – in order to gain some insights as to whether they might be inducing systematic errors when certain subpopulations are under study. If this is the case, it might be possible to make "corrections" when the stress–distress model is analyzed. This would be useful for studies using cross-sectional surveys with only retrospective life history data.

The strategy for estimating the systematic recall error and for constructing corrections is as follows. We hypothesize that recall error is a function of systematic biases due to a person's psychological and social characteristics. The task, therefore, is to construct an estimation equation that predicts the extent of recall errors, given certain psychological and social characteristics of an individual. Once such an estimation equation is constructed, it may be possible to use it to predict the likelihood of recall errors, given the particular social and psychological characteristics of each respondent. The prediction equation becomes the correction variable, to be taken into account in the estimation of the lagged effects of recalled stressors on current distress.

There are two requirements for the estimation procedure. First, we must restrict the exogenous variables to constructs assessed in the cross-sectional study, so that the prediction equation can be used in cross-sectional studies. Second, the exogenous variables should represent the most critical correlates of the recall error variable. At this point, we do not have a theory or specific data guiding the selection of such variables, so we can only use what is available in the 1993 study.

With these requirements in mind, we first construct two estimation equations for recall errors, for underreporting and overreporting separately.[2] The dependent variable in each case is the number of discrepancies between (1) each actual experience reported in 1979–80 in each category of experiences (as shown in Table 2) and (2) the presence or absence of the experience recalled in 1993.

The predictors are selected from among the social and psychological factors usually associated with the stress process and routinely gathered in stress research. The final list includes: self-competence, self-esteem, gender (male), race (white), married, employed, education, occupational prestige, individual income, household income, number of children, and presence of young children (0–5 years of age) in the home. These variables have been found to associate with mental distress in the research literature. All predictors are from the 1993 survey. Ordinary linear regression for each category of life experiences is performed. The results (significant predictors and R^2) are presented in Table 5.

The task here is to assess the nonrandomness of the recall. We will defer to another paper any conceptual or theoretical analyses regarding the substantive meanings of the significant correlates for recall errors concerning each type of life experience. In general, for the given set of exogenous variables, systematic errors seem minimal to moderate, as the explained variances (R^2) for the equations range from 0.03 to 0.11. Systematic errors tend to occur in recall of experiences concerning financial/legal/work changes (0.11) or recreational and social activities (0.09). Of the selected twelve exogenous variables, only four are statistically significant in one or more recall error equations. Marital status change appears in four equations and age in three equations.

We cannot conclude that recall errors are generally not systematic, as the predictors used may not reflect all the possible sources inducing recall errors with respect to the life history calendar. However, we would tentatively suggest that, in the usual stress–distress modeling, *estimation of recall errors does not seem to induce significant systematic biases.* To the extent that such biases do occur, they tend to be related to marital status and age. Additional sociodemographic variables such as employment status and self-esteem may also be relevant.

Constructing and using correction variables

Although the evidence of systematic errors associated with recall is limited, we proceed with an exercise demonstrating how information concerning potential systematic recall errors can be taken into account in the usual stress–distress analysis. The question to be addressed is: In a cross-sectional survey to assess the presumed lagged effects of stressors on distress, how does the researcher account for possible recall errors in using data from the life history calendar and then make corrections for them? Such corrections should be estimated from variables collected in the cross-section survey.

We carry out this exercise in two steps. In the first step, we construct "correction" variables. These correction variables are constructed from: (1) the short-form equations involving the minimal number of predictors (marital status and age) and (2) the full-form equations involving the four variables in Table 5 that are significant in at least one equation. Each equation is the predicted extent of recall errors from the set of independent variables. The constructed correction equations or variables, to be called recall error indexes (REI), are as follows:

(1) recall error index, short-form (REI-S) = B1 (age) + B2 (married);
(2) recall error index, full-form (REI-F) = B1 (age) + B2 (married)
      + B3 (self-esteem) + B4 (employed).

Here, the Bs are standardized partial regression coefficients (beta weights).

Table 5. *Estimations for recall errors[a] (beta),*
1979–80

Life experiences	Significant predictors[b]	R^2
Marital status		
Underreporting	married (−0.15)	0.03
Overreporting	N.A.	
Birth		
Underreporting	N.S.	0.03
Overreporting	age (−0.20)	0.06
Residential move		
Underreporting	age (−0.16)	0.05
Overreporting	N.A.	
Education		
Underreporting	self-esteem (0.14)	0.07
Overreporting	N.A.	
Employment		
Underreporting	N.S.	0.04
Overreporting	N.A.	
Deaths		
Underreporting	N.S.	0.04
Overreporting	N.A.	
Financial/legal/work		
Underreporting	married (−0.17)	0.11
Overreporting	N.A.	
Health		
Underreporting	N.S.	0.03
Overreporting	N.A.	
Personal 1		
Underreporting	N.S.	0.04
Overreporting	N.A.	
Personal 2		
Underreporting	married (−0.15)	0.09
Overreporting	N.A.	
Total		
Underreporting	married (−0.18)	0.10
	employed (0.14)	
Overreporting	age (−0.20)	0.06

Notes: Regressors in all equations (all measured in 1993):
self-competence; self-esteem; gender (men); race (white);
married; employed; education; occupational prestige; personal income; household income; number of children; young
child at home (5 years or younger). N.A. denotes "equations
not applicable." N.S. denotes "none of the regressors are statistically significant."
[a] Recall errors is a count of errors made in respective categories.
[b] $p < .05$.

Table 6. *Recall error indexes (1993 reported changes in 1979–80)*

1. REI-S (recall error index – short form)
   A. REI-S (underreporting) = $-(0.236)$(age) $-(0.139)$(married)
   B. REI-S (overreporting) = $-(0.161)$(age) $+(0.074)$(married)
   C. REI-S (total) = $-(0.251)$(age) $-(0.132)$(married)
2. REI-F (recall error index – full form)
   A. REI-F (underreporting) = $-(0.126)$(age) $-(0.155)$(married) $+(0.046)$(self-esteem)
        $+(0.158)$(employed)
   B. REI-F (overreporting) = $-(0.195)$(age) $+(0.085)$(married) $-(0.071)$(self-esteem)
        $-(0.031)$(employed)
   C. REI-F (total) = $-(0.145)$(age) $-(0.146)$(married) $+(0.039)$(self-esteem) $+(0.154)$(employed)

Such equations are constructed for each category of life experiences and also for a total summary of life experiences. For this exercise, we construct equations for underreporting and overreporting separately. These equations, with the 1993 variables as predictors for recall errors (difference between actual experiences in 1979–80 and recalled experiences for 1979–80 in the 1993 data set), appear in Table 6. Only standardized coefficients are reported here.

The second step takes into account the corrections for recall errors in estimating the relationship between the effects of recalled life experiences in 1979–80 on distress. In this exercise, the stress–distress model is analyzed with the Center for Epidemiologic Studies depression scale (CESD) as the dependent variable and the life experiences as the independent variable. The life experiences are measured in two ways: actual reported experiences in the 1979 and 1980 surveys; and recalled experiences for these two years in the 1993 survey. Distress is also measured in two ways: the CESD as measured in the 1980 survey; and the CESD as measured in the 1993 survey. The 1993 CESD measure is a dependent variable in the lagged effect model. However, the time gap is so long that it is impractical to expect a significant direct impact from the life changes experienced 13 years previously.

We will compare the results between the equations involving the actual experiences and the recalled experiences. Our expectation is that the coefficient for the recalled experiences will be an underestimate of the coefficient for the actual experiences. Then, a correction variable will be added to the equation for the recalled experiences, to see if the estimation will improve and more realistically approximate the effect for the actual life experiences. These results and comparisons appear in Table 7.

The first panel (A) estimates the effect of 1979–80 life stressors on the 1980 CESD. The standardized coefficient for actual 1979–80 experiences is 0.27 and that for recalled 1979–80 experiences is 0.09, showing that the recalled stressors substantially underestimate the "true" effect. When any one of the recall error

Table 7. *Regression of CESD on life experiences 1979–80 with corrections for recall errors*[a]

Life experiences, 1979–80	Estimate	Correction variable	Corrected estimate
A. Effects on 1980 CESD			
Actual	0.27 (1.08)***		
Recalled	0.09 (0.65)		
Recalled with corrections for:[b]			
REI-S: overreporting	0.09 (0.64)	0.005 (0.04)***	0.10
REI-F: overreporting	0.06 (0.44)	0.09 (0.82)	0.15
REI-S: underreporting	0.05 (0.37)	0.14 (1.25)**	0.19
REI-F: underreporting	0.07 (0.50)	0.10 (0.83)	0.17
REI-S: total errors	0.05 (0.37)	0.14 (1.21)**	0.19
REI-F: total errors	0.07 (0.48)	0.10 (0.87)*	0.17
REI-S: both	0.07 (0.49)		
overreporting and		−0.10 (−0.86)	
underreporting		0.20 (1.70)***	0.17
REI-F: both	0.05 (0.37)		
overreporting and		0.07 (0.60)	
underreporting		0.08 (0.65)**	0.20
B. Effects on 1993 CESD			
Actual	0.07 (0.30)		
Recalled	0.07 (0.49)		
Recalled with corrections for:[b]			
REI-S: overreporting	0.12 (0.90)*	−0.18 (−1.65)***	−0.06
REI-F: overreporting	0.07 (0.52)	−0.01 (−0.12)	0.06
REI-S: underreporting	0.05 (0.36)	0.06 (0.59)	0.11
REI-F: underreporting	0.08 (0.56)	−0.04 (−0.37)	0.04
REI-S: total errors	0.05 (0.39)	0.05 (0.47)	0.10
REI-F: total errors	0.08 (0.56)	−0.04 (−0.37)	0.04
REI-S: both	0.10 (0.74)		0.03
overreporting and		−0.29 (−2.74)***	
underreporting		0.22 (2.01)***	
REI-F: both	0.08 (0.56)		0.07
overreporting and		0.003 (0.003)	
underreporting		−0.04 (−0.37)	

[a] Recall errors is a total count of errors made in reporting life experiences. Coefficients are standardized estimates (metric coefficient in parentheses).
[b] REI: recall error index (see Table 6 for details). In each equation with a correction, only the specified index is added to the equation. Only the standardized coefficients are computed.
*p < .05.   **p < .01.   ***p < .001.

indexes is incorporated, the estimation of the corrected stressor effect is improved. For example, when the REI-S (short-form) for overreporting is incorporated, the corrected stressor effect becomes 0.10 (0.09 + 0.005). This coefficient still underestimates the actual effect (0.27). On the other hand, when the REI-S for underreporting is incorporated, the corrected stressor effect becomes 0.19 (0.05 + 0.14), still underestimating the actual effect but a significant improvement over the first equation. Other equations incorporating the various recall error indexes all show consistent improvement in approximating the true effect. As expected, corrections for underreporting generally improve more than those for overreporting.

In the second panel (B), estimates for regressing the 1993 CESD on the 1979–80 stressors are performed. As expected, the "actual" lagged effect is not significant (0.07), and recalled experiences also show a nonsignificant coefficient (0.07). Hence there is no point in carrying the analysis further. However, as can be seen, the correction with the incorporation of a recall error index fluctuates (0.03–0.11) around the true effect of 0.07. Thus, the incorporation of correction variables did not substantially increase the bias even when the true effect is insignificant.

Summary and recommendations

This chapter addressed two methodological issues central to the study of stress in the life course: the construction of a life history calendar, and assessment of its reliability and validity. With a panel data set, we showed that recall errors usually reflect underreporting rather than overreporting, and that the extent of recall errors tends to be greater for chronic and routine changes and less for personal and family experiences. Thus, recalled information from the life history calendar will underestimate rather than inflate the potential lagged effects of such life experiences on later distress experienced. We also showed that recall errors tend to be a function of forgetting the experiences rather than misplacing the experiences in time. We demonstrated that recall errors do not seem to present substantial systematic biases, as their variances are only minimally or moderately explained by an array of social and psychological variables. Finally, we constructed a series of recall error indexes to correct the underestimated effects of recalled experiences.

This study represents an exploratory assessment for accounting for errors in retrospective life history data. Limitations on the data sets, measurements, and decisions on life experiences studies preclude any definitive conclusions. Nevertheless, we are encouraged by the results and feel that the life history calendar can be a very useful tool in the retrospective reconstruction of life events and social role changes. Elsewhere, for example, we have shown that clusters of distal stressors (recalled changes in 1979–83, in 1984–88, and in 1989–93) contribute to explaining current distress (1993) after current stressors are accounted for (Ensel et al. 1996; Lin & Ensel 1994). Further, distal stressors in 1979–83 (especially residential moves and deaths) show long-term effects for respondents aged 65 or older. Because this analysis incorporates no recall error corrections, it tends to underestimate such experiences, thus representing a conservative estimate of their potential stressful effects. With caution and planning, it seems feasible to account for recall errors and so improve estimation of the lagged effects of stressors on distress.

Notes

1. One suspicion was that errors may be more prone for changes involving nonfamily members or situations. Further analysis for the specific change in each of the categories where substantial errors are made did not show clear trends. For example, errors in reporting deaths include 8% for family members and 4% for friends. Errors in recalling financial/legal/work changes occurred equally for financial problems (6%), major mortgate or loan (5%), and trouble with boss or co-worker (5%). Errors in the health category involve both personal injuries or illnesses (12%) and injuries or illnesses among family members (12%).
2. Even though overreporting is shown to be minimal, we decided to carry out the more comprehensive analysis in this exploratory and illustrative exercise.

Appendix: The Albany life history calendar

Changes in status

Now, I would like to ask you a few questions about things that may have happened to you since April of 1979.

1. CHANGE IN MARITAL STATUS
   a. First of all, in April 1979, were you married, divorced, separated, widowed, or had you never been married?
      1. married (CONTINUE)
      2. divorced (CONTINUE)
      3. separated (CONTINUE)
      4. widowed (CONTINUE)
      5. never married (CONTINUE)
   b. Since then, was there any change in your marital status? That is, did you get married, or become divorced, separated, or widowed?
      1. yes (CONTINUE)
      2. no (GO TO Q # 2)
(*Note:* If there was a change, get sequence of events in proper order.)
   c. What happened? Did you get married, become divorced, separated, or were you widowed?
      1. got married (CONTINUE)
      2. became divorced (CONTINUE)
      3. became legally separated (CONTINUE)
      4. became widowed (CONTINUE)
   d. When did this happen?
      (PLACE "M" IN APPROPRIATE YEAR IF RESPONDENT GOT MARRIED)
      (PLACE "D" IN APPROPRIATE YEAR IF RESPONDENT GOT DIVORCED)

(PLACE "S" IN APPROPRIATE YEAR IF RESPONDENT GOT SEPARATED)

(PLACE "W" IN APPROPRIATE YEAR IF RESPONDENT BECAME WIDOWED)

e. Were there any other changes in your marital status after this?
  1. yes (GO BACK TO c)
  2. no (GO TO Q # 2)

1979	1980	1981	1982	1983	1984	1985	1986	1987	1988	1989	1990	1991	1992	1993

2. BIRTH OF CHILDREN

(*Note:* If respondent previously reported not having any children, skip to Q # 3)
  a. Since April 1979, have you had any children?
    1. yes (CONTINUE)
    2. no (GO TO Q # 3)
  b. In what year was each child born?
    (PLACE A "1" IN THE YEAR 1ST CHILD WAS BORN,
      "2" IN THE YEAR 2ND CHILD WAS BORN, ETC.)

1979	1980	1981	1982	1983	1984	1985	1986	1987	1988	1989	1990	1991	1992	1993

3. CHANGE IN RESIDENCE

  a. Since April 1979, have you moved?
    1. yes (CONTINUE)
    2. no (GO TO Q # 4)
  b. Was it a local move or an out-of-state move?
    1. local move (CONTINUE)
    2. out-of-state move (CONTINUE)
  c. In what year did you move?
    (PLACE AN "L" IN APPROPRIATE YEAR IF IT WAS A LOCAL MOVE)
    (PLACE AN "O" IN APPROPRIATE YEAR IF IT WAS AN OUT-OF-STATE MOVE)
  d. Were there any other moves?
    1. yes (GO BACK TO b)
    2. no (GO TO Q # 4)

1979	1980	1981	1982	1983	1984	1985	1986	1987	1988	1989	1990	1991	1992	1993

4. CHANGE IN EDUCATION

  a. In April 1979, were you going to school?
    1. yes (GO TO b)
    2. no (GO TO c)
  b. Was it part-time or full-time?
    1. part-time (GO TO f)
    2. full-time (GO TO f)

c. Have you gone to school since then?
  1. yes (CONTINUE)
  2. no (GO TO Q # 5)
d. Was it part-time or full-time?
  1. part-time (CONTINUE)
  2. full-time (CONTINUE)
e. In what year did you start this?
  (PLACE A "P" IN YEAR RESPONDENT STARTED SCHOOL PART-TIME)
  (PLACE A "F" IN YEAR RESPONDENT STARTED SCHOOL FULL-TIME)
f. Have you left since then, or have you been continuously going to school since then?
  1. left (CONTINUE)
  2. still attending school (GO TO Q # 5)
g. When did you leave?
  (PLACE AN "L" IN THE YEAR RESPONDENT LEFT SCHOOL)
h. Did you go back to school since then?
  1. yes (GO BACK TO d)
  2. no (GO TO Q # 5)

1979	1980	1981	1982	1983	1984	1985	1986	1987	1988	1989	1990	1991	1992	1993

5. CHANGE IN EMPLOYMENT
  a. In April 1979, did you have a paying job?
    1. yes (GO TO b)
    2. no (GO TO c)
  b. Was it part-time or full-time?
    1. part-time (GO TO f)
    2. full-time (GO TO f)
  c. Have you had a paying job since then?
    1. yes (CONTINUE)
    2. no (GO TO Q # 6)
  d. Was it part-time or full-time?
    1. part-time (CONTINUE)
    2. full-time (CONTINUE)
  e. When did you start this job?
    (PLACE A "P" IN YEAR RESPONDENT STARTED PART-TIME JOB)
    (PLACE A "F" IN YEAR RESPONDENT STARTED FULL-TIME JOB)
  f. Did you ever leave this job?
    1. yes (CONTINUE)
    2. no (GO TO Q # 6)
  g. When did you leave this job?
    (PLACE AN "L" IN THE YEAR RESPONDENT LEFT THE JOB)

h. Did you get another paying job since then?
   1. yes (GO BACK TO d)
   2. no (GO TO Q # 6)

1979	1980	1981	1982	1983	1984	1985	1986	1987	1988	1989	1990	1991	1992	1993

Significant events

Now, I would like to ask you about a number of major events that people experience in their lives. Have any of these events occurred to you since 1979?
(PLACE A "1" IN ALL YEARS IN WHICH EVENT OCCURRED)

DEATHS
6. Death of close friend
7. Death of close family member
8. Death of a child

1979	1980	1981	1982	1983	1984	1985	1986	1987	1988	1989	1990	1991	1992	1993

FINANCIAL/LEGAL/WORK
 9. Gone to jail
10. Serious financial problems
11. Foreclosure of mortgage or loan
12. Took on a major mortage or loan
13. Serious trouble with boss/worker

1979	1980	1981	1982	1983	1984	1985	1986	1987	1988	1989	1990	1991	1992	1993

HEALTH
14. Serious injury or illness
15. Serious injury/illness to family member

1979	1980	1981	1982	1983	1984	1985	1986	1987	1988	1989	1990	1991	1992	1993

	79	80	81	82	83	84	85	86	87	88	89	90	91	92	93
CHANGES IN STATUS															
1 CHANGE IN MARITAL STATUS															
2 BIRTH OF CHILDREN															
3 CHANGE IN RESIDENCE															
4 CHANGE IN EDUCATION															
5 CHANGE IN EMPLOYMENT STATUS															
SIGNIFICANT EVENTS															
DEATHS															
6. DEATH OF CLOSE FRIEND															
7. DEATH OF CLOSE FAMILY MEMBER															
8. DEATH OF A CHILD															
FINANCIAL/LEGAL/WORK															
9. GONE TO JAIL															
10. SERIOUS FINANCIAL PROBLEM															
11. FORECLOSURE-MORTGAGE/LOAN															
12. TOOK ON MAJOR MORTGAGE/LOAN															
13. SERIOUS TROUBLE - BOSS/COWORKER															
HEALTH															
14. SERIOUS INJURY/ILLNESS															
15. SERIOUS INJURY/ILLNESS-FAMILY MEMBER															
PERSONAL															
16. SEXUAL DIFFICULTIES															
17. INCREASE ARGUMENTS-SPOUSE															
18. MAJOR CHANGE IN SOCIAL ACTIVITIES															
19. MAJOR CHANGE IN AMT OF RECREATION															

The life history calendar.

PERSONAL

16. Sexual difficulties
17. Increase in arguments with spouse
18. Major change in social activites (I)ncrease (D)ecrease
19. Major change in amount of recreation (I)ncrease (D)ecrease

1979	1980	1981	1982	1983	1984	1985	1986	1987	1988	1989	1990	1991	1992	1993

References

Brown, George W., & Tirrill, Harris (1978). *The Social Origins of Depression: A Study of Psychiatric Disorder in Women.* New York: Free Press.

Elder, Glen H., Jr. (1986). Military times and turning points in men's lives. *Developmental Psychology* 22: 233–45.

Elder, Glen H., Jr., Caspi, Avshalom, & Downey, Geraldine (1986). Problem behavior and family relationships: life course and intergenerational themes. In Aage B. Sorensen, Franz E. Weinert, & Lonnie R. Sherrod (eds.), *Human Development and the Life Course: Multidisciplinary Perspectives.* Hillsdale, NJ: Erlbaum, pp. 293–340.

Elder, Glen H., Jr., George, Linda K., & Shanahan, Michael J. (1994). Psychosocial stress over the life course. In Howard B. Kaplan (ed.), *Psychosocial Stress: Perspectives on Structure, Theory, Life Course, and Method.* San Diego, CA: Academic Press, pp. 247–92.

Ensel, Walter M., Peek, M. Kristen, Lin, Nan, & Lai, Gina (1996). Stress in the life course: a life history approach. *Journal of Aging and Health* 8: 389–416.

Freedman, D., Thornton, A., Camburn, D., Alwin, D., & Young-DeMarco, L. (1988). The life history calendar: a technique for collecting retrospective data. In Clifford Clogg (ed.), *Sociological Methodology.* New York: Academic Press, pp. 37–68.

George, Linda K. (1993). Sociological perspectives on life transitions. *Annual Review of Sociology* 19: 353–73.

Holmes, Thomas, & Rahe, R. (1967). The social readjustment rating scale. *Journal of Psychosomatic Research* 11: 213–18.

Jenkins, C. David, Hurst, Michael W., & Rose, Robert M. (1979). Life changes: do people really remember? *Archives of General Psychiatry* 36: 379–84.

Lin, Nan, Dean, Alfred, & Ensel, Walter (1986). *Social Support, Life Events, and Depression.* Orlando, FL: Academic Press.

Lin, Nan, & Ensel, Walter M. (1994). Social stress in the life course. Paper presented at the Eighth World Congress of Sociology (July, Bielefeld, Germany).

Moen, Phyllis, Dempster-McClain, Donna, & Williams, Robin M., Jr. (1992). Successful aging: a life-course perspective on women's multiple roles and health. *American Journal of Sociology* 97: 1612–38.

Pearlin, Leonard I., Liberman, Morton A., Menaghan, Elizabeth G., & Mullan, Joseph T. (1981). The stress process. *Journal of Health and Social Behavior* 22: 337–56.

Peters, H. Elizabeth (1988). Retrospective versus panel data in analyzing life cycle events. *Journal of Human Resources* 23: 489–501.

Powers, Edward A., Goudy, Willis J., & Keith, Pat M. (1978). Congruence between panel and recall data in longitudinal research. *Public Opinion Quarterly* 42: 380–9.

Romney, A. Kimball, & Weller, Susan C. (1984). Predicting informant accuracy from patterns of recall among individuals. *Social Networks* 6: 59-77.

Rossi, Alice S., & Rossi, Peter H. (1990). *Of Human Bonding: Parent-Child Relations Across the Life Course*. New York: Aldine.

Thoits, Peggy A. (1983). Dimensions of life events that influence psychological distress: an evaluation and synthesis of the literature. In Howard B. Kaplan (ed.), *Psychosocial Stress*. New York: Academic Press, pp. 33-103.

Wheaton, Blair (1990). Life transitions, role histories, and mental health. *American Sociological Review* 55: 209-23.

14 Using discrete-time survival analysis to study event occurrence across the life course

John B. Willett & Judith D. Singer

As the chapters in this volume illustrate, an important class of questions arising in life-course research ask "whether" and, if so, "when" a variety of events occur. Researchers investigating the consequences of childhood traumas on later well-being, for instance, ask whether an individual ever experiences depression and, if so, when onset first occurs (see Chapter 3). Other researchers ask questions about whether and when street children return to their homes (Chapter 4), whether and when high school dropouts find work (Chapter 5), whether and when high school graduates enroll in college, get married, and begin a family (Chapter 10), and whether and when young children make the transition between adult-supervised care and self-care (Chapter 8).

Familiar statistical techniques, such as regression and analysis of variance, and their more sophisticated cousins, such as structural equation modeling, are ill-suited for addressing questions about the timing and occurrence of events. These usually versatile methods fail because they are unable to handle situations in which the value of the outcome – whether and when the event occurs – is unknown for some people under study. When studying event occurrence, this type of information shortfall is inevitable. No matter how long a researcher collects data, some people in the sample will not experience the target event while under observation; some adults will not have a depressive episode, some street children will not return to their homes, some high school graduates will not marry, and some young children will not be left alone unsupervised. Statisticians say that such observations are *censored*.

Censoring creates an analytic dilemma. Although the researcher knows something about individuals with censored event times – if they do ever experience the event then it will be *after* the period covered by data collection – this knowledge is imprecise. If a high school graduate does not marry by age 30, for example, we would not want to conclude that he or she will *never* marry. All we can say is that, at age 30, the individual remains single. Yet the need to analyze simultaneously the data from individuals with censored and noncensored event

The order of the authors was determined by randomization.

273

times is apparent because the former are a key group of people: those least likely to experience the event.

Sound investigation of event occurrence requires an analytic method that deals consistently and evenhandedly with noncensored and censored observations. During the past 25 years, biostatisticians modeling human lifetimes (time to death) have developed a class of appropriate methods because they were faced with a related problem, in which some of the individuals in their studies (thankfully) did not die by the end of data collection (Allison 1984; Cox 1972; Kalbfleisch & Prentice 1980). Despite the foreboding appellations of these techniques – known variously as survival analysis, event history analysis, and hazard modeling – we believe that they constitute invaluable tools for stress researchers because they provide a sound mathematical basis for exploring the "whether" and "when" of any type of event.

In this chapter we provide a conceptual introduction to survival methods, focusing on the principles of discrete-time survival analysis. After distinguishing between discrete-time and continuous-time survival methods and describing why we emphasize the former approach, we use data describing the age of first onset of depression to introduce the fundamental building blocks of the methods: the hazard and survivor functions. We then describe the statistical models that can be used to link the pattern of temporal risk to predictors, commenting on the types of predictors that can be included in these models and how to interpret the results of statistical modeling. Finally, we show how researchers can be misled if they use traditional analytic techniques instead of survival methods. Our presentation here is nontechnical and conceptual. Readers seeking practical information and data-analytic advice should consult one of our companion papers (Singer & Willett 1991, 1993; Willett & Singer 1991, 1993, 1995) before using survival analysis in their research.

How do you measure time and record event occurrence?

To study event occurrence and its predictors, a researcher must record how long it takes, from some common starting time, for each individual in a sample to experience the target event. Researchers have a great deal of flexibility in identifying the "beginning of time." Because birth is both handy and meaningful across a wide variety of contexts, most researchers choose to use it as the beginning of time, using an individual's age (time since birth) as the marker of when the event occurred (see e.g. Chapter 3 in this volume). But researchers need not restrict themselves to the metric of chronological age. When modeling street children's return to a parental home, for example, the beginning of time may be defined as the time when the child first left the parental home (making "time on the street" the metric for analysis). Or, when modeling employment prospects among high school dropouts, "time since dropping out" might be used.

Once a common start time is defined, the researcher follows individuals (either prospectively on a periodic basis or through retrospective event history reconstruction) to record whether and, if so, when the target event occurs. All individuals who experience the target event during the period covered by data collection are assigned event times equal to the value of time when they actually experience the event. Individuals who do not experience the target event during the period covered by data collection are assigned *censored* event times, set equal to the value of time when data collection ended or when the individual was no longer at risk of experiencing the event. This censored event time, although seemingly imprecise, tells us a great deal about event occurrence: it tells us that the individual did not experience the target event at any earlier time.

Some researchers can record event occurrence data very precisely. When studying the relationship between experiences of childhood adversity and death, for example, Friedman et al. (1995) used public records of vital statistics to determine the precise time (year, month, and even day) when each deceased individual had actually died. More commonly, however, researchers record that the target event occurred within some finite time *interval*. A researcher might know, for example, the year when a person first experienced depressive symptoms, the month when an individual began a new job, or the grade when a youngster made the transition from adult-supervised care to self-care. We distinguish between these two scales of measurement (very precise and somewhat coarser) by calling the former *continuous-time* data and the latter *discrete-time* data.

In this paper, we focus on statistical methods for analyzing data recorded in discrete time. We have six reasons for this emphasis. First, we believe that these methods are more appropriate for much of the event history data collected by life-course researchers because, for logistical and financial reasons, data are usually recorded only in terms of intervals (see Chapter 13). Second, we have found that discrete-time methods are intuitively more comprehensible than their continuous-time cousins, facilitating initial mastery and later transition to continuous-time methods (if required). Third, this approach facilitates inclusion of both *time-invariant* and *time-varying* predictors, whereas inclusion of the latter can be difficult under the continuous-time approach. Thus, with discrete-time models, researchers can easily examine the effects of predictors whose values fluctuate naturally over the life course – for example, family structure and employment status. Fourth, discrete-time survival analysis fosters inspection of how the pattern of risk shapes up over time. The most popular continuous-time survival analysis strategy ("Cox regression"; Cox 1972) ignores the shape of the temporal risk profile entirely in favor of estimating the influence of predictors on risk under a restrictive assumption of "proportionality." Fifth, under the discrete-time approach, the proportionality assumption is easily checked and nonproportional models may be fitted. Finally, in discrete-time survival analysis, all estimation can be conducted using standard statistical

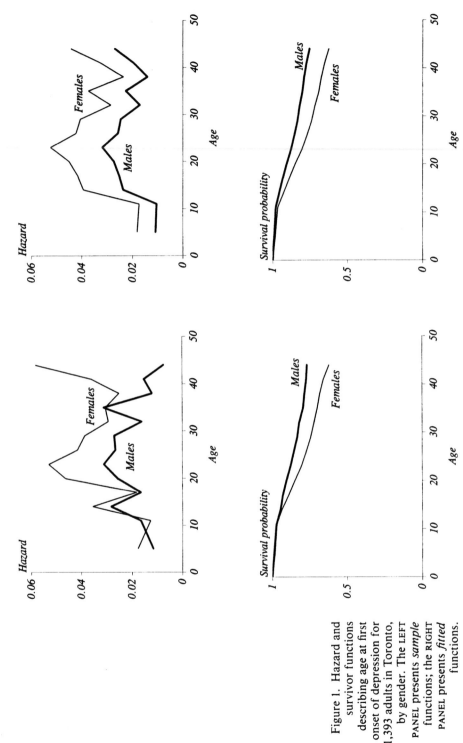

Figure 1. Hazard and survivor functions describing age at first onset of depression for 1,393 adults in Toronto, by gender. The LEFT PANEL presents *sample* functions; the RIGHT PANEL presents *fitted* functions.

software packages that fit logistic regression models. This avoids reliance on the dedicated computer software required for continuous-time survival analyses.

Describing survival data

The *hazard function* and the *survivor function* are the two fundamental tools for describing the occurrence and timing of events. Estimates of these functions provide answers to the two key descriptive questions: "When is the target event most likely to occur?" and "How much time passes before people are likely to experience the event?"

The hazard function

When examining the occurrence of an event – such as "experiencing an initial episode of depression" – for a random sample of individuals, we begin by asking about the pattern of event occurrence over time. We might ask, for example, when individuals are at greatest risk of first experiencing a depressive episode: during childhood, during their teens, or during their twenties, thirties, or forties? When we pose such questions, we are implicitly asking about the risk of event occurrence across time periods. Knowing how the risk of experiencing a depressive episode fluctuates over time provides answers to questions about the "whether" and "when" of event occurrence.

How can we summarize the risk of event occurrence among individuals in a sample, especially if some of these people have censored event times – by the end of data collection, they had never been clinically depressed? In discrete-time survival analysis, the fundamental quantity that represents the risk of event occurrence in each time period is called the *hazard probability*. Its computation in the sample is straightforward: in each time period, identify the pool of people still at risk of experiencing the event (the *risk set* – those who have reached this time period without experiencing the event) and compute the proportion of this group that experiences the event during the time period. Notice that this definition is inherently conditional; once someone experiences the event (or is censored) in one time period, that individual is no longer a member of the risk set in a future time period. The plot of the set of hazard probabilities against time yields the *hazard function,* a chronological summary of the risk of event occurrence.

In the top panel of the left-hand side of Figure 1, we present an illustrative hazard function using retrospective data gathered from a probability sample of 1,393 adults in metropolitan Toronto who were asked whether (and, if so) when they first experienced a depressive episode. (For a complete description of these data, see Chapter 3.) The panel presents two sample hazard functions, computed separately for men and women, describing the risk of initially experiencing a depressive episode in each of thirteen successive time periods: age 9 or younger, age 10–12, 13–15, 16–18, and so on in three-year increments through the age interval 40–42 and age 43 and older. Inspection of the sample hazard function helps pinpoint when events are most likely, and least likely, to occur. Examining these two hazard functions we see that, for both males and females, the risk of experiencing an initial episode of depression is relatively low in childhood, increases during adolescence, and then peaks in the early twenties. After this point in time, the risk of initial onset of depression *among those individuals who have not yet had a depressive episode* is much lower; by the early forties, it declines to preadolescent levels for men, although it rises again for women. Beyond this overall pattern of risk, also notice that in all but two time periods there is a sex differential: in general, women are at greater risk of experiencing a depressive episode than are men.

The conditionality inherent in the definition of hazard is critical. It ensures that all individuals remain in the risk set until the last time period in which they are eligible to experience the event (at which point they are either censored by the end of data collection or they experience the target event). For example, the hazard probability for initial onset of depression during the age period 31–33 is estimated conditionally using the data from all those individuals (852 of the initial sample of 1,393) who were at least age 31 when data were collected but who had not yet experienced a depressive episode during any earlier time period. Individuals who were not yet in their early thirties ($n = 227$) or who had already experienced a depressive episode ($n = 314$) are no longer at risk and are therefore excluded from the calculation of hazard in this time period and all subsequent time periods. This conditionality is crucial, for it ensures that the sample hazard probability deals evenhandedly with censoring – using all the information available in the sample event histories but not overextending this knowledge beyond the time for which the researcher has data.

The survivor function

In addition to using the hazard function to explore the conditional risk of event occurrence in each time period, it is useful to cumulate these period-by-period risks to display the proportion of the sample that "survive" through each time period – that is, the proportion of subjects who do *not* experience the event. The term *survival probability* refers to this proportion, and the term *survivor function* refers to plots arraying the survival probabilities against time. Sample survivor functions summarize aggregate event histories. They are easily computed by cumulating the entries in the sample hazard function over time (see Willett & Singer 1993).

In the bottom panel of the left-hand side of Figure 1, we display the sample survivor functions for men and women corresponding to the sample hazard functions displayed in the top panel. These survivor functions indicate the proportion of adults who "survived" (did not experience an initial depressive episode) through each successive time period – ages 1-9, 10-12, 13-15, and so on. Notice that the curves remain high in the beginning of time and then drop more sharply as time passes. At birth, all individuals are "surviving" – none of them has experienced a depressive episode – and so the survival probabilities are 1.00. Over time, as individuals experience depressive episodes, the survivor functions drop. Because most adults do not experience a depressive episode at any time in their lives, the curves do not reach zero, ending in this sample at 0.77 for men and 0.62 for women. These proportions indicate that, by the end of their late fifties, an estimated 77% of men and 62% of women had not yet experienced a depressive disorder. By subtraction, we estimate that 23% of men and 38% of women *have* experienced a depressive episode at some point before their sixties.

All sample survivor functions have a similar shape, a monotonically nonincreasing function of time. The rate of decline, however, can differ across groups. For example, although the two sample survivor functions in Figure 1 have similar shapes, the sharper decline among women suggests that, in comparison to men, they are at greater risk of experiencing a depressive episode.

Detecting predictors of event occurrence using a discrete-time hazard model

Estimated hazard functions and survivor functions describe when (and whether) a group of individuals is likely to experience a target event. These descriptive statistics can also be used to answer questions about differences between groups. Are maltreated children more likely than nonmaltreated children to repeat a grade in school (Rowe & Eckenrode 1995)? Are children of divorced parents more likely than children of intact families to experience a divorce themselves? Are individuals from larger families less likely to experience a depressive episode than individuals from smaller families?

Each of these examples implicitly uses individual characteristics – child maltreatment, parental divorce, and family size – to predict the risk of event occurrence. When we examine the pair of sample hazard and survivor functions displayed in the left-hand side of Figure 1, we too are implicitly treating gender as a predictor of age at first onset of depression. But implicit comparisons like these are limited. Using such plots, how can we examine the effects of continuous predictors? How can we examine the effects of several predictors simultaneously, or explore statistical interactions among predictors? How can we make inferences about the population from which the sample was drawn? With survival analysis, we achieve these goals by postulating and fitting statistical models of the hazard function and by conducting hypothesis tests about the values of population parameters in these models.

Statistical models of hazard express hypothesized population relationships between entire hazard profiles and predictors. To motivate our representation of these models, examine the two sample hazard functions in the top panel of the left side of Figure 1, and imagine that we have created a dummy variable, FEMALE, which can have but one of two values (0 for males, 1 for females). In this formulation, we are making the entire hazard function the conceptual "outcome" and the dummy variable FEMALE the potential "predictor."

What is the relationship between the predictor and the outcome? Ignoring differences in the shapes of the profiles for the moment, when FEMALE = 1, the sample hazard function is generally "higher" relative to its location when FEMALE = 0, indicating that in virtually every time period, women are more likely to experience an initial depressive episode. So conceptually, at least, the effect of the predictor FEMALE is to shift one sample hazard profile vertically relative to the other. A population hazard model formalizes this conceptualization by ascribing the vertical displacement in hazard profiles to variation in predictors in much the same way as an ordinary linear regression model ascribes differences in mean levels of a continuous noncensored outcome to variation in predictors.

The difference between a hazard model and a linear regression model, of course, is that the entire hazard profile is no ordinary continuous outcome. The discrete-time hazard profile is a set of conditional probabilities, each bounded by 0 and 1. Statisticians modeling a bounded outcome as a function of predictors generally do not use a linear function to express this relationship, but rather use a *nonlinear link function* that has the net effect of transforming the outcome so that it is unbounded. This prevents derivation of fitted values that fall outside the range of permissible values – in this case, between 0 and 1. When the outcome is a probability, the *logit* link function is especially popular (Collett 1991). If p represents a probability, then logit(p) is the natural logarithm ($\log_e$) of $p/(1-p)$ and, in the case of these data, can be interpreted as the *log-odds* of initial onset of depression.

Letting $h(t)$ represent the entire population hazard profile, a statistical model that relates the logit transform of $h(t)$ to the predictor FEMALE is thus

$$\text{logit } h(t) = \beta_0(t) + \beta_1(\text{FEMALE}). \tag{1}$$

The parameter $\beta_0(t)$ is the *baseline logit-hazard profile*. It represents the value of the outcome (the entire logit-hazard profile) when the value of the predictor FEMALE is 0 (i.e., it specifies the profile for men). We write the baseline as $\beta_0(t)$, a function of time, and not as β_0, a single term unrelated to time (as in regression analysis), because the outcome (logit $h(t)$) is an entire temporal profile. The discrete-time hazard model in (1) specifies that differences in the value of the predictor shift the baseline logit-hazard profile up or down. The slope parameter β_1 captures the magnitude of this shift; it represents the vertical shift in logit hazard associated with a one-unit difference in the predictor. Because the predictor here is a dichotomy, FEMALE, β_1 captures the differential risk of onset (measured in the logit-hazard scale) for women in comparison to men.

Discussion of methods for estimating the parameters of discrete-time hazard models, evaluating goodness-of-fit, and drawing inferences about the population is beyond the scope of this chapter. All of these goals are easily achieved using standard software for fitting logistic regression models (for a technical discussion see Singer & Willett 1993; for a hands-on applied discussion see Willett & Singer 1993). Without delving into details, suffice it to say that once a discrete-time hazard model has been fit, its parameters can be reported along with standard errors and goodness-of-fit statistics in much the same way that the results of familiar regression analyses are reported. And, just as fitted lines can be used to illustrate the influence of important predictors in the context of multiple regression, so too can fitted hazard functions (and survivor functions) be displayed for prototypical people – those who share substantively important values of statistically significant predictors.

We illustrate the results of this estimation process in the right-hand panel of Figure 1, which presents fitted hazard and survivor functions for the model presented in (1). Comparing the right and left panels, notice that the *fitted* plots on the right side are far smoother, without the crossing and zig-zagging characteristic of the *sample* plots on the left side. This smoothness results from the constraints inherent in the population hazard model stipulated in (1), which forces the vertical separation between the two hazard functions to be identical (in logit-hazard scale) in every time period. Just as we do not expect a fitted regression line to touch every data point in a scatterplot, we do not expect a fitted hazard function in survival analysis to match every sample value of hazard. Indeed, analyses using procedures described in our companion papers reveal that the discrepancies between the sample and fitted plots presented in Figure 1 can be ascribed to nothing more than sampling variation.

What have we learned by fitting this statistical model to these data? First, we can see the more clearly articulated profile of risk across time that is revealed by pooling information across individuals and asking questions about the population that gave rise to these sample data. This reveals a clear pattern of risk, resembling that found by many researchers studying the initial onset of depressive disorders (e.g., Sorenson, Rutter, & Aneshensel 1991; see also Chapter 2 in this volume): the risk of onset is relatively low in childhood, rises steadily through adolescence, and reaches a peak in the early twenties – at which point it declines, falling back not to zero but to moderate levels that never quite reach the peak risks of early adulthood.

Second, we can quantify the increased risk of initially becoming depressed among women in comparison to men, and we can conduct a hypothesis test of whether this gender differential may be a result of sampling variation. Our analyses yield a parameter estimate for β_1 of 0.52, which indicates that the vertical separation, in the logit-hazard scale, between the profiles of risk for men and women is 0.52. Conducting the appropriate hypothesis test (described elsewhere) we obtain a χ^2 test statistic of 23.20 on 1 degree of freedom ($p < .0001$), indicating that we may reject the null hypothesis that the predictor FEMALE has no effect on the population hazard profile (i.e., we reject the null hypothesis $H_0: \beta_1 = 0$). Because few researchers have an intuitive understanding of the logit-hazard scale, we recommend using the same data-analytic practice that researchers use when fitting ordinary logistic regression models: *antilog* the coefficient and interpret it in terms of odds and odds ratios (Hosmer & Lemeshow 1989). Antilogging 0.52 (i.e., evaluating $e^{0.52}$), we conclude that the estimated odds of experiencing a depressive episode in any given time period are 1.67 times higher for women than men.

The fitting of discrete-time hazard models provides a flexible approach to investigating predictors of event occurrence, one that appropriately includes data from both censored and noncensored individuals. Although hazard models may appear unusual, they actually resemble familiar multiple linear and logistic regression models. Like these familiar models, hazard models can incorporate several predictors simultaneously, simply through the inclusion of additional predictors. Inclusion of multiple predictors permits examination of the effect of one predictor while controlling statistically for the effects of others. Similarly, we can examine the synergistic effect of several variables by including statistical interactions between predictors.

Rather than describe the similarities between hazard models and familiar regression models (for these are presented extensively elsewhere), let us turn now to the unique analytic possibilities offered by hazard models – possibilities unavailable with standard statistical methods. We do so because we believe that it is these unique features of hazard models (such as the ability to investigate time-varying effects) that make them so exciting for the life-course researcher.

What if the *values* of predictors vary over time?: including time-varying predictors

Hazard models can include two very different types of predictors: those that are time-invariant and those that are time-varying. As befits their labels, the former describe immutable characteristics of people, such as their sex or race, whose values are stable across the lifetime; the latter describe characteristics of people that may fluctuate with time, as might an individual's self-esteem, marital status, or income. For clarity, when writing statistical models that include time-varying predictors, we include a parenthetical t in the variable name to distinguish such predictors from their time-invariant cousins.

There are at least two reasons why we believe that the ability to include time-varying predictors represents an especially exciting analytic opportunity for researchers studying the predictors and consequences of events across the life course. First, as the chapters in this volume illustrate, life-course researchers often find themselves studying behavior across extended periods of time, sometimes encompassing more than 20, 30, or even 40 years. Although researchers studying behavior across short periods of time may reasonably argue that the values of time-varying predictors will be relatively stable during the study period (enabling them to use time-invariant indicators of these time-varying features), the tenability of this assumption decreases as the length of time studied increases. Second, many of the research questions in this domain focus on the links between the occurrence of *several different events.* Researchers ask questions about whether the occurrence of one stressful event (e.g., parental divorce or death of a spouse) predicts the occurrence of another stressful event (e.g., one's own divorce or the onset of depression). Although it is possible to address such questions by comparing the trajectories of individuals who have had, and who have not had, the precipitating event at any time during the interval covered by data collection, this approach requires the researcher to set aside data on all individuals who experienced the precipitating event *during* the period of data collection. By coding the precipitating event using a time-varying predictor, data from all individuals may be analyzed simultaneously.

We illustrate the use of a time-varying predictor by considering the dummy variable PARDIV(t), which indicates whether the individual's parents had divorced by time t (0 = not yet divorced; 1 = divorced). We could investigate the effects of adding this time-varying predictor to model (1) by fitting the model:

$$\text{logit } h(t) = \beta_0(t) + \beta_1(\text{FEMALE}) + \beta_2(\text{PARDIV}(t)). \tag{2}$$

This model allows the *values* of the dummy variable PARDIV(t) to vary over time (beginning at 0 among intact families and switching to 1 if and when the individual's parents divorce). However, it also stipulates that the *effect* of parental divorce on the risk of onset is constant over time, represented by the single parameter β_2. If β_2 is positive then individuals whose parents divorced are more likely to develop depressive symptoms (after the divorce occurs); if it is negative, they are less likely; if it is zero, then parental divorce has no effect on risk.

The top panel of Figure 2 presents the results of fitting the population discrete-time hazard model postulated in (2) to these sample data. We present the results of this "main effects model" because analyses (not presented here) confirmed that there was no statistical interaction between these predictors – in other words, the effect of parental divorce on risk was identical for men and women. Comparison of the four fitted hazard functions clearly illustrates the large and statistically significant effects of the two predictors: women are at greater risk of experiencing depression, as are individuals whose parents divorced.

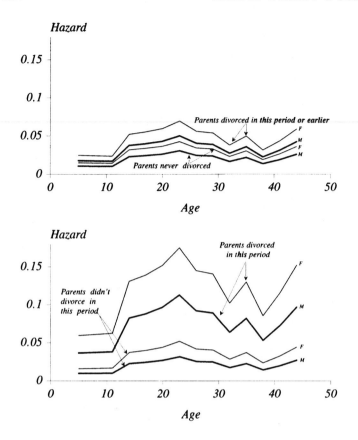

Figure 2. Fitted hazard functions describing age at first onset of depression, by gender, for children whose parents *had* or *had not* divorced. In the TOP PANEL, divorce effects are coded so that they *persist* throughout an individual's lifetime; in the BOTTOM PANEL, divorce effects are coded so that they are *interval-specific*.

Because PARDIV(t) is a time-varying predictor, these fitted plots cannot be interpreted in exactly the same way as the fitted plots presented in Figure 1. To learn how to interpret these plots, focus first on the bottom fitted hazard profile, which depicts the risk of experiencing a depressive episode among men whose parents never divorced. This is the lowest of the four fitted hazard profiles because this group of individuals is at lowest risk for experiencing a depressive disorder. Now consider the profile that would result if a boy's (or man's) parents divorce. While the parents were married, the boy's risk profile would still be represented by the lowest of the four hazard functions. When they divorce, however, the later portion of this boy's risk profile (the portion occurring after the divorce) would be described by the *other* fitted hazard profile for males, which is substantially higher and captures the increased risk of depression among males whose parents had divorced. In essence, then, the fitted hazard profiles presented in the top panel of Figure 2 provide an *envelope* of all possible hazard profiles corresponding to the many different possible times when parents may divorce. Individuals whose parents are not divorced remain on the lower profile (for their gender); if (and when) their parents divorce, their risk of becoming depressed rises to the level represented by the higher hazard profile for their gender.

Another analytic opportunity made possible through hazard modeling is the option of exploring different ways of parameterizing the effects of time-varying predictors. In the model we have just fit for parental divorce, we have assumed that the effect of parental divorce on the risk of depression remains with a person throughout his or her lifetime. But consider an alternative possibility: parental divorce may increase an individual's risk of depression but *only* during the time period when the parental divorce occurs. Letting the dummy variable DIVNOW(t) indicate whether the individual's parents had divorced at time t (0 = not divorced in this time period; 1 = divorced in this time period), we could investigate the effects of this time-varying predictor by fitting the model:

$$\text{logit } h(t) = \beta_0(t) + \beta_1(\text{FEMALE}) + \beta_2(\text{DIVNOW}(t)). \tag{3}$$

As with the model postulated in Equation (2), the values of the dummy variable DIVNOW(t) may vary over time (0 among individuals whose parents did not divorce during this time period and 1 for those whose parents did). So, too, we continue to hypothesize that the effect of parental divorce on the risk of initial onset of depression is constant over time, and is represented by the single parameter β_2. The difference between the two models is that once the variable PARDIV(t) takes on the value 1 for an individual, it remains at that value for the remainder of that individual's record; in contrast, the variable DIVNOW(t) would take on the value of 1 *only* during the time period when the individual's parents actually divorced. Thus, model (3) postulates that the effects of parental divorce are *interval-specific*: if β_2 is positive, individuals whose parents divorced in this interval are at greater risk of depression in this interval. This model does not allow the effects of parental divorce to carry over into any interval subsequent to the divorce.

The bottom panel of Figure 2 presents the results of fitting this alternative model to these data. We have plotted these fitted functions on a scale identical to that used in the top panel so that the differential effect associated with parental divorce in the two models is apparent. Once again, begin with the bottom hazard profile, which represents the risk of onset of depression among males whose parents did *not* divorce during the time period in question. Our model specifies that a male whose parents remained married would have this profile of risk over time. If and when that male's parents divorce, however, his risk of onset during that time period would skyrocket, jumping up to the upper hazard profile for men. The difference between the previous model and this model is that for the latter, after the time period in question, the male's risk profile would return to the lower level represented by the bottom hazard function.

Why are these models so different? Both confirm that the effect of parental divorce is statistically significant, but the magnitude of the effect differs because they code the parental divorce variable in dramatically different ways. The first model allows the effect of parental divorce to persist throughout a person's lifetime. It yields an estimated coefficient of 0.34, which indicates that the odds that children of divorced parents become depressed are $e^{0.34} = 1.41$ times higher than the corresponding odds for children of nondivorced parents. The second model, in contrast, stipulates that the effect of parental divorce "kicks in" only during the time period when the divorce occurred. It yields a much larger coefficient (1.36), which implies that the effect of parental divorce on the risk of depression is much higher during that particular interval. Antilogging this coefficient, we find that the odds of depression among children of divorced parents are 3.88 times higher at the time of divorce but thereafter revert to risk profiles indistinguishable from those whose parents never divorced. The first model essentially amortizes the dramatically elevated period-specific risk across an individual's post–parental-divorce life, while the latter focuses exclusively on what happens to an individual during the time period when his or her parents actually divorced.

The ease with which time-varying predictors can be incorporated into hazard models offers life-course researchers an innovative analytic opportunity. Many important predictors of trajectories and turning points fluctuate naturally with time: family and social structure, employment, opportunities for emotional fulfillment, and (perhaps most importantly) the occurrence and timing of other events. In traditional statistical analyses, temporal fluctuation in such predictors must be reduced to a single measure across time. With the advent of hazard modeling, this is no longer the case. Researchers can examine relationships between event occurrence and dynamically changing predictors.

What if the *effects* of predictors vary over time?: including interactions with time

When processes evolve dynamically, the effects of both time-invariant and time-varying predictors may fluctuate over time. A predictor whose effect is constant over time has the same impact in all time periods. A predictor whose effect varies over time has a different impact on hazard in different time periods.

Both time-invariant and time-varying predictors can have time-varying effects. Consider the effects of parental divorce, as measured by the variable PARDIV(t), on the risk of depression. PARDIV(t) is a time-varying predictor – its value moves from 0 to 1 if and when parents divorce – but its *effect* on hazard might be constant over time (as we have stipulated so far). If the effect is time-invariant, this means that the effect of parental divorce on the risk of onset is the same regardless of whether the divorce takes place during childhood, adolescence, or adulthood. However, if the effect of parental divorce varies over time, then divorce might have a larger effect on the risk of depression among children (who are still living at home) than among adults (who have already moved out of the house).

The discrete-time hazard models posited so far have not permitted a predictor's effect to vary with time; they are called *proportional-odds* models. Hazard profiles represented by such models have a special property: in every time period t under consideration, the effect of the predictor on logit hazard is exactly the same. In Equation (1), for example, the vertical shift in the logit-hazard profile for women is always β_1 and so the hypothesized logit-hazard profiles for women and men have identical *shapes,* since their profiles are simply shifted versions of each other. Generally, in proportional-odds models, the entire family of logit-hazard profiles represented by all possible values of the predictors share a common shape and are mutually parallel, differing only in their relative elevations. If the logit-hazard profiles are parallel and have the same shape, the corresponding raw hazard profiles are (approximate) magnifications and diminutions of each other – they are *proportional*.[1] Because the models presented so far include predictors with only time-constant effects, the fitted hazard functions displayed appear to have the required proportionality.

But is it sensible to assume that the effects of all predictors are unilaterally time-constant and that all hazard profiles are proportional in practice? In reality, many predictors will not only displace the logit-hazard profile but will also alter its shape. If the effect of a predictor varies over time, we must specify a nonproportional model that allows the shapes of the logit-hazard profiles to differ. When the effect of one predictor differs by the levels of another, we say that the two predictors *interact*; in this case, we say that the predictor interacts with time. To add such an effect into our hazard models, we include the cross-product of that predictor and time as an additional predictor (see Willett & Singer 1993).

In order to illustrate the types of information that can be gleaned from determining whether a predictor interacts with time, Figure 3 presents the results of fitting two discrete-time hazard models to the depression data using the time-invariant predictor NSIBS.[2] Because NSIBS is a continuous variable (its values vary from 0 to 26), we present fitted hazard profiles for two prototypical individuals: those who were an only child (0 sibs) and those who came from larger

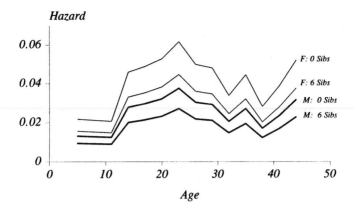

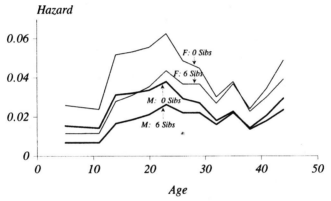

Figure 3. Fitted hazard functions describing the age at first onset of depression, by gender and the individual's number of siblings, from two discrete-time hazard models: TOP PANEL is a main-effects model, in which the effect of number of siblings is *constant* over time; BOTTOM PANEL is an interaction-with-time model, in which the effect of number of siblings *varies* over time.

families (6 sibs). The figure presents fitted hazard profiles from two distinct models: a main-effects model (top panel) and an interaction-with-time model (bottom panel). The main-effects model suggests that siblings protect against depression: for both men and women, the greater the number of siblings, the lower the risk of onset. The four fitted hazard profiles appear proportional because the main-effects model constrains the effect of NSIBS to be the same in each time period.

But a more accurate and complex story emerges from the interaction-with-time model displayed in the bottom panel, where the effect of NSIBS is allowed to vary over time. Comparing the fitted hazard functions from the interaction-with-time model with those from the main-effects model illustrates the untenability of the proportionality assumption, owing to the statistically significant interaction between NSIBS and time. The hazard functions in the bottom panel are clearly not proportional. In childhood, when individuals are still living at home, family size *does* have a protective effect: boys and girls from larger families are at lower risk of having a depressive episode. Over time, however, the protective effect of family size diminishes; by the time an individual reaches the early thirties, the effect is virtually non-existent. Instead of having a constant vertical separation in logit-hazard space, the relative differences between the hazard functions vary, being larger in childhood and trivial in adulthood.

We believe that the ability to include – and test the importance of – interactions with time represents a major analytic opportunity for researchers investigating the sequelae of trauma and adversity. When studying the behavior of individuals over very long periods of time (as many life-course researchers do), it seems reasonable to hypothesize that the effects of predictors will vary as people pass through different life stages. Although the effects of some predictors will remain with an individual throughout his or her lifetime, the effects of others may dissipate, or increase, over time. Our example of the changing effects of family size is but one of hundreds of reasonable possibilities that depression researchers might want to investigate. Were we to look for predictors of depression whose effects might *increase* over time, we might find that characteristics of the individual's own family in adulthood (number of children, say) might be an important predictor of depression in this phase of life.

We believe that it is not hyperbole to state that interactions with time are everywhere, if only researchers took the time to look for them. Present data-analytic practice (and the widespread availability of prepackaged computer programs) permits an almost unthinking (and often untested) adoption of proportional hazards models ("Cox" regression), in which the effects of predictors are constrained to be constant over time. Yet we have found – in a wide variety of substantive applications that include not only our own work on employment duration (Murnane, Singer, & Willett 1989; Singer 1993a,b) but also others' work on topics such as age at first suicide ideation (Bolger et al. 1989) and child mortality (Trussel & Hammerslough 1983) – that interactions with time seem to be the rule rather than the exception. We have every reason to believe that once researchers start looking for interactions with time, they will arise commonly. The key is to *test* the tenability of the assumption of a time-invariant effect. Although we have not outlined the statistical procedures for doing so here, we refer the interested reader to Singer and Willett (1993) and Willett and Singer (1993).

Is survival analysis really necessary?

In this paper, we have introduced a class of statistical methods for analyzing longitudinal data on the occurrence and timing of events. Our presentation so far has encouraged researchers to learn more about these methods because they offer analytic capabilities that other methods do not. But now we turn to another reason for learning about survival methods: failure to use them when appropriate can mislead a researcher alarmingly.

How can traditional methods for analyzing event occurrence deceive the investigator? The answer to this question depends upon which traditional approach replaces the survival method and how that approach responds to the problem of censoring. Survival methods deal evenhandedly with censored cases – they contribute information to the analysis up until the time at which they are censored. Traditional analytic methods, in contrast, deal with censoring in an ad hoc way, which can create a series of problems we now describe.

One common way of "resolving" the censoring dilemma is to ignore the censored cases completely, treating them as if they were missing. Traditional statistical analyses can then be conducted in the subsample of noncensored individuals, with event time (or perhaps its logarithm) playing the role of the dependent variable. Descriptive statistics can be used to summarize subsample variability in event time. Correlation analysis, regression analysis, and analysis of variance can be used to investigate the relationship between event time and predictors. Unfortunately, this approach reduces statistical power (due to the smaller sample size) and leads to negatively biased estimates of aggregate event time (with a corresponding impact on estimates of the relationship between event time and predictors). When studying age at first divorce, for example, an investigator might be tempted to subsample only those individuals who had divorced by the end of data collection. But omitting individuals who remain married modifies the sample in an unfortunate way, reducing its size by eliminating the very individuals at lowest risk of divorce! After all, some of these individuals *will* divorce; they will just do so after data collection ends. The average time-to-divorce among the full population of "ever marrieds" must be longer than that found among the noncensored ("divorced") subsample analyzed.

An alternative to this "convert all censored cases into missing values" approach involves imputing their unknown event times and regressing its logarithm on predictors in the traditional fashion. The imputation allows the censored cases (for whom continuous duration data are unavailable) to be included in analyses with noncensored cases. The basic idea is well-intentioned – there must be equivalent information available on both groups if they are to be included in the same traditional analysis. Although the approach maintains the sample at its original size (thereby apparently avoiding a loss of statistical power), it does not resolve the problem of bias. The censored event times are usually imputed arbitrarily or simply set equal to the length of data collection. Such a decision is not completely unreasonable, because none of the censored individuals experienced the target event until that point in time. But many did not experience the target event for many more years to come. Full sample summaries of event times based on such data necessarily underestimate the true length of "time to event" because, for an unknown proportion of the sample, the ultimate event times must be greater than the imputed value.

To avoid arbitrary data imputation while retaining both censored and uncensored cases, many investigators set aside the continuous event-time information (which is unknown for one of the subgroups) and focus on the categorical data that is known for both groups – data on whether each member of the sample experienced the target event by a particular point in time, usually the end of data collection. Dichotomization provides a new analytic outcome for which individuals who experienced the target event prior to the chosen cutoff are assigned a value of 1 and those who did not (the censored cases) are assigned the value 0. Descriptive statistics can summarize the proportion of cases experiencing the event prior to the chosen time, and logistic regression can be used to investigate the relationship between event occurrence and predictors.

Dichotomization can be viewed as the coarsest form of discrete-time survival analysis available. But its coarseness creates problems that can obscure knowledge about transitions. First, the approach destroys perfectly good continuous duration data to create the new dichotomous outcome. Consider what would happen, for example, if we followed a sample of individuals for 50 years and asked whether and (if so) when they first experienced a depressive episode. Dichotomization would eliminate known and potentially meaningful variation in event times by clustering together everyone whose onset was prior to the cutoff age of 50. People whose initial depressive episodes occurred in early childhood would be pooled with those who did not become depressed until their late forties, even though such individuals undoubtedly differ enormously in the causes of their depression and in their ultimate prognosis.

A further problem is that any particular cutoff time – even one seemingly relevant to the process under study – is somewhat arbitrary. A researcher studying the predictors of obtaining employment after dropping out of high school, for example, might follow a sample of people for two years to see whether they successfully secured a first job (as in Chapter 5 of this volume). But highly disparate temporal profiles of risk can lead to similar employment rates at a specific point in time. Just because individuals with high self-esteem and low self-esteem were equally likely to have found jobs after two years does not mean that they got there by following similar trajectories. Perhaps most of the high-self-esteem individuals obtained their jobs relatively quickly, soon after dropping out, while the low–self-esteem individuals may have found jobs only after months and months of searching. The two-year cutoff point is convenient but not purposeful. By avoiding dichotomization and using survival analysis to disaggregate risk, we can better document variation in risk over time; by discovering what predicts variation in risk, we can better understand why some individuals find jobs early and others do not. Traditional methods disregard the temporal profile of risk; with survival methods, the risk profile becomes the primary analytic focus.

Disregard for the temporal variation in risk leads to yet another problem with the dichotomization approach: contradictory conclusions can result from nothing more than differences in the particular cutoff time adopted. Not only will the overall proportion of the sample experiencing the event differ as the cutoff is modified, but the relationship with predictors may also change. In our previous example, choosing cutoffs of two months, one year, and two years (say) may lead to three entirely discrepant conclusions about the rate at which high-school dropouts find jobs. The two-month rates might erroneously indicate that *low*–self-esteem individuals are more likely to find jobs (because they will take the first job that comes along), the one-year rates might register no difference, and the two-year rates might suggest that *high*–self-esteem individuals are more likely to find jobs (because they persist and ultimately do secure employment). By using survival analysis to look at the relationship between hazard and self-esteem, the source of these cumulative differences in risk may be revealed as a statistically significant interaction between self-esteem and time. Researchers using traditional methods must constantly remind themselves that their conclusions can fluctuate as they modify their cutoff. Although such caveats usually appear in the "Results" section of an article, they often disappear by the "Discussion" section. In survival analysis, the time frame itself is an integral part of the answer; it highlights, rather than obscures, variation in risk over time.

The dichotomization "solution" is rendered even more ineffective if censoring occurs at different times for different members of the sample. This occurs when sampled individuals are observed for different lengths of time, perhaps because of the research design (as when interviewing an age-heterogeneous sample and obtaining retrospective event history data) or because of the gradual onset of attrition (a common problem in longitudinal research). If censoring times differ across sample members, then both cutoff time and opportunity for event occurrence differ as well. People followed for longer periods of time have greater opportunity to experience the target event than do those who are followed for shorter periods of time. Hence, observed differences in cumulated risk might be attributable to nothing more than research design. Although it is possible to make risk periods equivalent across all sample members by discarding data describing behavior that occurred after the earliest possible censoring point for any member of the sample, such an approach will eliminate large quantities of perfectly good data already collected. With survival analysis, a person who does not experience the event of interest is censored at the particular time that his or her data record ends; censoring times need not be identical for everyone under study.

Finally, traditional analytic methods offer few mechanisms for including predictors whose values vary over time or for permitting the effects of predictors to fluctuate over time. To overcome this limitation, researchers studying the effects of such variables as family functioning, socioeconomic status, or marital status often use predictor values corresponding to a single point in time, the average of the several values over time, or perhaps a rate of change in values over time. Survival analysis makes this approach unnecessary. The analytic effort is identical whether including predictors that are static over time or predictors that change over time; so, too, it is easy to determine whether the effects of predictors are constant over time or whether they differ over time. Traditional methods force researchers to build static models of dynamic processes; survival methods allow researchers to model dynamic processes dynamically.

For all these reasons, we believe that life-course researchers should investigate the possibilities offered by survival methods. In the recent past, when these methods were in their infancy and statistical software was neither available nor user-friendly, researchers reasonably adopted other approaches. But survival methods, originally developed to model an event seemingly beyond a person's control (i.e., death), lend themselves naturally to the study of individual behavior and development. The time has come for researchers investigating the life course to explore the utility of survival analysis. We are convinced that there is much that these methods can reveal.

Notes

1. For pedagogic reasons, we have taken some mathematical liberties here. In discrete-time models, the proportionality of the raw hazard profiles is only approximate because vertical shifts in logit hazard correspond to magnifications and diminutions of the untransformed hazard profile only when the magnitude of the hazard probability is small (say, less than 0.15 or 0.20). In much empirical research, as in the example we present here, discrete-time hazard is about this magnitude or less, and therefore the approximation tends to hold quite well in practice (see Singer & Willett 1993 for further discussion of this issue).
2. Because of data limitations, the values of this predictor are assumed to be constant during an individual's lifetime. If we had access to data indicating when the respondent's siblings were born, we could have coded this as a time-varying predictor.

References

Allison, P. D. (1984). *Event History Analysis: Regression for Longitudinal Event Data* (Sage University Paper Series on Quantitative Applications in the Social Sciences, ser. no. 05-046). Beverly Hills, CA: Sage.

Bolger, N., Downey, G., Walker, E., & Steininger, P. (1989). The onset of suicide ideation in childhood and adolescence. *Journal of Youth and Adolescence* 18: 175–89.

Collett, D. (1991). *Modelling Binary Data*. London: Chapman and Hall.

Cox, D. R. (1972). Regression models and life tables. *Journal of the Royal Statistical Society B* 34: 187–202.

Friedman, H. S., Tucker, J. S., Schwartz, J. E., & Tomlinson-Keasey, C. (1995). Psychosocial and behavioral predictors of longevity: the aging and death of the "Termites." *American Psychologist* 50: 69–78.

Hosmer, D. W., & Lemeshow, S. (1989). *Applied Logistic Regression.* New York: Wiley.
Kalbfleisch, J. D., & Prentice, R. L. (1980). *The Statistical Analysis of Failure Time Data.* New York: Wiley.
Murnane, R. J., Singer, J. D., & Willett, J. B. (1989). The influences of salaries and "opportunity costs" on teachers' career choices: evidence from North Carolina. *Havard Educational Review* 59: 325–46.
Rowe, E., & Eckenrode, J. (1995). The timing of academic difficulties among maltreated and non-maltreated children. Paper presented at the Society for Research in Child Development meetings (31 March, Indianapolis).
Singer, J. D. (1993a). Are special educators' career paths special?: results of a 13-year longitudinal study. *Exceptional Children* 59: 262–79.
Singer, J. D. (1993b). Once is not enough: special educators who return to teaching. *Exceptional Children* 60: 58–73.
Singer, J. D., & Willett, J. B. (1991). Modeling the days of our lives: using survival analysis when designing and analyzing longitudinal studies of duration and the timing of events. *Psychological Bulletin* 110: 268–98.
Singer, J. D., & Willett, J. B. (1993). It's about time: using discrete-time survival analysis to study duration and the timing of events. *Journal of Educational Statistics* 18: 155–95.
Sorenson, S. B., Rutter, C. M., & Aneshensel, C. S. (1991). Depression in the community: an investigation into age of onset. *Journal of Consulting and Clinical Psychology* 57: 420–4.
Trussel, J., & Hammerslough, C. (1983). A hazards-model analysis of the covariates of infant and child mortality in Sri Lanka. *Demography* 20: 1-26.
Willett, J. B., & Singer, J. D. (1991). From whether to when: new methods for studying student dropout and teacher attrition. *Review of Educational Research* 61: 407–50.
Willett, J. B., & Singer, J. D. (1993). Investigating onset, cessation, relapse and recovery: why you should, and how you can, use discrete-time survival analysis to examine event occurrence. *Journal of Consulting and Clinical Psychology* 61: 952–65.
Willett, J. B., & Singer, J. D. (1995). It's déjà-vu all over again: using multiple-spell discrete-time survival analysis. *Journal of Educational and Behavioral Statistics* 20: 41–67.

Index

Printed in the United Kingdom
by Lightning Source UK Ltd.
119073UK00001BA/227

9 780521 029711